Aiding Empowerment

The Carnegie Endowment for International Peace offers decision makers global, independent, and strategic insight and innovative ideas that advance international peace. Founded in 1910 as the first international affairs think tank in the United States, it is a global institution with centers in Beijing, Beirut, Brussels, Moscow, New Delhi, and Washington. Carnegie's network works together to provide analysis, shape policy debates, and propose solutions to the most consequential global threats.

The Carnegie Endowment for International Peace does not take institutional positions. Its scholars embody a variety of national and regional outlooks as well as the issues that transcend them. All views expressed in its publications are solely those of the author or authors.

Aiding Empowerment

Democracy Promotion and Gender Equality in Politics

SASKIA BRECHENMACHER
and
KATHERINE MANN

OXFORD
UNIVERSITY PRESS

Oxford University Press is a department of the University of Oxford. It furthers
the University's objective of excellence in research, scholarship, and education
by publishing worldwide. Oxford is a registered trade mark of Oxford University
Press in the UK and certain other countries.

Published in the United States of America by Oxford University Press
198 Madison Avenue, New York, NY 10016, United States of America.

© Oxford University Press 2024

All rights reserved. No part of this publication may be reproduced, stored in
a retrieval system, or transmitted, in any form or by any means, without the
prior permission in writing of Oxford University Press, or as expressly permitted
by law, by license, or under terms agreed with the appropriate reproduction
rights organization. Inquiries concerning reproduction outside the scope of the
above should be sent to the Rights Department, Oxford University Press, at the
address above.

You must not circulate this work in any other form
and you must impose this same condition on any acquirer.

Library of Congress Cataloging-in-Publication Data
Names: Brechenmacher, Saskia, author. | Mann, Katherine, author.
Title: Aiding empowerment : democracy promotion and gender equality in politics /
Saskia Brechenmacher and Katherine Mann.
Description: New York, NY : Oxford University Press, [2024] |
Includes bibliographical references and index.
Identifiers: LCCN 2023043719 (print) | LCCN 2023043720 (ebook) |
ISBN 9780197694282 (paperback) | ISBN 9780197694275 (hardback) |
ISBN 9780197694299 (epub)
Subjects: LCSH: Women in development—Developing countries. |
Women—Political activity—Developing countries.
Classification: LCC HQ1240.5.D44 B743 2024 (print) | LCC HQ1240.5.D44 (ebook) |
DDC 305.4209172/4—dc23/eng/20240110
LC record available at https://lccn.loc.gov/2023043719
LC ebook record available at https://lccn.loc.gov/2023043720

DOI: 10.1093/oso/9780197694275.001.0001

CONTENTS

Acknowledgments ix
Abbreviations xi

PART I SITUATING THE INQUIRY

1. **Introduction** 3
   A GROWING AID PRIORITY 4
   TAKING STOCK OF PROGRESS 6
   CAPTURING LEARNING 8
   OUR ARGUMENTS 10
   OUR APPROACH 14
   OUTLINE OF THIS STUDY 19

2. **The Global Aid Ecosystem** 21
   THE RISE OF A NEW GLOBAL NORM 22
   A GRADUAL AID EVOLUTION 25
   MAPPING THE CURRENT ASSISTANCE LANDSCAPE 27
   UNDERSTANDING THE KEY ACTORS 31
   A FRAGILE CONSENSUS? 32
   CRITICAL VOICES 35
   CONCLUSION 37

3. **Introducing the Cases** 38
   SITUATING OUR CASES 39
   NEPAL: THE STRUGGLE FOR POSTCONFLICT INCLUSION 43
   KENYA: CONFRONTING "WINNER-TAKES-ALL" POLITICS 46

MOROCCO: THE CHALLENGE OF PARTIAL REFORM 49

MYANMAR: THE RESURGENCE OF AUTOCRACY 52

CONCLUSION 55

PART II   THE STATE OF THE FIELD

4. First Generation: Getting Women in the Room 59

BOLSTERING WOMEN'S POLITICAL PARTICIPATION 61

THE GLOBAL PUSH FOR GENDER QUOTAS 65

BUILDING WOMEN'S CAPACITY 68

ASSISTANCE TO WOMEN'S ORGANIZATIONS 70

A STORY OF FORMAL GAINS 72

ADDING WOMEN AND STIRRING? 75

THE PERSISTENCE OF SILOED APPROACHES 76

CONCLUSION 78

5. Second Generation: Transforming Systems 79

TRANSFORMING THE ECOSYSTEM 80

THE EXPANDED TOOLBOX 81

ENGENDERING ELECTIONS 85

ENGAGING POLITICAL PARTIES 87

BOLSTERING WOMEN'S INFLUENCE 88

COUNTERING RESISTANCE AND VIOLENCE 90

AN INCOMPLETE EVOLUTION 91

CONCLUSION 96

6. The Limits of Candidate Training 98

A SUPPLY-SIDE MODEL 99

THE CHALLENGE OF MEASURING SUCCESS 100

THE DRAWBACKS OF ONE-OFF INITIATIVES 103

INVESTING IN LONG-TERM ACCOMPANIMENT 104

BROADENING THE SCOPE 106

A LIMITED APPROACH 109

CONCLUSION 113

7. Confronting the Gatekeepers 115

GENDER BIASES IN POLITICAL PARTIES 116

FROM TRAINING TO ORGANIZATIONAL CHANGE 118

FOSTERING CROSS-PARTY LINKAGES 122

CONTENTS　　vii

INCREMENTAL REFORMS　123

STUBBORN STUMBLING BLOCKS　125

CONFRONTING THE COST OF POLITICS　127

THE NEED FOR PRAGMATISM　130

CONCLUSION　132

8. From Presence to Power　134

AN INDIRECT LINK　135

LEARNING THE RULES OF THE GAME　137

COLLECTIVE POWER THROUGH WOMEN'S CAUCUSES　140

CRITICAL ACTORS: A MISSING PIECE?　143

BUILDING COOPERATIVE CONSTELLATIONS FOR CHANGE　146

TRANSFORMING PARLIAMENTARY INSTITUTIONS　148

CONCLUSION　151

PART III　NEW FRONTIERS

9. Tackling Patriarchal Gender Norms　155

THE LONG SHADOW OF PATRIARCHAL NORMS　156

ENGAGING MEN AS STAKEHOLDERS　159

TRANSFORMING MASCULINITIES　162

THE NEED FOR LEARNING　164

FIGHTING VIOLENCE AND BACKLASH　166

A MULTIDIMENSIONAL PROBLEM　168

ADAPTING TO NEW THREATS　171

CONCLUSION　173

10. Widening the Lens　175

RECKONING WITH HIERARCHIES　176

TRANSLATING INTERSECTIONALITY INTO PRACTICE　178

A DEPOLITICIZED AGENDA?　181

CONFRONTING THE GLOBAL DEMOCRATIC RECESSION　183

RISKS OF AUTOCRATIC CO-OPTATION　187

FORGING MORE POLITICALLY INFORMED APPROACHES　190

CONCLUSION　193

11. Toward a Different Assistance Model　195

CHRONIC SHORT-TERMISM　196

ENDURING SILOS　198

AN EXTERNALLY DRIVEN AGENDA? 201

SHIFTING RESOURCES AND POWER 204

REFORMING AID BUREAUCRACIES 206

A GROWING FEMINIST TIDE 209

CONCLUSION 212

12. Building Gender-Inclusive Democracies 214

RECAPPING OUR ARGUMENTS 215

STRENGTHENING THE AID ECOSYSTEM 219

DEEPENING SECOND-GENERATION APPROACHES 223

TACKLING NEW FRONTIERS 229

CONCLUDING REFLECTIONS 235

Notes 239
Index 285

ACKNOWLEDGMENTS

This book would not have been possible without the support, assistance, and participation of dozens of colleagues, scholars, practitioners, activists, and friends. First and foremost, we thank our colleagues at the Carnegie Endowment for International Peace, who accompanied this project from its conception up to the finish line. We owe particular thanks to Tom Carothers for encouraging us to embark on this research journey, believing in the project, and providing incisive feedback along the way. He nudged us to turn our ideas into a book, an initially daunting task that we would not have accomplished without his advice, trust, and support. We are thankful for his generosity and mentorship.

We are also grateful to the entire Democracy, Conflict, and Governance program at Carnegie for providing a warm and intellectually stimulating institutional home and for offering encouraging feedback and advice when we needed it. Special thanks go to five talented and dedicated Junior Fellows who provided critical background research, fact-checked information, transcribed interviews, and carefully edited our chapters: David Wong, Lauren Meadows, Nikhita Salgame, Caroline Crystal, and Francesca Nyakora. All of you helped sharpen our ideas and made our writing better.

At the core of this book are the insights of many women's rights activists, politicians, aid officials, and policymakers who took the time to candidly share their experiences with us. We are deeply grateful for their willingness to speak with us on Zoom, WhatsApp, and in person, particularly during those difficult first few months of the global Covid-19 pandemic. We cite some of these individuals by name in the book; others wished to remain anonymous. Our hope is that our book does justice to their knowledge and experiences and provides useful tools to strengthen their important work going forward. We also thank Erica Adhikary for assisting us with translation and interpretation during our conversations with interviewees in Nepal.

Several researchers and experts provided immensely useful feedback on our writing along the way. We are particularly grateful to Jonna Haapanen, Caroline Hubbard, Dr. Ragnhild L. Muriaas, Dr. Juliana Restrepo Sanín, and Heleen Schrooyen for agreeing to review different chapters of the book and providing substantive comments. Two anonymous reviewers also offered excellent suggestions on our proposal and initial chapters. We are thankful for their constructive comments and advice.

This book was made possible by the generous financial support of several funders that helped sustain our work at Carnegie, including the Ford Foundation, the UK Foreign, Commonwealth & Development Office (then DFID), and the Charles Stewart Mott Foundation. The Department of Politics and International Studies at the University of Cambridge supported Saskia's field research in Kenya, which enabled us to supplement our virtual interviews in the country with in-person follow-ups and participant observation. We also thank Dave McBride and Alexcee Bechthold, our editors at Oxford University Press, for guiding us through the peer review, submission, editing, and production process.

Finally, we thank the people in our lives who accompanied and supported us throughout the research and writing of this book.

Katie: I am extremely grateful to my parents, Marcy and Peter Mann, for their unwavering support for my education, research, and wider interest in international politics. If not for their own curiosity about the world and devotion to promoting social good, I likely would not have found my way into political science. Immense gratitude also goes to Samantha Aviles, Adrienne Propp, Juliette Chausson, Laura Courchesne, and Ryan Crowley, who have been a constant source of encouragement and friendship along the winding journey of writing this book.

Saskia: my gratitude goes to my parents, Birgit and Joachim, for believing in me and my work and nurturing my interest in politics and in our world— even when this pursuit has taken me farther and farther away from home. And to Phil, for always being ready to talk through my ideas, for endlessly cheering me on, and for surrounding me with laughter and love: I could not have done it without you.

ABBREVIATIONS

CA	Constituent Assembly (Nepal)
CEDAW	Convention on the Elimination of All Forms of Discrimination against Women
CEPPS	Consortium for Elections and Political Process Strengthening
DAC	Development Assistance Committee
DFAT	Department of Foreign Affairs and Trade (Australia)
DIPD	Danish Institute for Parties and Democracy
ECN	Election Commission Nepal
EMBs	Electoral Management Bodies
EU	European Union
FCDO	Foreign, Commonwealth & Development Office (United Kingdom)
GAD	Gender and Development
GSP	Gender-sensitive Parliaments
IFES	International Foundation for Electoral Systems
INGO	International Nongovernmental Organization
IDEA	International Institute for Democracy and Electoral Assistance
IPU	Inter-Parliamentary Union
IRI	International Republican Institute
IWDA	International Women's Development Agency
KEWOPA	Kenya Women Parliamentary Association
MCA	Member of County Assembly (Kenya)
NDI	National Democratic Institute
NIMD	Netherlands Institute for Multiparty Democracy
NLD	National League for Democracy (Myanmar)
OAS	Organization of American States

OECD	Organisation for Economic Co-operation and Development
OSCE	Organization for Security and Co-operation in Europe
SIDA	Swedish International Development Cooperation Agency
SDGs	Sustainable Development Goals
UN	United Nations
UNDP	United Nations Development Programme
USAID	United States Agency for International Development
V-Dem	Varieties of Democracy
WID	Women in Development
WPS	Women, Peace and Security

PART I

SITUATING THE INQUIRY

1

Introduction

In early 2017, Nepal was gearing up for an important election. For the first time in two decades, voters were going to the ballot to choose their local government representatives. The election was the first to be held under the country's new federal constitution, passed in 2015 after a decade-long internal conflict followed by years of difficult political negotiations. Across the country, almost 44,000 candidates were competing for 13,556 municipal posts.[1] And, for the first time in the country's history, there were thousands of women among them. As a result of the new legal framework, political parties were no longer allowed to exclusively nominate men: either the mayoral or deputy mayoral position in each municipality had to go to a woman, as did half of the seats on every ward committee. One position on each committee was specifically reserved for women from the Dalit community, the country's most disadvantaged caste.[2]

For local and international organizations seeking to promote women's political participation, the election represented a pivotal moment. Thousands of women who had never served in formal political office suddenly stood a chance of shaping the country's democratic future. In the lead-up to the polls, the National Democratic Institute (NDI), a US democracy assistance organization supported by the United States Agency for International Development (USAID), launched a nationwide effort to train women candidates on how to run their campaigns: how to raise resources, how to build their political networks, and how to shape their public message. "We trained around 800 women around the country, out of whom 300 or 400 got elected," recalls an NDI representative involved in the program. "We thought this worked very well. We would definitely use a similar approach again in the future."[3]

Every year, bilateral donor agencies partner with local and international organizations to fund hundreds of similar efforts aimed at bolstering women's political participation and leadership. They train women to run for office, support newly elected women parliamentarians, and build women's caucuses in

Aiding Empowerment. Saskia Brechenmacher and Katherine Mann, Oxford University Press.
© Oxford University Press 2024. DOI: 10.1093/oso/9780197694275.003.0001

political parties and parliaments. They fund campaigns by women's organizations calling for gender quotas, advocate for gender mainstreaming in elections, and channel aid to voter education targeting female citizens. The overarching aim is a simple one: to overcome women's persistent political exclusion in most parts of the world.

Today, these donor-funded initiatives span all regions of the developing world—from countries wracked by ongoing conflict to relatively stable democracies. They involve an ever-widening array of experts and organizations, from United Nations (UN) agencies and global foundations to local women's groups. And although funding dedicated to women's political empowerment remains a small component of global aid budgets, it has increased substantially over the past two decades. In 2021 alone, the world's thirty largest development aid donors spent approximately US$865 million on democracy assistance projects that listed gender equality as their primary objective.[4] In many countries, donor-funded training workshops, manuals, and consultants have become a recurring and palpable presence in the lives of women politicians and activists.

What ideas about gender, power, and political change guide these aid programs? What have practitioners and advocates learned about their effectiveness, and how have they adapted their assumptions and approaches over time? How might aid actors improve their work in this domain going forward? These are the questions at the core of this book. As in many other areas of development assistance, the proliferation of women's political empowerment programs over the past three decades has led to a growing gap between donor activities and analytical work examining these initiatives. To address this gap, this book builds a conceptual and empirical map of this understudied domain of international aid. We trace the evolution of international support for women's political empowerment over the past thirty years: critically probing areas of progress, examining persistent challenges, and highlighting new frontiers. At a time of both renewed feminist mobilization and global concerns about illiberal attacks on gender equality gains, we aim to synthesize past learning and help gender equality advocates, policymakers, and practitioners chart a more hopeful path forward.

A growing aid priority

Peruse the websites and strategy documents of major international aid agencies and you will find countless references to bolstering gender equality and women's empowerment around the world. Many donors have also made specific commitments to strengthening women's political leadership. However, this was not always the case. The rise in donor support for women's political

Introduction   5

empowerment is part of the exponential growth of international democracy aid over the last thirty years.

Democracy assistance programs first proliferated after a wave of democratic transitions swept across central and eastern Europe, Latin America, and many parts of Sub-Saharan Africa and Asia in the late 1980s and early 1990s. As the Cold War came to a close, many advanced democracies began pivoting their foreign policies away from anticommunism and toward democracy promotion, based on the enticing notion that the long-standing tension between *realpolitik* and liberal democratic ideals had been overcome.[5] In tandem with this geopolitical shift, Western governments and international organizations launched new aid programs seeking to sustain nascent democratic openings, powered by a strong sense of optimism about the potential for transnational democratic learning. Through a growing network of nonprofits, institutes, and consulting groups, they began channeling aid to newly created electoral commissions, political parties, parliaments, civil society groups, and other entities viewed as essential for democratic consolidation.[6]

This first wave of democracy aid programs integrated women's political rights and participation in a mostly peripheral manner. But the spread of democracy assistance in the 1990s took shape in parallel to another global trend: a surge in local and transnational activism for gender equality change. In countries where women's movements had previously been co-opted by authoritarian single-party regimes, new autonomous women's groups multiplied. Emboldened by increasing political liberalization, they began mobilizing more openly for a seat at the decision-making table. In 1995, activists from around the world assembled at the Fourth World Conference on Women in Beijing to press governments for greater gender equality across all areas of public life, including in the political sphere. "Without the active participation of women and the incorporation of women's perspective at all levels of decision-making, the goals of equality, development and peace cannot be achieved," warned the resulting Beijing Platform for Action.[7]

Over the past two and a half decades, gender equality advocates have successfully pushed for greater attention to gender equality across foreign policy and development aid, including in international democracy support. International policy and normative frameworks on women's political participation have also multiplied. For instance, UN Security Council Resolution 1325 on women's role in conflict prevention and resolution has given rise to a global Women, Peace and Security (WPS) agenda that seeks to strengthen women's participation in peace and security efforts. The United Nations' Sustainable Development Goals (SDGs) also include a worldwide target for strengthening women's participation and leadership.[8] An increasing number of countries—including Canada, Chile, Colombia, France, Germany, Luxembourg, Mexico, the Netherlands, Spain and, until recently, Sweden—have formally adopted "feminist foreign policies" or "feminist international assistance policies" that elevate gender equality and women's rights to a central foreign policy objective.[9]

Governments have various tools at their disposal to advance these commitments internationally. They can push for women's inclusion in bilateral and international negotiations, raise issues related to women's political rights in political dialogues with partner countries, and use their diplomatic presence in other countries to raise the public profile of women's rights advocates and organizations. They can act as role models by promoting women's political leadership at home and ensuring diversity within their own senior diplomatic corps and multilateral delegations. Beyond these diplomatic strategies, however, aid programs that seek to bolster women's political empowerment have emerged as the primary avenue for cross-national engagement. Most of the world's largest development aid donors today fund initiatives to advance women's political empowerment as part of their rising investments in gender equality aid, and channel these resources to multilateral organizations like UN Women, international nongovernmental groups, as well as women's organizations in aid-recipient countries.

Taking stock of progress

These assistance efforts have contributed to important global gains. One of the most repeated data points is the remarkable increase in women's legislative representation around the world. The average share of women parliamentarians has more than doubled over the past twenty-five years, from 11.3 percent in 1995 to 26.7 percent in 2023.[10] Across 136 countries for which data is available, women now also make up 34 percent of elected members in local deliberative bodies.[11] Although executive leadership positions have proven more difficult for women and other marginalized groups to break into, women have gained ground within cabinets. As of 2023, they held 22.8 percent of ministerial positions globally, and there were twenty-six countries where women served as heads of state and/or government.[12]

These worldwide averages inevitably obscure significant regional variation. Globally, the Americas and Europe have fared substantially better with respect to women's parliamentary representation than the Middle East or the Pacific region.[13] Yet it is not the case that all donor countries that promote women's political empowerment through their foreign aid investments outperform aid recipients. Take the example of the United States: with a Congress that remains over 70 percent male, the country ranks seventy-first on the Inter-Parliamentary Union's (IPU) index of women in parliament globally, far behind Armenia,

Bolivia, Namibia, and South Africa (to name a few). Other prominent donor governments such as Canada, Italy, and the United Kingdom also remain far from gender parity, with women's parliamentary representation lingering below 35 percent.[14] Even though international democracy assistance flows primarily to fragile and developing democracies, the challenge of women's underrepresentation in politics remains a global one.

Of course, gender-inclusive democracy is not only about women's high-level leadership. When it comes to other dimensions of women's political empowerment, however, global and regional trend lines are more difficult to assess. Data by the Varieties of Democracy (V-Dem) project show that women's civil liberties—measured by examining access to justice, private property rights, freedom of movement, and freedom from forced labor—have improved substantially since the 1960s, paving the way for other forms of political participation.[15] Voting patterns vary across regions: whereas women tend to vote at higher rates than men in some central and eastern European countries, the opposite is true in most of the Middle East and North Africa and in parts of Asia.[16] However, even in some traditionally conservative societies, gender gaps in voting have started to decrease. In India, for example, women are now casting their ballots in higher numbers than ever before.[17] Around the world, women's mobilization in civil society has also achieved remarkable successes over the past several decades, including the adoption of gender quotas, new laws countering gender-based violence, and reforms to discriminatory family codes.[18]

Despite these important advances, however, it is possible to look at global trend lines and paint a much more dispiriting picture. For one, the overall pace of gender equality change in politics remains frustratingly slow. No country has achieved full political parity across all branches of government, and at the current rate of progress, gender parity in national legislative bodies will not be attained before 2063.[19] Although electoral gender quotas in many countries have fast-tracked more women in political office, they have sometimes turned into de facto ceilings that women are struggling to break through. Even in many consolidated democracies, the most powerful political positions and policy portfolios are still overwhelmingly held by men. Women politicians and activists also routinely experience gendered harassment and violence, including disproportionate levels of online abuse. Rather than ebbing as more women enter the political sphere, this type of pushback has only become more visible.[20]

The past decade has also brought global democratic backsliding and worrisome signs of backlash against past gender equality gains. In Hungary, Nicaragua, Turkey, and elsewhere, illiberal leaders are forcefully pushing back against feminist and LGBTQ+ demands for equality and inclusion. New antirights groups are mobilizing locally and transnationally to roll back past legislative and policy measures on women's rights and gender equality. More and more countries are cracking down on international democracy assistance and imposing new restrictions on autonomous civil society groups, thereby limiting women's ability to advance change through activism and protest.[21] Recent data on women's political leadership also show signs of stagnation. The World Economic Forum's Women's Political Empowerment Index, for instance, indicates no global progress over the course of 2021 and only modest improvements in 2022.[22] In some countries, women's legislative representation has *decreased* significantly, including in Afghanistan, Algeria, Qatar, and Zambia.[23] At the same time, some authoritarian governments have learned that they can curry international favor by promoting women into positions of leadership, even as they crack down on other forms of political mobilization and activism.[24] Women's political gains in countries such as Rwanda and the United Arab Emirates raise new challenges for democracy assistance providers, by highlighting that efforts to "deepen democracy" and "support women's political leadership" may not always go hand-in-hand.

Capturing learning

This paradoxical moment, marked by both progress and threats of backsliding, presents an opportunity for critical stocktaking. More than twenty-five years after the Beijing Conference, practitioners and policymakers working to support women's political empowerment have accumulated significant knowledge and experience about the strengths and limitations of different types of interventions. Yet their insights have not been systematically captured. Despite the vast body of research on women's political participation around the world, there are still few analyses of international aid in this domain. Practitioners tend to have limited time and resources to engage in reflection. They may collect and distill their lessons learned internally, but they rarely share these findings with the wider public or even with other organizations working in the field. Due to the competitive nature of the aid industry and concerns about jeopardizing relationships with local partners, public-facing reports often highlight success stories rather than engaging in critical analysis.

The bulk of existing practitioner research thus consists of "best practice" guides for implementing organizations and donor-commissioned evaluations of specific projects. The latter (which are not always published) often measure progress against narrow indicators and outputs, such as the number of women trained or gender policies passed. They generally do not take a step back to put these findings into a broader comparative context. Moreover, aid activities related to women's participation are sometimes a small part of larger democracy aid initiatives, which means that evaluations only discuss them in passing. In recent years, some donor agencies and multilateral organizations have tried to strengthen their evidence base by commissioning meta-reviews that seek to synthesize findings across multiple aid programs.[25] However, these reviews tend to be technical documents that focus on high-level bureaucratic constraints and enablers, rather than providing nuanced insights into programming "on the ground."

Within the academic sphere, gender and politics scholars have extensively researched the drivers of women's political empowerment around the world. Existing accounts emphasize the role of cultural and religious norms, levels of economic development, and the effects of political institutions, particularly the design of electoral systems and gender quotas.[26] But international influences also feature prominently. One important strand of research underscores the role of international actors in driving the transnational diffusion and adoption of quota reforms, through both their partnerships with local women's organizations and direct pressure on governments.[27] Some scholars also find that international linkages and assistance have led autocratic regimes to adopt gender quotas and promote women's political representation.[28] Yet the bulk of these studies investigate macrolevel relationships between foreign aid and women's rights reforms, rather than focusing on the design and implementation of specific aid initiatives. Moreover, they do not explore the much wider range of aid programs that are unrelated to electoral quotas, such as efforts to train women candidates, bolster women's caucuses, and reform political parties.

A second, smaller body of research focuses on women's political empowerment programs within specific countries, or investigates the theories of change guiding specific types of donor initiatives. These microlevel analyses highlight a disconnect between the predominant aid strategies and the political and structural constraints that limit women's political representation in aid-receiving countries. Piscopo (2018), for instance, theorizes the limits of candidate training programs in tackling institutional, organizational, and structural barriers to women's political leadership in new or developing democracies.[29] Wood (2015) and Geha (2019) similarly observe a mismatch between international training programs and the primary challenges facing women candidates in the Solomon Islands and in Lebanon, respectively.[30] Carapico (2014), on the other hand, observes how democracy aid providers in the Middle East often frame Arab women as victims of a patriarchal culture rather than full political agents and favor professionalized women's organizations and state-managed women's movements over more contentious forms of feminist mobilization.[31] These findings echo insights from the broader academic literature on international democracy support, which also critiques donors for relying on technical projects and reform templates that are often out of sync with local struggles for political change.[32]

Our book seeks to bring together these presently disparate strands of scholarship. Cross-national analyses examining foreign aid and quota adoption, as well as country-specific analyses of training programs or civil society support, tackle important dimensions of the current assistance landscape. They do not, however, capture the full diversity and complexity of aid programs focused on women's political empowerment. Drawing on both existing research and original data, we therefore seek to build a more comprehensive analytical map of the field, conceptualizing it as a distinct domain of international democracy promotion worthy of independent analysis. To chart out the boundaries of this field and its current characteristics, we focus on several guiding questions:

1. First, how has international support for women's political empowerment evolved over time and why? What are the primary areas of progress and learning?
2. Second, what can we conclude about the strengths and weaknesses of the most common programming models and their underlying theories of change?
3. Third, what are the main challenges facing this area of international support— and how do they unsettle existing assistance approaches?

To answer these questions, we direct our focus to the community of international nongovernmental organizations, aid officials, policymakers, and gender equality activists that fund, design, implement, and evaluate aid programs centered on women's political inclusion across the developing world. We draw on over 180 interviews with policymakers, practitioners, civil society advocates, and politicians in Western donor countries and across four aid-receiving countries, namely Kenya, Morocco, Myanmar, and Nepal. To investigate how aid programs unfold in practice, we center the perspectives of women's rights advocates and organizations that are often at the receiving end of international aid, both as targets and implementers of international funding. In doing so, we seek to move beyond black-and-white narratives that frame aid as either normatively desirable and thus beyond critical empirical scrutiny or that dismiss it upfront as ineffective or counterproductive. Our aim instead is to tell a nuanced story about the actors, approaches, and ideas that characterize the field.

Our arguments

This book tells a story of gradual learning as well as persistent shortcomings. We argue that international aid for women's political empowerment has undergone a significant evolution over the last three decades, from a first generation of efforts that aimed to integrate women into nascent democratic institutions to a second generation that focuses on transforming the broader political ecosystem hindering women's equal political influence. Yet this evolution remains incomplete, and efforts to deepen existing work are running into thorny obstacles.

Engendering democracy

In the 1990s and 2000s, many aid providers supported the implementation of gender quotas and trained women to run for office, typically in partnership with politically oriented women's groups. Mirroring the insights of earlier research on women's political representation, international actors hoped that gender quotas would increase political parties' "demand" for women leaders, while training initiatives would simultaneously bolster the "supply" of qualified women candidates. Yet although the global push for quotas proved very successful, this first generation of aid had significant limitations. Most importantly, it paid only limited attention to entrenched institutional and sociocultural barriers to women's political empowerment, and it often took the form of scattered, stand-alone initiatives that were disconnected from broader democracy promotion activities.

Over the past decade, the search for new entry points has given rise to a second generation of assistance characterized by two important shifts. First, rather than merely integrating women into existing structures, these newer initiatives place greater emphasis on making the entire political ecosystem more gender-inclusive. They are supporting not only women's individual confidence and capacity but also a wide range of institutional reforms. They are also increasingly tackling persistent patriarchal gender norms and violence targeting women in politics. Second, both donor agencies and implementing organizations are increasingly complementing stand-alone "women-in-politics" activities with efforts to mainstream gender equality across all areas of democracy support, including electoral assistance, political party aid, and parliamentary support.

However, this shift toward an "ecosystem" approach is still unfolding, and changes in thinking have in many ways outstripped changes in actual aid practice. For one, efforts to tackle discriminatory gender norms and informal institutions remain much more incipient than interventions focused on capacity-building and institutional or legal reform. Not only are these areas outside of the traditional comfort zone of many democracy support organizations but they are also more difficult to influence than formal institutions and frameworks, particularly within the timespan of an assistance program. Moreover, aid actors have made less progress adapting their programmatic templates to challenging political landscapes, such as those marked by entrenched inequalities among women or those affected by democratic erosion or authoritarian co-optation. Finally, current assistance modalities in some ways remain at odds with an ecosystem approach. Most funding for targeted women's political empowerment programs is still short-term, project-based, and thematically siloed, and thus fails to empower grassroots actors fighting at the frontlines of gender equality change. Gender mainstreaming, on the other hand, often remains superficial, hampered by weak political commitments and aid providers' insufficient expertise on gender and democracy issues. Taken together, these dynamics disincentivize the long-term, flexible interventions needed to generate transformative change.

A closer look at three common areas of programming across our four cases—training for women candidates, efforts to reform political parties, and initiatives bolstering the influence of women legislators—reinforces and deepens these findings. Many programs fall back on short-term capacity-building, whereas sustained and problem-oriented coaching and mentorship remain scarce. No matter how well designed, these training initiatives targeting women cannot dismantle hostile institutions or tackle the discriminatory norms and biases of male gatekeepers. Although some innovative programs are attempting to challenge exclusionary structures within political parties and parliaments, their track record has been mixed. So far, aid actors have had more success bolstering women's political networks, facilitating gender assessments, and (in some cases) securing changes in policies and rules than they have ensuring the latter's implementation. Moreover, programs rarely measure longer-term shifts in gender norms, behaviors, and practices within institutions, making it difficult to assess progress. One recurring hurdle is aid organizations' weak attention to the politics of gender equality reform, including the political incentives of and institutional constraints on various political actors.

Building on this analysis, we examine several critical challenges facing the field: the persistence of patriarchal norms within the political sphere, the challenges posed by systemic inequities *between* women as well as democratic erosion, and a global funding system ill-suited to driving gender-transformative change. In recent years, democracy support actors have launched new initiatives to tackle some of these frontiers. Emerging interventions seek to engage men as agents of gender equality change, and international actors are increasingly investing in data collection, norm-building, and advocacy focused on fighting violence against women in politics. Additionally, references to intersectionality and the inclusion of marginalized women have multiplied in policy frameworks and programs. New funding models also seek to shift more resources and power into the hands of feminist and women's rights movements and organizations.

These are promising avenues for engagement that represent a natural deepening of the second-generation approaches. At the same time, most of this work is still nascent, and aid providers and researchers have much to learn about which approaches work where and how to adjust their support to contexts of

Introduction 13

backsliding or co-optation. Moreover, as democracy support actors attempt to build on past successes and expand their assistance in these new areas, they have to change their ways of operating. Aiding gender norm change, supporting processes of intersectional empowerment, and countering patriarchal authoritarianism requires them to move beyond their traditional focus on formal institutions and cooperative partnerships with government counterparts and take on greater political risk, particularly to invest in women's collective leadership and mobilization.

Concepts and boundaries

Democracy aid providers and practitioners use a wide range of terms to describe their work on gender equality, from promoting "women's political participation and leadership" to advancing "gender-inclusive democracy." In general, however, international assistance programs carried out under these different rubrics concentrate on changes across three main spheres: (1) women's individual political engagement, primarily as voters; (2) women's political mobilization in civil society, as members and leaders of nongovernmental groups; and (3) women's political participation and representation as candidates and elected or appointed officials.

Throughout the book, we use "aid for women's political empowerment" as an umbrella term to describe these different activities, for several reasons. For one, the term is broad enough to encompass the individual, civic, and formal political spheres, without emphasizing one over the other. Moreover, it puts the spotlight on *power*, thereby signaling that the end goal of gender equality change is not only formal political or legal equality between men and women, but also women's increased capacity to *influence* political decision-making. We thus follow Alexander, Bolzendahl, and Jalalzai (2018) in conceptualizing women's political empowerment as "the enhancement of assets, capabilities, and achievements of women to gain equality to men in influencing and exercising political authority worldwide," through their inclusion in elite institutions, their mobilization in civil society, and their empowerment as citizens.[33]

Our analysis examines aid programs that concentrate on *political* institutions and processes, including elections, political parties, legislatures, and politically oriented civil society organizations. At the same time, the boundaries of what is or is not "political" can be murky. To limit the scope of our book, we excluded several areas of assistance that are related to and contribute to women's political empowerment but that often fall beyond the traditional scope of democracy aid. For one, we do not examine in detail initiatives that focus on increasing the number of women serving in state bureaucracies or in the judiciary, or on nurturing gender-responsive state governance more broadly. We also do not analyze assistance programs implemented under the umbrella of the global WPS agenda, including efforts to bolster women's participation in peace negotiations or increase their presence among the ranks of security force personnel. Finally, our analysis does not include the much wider range of development aid programs that seek to advance women's socioeconomic empowerment and prevent gender-based violence.

By excluding these forms of aid from our analysis, we do not mean to suggest that they are apolitical in nature. Our approach instead reflects the current structure of international assistance: in practice, democracy support is often funded and implemented separately from aid focused on conflict stabilization and peacebuilding and on women's socioeconomic and legal empowerment. There are, of course, instances when these different assistance realms overlap, and we draw attention to these intersections throughout our analysis. Indeed, the book shows that entrenched thematic and sectoral silos are often at odds with advancing women's political empowerment in a holistic fashion.

It is also worth noting that efforts to protect and advance the political rights and representation of LGBTQ+ individuals and organizations have expanded in recent years. We view these efforts as related to and intersecting with initiatives targeting women's political empowerment: both seek to challenge and transform existing gender hierarchies and build more gender-inclusive democracies. At the same time, the challenges facing LGBTQ+ communities in politics are often distinct and far more severe, rooted in criminalization and persecution in many societies. For this reason, we do not cover them in this analysis but invite other scholars to study these assistance efforts in greater depth.

Our approach

This book draws on qualitative data collection and analysis. It combines in-depth interviews with aid officials and policymakers and reviews of assistance documents across donor countries with case studies of women's political empowerment aid in Kenya, Morocco, Myanmar, and Nepal.

On sources and methods

We began our research by reviewing and analyzing the existing academic and gray literature on donor support for women's political empowerment and analyzing publicly available donor strategies, programming guides, annual reports, evidence reviews, and program evaluations. As a second step, we interviewed thirty-five gender and democracy experts working in the headquarters of multilateral organizations, bilateral donor agencies and foreign ministries, and international nongovernmental organizations (INGOs) specialized in democracy assistance, located mostly in Europe and North America. These experts are charged with developing new gender equality strategies and overseeing their implementation, as well as developing targeted programming guidance and providing substantive advice to country offices. As a result, they have a unique overview of the field. Together, these two sources of data inform our analysis of the overarching evolution of international aid and the new challenges confronting aid officials and practitioners at the global level.

Building on these initial interviews, we then selected four countries—Kenya, Morocco, Myanmar, and Nepal—to explore in more detail how international programs are implemented in practice. International support for women's political empowerment today reaches a wide range of political regimes, from conflict-affected and fragile democracies to backsliding electoral autocracies. We chose our four case studies to reflect some regional diversity as well as different types of aid recipient countries: although all four have received significant democracy aid over the last two decades, they are characterized by varying levels of women's political representation and democratic space. By examining international assistance across these four different contexts, we can identify common trends in donor programming and explore how wider contextual factors shape their implementation on the ground.

In each of our case study countries, we closely reviewed existing program evaluations, aid strategies, and secondary research on women's political empowerment. We then conducted between thirty-five and forty-five semistructured interviews with international donor officials, local and international staff working at international democracy assistance organizations, gender equality activists, and women politicians. These interviewees were identified using a snowball sampling technique. We began by reaching out to country experts or local staff of major aid organizations and then used these initial contacts to identify further research participants. In our interviews with practitioners, we asked open-ended questions about the reasoning behind different activities and their experiences with implementation, including successes, challenges, and shifts in programming over time. We inquired why they felt certain interventions worked well and others did not, paying attention to how our interlocutors defined "impact" or "success." We also sought out the perspectives of those on the other side of these programs, including local civil society organizations, gender experts, and women politicians themselves. We interviewed some women who had participated in donor-funded activities, as well as some who only had limited exposure to these efforts, and asked which approaches they felt were most and least useful and why. We used an interpreter for some of the interviews conducted in Nepalese; all other interviews were conducted by us in either English or French.

Here, it is worth briefly returning to the nature and scope of our analysis. Any study of international aid inevitably raises the question: does such assistance work? Yet answering this question systematically is remarkably difficult. If researchers compare aid-receiving countries to those that do not receive such aid, they run into the problem that foreign aid is not a random treatment. Instead, different types of countries receive different types and levels of support. For example, democracy support is often designed to take advantage of political openings, such as constitutional negotiation processes. This dynamic makes it difficult to assess whether positive outcomes can be (fully or partially) attributed to the assistance in question. At the program level, assessing outcomes is not necessarily easier. Although it is possible to randomize certain interventions to rigorously assess their impact, the same method cannot be applied to other forms of international support, particularly in the political realm. For example, aid organizations can evaluate whether a randomized voter education initiative changes citizens' political behavior in a particular locality. However, they cannot randomize their technical assistance to and dialogue with electoral institutions and political parties in a given country. There are, of course, other ways of evaluating impact, including qualitative process tracing. But establishing a direct causal link between a specific aid program and broader political developments is often difficult, particularly in complex and rapidly evolving political environments. In some cases, it can also be difficult to determine what should count as "success," particularly if the intended changes are unlikely to unfold rapidly or in a linear fashion.

Given these challenges, our analysis does not seek to measure the overall effect of women's political empowerment assistance in aid-receiving countries compared to contexts that did not receive such aid. Our research design is not set up to do this, as all four of our case study countries have received significant amounts of democracy support. Nor do we evaluate the causal impact of any one program. Instead, our aim is both more expansive and more limited: we seek to develop a broader analytical framework for understanding progress and challenges in this field of assistance. We distill recurring themes among practitioners' and advocates' insights, program evaluations, and existing research, and investigate whether the rationales underlying donor-funded programs match local political realities.

By excluding "negative cases" that have not received international democracy aid from our analysis, we limit the applicability of our findings to aid-receiving contexts that resemble our cases. As such, we are unable to draw conclusions about how women's political empowerment can best be promoted in contexts that international democracy aid does not reach, such as closed autocracies, countries affected by high levels of armed conflict, or middle-income countries that receive little foreign aid. This question, while important, falls outside the scope of this analysis.

The reader may wonder about our own relationship to the programs under study. While we do not have any formal affiliation with an aid organization, we view our position as researchers as that of "feminist critical friends," a term coined by Chappell and Mackay (2021) to describe the relationship between "feminist academics and researchers who are 'entangled' with international organisations."[34] As such, we share a normative commitment to challenging gender inequities in politics with many of the actors that appear in this book. We also aim for our research to be useful and accessible to practitioners and policymakers in the international democracy assistance community, and for our criticisms of the field to be constructive. At the same time, throughout the course of our research, we have strived to maintain a critical distance from the policy world in order to highlight recurring shortcomings, faulty or untested assumptions, and policy trade-offs that those operating within aid agencies are often not well-positioned to recognize or openly acknowledge.

That being said, it is possible that some of our interviewees believed that we were somehow affiliated with international aid organizations. We were careful to explain our role as independent researchers working with a nongovernmental research institute when requesting and conducting interviews. We also noted that our goal was not to evaluate any particular program or organization. Research participants who are frequently surveyed and interviewed by aid organizations and evaluators may nevertheless have associated our research project with the United States government or other donor agencies.[35] In practice, this could mean that some research participants—especially those who receive donor funding—felt pressure to speak about program outcomes in a positive light, in the hope of increasing their chances of receiving future funding. To mitigate any such bias in our interview data, we triangulated our findings with multiple sources, including program evaluations and interviews with local gender equality experts and women politicians who had never participated in aid programs. In general, however, we observed that interviewees from both local and international implementing organizations openly voiced criticism of international actors and shared why they thought certain programs had not achieved their intended effects.

Research during a global pandemic

Our data collection for this study was shaped by the global coronavirus pandemic. We began our interviews with policymakers and aid officials in the United States, Brussels, and the United Kingdom in the fall of 2019 and planned to complete the bulk of our case study research in Kenya, Morocco, Myanmar, and Nepal during the early spring and summer of 2020. Following the onset of the Covid-19 pandemic, however, we quickly decided not to move forward with our research trips. Global travel became difficult due to new entry restrictions, and we did not want to put any of our research participants at risk.[36] Instead, we proceeded with remote interviews using Zoom and WhatsApp to connect with our research participants.[37]

Like other scholars who have written about the shift from in-person to digital research, we found that our reliance on remote interviewing had both advantages and drawbacks. Given that our interlocutors were mostly politicians, aid workers, and civil society activists, access to computers and Internet service was generally not an obstacle. Virtual conversations enabled us to speak with a wide variety of participants with much more scheduling flexibility and less time pressure. Like Howlett (2022), we also found that video calls often facilitated more relaxed, symmetrical, and informal conversations than perhaps would have been possible in an office setting.[38] We were able to establish a rapport with our interlocutors by sharing our respective experiences during this unusual period and reflecting on the shifts the pandemic had caused in our work and our personal lives.

The biggest disadvantage of this virtual approach was our lack of physical immersion in our research sites. We were familiar with the democracy aid world that we were studying, having visited many donor headquarters and overseas aid offices and observed different types of democracy aid activities for previous research projects. Yet in this case, we were unable to complement our interviews with ethnographic observation of the spaces and activities we were studying, nor could we participate in spontaneous conversations and chance encounters. To make up for these gaps, we complemented our interviews with additional sources whenever possible, including program evaluations and activity reports provided by aid officials and expert interviews with local academics who could provide contextual knowledge. Throughout 2021 and 2022, we also conducted a series of in-person follow-up interviews with women candidates, politicians, and aid workers in Kenya, and observed several training activities in different parts of the country. These additional forms of data collection allowed us to deepen parts of our analysis.

The Covid-19 pandemic also impacted women's political empowerment and the assistance programs we were studying, both in our case study countries and globally. The pandemic's harmful effects on gender equality have been widely documented: around the world, women and girls lost their jobs, dropped out of school, and experienced gender-based violence at higher rates than men and boys.[39] Although the consequences of the pandemic for women's political participation were not immediately clear or directly observable, they were on our minds and the minds of our interlocutors while we conducted our research. Some women politicians we spoke with told us that their work had shifted online and worried about supporting their constituents through the crisis. Many women's rights activists were lobbying their governments to ensure gender-sensitive pandemic responses. Democracy aid providers, on the other hand, described temporarily putting their programs on hold or moving activities online. In terms of our own data collection, however, we felt that the pandemic was still too new and its trajectory too uncertain to investigate its effects on assistance. Our analysis, therefore, centers on programs that were designed and implemented prior to the crisis. Anecdotal impressions and follow-up interviews suggest that many aid providers did not radically shift their ambitions, strategies, and tactics after initial lockdowns and restrictions eased. As a result, we believe that our findings remain valid and useful to researchers interested in learning more about the field and practitioners seeking to rethink and refine their activities in the future.

Outline of this study

The book proceeds in three parts. The rest of Part I sets the stage for our empirical inquiry. Chapter 2 describes how and why women's political empowerment evolved from a nascent, sometimes grudging line of effort within the democracy assistance community to a growing donor priority. We show that aid for women's political empowerment has grown from a niche endeavor to a significant area of cross-border assistance that involves a global network of actors and organizations, ranging from UN institutions and major donor agencies to grassroots women's groups. However, behind this apparent global consensus lie unresolved questions about commitments, strategies, and goals. Chapter 3 introduces our four case studies—Nepal, Kenya, Morocco, and Myanmar—and highlights their similarities and differences. For each country, we describe the evolution of women's political representation over the past three decades and briefly review the role of international democracy support in this process.

Part II of the book develops our core analytical framework and explores the question of impact. Chapter 4 analyzes the first generation of programs focused on women's political empowerment, covering both the achievements and limitations of donor support for gender quotas, capacity building for female candidates and elected officials, and support for women's organizations. Chapter 5 examines the emergence of a second generation of aid programs, analyzing the shift in aid actors' priorities from a narrow focus on women's political participation to a broader emphasis on transforming the institutions and norms that perpetuate women's political exclusion. Chapters 6, 7, and 8 tackle the question of effectiveness in further detail. We turn the lens to three areas of action that have received extensive international support: training programs for women aspirants and candidates, initiatives to advance gender equality in political parties, and efforts to bolster women's political influence and leadership once in office. Drawing on academic research, donor evaluations, and interviews conducted across our four case studies, we review existing intervention models, examine their underlying theories of change, and trace what advocates and practitioners have learned about their strengths and weaknesses over time.

Part III of the book tackles the frontiers of the field—new areas of actions that build on and deepen second-generation approaches. Confronted with the limits of capacity-building and formal institutional change, aid officials and advocates are increasingly paying attention to the deeper causes of gender inequities in politics. In Chapter 9, we describe new efforts to challenge deeply embedded gender norms and informal practices that undermine women's equal political power, focusing on initiatives that engage men as agents of change and tackle violence and backlash against women in politics. Chapter 10 interrogates how current assistance models address intersecting forms of exclusion and discrimination and explores the challenges posed by global democratic erosion and autocrats' efforts to advance women's political representation and leadership. Chapter 11 turns to several overarching shortcomings of the current aid system, including chronic short-termism, entrenched thematic silos, and project-based aid that is ill-suited to bolstering women's grassroots political mobilization. In the final chapter, we summarize our key arguments and findings, and offer detailed policy recommendations for aid officials, implementing organizations, and local civil society advocates looking to strengthen the field moving forward.

2

The Global Aid Ecosystem

In 1890, women did not have the right to vote anywhere in the world. No women served in elected office, and most were shut out of public roles as state representatives or civil servants. Finland became the first country to elect a woman to parliament—in 1907. Today, women have served as heads of state and government in fifty-nine countries and make up just over 25 percent of legislators worldwide.[1] With the exception of Vatican City, women can vote and run for office in every country that holds national elections, and most states have established ministries or public bodies dedicated to advancing women's concerns in the policy process.[2] Although women's political underrepresentation persists, the global picture looks markedly different than it once did.

International actors and exchanges have been crucial drivers of these shifts. Long before multilateral institutions and bilateral aid agencies took up the issue of women's political leadership, women formed transnational alliances to advance their political inclusion. Over the course of the twentieth century, their campaigns morphed into a global movement encompassing thousands of activists and organizations. As the international women's movement gained in influence, it increasingly collaborated with international organizations and donor governments to advance women's political empowerment, thereby laying the foundations for many of the aid policies and programs that exist today.[3]

This chapter introduces the global aid ecosystem focused on women's political empowerment. We start by describing how women's rights activists mobilized to establish a global norm for women's political inclusion, as well as the changes this norm triggered in international development policy and assistance over time. The second half of the chapter maps out the network of actors involved in funding, designing, and implementing women's political empowerment interventions today. We conclude the chapter by discussing the depth of existing policy and aid commitments and addressing critical questions raised

Aiding Empowerment. Saskia Brechenmacher and Katherine Mann, Oxford University Press.
© Oxford University Press 2024. DOI: 10.1093/oso/9780197694275.003.0002

by skeptics. After more than a century of activism, women's political empowerment is now firmly entrenched in international legal and policy frameworks, and development aid funding in this area has steadily increased over time. Yet this apparent international consensus belies ongoing questions and tensions characterizing this growing area of democracy support—questions about commitment, credibility, and strategy.

The rise of a new global norm

On March 25, 1888, American suffragist Elizabeth Cady Stanton addressed the founding congress of the International Council on Women in Washington, DC. Speaking to an audience of American, European, Indian, and Russian women, she argued that "women of all nationalities, in the artificial distinctions of sex, have a universal sense of injustice, that forms a common bond of union between them."[4] This meeting in Washington was not an isolated event: beginning in the mid-nineteenth century, women who were active in different social movements devoted to abolitionism, socialism, pacifism, and women's rights began forging new transnational connections.[5] Their coalition-building efforts accelerated at the turn of the century, with women from different parts of the world coming together to create new organizations such as the International Woman Suffrage Alliance and the Women's International League for Peace and Freedom. Like Stanton, they argued that the path to gender equality had to be forged through cross-national cooperation—even as many emerging alliances remained heavily Euro-American in their composition and leadership, and often excluded the demands of nonwhite, enslaved, or colonized women.

The first wave of women's transnational activism primarily focused on the right to vote, with suffrage sometimes framed as an end in itself and other times as a means to pursue broader political goals. The creation of new international bodies after the First World War—namely the League of Nations and the International Labour Organization—opened new institutional arenas for women to advance these demands. Gender equality activists formed organizations to influence this emerging multilateral infrastructure, and transnational cooperation between women's groups intensified.[6] However, their push for equal political citizenship faced stiff resistance from male political leaders, who argued that issues of individual rights did not fall under the purview of international institutions. Women's rights activists themselves were far from united in their views, with some advancing a liberal reformist agenda and others demanding radical socialist transformation. Women's diverging demands also mirrored global power relations. Whereas white women in many Western countries gained voting rights following the First World War, women in most parts of the world were still fighting for basic political rights both as women *and* as members of colonized and oppressed communities.[7]

The end of the Second World War brought further openings for feminist advocacy, chief among them the establishment of the United Nations and the expansion of an international human rights framework centered on individual political rights. Although there were only four women represented among the 160 signatories of the UN Charter, women's rights activists influenced the body's earliest meetings. Feminists from Brazil, the Dominican Republic, and Mexico successfully pushed for gender equality to be included in the UN's founding document and lobbied for the creation of the UN Commission on the Status of Women, which has played a crucial role in setting international standards that challenge gender discriminatory domestic laws.[8] By institutionalizing gender equality at the international level, women's organizations generated stronger pressure on states to incorporate women as full political subjects.

By 1970, most countries around the world had dismantled formal legal barriers to women's right to vote and run for political office. However, women remained a small minority in decision-making roles. In response, women's transnational organizing shifted its focus to women's political *representation*, with advocates calling for not only "the right to vote" but also "the right to be elected."[9] The 1970s in particular generated an explosion of political activism. In many countries, a new generation of feminist activists started pushing for much more expansive social change, challenging patriarchy and inequality in all areas of life. The number of women's INGOs skyrocketed, producing an "increasingly dense network of actors mobilizing on behalf of equal representation."[10] Responding to this surge in activity, the UN declared 1975 the International Women's Year and 1975–1985 the Decade for Women. It also hosted a series of world conferences on women's rights that allowed activists to build stronger global and regional networks. Activists' new focus on women's political representation and leadership directly influenced the international treaties forged during this period. For example, the 1979 Convention on the Elimination of All Forms of Discrimination against Women (CEDAW) affirmed women's right "to hold public office and perform all public functions at all levels of government," and urged signatories to take "measures to ensure to women, on equal terms with men and without any discrimination, the opportunity to represent their governments."[11]

The 1990s brought another shift in women's transnational mobilization for political inclusion. Confronting a sluggish rate of global progress, advocates began demanding that governments adopt concrete legislative targets to advance women's political leadership.[12] This new priority was reflected at the

1995 Beijing World Conference on Women, which brought together a women's movement that was much more organized and global than in previous decades. At the conference, activists from Latin America and several postconflict countries shared their experience instituting legislative gender quotas, which helped propel the issue to the forefront of the conference agenda.[13] The Beijing Platform for Action, signed by all 189 participating states at the conference, called on governments to establish targets to include at least 30 percent women in political decision-making structures and to take proactive measures toward achieving this goal.[14] The conference marked the beginning of a new era in advocacy for women's political rights, by strengthening women's political representation as a core international norm and legitimizing activists' domestic demands for quota measures.[15]

The growing international consensus around women's right to political inclusion also opened up new avenues for gender equality activists to promote gender-balanced representation in peace processes and conflict responses. Building on a long history of women's mobilization for peace and disarmament, local and international women's organizations in the 1980s and 1990s pushed international organizations to pay greater attention to women's distinct experiences and roles in conflict zones—as well as their contributions to peacemaking.[16] In 2000, these efforts culminated in UN Security Council Resolution 1325 on Women, Peace and Security, which urges member states to promote women's participation in conflict prevention, conflict resolution, and peacebuilding processes. Since then, governments around the world have passed 107 WPS Action Plans, all of which emphasize women's right to political participation as a key pillar of gender equality in conflict prevention and peacebuilding.[17]

In brief, women's transnational mobilization—facilitated by the expansion of international organizations and global human rights frameworks—has gradually established a global norm of women's political participation and representation, anchored in a growing web of international conventions, organizations, and commitments. In the twenty-eight years since Beijing, advocates and policy entrepreneurs have continued strengthening this norm. Numerous regional organizations, including the African Union and the Organization of American States, have affirmed women's right to equal political participation and representation in regional treaties and resolutions and called on states to take positive action in this respect. Today, global commitments to political inclusion are also reflected in the SDGs adopted in 2015, which include a specific target focused on advancing women's "full and effective participation and equal opportunities for leadership at all levels of decision-making."[18] Although the implementation of these commitments remains weak and incomplete, the global normative and policy framework is firmly in place—with important implications for international development aid.

A gradual aid evolution

For most of the twentieth century, transnational advocacy for women's political inclusion evolved separately from international development cooperation. Attention to women's political rights and participation within bilateral aid agencies only took off in the late 1980s and 1990s, both in response to global geopolitical changes and shifts in thinking about gender, democracy, and development among policymakers and practitioners.

Early development aid programs set up by Western governments in the 1950s and 1960s focused narrowly on advancing economic growth. They sought to transform countries economically by injecting technocratic knowledge and capital, while staying removed from messy political questions about colonialism, governance, and democratic participation.[19] They also largely ignored questions of gender equality, a gap that reflected women's general absence from development scholarship and decision-making in Western democracies at the time.

This pattern began to change in the 1970s. Although donor governments remained reluctant to engage in questions of political reform, women working within these institutions began mobilizing to correct the gender-blindness of traditional aid programs. Drawing on the second-wave feminist movement that was gaining traction at the time, proponents of this new approach—termed "Women in Development" (WID)—argued that targeted investments in women would benefit economic development overall. Enhancing women's neglected productive capacity, rather than simply treating women as welfare recipients, would increase overall productivity and earnings.[20] In response, many aid agencies established units or bureaus that implemented projects exclusively targeting women.[21] In the United States, for example, legislative amendments passed in 1973 directed USAID to "give particular attention to those programs, projects, and activities which tend to integrate women into the national economies of foreign countries."[22]

In general, however, WID offices within aid agencies remained peripheral to the overall aid enterprise. Women-focused projects were sequestered into separate and underresourced units rather than integrated into mainstream assistance efforts.[23] Moreover, critics in both the Global South and North pointed out that WID policies largely ignored the systemic drivers of gender inequities. Feminist neo-Marxists and dependency theorists in particular challenged the lack of attention to global systems of capital accumulation and economic inequality that perpetuated women's disempowerment.[24] However, neither WID advocates nor their critics explicitly grappled with women's *political* participation or representation. Their focus on economic empowerment reflected the political climate of the period, with most of the world's population still living in authoritarian states. It also reflected the pervasive idea in development circles that political development, and in particular democratization, would naturally follow from economic development.[25]

Several shifts in the 1980s and 1990s opened the door for aid organizations to engage much more explicitly with women's political rights and participation. Most importantly, the end of the Cold War and the third wave of democratic transitions radically altered the global geopolitical context. No longer focused on supporting anticommunist regimes, Western donor governments began funding new aid programs that explicitly sought to bolster fragile democratic openings in eastern Europe, Latin America, Sub-Saharan Africa, and Asia, including assistance initiatives targeting elections, prodemocratic civil society organizations, and newly established political parties.[26] New intergovernmental and nongovernmental organizations emerged that specialized in international support for democratic reform, such as the International Institute for Democracy and Electoral Assistance (International IDEA), the International Foundation for Electoral Systems (IFES), and the Westminster Foundation for Democracy. Various UN agencies also became more involved in democratization efforts, particularly in postconflict countries like Bosnia and Herzegovina, Cambodia, and Guatemala. The growth and increasing institutionalization of democracy support as a distinct assistance realm triggered more direct donor engagement with questions of women's political participation, particularly after the 1995 Beijing Conference put the issue firmly on the international agenda.[27]

In parallel to this changing geopolitical context, many aid agencies also underwent internal shifts that pushed them to integrate gender more systematically into their work. For one, some in the aid community began endorsing a human rights-based approach to development that (at least rhetorically) placed greater emphasis on the inclusion of marginalized and excluded groups in all development efforts.[28] In the gender realm, critiques of traditional WID approaches in the 1980s and 1990s gave rise to a new "Gender and Development" (GAD) approach that pushed for a stronger focus on addressing the systemic roots of women's subordination. In contrast to earlier WID programs, proponents of the GAD model argued that gender should be seen as a cross-cutting issue relevant to all political, social, and economic processes.[29] These changes in thinking prompted a new focus on gender mainstreaming within aid agencies. Mainstreaming typically had two components: first, integrating gender perspectives across the entire spectrum of aid projects, and second, diffusing responsibility for gender issues beyond isolated "women's units" through gender training, focal points, and agency-wide guidelines.[30]

Nordic governments were the first to experiment with this approach; other bilateral funders followed suit in the early 1990s. The Beijing Conference further accelerated the trend, with many donor governments and multilateral organizations hiring gender specialists, developing new gender strategies, and launching new forms of gender training for their staff.[31] In practice, these changes remained contested, with gender equality advocates criticizing aid agencies for instituting only superficial fixes without fundamentally rethinking existing aid models.[32] But the shift to gender mainstreaming was nevertheless significant. It led many bilateral and multilateral aid organizations to expand their internal capacity for integrating gender into program design, including into the growing field of democracy and governance assistance.

Mapping the current assistance landscape

Today, all major donor governments and multilateral institutions cite gender equality as one of their top international policy priorities and as an important dimension of their commitment to strengthening democracy globally. Building on the Beijing Platform for Action and the SDGs, most have adopted dedicated gender equality strategies that guide how different ministries and government agencies engage on gender issues, both domestically and abroad. Various countries have gone further and announced feminist foreign policies that seek to prioritize women's rights and gender equality across different areas of international engagement. Rising policy attention has also fueled a steady increase in development funding: in 2021, official development assistance targeting gender equality reached US$57.4 billion, a 153 percent increase relative to 2011.[33]

In this wider context, women's political empowerment and leadership has become an increasingly important plank of international democracy support and gender equality aid (see Table 2.1). This shift reflects the recognition that democratic institutions alone do not automatically ensure inclusion: instead, extending democratic rights to historically excluded groups requires targeted efforts. It also reflects a growing commitment to the idea that women's representation in decision-making is essential to achieving other policy goals. In a recent speech at the UN Commission on the Status of Women, US Vice President Kamala Harris affirmed this view, noting that "the status of democracy [. . .] depends fundamentally on the empowerment of women—not only because the exclusion of women in decision-making is a marker of a flawed democracy, but because the participation of women strengthens democracy."[34]

Of course, international policy commitments often mean little unless they are matched with dedicated resources. However, tracking how much different funders spend on women's political empowerment is a difficult task. For one, different governments and organizations lack a common definition of what "counts" as support in this area. For example, does it include all international aid for women's rights organizations, regardless of their specific focus area, or only aid for activities strictly related to women's political rights and participation? Moreover, most aid providers do not sufficiently break down their own gender

Table 2.1 **Gender Strategies of the Ten Largest Bilateral Donors of Development Aid**

Donor Country	Most Recent Gender Policy or Strategy (Year)	Objectives Related to Women's Political Empowerment
United States	USAID Gender Equality and Women's Empowerment Policy (2023)	"Increase the capability of women and girls to fully exercise their rights, determine their life outcomes, assume leadership roles, and influence decision-making in households, communities and societies" listed as one of four strategic objectives.
United Kingdom	International Women and Girls Strategy (2023–2030)	"Women's political and social empowerment" listed as an area of focus
Sweden	Development Cooperation Strategy for Global Gender Equality and Women's and Girls' Rights (2018)	"Enhanced conditions for women's rights organisations, feminist movements and women human rights defenders to act independently and contribute to gender equality and the full enjoyment of human rights by all women and girls" listed as one of seven objectives.
Netherlands	Theory of Change on Women's Rights and Gender Equality (2018)	"Increasing women's leadership and participation in political decision-making" and "strengthening women's role in conflict resolutions and peacebuilding" listed as two of four core objectives.
Australia	Gender Equality and Women's Empowerment Strategy (2016)	"Enhancing women's voice in decision-making, leadership, and peacebuilding" listed as one of three priorities.
Canada	Feminist International Assistance Policy (2017)	"Inclusive governance" listed as one of six action areas.
Germany	Feminist Development Policy (2023)	"Realising the rights of women and marginalised groups, promoting their access to resources and strengthening representation" listed as one four action areas.
European Commission	Gender Action Plan III (2021–2026)	"Advancing equal participation and leadership" listed as one of six key thematic policy areas.

Table 2.1 **Continued**

Donor Country	Most Recent Gender Policy or Strategy (Year)	Objectives Related to Women's Political Empowerment
France	International Strategy for Gender Equality (2018–2022)	"Meaningful participation of women in economic, political and social decision-making forums" and "equal participation of women in peace and security processes" listed as two of five sectoral priorities.
Japan	Development Strategy for Gender Equality and Women's Empowerment (2016)	"Advancement of women's leadership in politics, economy and other public fields" listed as one of three thematic initiatives.

equality funding to allow for detailed analysis of their spending priorities. The fact that "strengthening women's participation" tend to be a cross-cutting priority makes it particularly difficult to analyze funding trends.

Given these limitations, the best available data source is the Organization for Economic Cooperation and Development (OECD) Development Assistance Committee's (DAC) Gender Equality Marker, which asks the world's largest development donors every year to report whether their various investments target gender equality as a "principal" or a "significant" objective.[35] This coding system is inevitably imprecise, as governments sometimes use divergent or faulty benchmarks to categorize their spending.[36] Moreover, not all donors screen all of their aid expenditures.[37] Nevertheless, examining how many activities in the "government and civil society" sector target gender equality provides a rough estimate of funding for women's political empowerment over time.

The OECD data show that donor spending on gender equality in politics has gradually increased over the past decade. In 2021, the world's thirty largest bilateral aid providers (including the European Union) categorized 61 percent of their spending in the overall "government and civil society" sector as gender-related, compared to only 37 percent ten years earlier.[38] This upward trend is also visible with respect to aid that is squarely focused on democratic governance, namely international support for elections, political parties and legislatures, democratic participation and civil society, media freedom, and women's rights organizations, movements, and institutions (described as "democracy assistance" going forward). In 2021, just over 73 percent of DAC donors' investments in this area—a total of US$2.8 billion—indicated gender equality as either a primary or a secondary goal, compared to 59 percent in 2011.[39]

In 2021, the Netherlands, Sweden, and the European Union were the largest donors of democracy assistance with gender equality as a *principal* objective,

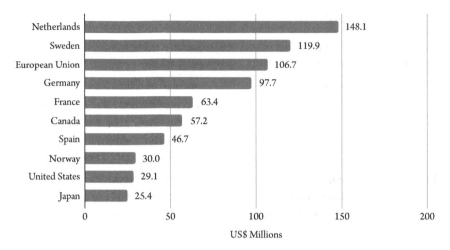

Figure 2.1 Top Ten Donors of Democracy Aid with Gender Equality as a "Principal" Objective in 2021 (in US$ millions 2020) Source: OECD.Stat, "Aid Activities Targeting Gender Equality and Women's Empowerment (CRS)," accessed February 9, 2023, https://stats.oecd.org/Index.aspx?DataSetCode=DV_DCD_GENDER.

followed by Germany, France, and Canada (see Figure 2.1). Several (though not all) of these donor countries have adopted or are in the process of adopting some version of a "feminist foreign policy" or "feminist assistance policy." Sweden was the front runner in this area, becoming the first country to launch a feminist foreign policy in October 2014. Its framework was based around three "Rs:" rights, representation, and resources. Canada's Feminist International Assistance Policy, adopted in 2017, places less emphasis on democracy, but it has significantly increased Canada's funding for women's rights organizations. For instance, in 2020-2021, Canada spent US$72 million to support women's organizations and institutions, compared to only US$9 million provided by the United Kingdom.[40]

Several private philanthropic foundations also support programs and initiatives focused on women's political empowerment, though at a smaller scale. According to a 2018 survey conducted by the OECD, private foundations spent US$3.7 billion on gender equality between 2013 and 2015. Although most of this aid targeted women's health, around 10 percent (or US$400 million) was allocated to initiatives related to women's rights, democratic participation, civil society development, and conflict prevention.[41] Over the past few years, several private funders have developed a particular focus on resourcing women's rights activism. At the 2021 Generation Equality Forum, for example, the Open Society Foundations and the Ford Foundation committed US$100 million and US$94 million in new funding to feminist movements, respectively.[42] Alongside these larger actors, a global network of women's funds—such as Mama Cash, the Global Fund for Women, and the African Women's Development

Fund—specializes in supporting grassroots women's organizations. However, their funding currently makes up a relatively small share of the total funding for women's political empowerment each year.[43]

Understanding the key actors

As international investments in women's political empowerment have increased, organizations and institutions involved in carrying out programs and initiatives in this area have also multiplied. Both donor governments and private philanthropic actors channel their funding to a wide network of actors—including multilateral organizations, partner governments, INGOs, and local civil society groups. These organizations are usually the ones that are proposing, designing, and implementing programs and activities, though their priorities and approaches are inevitably influenced by global funding trends and funders' calls for proposals.

At the multilateral level, UN Women has emerged as a particularly important actor. Established in 2011, the agency counts women's political empowerment as one of its four priority areas. Its work in this area is funded by voluntary contributions from UN member states, with Sweden acting as a key partner. [44] Globally, UN Women focuses on intergovernmental norm-building related to women's political participation by convening expert meetings, influencing high-level UN discussions and reports, and spearheading new data collection efforts. The organization further implements programs through its many regional and country offices, usually in partnership with local organizations and gender-focused ministries.[45] The United Nations Development Programme (UNDP) has also developed a stronger focus on women's political empowerment over time. For example, it regularly coordinates multidonor election aid funds that include support for gender-focused activities in electoral management and voter registration.[46] Beyond the UN system, the IPU and International IDEA are two leading intergovernmental organizations spearheading research, norm-building, and programs related to women's political empowerment around the world.

A second key group of actors are INGOs and multiparty institutes specialized in promoting democracy around the world. In the United States, this group includes NDI, IFES, and the International Republican Institute (IRI), all three of which have a wide network of country offices around the world. In Europe, the German political foundations, the UK-based Westminster Foundation for Democracy, the Netherlands Institute for Multiparty Democracy (NIMD), the Danish Institute for Party Democracy (DIPD), and Demo Finland play similar roles. Although none of these organizations focus exclusively on women's political participation, many have gradually built out their internal expertise on gender issues. NDI, for example, first began working on women's political participation in the 1990s and set up a dedicated gender team in response to increasing donor demand for gender-related democracy programming. In addition to advising NDI's country offices, the team now coordinates cross-national programs, spearheads global advocacy campaigns, and develops new research and programming guidance.[47] A few large INGOs specialized in international development—such as Oxfam and Care International—also work on women's leadership, though often with a focus on grassroots empowerment rather than formal electoral politics.

The final link in this global chain are local women's organizations, which are far from uniform. Some are urban, professionalized organizations working primarily on policy and legislative reforms; others are smaller, informal groups focused on awareness-raising and service delivery. Whereas some identify as feminist organizations fighting for radical structural change, others operate firmly within the political mainstream, with limited ties to grassroots constituencies.

Relationships between local organizations and international actors also vary widely. Some organizations receive direct support from foundations, donor agencies, and international funding mechanisms, like the European Instrument for Democracy and Human Rights. This support sometimes takes the form of flexible, core support grants that allow organizations to decide how the money is spent. More often, however, organizations are asked to submit project ideas when donor agencies issue a "call for proposals," and are then funded to carry out specific activities within the framework of a program, such as advocacy campaigns or training workshops. It is also common for groups to receive *indirect* donor support, in the form of implementation partnerships with larger INGOs or multilateral organizations. In these cases, local groups may be involved in shaping and carrying out specific activities, but they are not necessarily the ones defining the project design and its goals.

One recurring critique of international development cooperation is therefore donors' insufficient direct support for local feminist and women's rights organizations.[48] Globally, less than 1 percent of gender equality funding reaches such groups, while the rest circulates between development agencies, multilateral organizations, and INGOs.[49] In recent years, several new initiatives have tried to shift this pattern—a trend we return to in Chapter 11.

A fragile consensus?

Although the consensus underlying international support for women's political inclusion appears to be broad, it is by no means absolute. And notwithstanding the growing number of organizations and institutions working on the issue, both policy and aid commitments are shallower than indicated in official documents.

For one, governments rarely prioritize women's political rights and inclusion when they conflict with core foreign policy interests, no matter their formal aid commitments. After all, women's political empowerment sits at the intersection of two agendas that are frequently downgraded in strategic deliberations with other states: democracy and human rights, on the one hand, and gender equality on the other. This challenge is particularly visible with respect to women's participation in peace negotiations. Despite the proliferation of international commitments and WPS national action plans over the last twenty years, efforts to include women in peace talks remain limited. Between 2015 and 2019, women constituted only 7 percent of signatories and 14 percent of negotiators in international peace negotiations.[50] The same dynamics play out in more politically stable contexts. There is little data on how often concerns about women's political rights—or gender equality more broadly—are integrated into policy and political dialogues with partner countries. Studies of specific donors' diplomatic action suggest that inconsistent engagement is common. For example, advocates have noted that the European Union has often failed to leverage its negotiating power to push for women's participation in preaccession negotiations with countries in the Western Balkans.[51] Similarly, France has rarely raised concerns about women's rights in its bilateral exchanges, despite publicly announcing its commitments to "feminist diplomacy" since 2018.[52]

Shallow commitments also seep into assistance efforts to promote women in politics. Although aid spending in this area has increased over time, this upward trend has primarily been driven by democracy aid programs that include gender equality as a secondary rather than a primary objective. In some ways, these growing investments in gender mainstreaming are encouraging: they suggest that gender equality is increasingly integrated into broader democracy support activities, rather than being treated as a niche and isolated issue. However, gender mainstreaming can be superficial in practice. Gender-related objectives are tacked on to projects to "tick the box," with limited analysis, planning, and follow-through. A recent Oxfam study, for example, examined seventy-two projects that donors had categorized as including gender equality as a "significant" objective and found that only two of them met the OECD criteria for classifying them as such.[53] These findings suggest that donors may be significantly overreporting their investments in gender equality, including in the democracy and governance realm. Meanwhile, spending on programs that count women's political empowerment as a primary goal still makes up a relatively small share of the overall democracy assistance bucket—around 22.7 percent, or US$865 million in 2021. This share has grown only minimally over time.[54]

Moreover, policymakers, aid officials, and gender equality advocates do not necessarily share the same rationale for supporting women's political empowerment. Historically, development agencies have leaned on "efficiency" arguments to justify their funding for gender equality. WID programs, for example, emphasized investments in women as a means to achieving greater economic growth. This instrumental approach, however, stands in stark contrast to feminist calls for an *intrinsic* commitment to gender equality, as part of a broader struggle for equality, justice, and emancipation. Not surprisingly, feminist scholars and advocates have criticized donor agencies for depoliticizing radical concepts like "women's empowerment" and "participation," noting that aid agencies only embrace these principles when they fit their economic growth agenda—and without questioning that agenda itself.[55]

The same tension between intrinsic and instrumental rationales also shapes aid focused on women's political empowerment. Intrinsic arguments frame women's political inclusion as a matter of justice: women are a socially meaningful—albeit diverse and contested—identity group with a right to influence the political decisions that shape their lives. The instrumental approach, on the other hand, emphasizes how women's representation contributes to broader political and socioeconomic outcomes, including political stability, reduced corruption, and greater human development. Although most donor governments and organizations officially embrace a mix of intrinsic and instrumental rationales, advocates note that in some aid agencies, rights-based commitments remain relatively superficial. They worry that women's participation only matters if women are shown to be making a difference—and that it can be discarded as a priority if it becomes inconvenient or endangers relationships with partner countries.

This debate is, of course, not unique to this area of assistance. It reflects longstanding tensions within aid circles between those pushing for rights-based approaches and those embracing a narrower socioeconomic development mandate. It is also not limited to aid agencies. Even within democracy organizations, which are populated with staff who are normatively committed to political and civil rights, those working on gender equality sometimes feel that they need to prove why their work is essential to meaningful democracy-building. This is partly because democracy assistance organizations, like most of the development and foreign policy establishment, have traditionally been male-dominated organizations.[56] They have sometimes viewed women's political participation as a nice addition, but not necessarily as an essential dimension of democracy on par with free and fair elections, multiparty competition, and an independent judiciary.[57] In other words, countries could be considered "democratizing" even if women remained excluded from positions of power. Although this attitude has become less common with time, its persistence still motivates feminists within these organizations to stress how and why women's political inclusion matters for broader political outcomes, such as peace and stability. This can, at times, detract from more open discussions of the complex relationship between democracy and women's political empowerment, including the ways in which illiberal actors use women's political leadership as a cover for fundamentally undemocratic and exclusionary agendas.

Critical voices

The critiques discussed above focus primarily on the depth of international commitment, or whether policy declarations have translated into meaningful changes in diplomacy and aid practice. There are, however, other critical voices that have raised more fundamental questions about the whole endeavor of international support for women's political empowerment and gender equality more broadly.

One line of critique suggests that efforts to promote women's political participation across borders represent a form of cultural imperialism, as they impose predominantly Western values, norms, and institutions on other societies— often those in the global South. In its most simplistic form, this narrative is typically espoused by those resisting gender equality reforms within their own societies and at the international level. It conveniently ignores the long and rich history of locally rooted women's rights activism in all regions of the world, which has always drawn on transnational networks and exchanges. Moreover, far from only being the "recipients" of external gender equality norms, women's movements in the global South have played central roles in shaping international debates around women's political participation, including about gender quotas, gender mainstreaming, and women's right to participate in peace negotiations.[58]

At the same time, assistance for women's political empowerment, like all forms of international development aid, *is* clearly embedded in a context of unequal global power relations, characterized by transfers of resources and "technical expertise" from developed countries to the developing world. Interventions are sometimes based on standard institutional and programming templates that are created with only superficial input from their intended beneficiaries. Even when aid programs are designed by local actors, their options are (directly or indirectly) constrained by the priorities of international funders, which influence the local political economy of experts, consultants, and organizations. Exchanges of knowledge and experience, let alone resources, in the other direction are much less common.

This imbalance speaks to a second critique, namely that Western donor governments lack the credibility to promote women's political empowerment abroad. After all, many developing countries have more women in political office than Western democracies. Perennial barriers that hinder women's access to political leadership—such as inequities in caregiving, financial hurdles, and women's experiences of sexism on the campaign trail—also plague many wealthy, established democracies. Recent trends of democratic backsliding in the United States and in Europe have further highlighted the one-sidedness of the current democracy aid infrastructure.[59] Of course, not all international support for women's political empowerment fits this model. Some international nongovernmental and intergovernmental organizations like the IPU work globally to share best practices around women's political inclusion, and several philanthropic foundations fund advocacy related to women's political rights in both developed and developing countries. Nevertheless, the bulk of assistance is not set up to facilitate multidirectional learning.

A final critique is that international support for women's political empowerment is fundamentally *depoliticizing*. According to this view, such aid reduces collective struggles over power and resources to technical and professionalized programs and interventions, which frame women as recipients of aid rather than full political agents.[60] Critical feminist scholars, for example, criticize donor programs for reproducing liberal assumptions about social change and relying on partnerships with state institutions, rather than questioning how existing state structures perpetuate women's oppression and the oppression of other marginalized groups.[61] They also note that the aid agenda is largely divorced from the global economic and geopolitical structures that perpetuate gender inequities, whether through conflicts brought about by the War on Terror or through neoliberal trade agreements.[62] In sum, international development cooperation seeks to integrate women into an inequitable global system rather than fundamentally transforming it.

This critique brings to the fore a crucial point: gender relations in any society are deeply entrenched, and major changes often occur as a result of structural shifts, such as disruptions brought about by conflict, economic growth, mass mobilization, or urbanization. Any short-term project is unlikely to bring about radical transformation. At the same time, as the beginning of this chapter shows, gender equality change in politics has routinely been influenced by transnational and international exchanges, with local reformers and activists drawing on global frameworks, norms, and advocacy tools (and reshaping them in return). Framing all forms of international democracy support as inherently depoliticizing also ignores the diversity of strategies and approaches that exist within the sector, including those born from learning over the past three decades. Although we do not assume that international aid programs targeting women's political empowerment are inherently effective or beneficial, we therefore argue that dismissing the field as a whole would be a mistake. Instead, the strengths and limitations of existing approaches—and how they have evolved over time—merit careful analysis.

Conclusion

International aid for women's political empowerment has its roots in decades of transnational mobilization for women's political inclusion. Over the course of the twentieth century, advocacy by women's rights movements gradually solidified the norm that women should have an equal voice in political decision-making. Today, this norm is anchored in numerous international agreements and commitments. It has also become a growing priority for international development cooperation, particularly since the rise of politically oriented aid in the late 1980s and 1990s. Not only does women's political leadership feature prominently in most donors' democracy promotion and gender equality strategies; funding in this area has also substantially increased over the past decade. Today, a global network of actors is involved in bolstering women's political empowerment globally, from donor governments and UN agencies to specialized democracy aid organizations and women's rights groups and institutions in aid-recipient countries. There is now an entire ecosystem of aid organizations and experts that have accumulated extensive cross-national knowledge on women's political participation and related policy responses and programming models.

At the same time, however, there are still tensions and uncertainties surrounding this area of international democracy support. A closer look reveals inconsistent political and aid commitments by donor governments. Some advocates doubt that the issue has truly become a foreign policy and aid priority and worry that gender mainstreaming in democracy assistance is leading to superficial activities that check the gender equality box but fail to advance meaningful change. Moreover, not all donor agencies share a strong rights-based commitment to women's political inclusion, nor do all democracy aid organizations treat gender inclusion as a core component of their mandate and work. Beyond the aid community itself, some skeptics wonder whether Western donor governments can or should help advance gender equality in politics in the global South, particularly if they are also falling behind on women's political leadership at home. We take these doubts and critiques as a starting point for our investigation. In the next chapter, we introduce the core country cases that anchor our analysis, before delving deeper into the evolution of the field.

3

Introducing the Cases

Having described the global aid ecosystem focused on women's political empowerment, we now turn to the four countries that anchor our analysis: Kenya, Nepal, Morocco, and Myanmar. Located in different parts of the world, these countries appear at first glance to have little in common. However, despite their different political histories and varying trajectories of democratic change, they do share one important feature. Looking back to the 1990s, all four countries were characterized by women's near-total political exclusion. In Kenya and Nepal, women made up less than 4 percent of legislators; meanwhile, only two women served in the Moroccan parliament until 2001. In Myanmar, women were excluded entirely from the all-male military junta that ruled the country (Figure 3.1). Yet over the past several decades, all four countries have experienced profound political changes that have opened up new space for women to participate in political life. Significant constitutional and legislative reforms— or, in the case of Myanmar, the brief return of parliamentary politics—have enabled women to secure a greater foothold within political parties, parliaments, and other political spaces.

International assistance has played an important part in these trajectories of progress. As each country underwent its political transition, various donor governments and multilateral organizations funded politically oriented aid programs in the hopes of solidifying fragile democratic openings. These efforts had varying goals—from supporting multiparty elections to strengthening the rule of law. Yet across all four countries, international actors integrated a greater focus on women's political inclusion into their aid over time. Particularly around elections and other key political junctures, they began funding programs to train women candidates, support women's civil society advocacy, and mentor newly elected women legislators.

In the remainder of this chapter, we introduce these country cases in more detail. We begin by explaining our case selection and highlighting important

Aiding Empowerment. Saskia Brechenmacher and Katherine Mann, Oxford University Press.
© Oxford University Press 2024. DOI: 10.1093/oso/9780197694275.003.0003

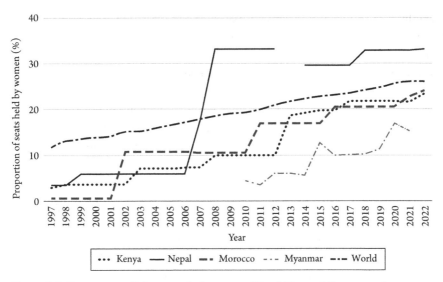

Figure 3.1 Proportion of Women in Parliament in Nepal, Kenya, Morocco, and Myanmar (1997–2022) Sources: World Bank, "Proportion of Seats Held by Women in National Parliaments (%)," accessed January 27, 2023, https://data.worldbank.org/indicator/SG.GEN.PARL.ZS, and IPU Parline, "Global and Regional Averages of Women in National Parliaments," accessed January 27, 2023, https://data.ipu.org/women-ranking.

similarities and differences across our cases. We then offer a short historical overview of women's political inclusion in each country to help the reader situate the various programming examples and illustrations in the remaining chapters. We describe how women's political empowerment has evolved over the last three decades, outlining important political junctures as well as stubborn hurdles limiting women's equal access to decision-making power. We also briefly review the evolving role of international actors and aid programs in these processes, chronicling how international attention to questions of women's inclusion fluctuated over time.

Situating our cases

We chose Kenya, Nepal, Myanmar, and Morocco as our core cases because they reflect the diversity of political contexts that receive international democracy assistance. As noted in the introduction, we looked at three main country features to guide our case selection. First, our cases are characterized by different patterns and degrees of women's political inclusion, measured by the share of women serving in national and subnational legislatures and the presence or absence of gender quotas. In addition, we chose cases that represent different intersections of women's political representation and regime type. Finally, we also sought to ensure some regional diversity by including countries from distinct areas of the world, North and East Africa and South and Southeast Asia.

Our case study approach was not designed to investigate whether aid-receiving countries demonstrate higher levels of women's political empowerment than countries that do not receive such assistance. We therefore did not include a "counterfactual" case that has not received international democracy support. Instead, we draw on our case studies to assess common programming models used by aid providers and their local partners as well as gaps in international assistance. Through our cases, we trace different interventions' theories of change, explore strengths and weaknesses in their design and implementation, and illustrate recurring tensions, challenges, and uncertainties confronting international practitioners and their local partners. By choosing cases that vary with respect to women's political representation and democratic institutions, we can examine whether and how interventions change depending on women's political gains and the political space available to both international actors and domestic reformers.

At the same time, Kenya, Morocco, Nepal, and Myanmar are not necessarily representative of all countries that receive gender-related democracy support. Wherever possible, we have therefore sought to complement and triangulate our case study research with insights gleaned from our interviews with policymakers and practitioners working at the global level, and with a careful review of donor reports, program evaluations, and other secondary sources. Particularly when analyzing newer areas of policy and programming, we also draw on examples from other countries. Together, these sources provide a comprehensive—but not exhaustive—overview of the field.

As we noted above, our cases reflect a critical global trend: over the past three decades, they have all witnessed an important increase in the number of women serving in elected office (Figure 3.1). This positive trend line is shared among many other countries around the world. Globally, the average share of women legislators has steadily increased over the past three decades, reaching 26.7 percent in 2023.[1] The World Economic Forum's (WEF) Women's Political Empowerment subindex, which also looks at the percentage of women in ministerial positions and women heads of state, similarly reflects a picture of gradual but positive change.[2]

At the same time, these averages mask significant regional differences. In fact, WEF data on women's political empowerment shows the widest range of dispersion among countries, more so than indicators related to women's economic participation, health, and educational attainment. Examining our cases more closely, they also reflect important variation. Despite a general upward trend, the pace and the intensity of change has varied from country to country. In Nepal, women's parliamentary representation has jumped most dramatically, from a mere 3 percent in 1997 to 33 percent in 2022.[3] Thanks to a strong subnational gender quota, women now also hold 41 percent of seats at the subnational level.[4] As a result, Nepal has the highest rates of women's political representation in South Asia. In Kenya and Morocco, on the other hand, changes have unfolded more gradually, and women still hold less than a quarter of national parliamentary posts. However, reserved seats in Kenya's county assemblies have secured women a higher legislative presence at the subnational level. Myanmar lags even further behind. The country saw an uptick in women's leadership following its partial democratic opening after 2011. Yet the country's majoritarian electoral system and political resistance against quota measures continued to exclude women from politics. In 2021, the sudden return of military rule led to the dissolution of parliament, once again pushing most women out of the decision-making sphere.

Our four cases also reflect different democratic trajectories and degrees of political and democratic space. In Nepal, dramatic increases in women's political representation have occurred alongside major political transformations, including the end of civil conflict and monarchical rule. Today, V-Dem classifies Nepal as an electoral democracy.[5] The country holds regular and competitive elections, even as corruption and entrenched sociopolitical hierarchies still limit citizens' equal political rights. Kenya is also a partial democracy, though it scores lower on global democracy indices. Over the past twelve years, far-reaching constitutional reforms have limited the power of the executive, decentralized governance, and strengthened citizen participation. Nonetheless, accountability systems between elections remain weak, and security force abuses persist. Morocco, on the other hand, is more autocratic. Despite a series of liberalizing reforms, including important women's rights measures, King Mohammed VI maintains his political dominance through substantial formal powers and informal networks of influence, and civil liberties in the country remain closely circumscribed. Gains in women's political representation have thus unfolded under the top-down control of the monarchy. Finally, Myanmar represents an even more difficult political environment. Even during the country's partial opening, the military retained high levels of influence in politics, and women's political rights were heavily curtailed by internal armed conflict.

How has international aid for women's political empowerment varied across these contexts? Before we delve into each case in greater detail, it is worth highlighting several broader patterns. First, even though all four countries have received substantial assistance targeting women's political empowerment over the past fifteen years, aid amounts have varied across countries and over time (see Figure 3.2). OECD data indicate that Kenya has received the highest amount

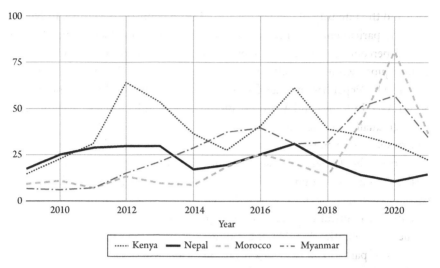

Figure 3.2 Total Gender-Related Democracy Aid (2009–2021, in US$ millions 2020) Source: OECD.Stat, "Aid Activities Targeting Gender Equality and Women's Empowerment (CRS)," accessed February 11, 2023, https://stats.oecd.org/Index.aspx?DataSetCode=DV_DCD_GENDER.

of democracy assistance with primary or secondary gender equality objectives, amounting to over US$480 million between 2009 and 2021. Myanmar ranks second, with US$369 million in assistance, followed by Morocco (US$299 million) and Nepal (US$285 million)—though both Morocco and Myanmar saw an uptick in gender-related democracy aid between 2018 and 2020. Until 2018, of the four countries, Kenya also received the most annual funding for programs with women's political empowerment as their *primary* goal. However, an injection of EU and French funding for women's rights institutions and organizations in Morocco in 2019 and 2020 has pushed it into the top spot.[6]

As Figure 3.2 shows, assistance in this area has often spiked around election periods, while decreasing in between. This pattern is not unique to women's political empowerment aid. International democracy support generally increases around elections, which are still considered core benchmarks of countries' democratic progress. Even so, across most of our cases, the overall share of democracy aid funding with gender-related objectives has increased over time, indicating that over the past decade, women's political empowerment has become a greater priority within international democracy support (see Figure 3.3). In fact, three of our four cases have generally scored above the global average over the past decade, which makes them ideal cases to study what such assistance looks like in practice. Having briefly reviewed these broader comparative patterns, we now turn to each of our cases in greater detail.

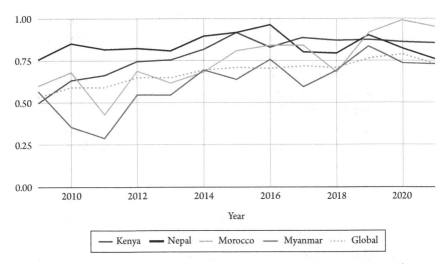

Figure 3.3 Share of International Democracy Assistance That Is Gender-Related (2009–2021, in percentage) Source: OECD.Stat, "Aid Activities Targeting Gender Equality and Women's Empowerment (CRS)," accessed February 11, 2023, https://stats.oecd.org/Index.aspx?DataSetCode=DV_DCD_GENDER.

Nepal: The struggle for postconflict inclusion

Nepal has experienced profound sociopolitical shifts over the past thirty years: a startling transition from a unitary, monarchical system to a democratic federal republic at the start of the 1990s; descent into civil war in 1996; emergence from conflict into a negotiated peace in 2006; and, since then, a pattern of continued pluralism that few would describe as democratic consolidation—yet one that has stayed clear of autocracy and illiberalism. Women have played central roles in these political struggles, and progressively pushed for much greater representation in the country's governance institutions.

From conflict to reform

After Nepal's initial transition from monarchy to multiparty democracy in the early 1990s, women remained largely excluded from the political sphere. Power rested firmly in the hands of a male, upper-caste elite, while discrimination based on gender, caste, ethnicity, and religion persisted across the country. Against this backdrop, the Maoist movement launched an insurgency in 1996 aimed at establishing a more egalitarian society. During the decade-long conflict that followed, the predominantly male Maoist leadership recruited thousands of women from rural communities to join the movement, many of whom embraced the struggle against patriarchal and upper-caste domination.[7] Women's active involvement as combatants challenged traditional gender roles in Nepali society, even as the war itself wrought hardship on vulnerable communities.[8] Yet despite women's widespread participation in the conflict and in the 2006 mass movement that paved the way to a peace agreement, their right to shape the country's political transition remained contested. They were excluded from the peace negotiations between the Maoists and the government, and it was only through women's concerted pressure and mobilization that male political elites agreed to expand the Interim Constitution Drafting Committee to include several female representatives.[9]

It was during this initial postconflict period that international assistance for women's political representation first mushroomed. Although international donors had provided democracy support to Nepal since the country's transition to multiparty politics in the 1990s, efforts to promote women's political leadership were limited to small-scale candidate training activities. International involvement grew as the country embarked on its fragile transition. One set of activities—led by the UN Mission in Nepal and the UN Peace Fund for Nepal—focused on supporting the peace process and the disarmament, demobilization, and reintegration of former combatants. However, these efforts largely failed to integrate a gender lens, and pushed many female Maoist fighters back into the traditional gender roles and livelihoods that they had sought to escape.[10] Another set of activities supported the first postconflict elections in 2008 and the constitutional reform process, including through technical assistance to the Electoral Commission of Nepal (ECN). During this period, international actors like UNDP, International IDEA, and NDI advocated for women's inclusion in the constitutional negotiations and funded civil society groups mobilizing for change. In the end, women's lobbying proved effective: they successfully pushed for a 33 percent gender quota for the Constituent Assembly (CA), which was charged with forging a new political settlement for the country.

Realizing hard-won constitutional gains

The 2008 CA elections became a milestone for women in Nepali politics. For the first time in the country's history, women—of different social classes and ethnic groups—held one-third of parliamentary seats. They were also included in each of the assembly's thematic committees and formed an informal caucus to advance their priorities. Nevertheless, most political power remained concentrated in the hands of a small circle of high-caste male leaders, who often made decisions outside of the formal political body.[11] As the drafting process dragged on and grew more contentious, these leaders increasingly deprioritized gender equality issues. The gradual reassertion of ideological and ethnic divisions also made it more difficult for women assembly members to collaborate across party lines.[12]

During the first phase of constitutional reform negotiations, various international actors launched activities to strengthen women's political influence in the Constituent Assembly and to integrate gender perspectives into the reform process. They benefited from high levels of civil society engagement and domestic elites' relative openness to political reform.[13] International IDEA, for instance, received British and Norwegian funding to launch the "Women and Constitution Building Initiative in Nepal," which produced research, organized exchanges with international constitutional reform experts, and facilitated dialogues among CA members, political parties, academics, and civil society.[14] In parallel, UN Women—in partnership with DiDiBahini, Sancharika Samuha, and other local organizations—implemented the "Making Politics Work with Women" project, which mobilized media support for women candidates, lobbied political parties, and created women's watch groups to monitor the Constituent Assembly elections. The project also sought to forge a common position among women on pressing political reform questions, including electoral system design.[15] However, as the constitutional negotiations devolved into a political stalemate, the Nepali government began pushing back against donors' and advocates' demands for ethnic and gender inclusion. The initial openness of senior political leaders gave way to accusations that international actors were encouraging factionalism and division.[16]

The final constitution, passed after two devastating earthquakes hit Nepal in 2015, fell short of women's rights advocates' reform aspirations. For example, they were unable to remove a discriminatory provision that prevents children born to single women or women married to foreign men from accessing full citizenship rights.[17] However, the document did institutionalize several important measures to advance women's political participation. It established a mixed electoral system, guaranteed women the right to proportional representation at all levels of governance, and mandated political parties to fill at least one-third of their parliamentary seats with women. Subsequent electoral reforms further established a gender quota in local government, with certain seats reserved for Dalit women. These legal measures precipitated a major uptick in women's representation, especially at the local level. After the 2017 elections, women gained 40.9 percent of local government seats and 32.7 percent of national parliamentary seats.[18]

Once the constitution was passed, most international donors shifted from a focus on national political reform to assisting the Nepali government in implementing the new federal governance framework. With respect to women's political empowerment, much support over the past several years has focused on capacity-building for women serving in subnational governments. For instance, the EU, Norway, Switzerland, the United Kingdom, and the UN have invested in a nationwide Provincial and Local Government Support Program, which targets all local and seven provincial governments and encompasses training for women representatives.[19] In contrast to the initial transition period, however, fewer targeted initiatives now center on advancing women's political representation at the national level, though some international actors continue to integrate gender issues into their work with the ECN, parliament, and political parties.[20] In recent years, closing civic space and the government's prioritization of large-scale development projects over sociopolitical empowerment have also created a more hostile environment for international actors working on issues of democratic reform.

Despite Nepali women's impressive political gains, profound social and political hierarchies persist. Men from privileged caste backgrounds still hold most decision-making positions in the country. None of the major political parties in Nepal have met the legally required 33 percent threshold for women's representation in their executive committees, and women struggle to exert influence within party and government structures.[21] Moreover, in Nepal's mixed electoral system, parliamentarians who are directly elected in single-member districts wield significantly more power than those elected through proportional representation. Yet parties almost never select women as candidates in competitive electoral districts; instead, they fill the national quota requirement by placing women on their proportional representation lists. Even though women now make up one-third of parliamentarians, they therefore find themselves in a marginalized position.[22] Beyond formal political institutions, wider structural barriers also inhibit women's equal political participation. Gender gaps in literacy endure, and many women lack the control over time and resources needed to engage in politics. Ethnic- and caste-based discrimination compounds these gender inequities, with Dalit, Janajati, Madhesi, and Muslim women experiencing distinct forms of social, economic, and political exclusion.[23]

Kenya: Confronting "winner-takes-all" politics

Despite its vibrant civil society and growing middle class, Kenya still lags behind its East African neighbors in terms of women's political representation. The return of multiparty politics in the early 1990s and subsequent constitutional reforms have created new pathways for women to access political office. At the same time, male political elites have repeatedly thwarted the full implementation of Kenya's constitutional framework. Legal reforms have also failed to transform the exclusionary logic of Kenyan politics. Expensive and often violent winner-takes-all electoral races, combined with ethnic power-sharing among influential male leaders, still impede women's full political inclusion.[24]

A protracted fight for democratic inclusion

Many Kenyan women participated in the country's independence struggle against British rule. Yet in the first decades following the independence in 1963, very few held high-level leadership roles. Women's organizations focused primarily on development and service delivery, as the ruling Kenyan African National Union allowed limited space for autonomous political activity.[25] This changed in the early 1990s, when the transition to multiparty politics enabled women to make more explicit demands for political rights. Gender equality advocates both inside and outside of government formed new coalitions to demand affirmative action measures. Faced with strong opposition, women built alliances across ethnic, religious, and regional divides, and successfully carved out an influential role in the country's constitutional reform negotiations.[26]

Kenya's transition to multiparty politics, spurred in part by international pressure, led to rising donor investments in democracy and governance. Following the first multiparty elections in 1992, international actors began channeling more support to parliament and to civil society, with the aim of advancing democratic consolidation and constitutional reform.[27] During this initial period, support for women's political participation primarily consisted of funding for women's groups, training for individual women leaders, and, beginning in the early 2000s, some work on gender equality in political parties.[28] USAID and UN Women were particularly instrumental in supporting women's lobbying for constitutional change and facilitating peer learning from reform processes in other countries.[29]

The organizing efforts of women's rights advocates bore fruit. Kenya's 2010 constitution—passed by referendum following large-scale electoral violence in 2007 and 2008—codified important gender equality reforms. In addition to devolving political and fiscal power to forty-seven newly created counties, the constitution affirms that no more than two-thirds of members of all elective and appointed public bodies can be of the same gender, thereby establishing a "constitutional limitation on the power or dominance of either gender" across political institutions (referred to hereafter as the "two-thirds gender principle").[30]

The document also sets out a postelection nomination process intended to ensure that this principle is met at the subnational level: if women hold less than one-third of county assembly seats after the election, parties nominate additional women representatives based on their share of the overall vote. However, the constitution fails to specify a similar quota mechanism at the national level, besides reserving forty-seven seats in the National Assembly and eighteen in the Senate for women.[31]

Progress amid resistance

Over the past twelve years, these constitutional reforms have spurred gradual increases in women's political representation. Today, women make up 23.3 percent of members in the National Assembly and 31.3 percent of Senators, as well as just over one-third of County Assembly members at the local level.[32] The 2022 election also marked the first time that seven women were elected as governors.[33] Women's organizations have played an active role in educating citizens about the new legal framework and bolstering public support for women's political engagement. They have launched social media campaigns, organized dialogues with community leaders, and offered direct support to women candidates. Afrobarometer survey data shows that most Kenyans today are supportive of women's political leadership—though men are still less likely than women to hold this view.[34]

At the same time, women continue to face significant hurdles in Kenyan politics. The parliament has repeatedly blocked attempts to pass legislation that would fully implement the two-thirds gender principle at the national level, despite court rulings ordering it to do so. The lack of action by senior political leaders speaks to persistent resistance against women's political inclusion.[35] Traditional gender norms, the high cost of running successful campaigns, and rampant political violence further discourage women from running for office. Women who do run for open seats struggle to make it past the primary stage.[36] At the highest levels of political leadership, women's exclusion from ethnic patronage networks weakens their ability to forge political coalitions and raise financial support.[37]

Due to these barriers, advances in women's political participation since 2010 have been driven almost entirely by women's nomination to reserved seats, whereas the number of women directly *elected* has mostly stagnated. Yet this quota mechanism has inadvertently created new hierarchies between political representatives similar to those in Nepal. Within legislatures at the national and local levels, women representatives in reserved seats are often treated as second-class politicians and sidelined from positions of political influence. This dynamic has in turn fueled some voters' perception that women are ineffective political leaders, thereby undermining the original intent of the quota measure.[38]

Since 2010, international support for women's political empowerment has focused on three areas: first, advancing the implementation of existing gender equality laws through continued advocacy and technical assistance to Kenya's electoral institutions and some advocacy targeting political parties; second, training women candidates and politicians, particularly at the local level, to increase the number of women running in elections; and third, advancing women's political participation through voter education and media campaigns.

Introducing the Cases 49

However, the degree of donor engagement has varied over time, and has generally spiked close to elections. For instance, women's limited political gains after the 2013 elections spurred more targeted investments in women's political participation ahead of the 2017 polls. USAID's 2016–2018 Electoral Assistance Program made women and youth participation a central priority, particularly through a countrywide push to recruit and train women candidates.[39] Other actors, including UN Women and the European Commission, funded efforts to integrate gender into voter education and registration, audit political party policies, raise awareness of gender-based violence during elections, and train electoral dispute resolution bodies on gender analysis.[40] Some aid officials felt that these and other investments paid off, as the number of women elected increased in 2017.[41] Yet the government's continued failure to implement the two-thirds gender principle, weak party compliance with official rules, and persistent problems of violence and corruption during elections have led both local and international actors to question the efficacy of existing support strategies. Ahead of the 2022 polls, many local women's organizations observed that international attention had turned to other issues, particularly in light of the ongoing Covid-19 pandemic and related food security crisis. As a result, they struggled to obtain funding for work related to women's political participation and leadership.[42]

Morocco: The challenge of partial reform

Over the past three decades, Morocco has undergone a gradual democratic reform process, yet without fundamentally shifting power away from the country's monarchy. In this context of partial opening, gender equality advocates have repeatedly benefited from the king's search for domestic and international legitimacy.[43] At the same time, socioeconomic inequities, patriarchal patronage politics, and calcified political parties still hold back women's political participation.

Incremental political change

As in Kenya, women's representation in Morocco's postindependence political institutions remained low, due to a combination of patriarchal norms, high rates of female illiteracy, and limited political space.[44] In the 1990s and 2000s, however, democratic reforms initiated by the king created new opportunities for women activists to press for their rights. They successfully pushed the government to ratify CEDAW, modified labor laws to recognize gender-based discrimination and harassment in the workplace, and, most importantly, reformed the country's discriminatory personal status code (the *Moudawana*).[45] Faced with continued political exclusion, they also mobilized for gender parity on electoral lists. Their efforts ultimately led political parties to reserve thirty seats in the House of Representatives for women.[46] In 2008, the government also passed an electoral law stipulating a local government quota, thereby increasing women's representation at the local level from a dismal 0.6 percent to 12.3 percent.[47] Throughout this period, the women's rights agenda largely aligned with the monarchy's top-down liberalization process, and King Mohammed VI publicly championed certain gender equality reforms.

Hybrid regimes like Morocco pose unique challenges to democracy assistance actors. Because these regimes have the basic political infrastructure of democracy, such as elections and political parties, they can usually absorb politically oriented aid without it threatening their power.[48] Despite this concern, a wide range of international actors have supported Morocco's "permanent political transition," rarely adopting a confrontational or regime-challenging approach.[49] In the 2000s, their efforts with respect to women's political empowerment focused squarely on promoting women's formal political representation. Some international actors channeled support to professionalized women's rights groups pushing for quota reforms; others focused on training women candidates and promoting party-level gender quota measures. For example, ahead of the 2002 polls, NDI initiated a public outreach campaign that included billboards and radio ads underlining the importance of women's political leadership and worked with political parties to implement voluntary quota measures.[50] Around the same time, IRI also expanded its democracy-strengthening activities in the country, including by training women leaders in the lead-up to the 2009 local elections.[51]

Between legal change and political stagnation

The Arab Spring protests that began in February 2011 created a momentary opening for more extensive political reforms. The uprising prompted a new wave of women's mobilization spearheaded by both secular and Islamist activists who linked gender equality to demands for social justice and wider institutional change.[52] King Mohammed VI reacted to rising domestic upheaval by quickly adopting a series of constitutional reforms that enshrined formal commitments to gender equality and nondiscrimination (among other changes), even as they left the king's sovereign powers intact. In addition, the government agreed to raise the number of seats reserved for women at the national level from 30 to 60, and to increase women's representation in local councils from 12 percent to 27 percent.[53]

The mass uprisings also renewed international interest in supporting prodemocratic political change. USAID, for instance, launched a significant new program focused on advancing the king's nascent democratic reforms. Yet with respect to women's political inclusion, there was no major change in strategy or funding amounts. Electoral reform remained a significant priority: both NDI and UN Women supported civil society advocacy to strengthen the share of seats reserved for women in municipal and regional councils.[54] The EU and UN Women, on the other hand, jointly launched a regional program called "Spring Forward for Women" that sought to advance marginalized women's economic and political empowerment using the "momentum for meaningful citizenship" created by the Arab uprisings. The program relied on a mix of advocacy, training for civil society advocates, knowledge exchanges, and reform dialogue; among other activities, it supported the regional Arab Women Parliamentarians Network for Equality.[55] In 2016, IRI also launched the Women's Support Network, a nonpartisan coalition that encourages women to learn about politics and get involved in public life.[56]

Looking back over the past decade, quota measures have bolstered Moroccan women's political representation and normalized their political leadership. Ahead of the 2021 elections, the Moroccan government further strengthened existing quota provisions. The new legal framework now allocates at least ninety parliamentary seats to women, who are elected from regional rather than national electoral lists. The share of seats reserved for women at the subnational level has also increased. As of 2023, women hold 24.3 percent of seats in the House of Representatives, and seven women serve as ministers.[57] For the first time in history, Morocco's three largest cities—Rabat, Casablanca, and Marrakech—are all governed by women mayors.

Yet these numbers only provide a partial picture. Patriarchal gender roles and women's economic marginalization remain strong barriers to their political engagement, particularly outside of major urban areas.[58] Moreover, although the quota system has increased gender inclusion in leadership, it has also siloed women into a separate pathway to political office. Echoing the patterns observed in Kenya, increases in women's representation have been driven almost entirely by the expansion of reserved seats, as most parties remain reluctant to run female candidates in open district races.[59] At a broader level, the absence of deeper democratic change has fueled a political culture marked by cronyism that disadvantages underrepresented groups. Candidate selection within weakly institutionalized political parties is often opaque and favors well-connected and wealthy politicians. Quota seats similarly tend to be filled based on patronage ties and familial networks, thereby sidelining women with activist credentials and commitments. Within parliament, women elected to reserved seats face significant pressure to conform to party lines, and the body as a whole still exercises only limited agenda-setting power vis-à-vis the monarchy.[60] Meanwhile, women's rights organizations remain important drivers of gender equality reform outside of formal politics. Yet they also operate in a context of limited (and, in recent years, shrinking) civic space, which has led some to avoid broader questions of democratic reform.[61]

Morocco's lack of democratic progress has not fundamentally changed its relationship to Western donor states. The EU, for example, has continued to expand its cooperation with the Moroccan government, valuing the country's relative stability and collaboration on migration and other issues.[62] At the microlevel, however, donor support has gradually shifted away from formal political reform toward a stronger focus on civil society assistance, local governance, and economic empowerment. Along these lines, several donors have moved more resources toward women's rights advocacy in recent years (as reflected in the uptick in funding shown in Figure 3.2). By contrast, fewer aid initiatives now explicitly focus on women's formal political participation, though a small number of democracy support actors continue to work with women parliamentarians and engage political parties on gender equality reform. Whereas some practitioners attribute this shift to changes in local advocacy priorities, others note that Western donor governments have become less interested in engaging the Moroccan government on democracy issues, viewing the country as a relative "success story" in a complex region and prioritizing greater socioeconomic development as the key to political stability.[63]

Myanmar: The resurgence of autocracy

After decades of military rule, Myanmar experienced a brief period of democratic opening between 2011 and 2020, during which the country held two rounds of multiparty elections in 2015 and 2020. Although women's representation in parliament increased during this period—from less than 5 percent in 2014 to over 15 percent in 2020—these gains occurred in a context of continued military dominance and ongoing internal conflict in various parts of the country. In February 2021, the military (known as the Tatmadaw) seized full power again in a coup that abruptly ended the country's uncertain transition process.

A short-lived opening

During the military junta's previous years in power, women were almost entirely excluded from Burmese politics. Although women's organizations had participated in the country's nationalist struggle against British rule, they were pushed out of politics following the Tatmadaw's 1962 coup d'état.[64] In the decades of autocratic rule that followed, systematic security force abuses against ethnic minority women catalyzed new waves of political activism, and women's organizations formed both inside the country and among communities in exile. The Women's League of Burma, for example, was founded in 1999, with twelve organizations of exiled women coming together to advance women's participation in the struggle for democracy.[65]

In the late 2000s, the spread of antigovernment protests—known as the Saffron Revolution—and growing international isolation prompted the military government to initiate a political reform process. A new constitution, adopted in 2008, precipitated a gradual political opening. However, the constitution preserved the military's dominant status, reserving a quarter of parliamentary seats as well as key ministerial posts for military representatives. It also codified impunity for the Tatmadaw's past human rights abuses and entrenched patriarchal rule by stating that certain political positions could only be filled by men.[66]

Myanmar's partial political liberalization spurred a rapid surge in donor assistance. Between 2011 and 2015 alone, donors committed US$13.7 billion in development aid.[67] Countless international NGOs, multilateral organizations, and bilateral donor agencies set up offices in the country. Although their primary focus was peacebuilding and socioeconomic development, investments in democratic governance also skyrocketed. In the lead-up to the 2015 polls, most of this assistance focused on ensuring free and fair elections, though a few programs also included an emphasis on women's political participation. For example, USAID and the Australian Department of Foreign Affairs (DFAT) funded IFES to help the Union Electoral Commission mainstream gender considerations into the election administration process, and various organizations implemented training programs for women leaders in political parties and at the grassroots level. After the election, several organizations also launched activities to support the new parliament, including training and mentorship programs for newly elected women parliamentarians.[68]

Dashed hopes and continued resistance

In the years that followed, some women made inroads into formal politics. The 2015 election brought to power the National League for Democracy (NLD) under the leadership of long-time activist Aung San Suu Kyi and more than doubled women's parliamentary representation. The number of elected women representatives in the Union Parliament rose from 6 percent to 13.7 percent, whereas women's representation in state and regional parliaments jumped from 3.8 percent to 12.7 percent.[69] Women's rights organizations also took advantage of the newly available civic space to push the government to deliver on its gender equality commitments. For example, a coalition of more than one hundred women's rights organizations known as the Gender Equality Network successfully advanced a stalled law on gender-based violence.[70] Ethnic women's organizations continued to play active roles in documenting human rights abuses and women's experiences of insecurity in the country.[71]

Some international actors had hoped that Aung San Suu Kyi's rise to power would open the door for more women to access senior leadership positions. But reality fell far short of expectations, as illustrated by Suu Kyi's failure to appoint a single woman to her executive cabinet.[72] In response, several international actors began focusing more systematically on women's political inclusion after 2015, primarily through the USAID-funded Consortium for Elections and Political Process Strengthening (CEPPS, which includes IRI, NDI, and IFES) and through the European Union's Support to Electoral Processes and Democracy (or STEP Democracy) program. For example, both DIPD and IRI provided training to female political party members and assistance to women's structures within political parties. NDI, the Asia Foundation, and the International Women's Development Agency (IWDA) all focused on leadership training and coalition-building among women legislators. IFES launched a "She Leads" program targeting women's political participation at the grassroots, including in conflict-affected regions.

A parallel—and largely separate—stream of international activities sought to bolster women's participation in Myanmar's peace process. This support was primarily channeled through the Joint Peace Fund (JPF), a pooled funding mechanism set up by various international donors. The JPF dedicated at least 15 percent of its project funding to "women's needs, equality, and empowerment, as active contributors to the peace process," typically in the form of grants to women's organizations.[73] International actors also lobbied the various parties to the conflict to increase the number of women involved in ceasefire monitoring bodies and other peacebuilding processes. However, these efforts had limited results, especially given that Burmese authorities strongly resisted external involvement in the peace process. In 2016, for instance, the government blocked the JPF's allocation of funds for gender inclusion in the peace negotiations.[74] Women's influence over the peace process therefore primarily took place through informal channels and networks.

Throughout this period, several barriers complicated progress on women's political inclusion. In many parts of the country, cultural norms about women's political leadership remained restrictive. The country's majoritarian electoral system combined with patriarchal party structures also disadvantaged women candidates, particularly since most parties—including the NLD—resisted any quotas to bolster women's political representation and remained ambivalent about women's rights generally.[75] Most importantly, however, women's formal political gains occurred within a broader system of militarized governance, with the Tatmadaw's continued political influence limiting democratic inclusion and fueling armed resistance in marginalized regions of the country. Although women's national political representation increased by another 4 percent in the 2020 elections, these gains occurred in a context of rising political tensions and spiraling conflict, particularly in Rakhine and Chin States.[76]

In February 2021, the military seized power, ushering in the return of a more repressive, violent, and patriarchal political order. In the years since, women have been at the frontlines of nonviolent protests against the military junta, mobilizing across ethnic, caste, and religious lines.[77] Many have been met with targeted violence, and in 2021 alone more than 1,300 women activists were arrested for protesting the military regime.[78] Although popular resistance against military rule continues, women's rights activists and political leaders have once again been forced into a much more precarious political position. The coup has also thrown into question much of the peacebuilding and democracy support provided to Myanmar over the past decade. Following the return of the junta, local women's rights activists called on international actors to take clear diplomatic action against the Tatmadaw, institute sanctions, and provide continued support for community-based initiatives.[79] Several major donors have since reviewed their engagement in the country, and some continue to fund women's rights organizations. However, whether and how international actors will remain engaged in the coming years remains an open question.

Conclusion

Our four country cases represent different trajectories of women's political mobilization and political change, though they also have some remarkable similarities. In Kenya and Nepal, democratic reform and decentralization have opened up more space for women in politics, but entrenched political hierarchies have proven difficult to dismantle. In both countries, political power remains concentrated in the hands of elite men, and advocates observe a disconnect between progressive legal frameworks and women's limited political influence. In Nepal, these patterns are further exacerbated by profound caste, regional, and ethnic inequities; in Kenya, expensive and ethnically based elections and weakly institutionalized parties pose significant hurdles.

Morocco and Myanmar, on the other hand, illustrate the obstacles hindering women's political empowerment in hybrid and authoritarian regimes. In Morocco, women's rights activism has benefited from the support of the monarchy at critical junctures. Yet the country's ongoing political stagnation— marked by patronage politics and weak political parties—constrains women's pathways to political power and their influence once in office. In Myanmar, ongoing armed conflict and the persistent political influence of the patriarchal and exclusionary Tatmadaw limited women's political inclusion throughout its fragile and ultimately failed political transition. Although women mobilized politically through both formal and informal channels, they remained institutionally and politically sidelined. Advocates and reformers in all four countries have secured important successes in strengthening women's electoral representation. At the same time, achieving a meaningful redistribution of political *power* has proven more challenging, with weak or undemocratic institutions, poorly designed quota measures, patriarchal norms, and entrenched structural inequities acting as recurring constraints.

Across Nepal, Kenya, Morocco, and Myanmar, international actors have channeled resources into programs targeting women's political empowerment. In many cases, these efforts have been particularly visible around critical elections and reform junctures, when international organizations backed local campaigns for gender quota reforms. Yet as this brief overview indicates, international organizations have also drawn on a wider set of approaches, from training women candidates to pushing political parties to reform their internal structures. In tandem with local women's rights advocates, they have had to contend with the successes and limits of gender quotas, and some have shifted their focus to newer areas in response. In the next two chapters, we unpack these various strategies in greater detail. Drawing on all four cases as well as a broader review of aid strategies and programming, we build a conceptual framework for understanding the broader evolution of international aid for women's political empowerment over the past several decades.

PART II

THE STATE OF THE FIELD

4

First Generation: Getting Women in the Room

In December 1991, Kenyan president Daniel arap Moi repealed Section 2A of the Kenyan constitution, which had turned the country into a one-party state in 1982. Faced with growing international pressure and domestic discontent, he agreed to hold multiparty elections. After years of state repression, Kenyan civil society groups took hold of this transitional moment to press for wider legal and constitutional reform. New women's organizations and coalitions formed to ensure women's inclusion in the emerging democratic reform agenda. They launched political education campaigns targeting women voters and organized training workshops to support women interested in running for political office.[1] In 1992, women from across the country gathered at a National Women's Convention in Nairobi to define a shared set of demands for a democratic Kenya.[2]

Yet despite this mushrooming of political activism, women's political representation continued to stagnate. In the first multiparty elections held in the same year, only six women were elected to the Kenyan parliament, a number far below the 30 percent threshold that advocates had hoped for. Only two more women joined their ranks in the next election. None of the dozens of newly formed political parties made space for women in their leadership ranks. Writing in 1997, Kenyan scholar and women's rights advocate Maria Nzomo gave voice to a growing sense of disillusion among gender equality activists. "Women must face up to the fact that the Kenyan political machinery and society are still dominated by men who are not willing to share power with women," she wrote. "Men resist the entry of women into the political arena; and when she does enter she is allocated positions of relative powerlessness and then ignored."[3]

A similar pattern unfolded in many other democratizing countries. On the one hand, the return of multiparty politics in most parts of the world gave rise

Aiding Empowerment. Saskia Brechenmacher and Katherine Mann, Oxford University Press.
© Oxford University Press 2024. DOI: 10.1093/oso/9780197694275.003.0004

to new forms of political debate and contestation, thereby opening up spaces for women to claim their political voice. On the other hand, greater political pluralism and freedom for civil society initially produced few tangible gains in women's high-level political representation. In fact, the global percentage of women representatives in lower houses of parliament fell from 14.8 percent in 1988 to 10.3 percent in 1993, even as many countries instituted multiparty elections.[4] It quickly became clear that democratization alone would not be enough to change the face of political leadership around the world.

In this period of political flux, a first generation of aid programs for women's political empowerment began to take shape. As questions of political participation and institutional reform took center stage in many countries, bilateral and multilateral donors began funding activities that sought to bolster women's inclusion in nascent democratic processes. The pattern of near-universal male overrepresentation in politics drove first-generation activities to focus on *numerical* gains: increasing the number of women voters, increasing the number of women candidates, and increasing the number of women elected officials. Underlying these efforts was the assumption that getting a "critical mass" of women—generally considered to be 30 percent—into positions of leadership would allow them to establish reform coalitions, advance women's rights, and ultimately transform discriminatory structures and norms.[5]

This chapter lays out the primary goals and achievements of this first generation of aid initiatives as well as their limitations. It begins by reviewing the main types of international support that emerged during the 1990s and 2000s: campaigns for gender quotas; capacity-building initiatives targeting women political candidates and political leaders, including some initial efforts to build women's caucuses within political institutions; and support for politically oriented women's organizations. These efforts brought about important gains. In many countries, they bolstered women's advocacy during critical constitutional reform junctures and advanced the global spread of gender quotas, which quickly became one of the most common electoral reforms around the world. However, by focusing on women's *presence* within political institutions, first-generation approaches paid less attention to the sociocultural and institutional environment hindering women's participation and influence in politics. Moreover, they often took the form of stand-alone "women in politics" programs that were poorly integrated into broader democracy assistance initiatives, which limited both their impact and reach. In many new or partial democracies, the first generation of aid programs targeting women's political participation thus proved relatively successful at advancing gender-sensitive legal frameworks and increasing the number of women elected to political office—while leaving the most entrenched obstacles to women's equal political power intact.

First Generation 61

Bolstering women's political participation

To challenge men's overrepresentation in newly democratic or democratizing institutions, first-generation efforts prioritized increasing the number of women elected to political office, typically referred to as women's *descriptive* representation. Some activities, of course, had other objectives, such as ensuring that women voted at similar rates to men or passing gender-sensitive legislation. Yet for many women's rights activists in new democracies as well as their international backers, the end goal was to get more women into the decision-making room. Baked into this strategy was the hope that women's inclusion in formal political institutions would gradually reinforce women's *substantive* representation, meaning that women legislators would act on behalf of the previously neglected interests of women citizens.

Development donors and their local and international partners embraced several core strategies to bolster women's electoral gains. To contextualize these strategies and their underlying theories of change, it is helpful to lay out a simple analytical model summarizing the central drivers of women's political exclusion. Globally, gender inequities in political life are rooted in a complex array of cultural, political, and socioeconomic factors, with patriarchal gender norms and institutions taking different forms in different contexts. Unsurprisingly, scholars therefore disagree about the relative importance of these variables in explaining women's political representation. Existing research nevertheless highlights several recurring patterns.

First, women's political representation is shaped by the overall "supply" of women with the ambition, experience, and skills to compete with men for positions of leadership. Across different political contexts, women tend to run for political office at lower rates than men. This pattern is partly rooted in entrenched gender roles that assign women the primary responsibility for unpaid domestic work. Charged with household and childcare duties, women lack access to key resources needed to succeed in political life, including time, mobility, money, education, and professional networks.[6] In highly patriarchal societies, gender discrimination in inheritance and property ownership further exacerbates this pattern, by depriving women of important sources of wealth and financial autonomy. Alongside these structural constraints, gendered socialization processes tend to reduce women's interest in participating in politics. For example, research in the United States shows that women are more likely to doubt their readiness to run for office than men with similar education and professional backgrounds—whereas men are more likely to be socialized to be politically ambitious.[7] One entry point for addressing women's political marginalization is thus to focus on expanding the overall pool of women aspirants and

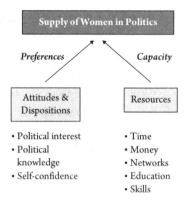

Figure 4.1 The Supply Side of Women's Political Representation

political leaders, by targeting both women's *capacity* to engage and their *attitudes and dispositions* vis-à-vis a political career (see Figure 4.1).

Yet gender gaps in political ambition and resources alone cannot explain women's global political marginalization. After all, once women decide to run for political office, they also need to be selected as candidates and voted into political office—and a vast body of research underscores that women politicians rarely face an equal playing field in this respect. In some cases, they experience direct discrimination by gatekeepers, whose attitudes and actions are colored by the same traditional gender norms that deter many women from participating in politics. For instance, the political party officials charged with selecting candidates are often men—and they tend to be more likely to value stereotypically masculine traits and experiences and to judge women as less qualified.[8] Beyond these individual gatekeepers, women's opportunities in politics are also shaped by the broader rules of the game. The electoral system, the structure and organization of political parties, and the nature of political competition all shape who is deemed a viable or promising candidate and what attributes are needed to win. These "demand-side" factors in turn influence the supply of women interested in engaging in politics. If women perceive the political system as rigged against them, it is no surprise that they are unwilling to throw their hat into the ring (see Figure 4.2).[9]

This model is, of course, an oversimplification. It ignores the role of intersecting identities—such as race, class, and ethnicity—that shape women's and men's access to political power. Yet it is helpful for situating the three primary strategies that development actors, reform-oriented policymakers, and advocates embraced to advance women's political empowerment: electoral gender quotas, capacity-building, and advocacy and awareness-raising. Training and capacity-building programs focused first and foremost on expanding the

First Generation 63

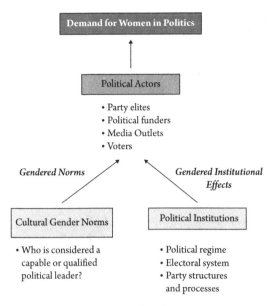

Figure 4.2 The Demand Side of Women's Political Representation

supply of women politicians by encouraging women to participate in politics and providing them with targeted skills and knowledge. Gender quotas, on the other hand, emerged as a compelling avenue for increasing the institutional *demand* for women candidates: by requiring political parties to recruit a set share of women candidates, or reserving a certain number of parliamentary seats for women, quota measures circumvent gender discriminatory practices and biases on the side of party gatekeepers and voters. Finally, advocacy and awareness-raising campaigns by civil society organizations can target both sides of the equation, by challenging cultural stereotypes about women in politics, pushing for gender-sensitive institutional reforms, and encouraging more women to get involved.

First-generation approaches to women's political empowerment shared several core characteristics, as shown in Table 4.1. First, they generally framed *women* as the primary targets of assistance and the drivers of gender equality change, while paying less attention to the *gender* roles and relations embedded in political institutions and the role of men as both drivers of and barriers to reform. Second, first-generation approaches primarily focused on bolstering women's participation and representation in formal political institutions and processes, whether as voters, candidates, or elected officials. Even when democracy aid actors targeted women's groups in civil society, they mostly supported activities geared toward women's inclusion in electoral politics, rather than, for example, feminist movement-building as a goal in and of itself. Underlying this

Table 4.1 **First-Generation Approaches to Women's Political Empowerment**

	Characteristics	*Assumptions*
Objective	Increasing women's political participation and representation in formal political institutions	Increasing the number of women elected to political office will ensure greater legislative and policy attention to women's interests and thus produce beneficial gender equality outcomes in society
Methods	Support for gender quotas and other temporary special measures	Implementing gender quotas that increase the institutional demand for women candidates will catapult more women into political office, thereby gradually transforming political institutions and eroding sociocultural barriers to women's participation
	Capacity-building for female candidates and elected officials	Reinforcing women's confidence, knowledge, networks, and skills will increase the overall supply of women candidates and bolster the influence of women legislators
	Assistance for politically oriented women's groups in civil society	Offering project funding and technical expertise to women's organizations will fuel bottom-up pressure for institutional reforms and help shift societal norms regarding women's leadership
Time frame	Elections as the focal point for interventions	Elections are the primary entry point for reinforcing women's political representation as electoral gains will translate into greater political power
Target	Women as the primary targets of assistance	Reinforcing women's power and capacity will help transform gender relations in politics, and the political and electoral gains of one group of women will help pave the way for others to gain greater political agency and voice
Modality	Stand-alone programs focused on women's political participation	Gender inequities in politics can be addressed through targeted interventions in specific areas

approach was the assumption that women's increased participation as voters and elected officials would gradually improve the quality of democratic representation, as women would use their increased electoral strength to promote greater attention to women's diverse interests.

This emphasis on formal institutional change encouraged a technocratic approach to gender equality in politics, with programs prioritizing questions of institutional and electoral system design over problems of political will, behavioral change, and social norms.[10] It also fueled a strong focus on elections (rather than, for instance, governance or movement-building) as the critical entry point to women's political empowerment. Quota campaigns, capacity-building programs, and civic education initiatives all centered on elections as *the* gateway to political power, which meant that women's electoral gains became central benchmarks of progress.[11] In the next part of the chapter, we turn to each of these strategies in more detail, examining why and how they emerged as areas of increased international investment.

The global push for gender quotas

First and foremost, the end of the Cold War and the third wave of democratization marked the onset of a global "quota fever," supported and encouraged by a wide range of international organizations and donor agencies.[12] Confronted with greater political pluralism and multiparty competition on the one hand, and women's continued political exclusion on the other, women's rights activists around the world turned to gender quotas as the primary mechanism for advancing women's political inclusion.[13] Shifting entrenched socioeconomic and attitudinal barriers, they recognized, would be a long and arduous process. Yet rather than waiting for these processes to unfold over the course of several decades, targeted institutional reforms could fast-track a critical share of women into political office, by compelling political parties to nominate women as candidates or reserving political seats for women. While advocates recognized that such measures in some ways represented a "shortcut" to gender inclusion, they also argued that "equal outcomes" should take priority over the classic liberal notion of "equal opportunity," which in practice was almost always undermined by hidden barriers and discrimination.[14] They also hoped that women politicians would help shift societal attitudes about women's leadership once in political office and thus pave the way for other women to follow.

Gender quotas were not a new idea. Over the course of the twentieth century, they had been used by various nondemocratic regimes around the world, including in many communist countries. Beginning in the 1980s, however, a growing number of left-leaning political parties in consolidated democracies—specifically in Germany, Austria, Belgium, and Canada—started adopting party-internal gender quotas in response to feminist activism within political parties. Informal networks between women politicians helped diffuse these measures into different political contexts, sometimes with the help of democracy promotion organizations. For example, in the late 1980s, contact between women in the Spanish Socialist Party and women politicians in Argentina and Costa Rica informed an initial push for gender quotas in Latin America. The German Friedrich Ebert Foundation also funded seminars and training booklets promoting gender quotas in Argentina, inspired by the experience of the German Social Democratic Party's own recent quota adoption process.[15] In 1991, Argentina became the first country to implement a binding gender quota law, which required all parties to place women in electable positions on their candidate lists.[16]

However, it was not until the 1995 Beijing Conference that the global push for gender quotas fully took off, triggering an explosion of international activities.[17] In Latin America alone, fourteen countries adopted quotas between 1996 and 2000.[18] Although these reforms were generally the result of domestic advocacy, international donors and organizations supported their efforts in three important ways. First, they helped establish global and regional normative frameworks that encouraged the adoption of gender quotas. Following Beijing, multilateral organizations such as the IPU, the Inter-American Development Bank, and UNDP endorsed gender quotas as the preferred mechanism for advancing gender equality in decision-making. These actors also convened international and regional conferences to exchange best practices and advance policy change. New international conventions and protocols—including the Millennium Development Goals and the 2003 Protocol to the African Charter on Human and People's Rights on the Rights of Women in Africa—also set specific, time-bound targets for the percentage of women that should hold elected office. These statements and activities provided domestic gender equality activists with new lobbying tools and legitimized their quota demands.[19]

Second, international organizations played an important role in tracking and disseminating comparative information about quota designs and implementation processes. In 1997, the IPU first began ranking countries based on the number of women in parliaments, thereby laying the groundwork for cross-national research and incentivizing competition between countries. One year later, the democracy assistance organization International IDEA launched its influential *Handbook on Women in Parliament*, which outlined the primary institutional enablers of women's political representation, including electoral system reforms and gender quota measures. The organization presented the handbook's findings at numerous seminars and conferences around the world, with the aim of disseminating best practices for increasing women's parliamentary representation.[20] In 2003, International IDEA also launched a global database of gender quotas and convened a series of regional workshops to gather information about the implementation of these measures. The initiative produced various case studies and reports examining the conditions under which gender quotas are most effective, which the organization then used to establish best practices for quota implementation.[21]

These research and monitoring initiatives fed directly into a third domain of international support, namely direct technical and financial assistance for electoral reform initiatives. In the late 1990s, international organizations and bilateral donors began organizing round tables, conferences, and seminars to share emerging best practices for quota design, and providing technical assistance to legislative drafting processes. In many cases, they also partnered with local women's organizations and women politicians, offering training and support for their quota campaigns. In postconflict states where international actors assumed more central roles, such as in Bosnia, Kosovo, and Afghanistan, international actors sometimes directly compelled local decision-makers to implement gender quotas as part of a broader template of "good governance" reforms. In Bosnia, for instance, the Organization for Security and Co-Operation in Europe (OSCE) Mission played a central role in pushing for a gender quota provision in the country's reformed electoral law, which was seen as a tool for "breaking out of the mold of nationalism" by catapulting new faces into Bosnian politics.[22] The law was adopted in 2001, despite significant domestic resistance, after the OSCE and the Office of the High Representative conditioned Bosnia's accession to the Council of Europe on the law's adoption.

Even in transitional contexts where donor governments and multilateral organizations had less direct political leverage, they advocated for gender quotas alongside broader gender equality provisions in constitutional reform processes. UNIFEM, the predecessor to UN Women, took on a particularly active role in this domain, supporting legal reforms in Liberia, Macedonia, Mexico, Morocco, and elsewhere.[23] In Morocco, the organization supported the Democratic Association of Moroccan Women ahead of the 2002 elections to mobilize women politicians in favor of electoral reform, which led to an amendment reserving 10 percent of national seats for women and pushed Morocco's six ruling parties to agree to a voluntary 20 percent candidate quota.[24] In 2007, UNIFEM launched a project called "Making Politics Work with Women" in Nepal to integrate gender perspectives into the country's postconflict constitutional negotiations. To this end, UNIFEM and its partners supported the participatory development of a gender-sensitive "model constitution," as well as several position papers on affirmative action and electoral system design that were then used to lobby the Constituent Assembly charged with drafting the country's new constitution.[25] During Kenya's constitutional reform process, on the other hand, UNIFEM seconded staff to government institutions to serve as technical advisors on gender mainstreaming and to integrate a gender perspective into various legislative and policy frameworks. It also organized consultations between different stakeholders involved in drafting and then implementing the gender equality provisions included in the new constitutional framework.[26]

Several factors explain why quotas took off as one of the preferred mechanisms to advance women's political empowerment. First, there was significant domestic demand for these measures. Local gender equality activists in many countries enthusiastically embraced the call for quota reforms, especially after observing weak commitments to women's political representation even among politically progressive and reform-oriented political parties. International efforts to advance gender quotas thus found committed partners in local women's groups. In addition, passing gender quotas—most often through electoral law reforms— represented a tangible objective with a clear endpoint and benchmarks for progress, which lent itself well to sharing technical transnational expertise. As such, aid providers viewed quota adoption as a more achievable goal than tackling more unwieldy obstacles like women's entrenched social and economic marginalization.

Lastly, in authoritarian or semiauthoritarian contexts, gender quotas were also less threatening to aid-receiving governments than many other types of democracy assistance. They rarely directly challenged the existing balance of power. After all, autocratic rulers and incumbent parties could use quotas to promote women loyal to the existing political regime, while at the same time signaling their commitment to democracy and development to the international community.[27] In Morocco, for example, King Mohammed VI supported the drive toward electoral reform: bolstering women's participation in a largely toothless parliament represented a welcome opportunity to bolster his domestic support as well as his international standing as a technocratic reformer. In short, bilateral donors, UN agencies, and other international organizations promoted quotas as a criterion of modern liberal statehood, and many governments had incentives to adopt these measures to boost their domestic and international legitimacy.

Building women's capacity

Electoral reforms, however, were not the only gender equality measure that gained popularity in the 1990s and early 2000s. Donor governments and multilateral organizations also invested in a growing range of grassroots training initiatives targeting women aspirants, candidates, and politicians. The idea of training women to become politicians had been pioneered by women's organizations in the United States. Beginning in the 1960s and 1970s, civil society organizations like EMILY's List emerged to assist female political candidates who supported abortion rights. In the decades that followed, these early groups were joined by others focused on advancing women's political leadership more broadly, for example by training community leaders and building a pipeline of young women interested in politics.[28] Their efforts were rooted in research showing that women in the United States were much less likely than men to consider themselves qualified for elected office and to put themselves forward as candidates—and that they were also less likely to be asked to run by political party operatives.[29] Training programs thus sought to boost the supply of women running for office by offering explicit encouragement and compensating for systemic disadvantages they might face as a result of their gender, such as weaker political and financial networks.

Beginning in the 1990s, democracy assistance organizations began incorporating similar training programs into their international work, based on the assumption that women in new democracies lacked the confidence, networks, and political experience to engage and succeed in politics. However, whereas training initiatives in the United States relied on a mix of recruitment, capacity-building, and funding for female candidates, their international equivalents consisted primarily of confidence- and skill-building workshops, with less of a focus on fundraising for women's campaigns.[30] Training curricula covered the benefits of women's political participation, information about the electoral and political system, and advice on campaigning skills and tactics. Donors also began funding training and exchanges for newly elected women parliamentarians and promoted the establishment of women's structures within parliaments and political parties, usually through a mix of capacity-building, funding, and logistical support. UNIFEM, for instance, backed the creation of women's caucuses in several postconflict contexts to strengthen women's collective influence in peace negotiations, including in the Democratic Republic of the Congo following the 1999 Lusaka Agreement and in Timor Leste in 2001.[31]

International training programs for women in politics reached Kenya, Nepal, and Morocco in the late 1990s (Myanmar, on the other hand, remained closed to this type of democracy aid until after the 2011 election). In Nepal, for instance, NDI began working on women's political participation ahead of the 1997 local government elections. At the time, Nepali women still held less than 1 percent of local government seats.[32] NDI launched a nationwide program to recruit and train women candidates and distilled the lessons learned into a campaign manual that was used in subsequent elections.[33] In 2008, following the end of armed conflict and the establishment of the Constitutional Assembly, NDI also launched a "Women's Leadership Academy" that provided training on substantive political issues for newly elected female Assembly representatives, government officials, and civil society actors. The organization also helped convene an Inter-Party Women's Alliance (IPWA) focused on advocating for political inclusion and encouraging women to get politically involved.[34]

Similar initiatives unfolded in Kenya and Morocco. In Kenya, many of the country's veteran female politicians, who first entered politics with the advent of multiparty politics in the 1990s, benefited from NDI training.[35] The League of Kenyan Women Voters, a local civil society organization focused on advancing women's political inclusion, also received international funding to identify and train women leaders, put together handbooks encouraging women to compete for elected office, and organize local-level "Democracy Forums" that brought women members of parliament together with their constituents in order to bolster their chances of re-election.[36] In Morocco, the implementation of a 12 percent gender quota in 2008 similarly led NDI and IRI—with funding from the US State Department's Middle East Partnership Initiative—to jointly launch a Women's Campaign Training program that targeted prospective women candidates, with the aim of "enhanc[ing] their skills in public policy, messaging, voter outreach and getting out the vote" ahead of the 2009 local elections.[37] In sum, throughout the 1990s and 2000s, donor-funded training programs for women aspirants, candidates, and politicians proliferated across new democracies, with the goal of encouraging more women to engage in politics, bolstering their campaigns, and strengthening their political skills once in office.

Assistance to women's organizations

Both international advocacy for gender quotas and capacity-building initiatives relied extensively on partnerships with local women's organizations and networks. Throughout the 1990s and early 2000s, a growing number of bilateral and multilateral donors began channeling support to these groups as part of a broader mushrooming of international civil society aid. Inspired by the important role that civic mobilization had played in overturning authoritarian regimes, many donors viewed civil society organizations as prodemocratic actors that could drive fragile reform processes while also nurturing citizens' bottom-up political participation.[38] Women's groups quickly emerged as one of the primary targets of such aid. Since women in many countries had a long history of formal and informal organizing, they were well positioned to take advantage of new organizational opportunities created by democratic transitions.[39] Of course, not all donor funding to women's organizations had an explicitly political bent. Many programs continued to focus on what feminist scholars have termed "women's practical interests," such as combating gender-based violence and supporting women's livelihoods.[40] But in many countries, international aid for women's rights advocacy increased at the same time that women's groups were using their newfound autonomy from state institutions to take on more explicitly political agendas.

International support for these organizations served dual goals: first, to strengthen women's voice and leadership in civil society as an end in itself and, second, to support civil society-led advocacy, education, and awareness-raising activities focused on bolstering women's political participation. Some donors offered direct support for specific projects and activities, for example by issuing calls for proposals through their embassies and country offices. Others, such as the Swedish International Development Cooperation Agency (Sida), channeled civil society aid through intermediary organizations, which then developed their own partnerships with local women's groups. In general, however, international actors gravitated toward and nurtured organizations that fit a certain organizational mold: NGOs that had specialized and educated (and therefore English-speaking) staff and experience with strategic planning and professionalized program design and management.[41] In many cases, international funding also came hand-in-hand with training in project and financial management to ensure that local partners would comply with the monitoring and reporting requirements of international donor agencies.

In Kenya, for instance, the Gender and Governance program—a US$12.1 million initiative supported by Canada, Denmark, Finland, the Netherlands, Norway, Spain, Sweden, and the United Kingdom—funded over two dozen women's organizations between 2004 and 2013. The program, which was managed by UNIFEM, issued calls for proposals for projects focused on women's participation in electoral processes and their leadership in subnational and national assemblies. Many of the selected groups used media campaigns and training workshops to change public perceptions of women in leadership and raise women's awareness of their political rights and opportunities. After the 2010 constitution was passed, they also focused on educating the public about the gender equality provisions in the new legal framework.[42] The program exemplifies the role of civil society support in first-generation approaches. Donors viewed women's organizations as important, nonpartisan channels to change community norms about women in leadership and encourage women to become politically involved. To this end, they facilitated time-bound projects consisting primarily of training workshops, conferences, and media campaigns focused on gender equality delinked from other political or ideological agendas.

A story of formal gains

The first generation of international support for women's political empowerment contributed to important changes around the world. Chief among them was the global proliferation of quota measures. By 2013, more than 60 states used some type of national gender quota; as of 2023, a total of 137 countries have instituted constitutional, electoral, or party-level gender quotas (see Figure 4.3).[43] The type of quota adopted has varied by region and electoral system. Countries in Latin and Central America and francophone Africa, which tend to have proportional representation systems, have mostly implemented legal quotas that require political parties to include a set share of women candidates on their party lists. By contrast, countries in Asia, East Africa, and the Middle East, many of which have majoritarian electoral systems, have more frequently opted for reserved parliamentary seats for women. In addition to electoral quotas, many countries have also incorporated broader gender equality provisions into their constitutional frameworks, often following domestic political transitions. Whereas past constitutions tended to be silent on matters of gender, many constitutions today include provisions on equality and nondiscrimination.[44] For example, according to Tripp (2015), 94 percent of constitutions in African postconflict countries now contain antidiscriminatory provisions based on sex and 75 percent reference gender quotas.[45]

International democracy aid and diplomatic pressure were certainly not the only catalysts for these reforms. Domestic women's movements, feminists within legislatures, political parties, state bureaucracies, and the political opportunities

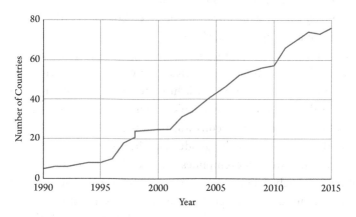

Figure 4.3 The Global Proliferation of Gender Quotas (2009–2015) Source: Melanie M. Hughes, Pamela Paxton, Amanda Clayton, and Pär Zetterberg, "Quota Adoption and Reform over Time (QAROT), 1947–2015," (Ann Arbor, MI: Inter-university Consortium for Political and Social Research, 2017).

afforded by democratic transitions all played critical roles. In many African countries, for example, cross-ethnic women's coalitions bringing together activists, scholars, and politicians helped drive quota adoption.[46] However, international aid reinforced local reform initiatives with funding, diplomatic backing, and technical assistance—and at times even advanced quota adoption in the absence of strong domestic advocacy campaigns.[47] Connections to bilateral and multilateral donors also lent advocacy coalitions greater legitimacy and expanded the domestic reform agenda by introducing comparative information about gender-sensitive legal frameworks adopted in other countries.[48] The influence of international actors is borne out in cross-national statistical analyses. For instance, Bush (2011) finds that countries with democracy-promoting UN peace operations, high levels of foreign aid dependence, and international election observation missions have been significantly more likely to adopt gender quotas, which underscores the importance of international actors and aid in these electoral reform processes.[49] In a more recent study, Edgell (2017) similarly finds that international democracy assistance has often contributed to quota adoption, both through aid interventions that bolster domestic reformers and by incentivizing (less democratic) aid-dependent countries to adopt quotas to highlight their reformist credentials.[50]

Quotas, of course, are not ends in and of themselves; they are merely a means to bolster women's representation. The past several decades have shown that they are largely effective at advancing this goal.[51] Women accounted for only 11.3 percent of members of parliament in 1995; this percentage had risen to nearly 16 percent by 2005 and 19.1 percent by 2010, primarily due to the adoption of quota measures.[52] Similar progress is evident across our case studies. As noted in the previous chapter, in Nepal, the number of women in parliament jumped from 6 percent in 2006 to 33 percent in 2008 following the adoption of a gender quota for the country's Constituent Assembly. In Morocco, women's parliamentary representation rose from 1 percent in 2001 to 11 percent in 2002 after political parties first agreed to reserve seats for women, and again to 17 percent in 2011 when the quota measure was codified into electoral law with a higher threshold. By 2021, women's representation reached 23 percent as advocates successfully lobbied for increasing the number of reserved seats.[53] For many aid officials as well as their local partner organizations, these electoral reforms represented a critical step forward, even if they did not resolve women's political marginalization on their own. "Having the right regulatory framework isn't enough, but it gives us a solid basis to move forward," said one international aid official in Morocco. "Especially in the context of wider legal reforms focused on gender equality, like the reform of the Family Code in 2004 and wider constitutional reforms. [...] Now we're focusing on the implementation phase, which is critical. Otherwise, it's just a statement with no actual impacts."[54]

Over time, international democracy organizations have accumulated greater comparative knowledge of the types of quotas that work best across different institutional contexts. International IDEA's 2007 "Designing for Equality" handbook, for instance, outlines which combinations of electoral systems and quota designs have proven most effective.[55] This study and other research projects underscore that candidate quotas are most impactful if they include high targets and specific placement mandates or ranking rules, in order to prevent parties from simply placing women at the bottom of their candidate lists. Meaningful sanctions for noncompliance are also essential. In majoritarian electoral systems, on the other hand, reserving a rotating set of electoral districts for women or electing women through national women-only lists tend to be more suitable options. These comparative insights have in turn informed the strategies of domestic advocates, who have increasingly turned their focus toward strengthening existing quota reforms and closing implementation loopholes.[56]

Beyond electoral and legal reforms, the impact of first-generation approaches to women's political empowerment is more difficult to measure. In politically fluid contexts, untangling the specific effects of awareness-raising and civic education initiatives can be an impossible task. However, it is likely that capacity-building and leadership training initiatives for women voters, aspirants, and politicians have helped disseminate knowledge about legal rights and institutional reforms, particularly during and after major political junctures. For women who lacked prior political experience and connections, such programs have also offered spaces to develop their confidence and forge relationships with like-minded leaders. Yet as we show in more detail in Chapter 6, their effects on bolstering women's political representation have often been less significant than donors, implementers, and advocates had hoped. At the individual level, they can provide valuable encouragement and advice, but they are not set up to counter institutional and structural barriers to gender equality in politics.[57]

Finally, international support certainly contributed to the growth of politically oriented women's organizations and networks that formed following the third wave of democratic transitions and the Beijing Conference.[58] A global survey of nearly one thousand women's organizations conducted by the Association for Women's Rights in Development (AWID) in 2005 found that most groups received the majority of their resources from bilateral and multilateral donors, followed by large private foundations, public foundations, individual donors, and women's funds.[59] As noted above, international support for domestic civil society mobilization was often critical for advancing legal and constitutional reforms, with donor funding and political backing reinforcing women's organizations' regional and domestic advocacy campaigns. In some cases, external support also encouraged greater professionalism and transparency among women's organizations and facilitated their autonomy from state patronage networks. But heightened dependence on donor funding has also raised new concerns about the sustainability and downward accountability of women's movements, as we explore further in the final part of this chapter.

Adding women and stirring?

Despite the achievements of first-generation approaches, several shortcomings quickly became apparent to aid actors and activists. Although legal reforms, combined with capacity-building and civic education, produced important gains in women's numerical representation in politics, these efforts often failed to challenge men's dominance in political life. For one, male gatekeepers in political parties frequently used their dominant status to resist or subvert the progressive electoral reforms, for example by channeling women to less desirable party list positions.[60] In addition, neither quotas nor training initiatives directly addressed many of the "demand-" and "supply-side" hurdles that discourage women from engaging in politics, from financial constraints to patriarchal resistance and violence. As a result, increases in women's representation rarely exceeded (and sometimes failed to meet) the minimum thresholds set by quotas, and women still found themselves excluded from the inner circles of political power.

In Morocco, as we noted above, the number of women parliamentarians increased substantially in the early 2000s following the expansion of reserved seats, which political parties filled through national candidate lists. At the same time, the number of women elected to (nonquota) district seats rose only minimally, from two (out of 325 directly elected representatives) in 1997 to seven (out of 305 representatives) in 2011.[61] This pattern shows that reserved seats for women did not fundamentally change the way parties selected their candidates. Since then, most have continued to place men in the top position on their electoral lists, while pushing women candidates into less electable positions. Women's selection to the national quota list, moreover, has remained driven by clientelism and kinship ties.[62] Many women legislators who make it onto the list are close relatives of men already active in politics, and their re-election to a large degree depends on their allegiance to (male) party leaders, rather than on their performance in parliament. In the most recent parliamentary election, around one-fifth of women elected to parliament had familial ties to senior party officials.[63] In sum, the example of Morocco illustrates how legal measures aimed at bringing more women into political office have struggled to dismantle gendered power hierarchies rooted in the wider institutional context.[64]

The focus of first-generation approaches on getting women into political institutions also meant that questions of *influence* and *interest representation* through democratic governance received comparatively less attention.

Although international actors in some countries supported gender caucuses, women's leagues, and training initiatives for female legislators, these efforts were not necessarily backed up by a broader theory of institutional change. As a result, increases in women's descriptive representation alone rarely guaranteed their equal political voice, nor did it ensure systematic attention to gender in policymaking. Whether within political parties or parliaments, women still faced blatant discrimination and informal exclusionary practices that limited their access to senior decision-making roles as well as their cross-party collaboration. Quotas sometimes reinforced these challenges, by placing women in institutionally disadvantageous positions. In Kenya, for example, women nominated to quota seats at the county level lack defined electoral constituencies, which means that they cannot spearhead the kinds of local development initiatives that allow politicians to build popular support. Instead, they find themselves beholden to the interests of party leaders, who control their access to committee and leadership roles.[65] Together, these dynamics help explain why increases in women's descriptive representation encouraged by first-generation approaches rarely had the transformative effects that advocates had hoped for.[66]

Instead, women's organizations in civil society remained critical drivers of gender equality change, pushing for gender-sensitive legislation and further institutional reforms. Yet in order to access international funds, women's organizations had to develop more specialized expertise, establish formal organizational structures, and build the internal capacity needed to comply with donors' cumbersome administrative requirements, all of which incentivized their professionalization as mostly urban and elite-based NGOs while disincentivizing a focus on grassroots mobilization and bottom-up movement-building. In addition, the unpredictable and short-term nature of donor funding fueled competition among women's groups and prevented longer-term coalition-building.[67] None of these pressures were unique to politically oriented women's organizations. They also varied from place to place; some countries had much more robust and unified women's movements than others. The overall tendency toward professionalization and fragmentation, however, meant that as countries embarked on the difficult journey of realizing ambitious legal commitments, they sometimes lacked a broad-based women's movement that could generate bottom-up pressure on political leaders.

The persistence of siloed approaches

A final shortcoming of first-generation approaches to women's political empowerment was the reliance on siloed and small-scale "women in politics" programs, which were often detached from broader democracy reform initiatives.[68] Donor agencies funded democracy assistance efforts without a clearly articulated gender lens or gender-related objectives, and then invested in separate activities targeting women. Even within the framework of gender-focused programs, different activities were not necessarily integrated into a coherent theory of change. Illustrating this pattern, a 2001 assessment of international assistance to women's groups across different postconflict countries found that programs funded and implemented by the international community had been "established in an opportunistic manner, without a carefully formulated policy framework."[69] A remarkably similar criticism appeared in a 2008 evaluation of the aforementioned Gender and Governance program in Kenya, which described the initiative as consisting of "discrete, sometimes competing projects, rather than a coherent programme pursuing shared goals."[70]

This fragmentation reflected the broader siloing of "women in politics" programs. Despite rhetorical commitments to gender mainstreaming, few donors and implementing organizations had instituted gender equality strategies that required them to integrate a gender lens across their democracy and governance programs, or that built the internal expertise, knowledge base, and programmatic tools necessary for such integration. Instead, many organizations and aid officials continued to treat women's political empowerment as a niche area, auxiliary to their core focus on elections, legislatures, and political parties. Gender-targeted programs, in turn, depended on the initiative of individual aid officials committed to the cause. "If there was a [Democracy, Rights and Governance] officer who happened to be passionate about these issues, then they were likely to integrate them into their program design," recalled a former USAID official. "But it wasn't really standardized, and there wasn't really guidance either."[71]

A similar dynamic played out within implementing organizations, many of which did not build gender considerations into program proposals unless explicitly prodded to do so by donors or individual program managers.[72] NIMD, for instance, only adopted an organization-wide approach to women's political empowerment in 2014, fourteen years after its founding.[73] A 2015 evaluation of its country programs found that NIMD had adopted a "highly decentralized and ad-hoc approach" to improving the political participation of excluded groups, with "no formal management commitment to mainstreaming, no guidelines, no central support and no M&E, risk management or 'do no harm policies' on what can be highly sensitive and complex issues."[74] This decentralized approach—which was by no means unique to NIMD—raised several challenges. Standalone projects tended to be small in scale and were rarely grounded in systematic research and strategic planning. Aid providers and their partners also missed opportunities to engage male stakeholders on gender equality issues and to integrate a focus on women's representation and influence into their existing initiatives and political dialogues. First-generation approaches to women's political empowerment thereby replicated many of the weaknesses that had characterized earlier "Women in Development" programs, including a programmatic focus on integrating women into existing structures and the reliance on targeted initiatives that neglected how gendered power relations are embedded in and reproduced by political institutions.

Conclusion

Emerging during a period of political opening around the world, the first generation of women's political empowerment programs primarily sought to increase the number of women in nascent democratic institutions. Rather than providing a full survey of the assistance activities initiated during this period, this chapter has focused on highlighting the dominant modes of support and their shared characteristics. Based on the belief that a critical mass of women in political positions would deepen democracy and enable more gender-sensitive governance, international actors prioritized the adoption and diffusion of gender-sensitive electoral reforms and capacity-building programs for women aspirants, candidates, and elected officials, while also funding politically oriented women's organizations to lobby decision-makers, implement trainings, and carry out civic education activities. Women's electoral participation and electoral gains stood at the center of these efforts, which mirrored the international community's broader focus on elections as key benchmarks for democratic progress.

Over the past three decades, the most significant contribution of these early initiatives has been the global proliferation of gender quotas, as well as the inclusion of broader gender equality and nondiscrimination provisions in constitutional and legislative frameworks. Through international norm-building, knowledge diffusion, and direct support to domestic reform initiatives, international actors played important supportive (and sometimes determinative) roles in advancing legal reform, with direct and positive effects on women's descriptive representation. Training and awareness-raising activities helped spread public knowledge of these reforms and provided support to many women venturing into political life for the first time. In most cases, however, these efforts were not as transformative as advocates had hoped. Even as more women entered political parties, parliaments, and other institutions, gendered power inequities and entrenched social and political hierarchies persisted, highlighting the need for additional strategies for change.

5

Second Generation:
Transforming Systems

In many countries, the first generation of assistance approaches helped catapult a critical mass of women into legislative seats. Yet in practice, legislative advances were often stymied by weak implementation and women's continued exclusion from meaningful decision-making. These patterns underscored the need for more holistic strategies to advance women's political empowerment, beyond quota reforms, capacity-building, and civil society advocacy. Over the past decade, the search for new entry points has gradually given rise to a second generation of assistance focused on women's political empowerment.

At its core, this second generation is characterized by two important shifts. First, whereas first-generation efforts focused on increasing women's presence in fledgling democratic processes and institutions, newer initiatives center the broader political ecosystem shaping women's political participation, including institutions, sociocultural norms, and individual resources and attitudes. Rather than inserting women into existing structures, they place greater emphasis on *transforming* patriarchal processes, norms, and institutions to make them more inclusive. Second, instead of relying only on stand-alone "women in politics" programs, donors and democracy-support organizations now integrate gender perspectives and goals across different areas of aid, including electoral assistance, political party aid, and parliamentary support. The idea that women's political equality is a central rather than peripheral element of democratic governance has gained significant ground.

This second generation does not, however, mark a wholesale rupture in thinking or practice. Instead, it should be understood as an expansion and deepening of existing activities, driven by research and advocacy by gender experts within aid organizations, the shifting priorities of women's rights advocates in aid recipient countries, and greater institutional prioritization of

Aiding Empowerment. Saskia Brechenmacher and Katherine Mann, Oxford University Press.
© Oxford University Press 2024. DOI: 10.1093/oso/9780197694275.003.0005

gender equality by some donors and multilateral organizations. Substantial areas of continuity remain, including a lasting focus on strengthening legal frameworks related to women's political participation and expanding the pool of women political leaders through training. Globally, however, international support for women's political empowerment today is characterized by a much larger and more sophisticated toolbox of interventions than fifteen or twenty years ago, with more nuanced theories of change. This ongoing evolution mirrors the broader transformation of the democracy assistance field, from an initial focus on standard institutional templates toward greater differentiation and appreciation of the complexities of political reform.[1] In this chapter, we trace what these shifts in international interventions have looked like in practice, and in which areas they remain incomplete.

Transforming the ecosystem

The rise of second-generation approaches is based on the core insight that gender equality in politics cannot be achieved by merely adding women into existing political structures. Women's growing presence within those institutions can make a difference, by normalizing women's political leadership in the eyes of citizens and bringing new issues onto the political agenda. But on its own, increasing women's political representation in formal political spaces is rarely sufficient to level the political playing field, particularly if wider socioeconomic, cultural, and political barriers to equality remain unchanged.[2] This insight is not new: since the 1960s and 1970s, feminist scholars and activists have cautioned against superficial inclusionary strategies that do not bring about systemic transformation.[3] In the political realm, however, the limits of tokenistic inclusion became more apparent after women's initial fights for legal reform had been won.

To illustrate these limitations, we return to the model of political inclusion introduced in Chapter 4, which focused on the "supply" of and "demand" for women in politics. First-generation efforts reflected this approach: they sought to expand the pool of women running for office and leverage gender quotas to bolster the institutional demand for women political leaders. However, training interventions only target individual constraints that are within women's control, such as their self-confidence and knowledge of political processes. They cannot transform structural gender inequities in wealth, income, and unpaid labor, or overcome hostile and sexist attitudes held by voters and politicians. Quota measures, meanwhile, can circumvent the gender biases of political gatekeepers, but they do not transform organizational practices and political cultures predicated on women's exclusion, or male leaders' ability to bend the political rules in their favor. These patterns highlight the shortcomings of the "supply and demand" model: it suggests a binary equation that underplays the systemic and self-reinforcing nature of men's political dominance.[4]

A greater focus on *gendered institutions* helps shed light on these complexities. Political scientist Mona Lena Krook, for instance, argues that gender inequities in access to political office are better understood as the product of three categories of institutions, broadly defined: rules (such as electoral systems), practices (such as campaign spending and candidate selection methods), and norms (such as prevailing ideas about equality, leadership, and representation). These institutions are "gendered" in the sense that they reflect societal gender roles and impact people differently depending on their gender. They are also interdependent: a change in formal rules, for example through a quota law, will have different effects depending on existing practices and norms, which can either hinder or enable the implementation process.[5] The same framework can be applied to women's political power once they are in elected office. Access to parliamentary influence depends not only on formal policies ensuring women's presence but also on workplace practices and widely held gender norms and expectations. In practical terms, these insights underscore the need for a more systemic approach to women's political empowerment, one that encompasses changes in systemwide rules, in political practices, as well as in institutional cultures and norms.

This conceptual shift influenced second-generation approaches to women's political empowerment (see Table 5.1). As practitioners sought to build on earlier gains, they began paying particular attention to the inner workings of political institutions, investigating how their rules and practices hindered women's influence.[6] They targeted the traditional pillars of democracy assistance—including electoral institutions, political parties, and parliaments—and started investing in new strategies of institutional and organizational reform, through a mix of advocacy, training, research, and network-building. In parallel, some aid providers and their local partners also turned their attention to the discriminatory gender norms and stereotypes that discourage women's participation and fuel patriarchal resistance and backlash. Embedded in these shifts was a stronger appreciation of and concern for the quality and meaning of women's political participation, and a move away from elections as the focal point for reform.[7] If the political ecosystem was the problem, elections alone could not resolve it. Instead, more diverse entry points were needed.

The expanded toolbox

As gender experts in multilateral organizations and INGOs turned their attention to the broader institutional changes required to advance gender equality

Table 5.1 From First- to Second-Generation Approaches to Women's Political Empowerment

	First Generation	*Second Generation*
Objective	Increasing women's political participation and representation in formal political institutions	Transforming the political ecosystem that inhibits women's political participation and influence
Time frame	Elections as the focal point for interventions	Interventions span the entire political cycle
Target	Women are the primary targets of assistance	Women remain the primary target group, in addition to new efforts to transform gender norms in political institutions and confront patriarchal resistance
Modality	Stand-alone programs focused on women's political participation	Increasing investments in gender mainstreaming across international democracy assistance programs

in politics, the dominant model of small-scale, stand-alone "women in politics" programs appeared increasingly problematic. It made little sense to train and empower women in a particular political party, for instance, if international actors failed to advocate for gender inclusion in their broader dialogues with the same party's leaders or even supported reforms that indirectly undermined women's participation. As long as women's participation was still treated as a marginal issue, rather than as a crucial building block of the democratic project, further progress seemed difficult to achieve. As a result, advocates began pushing for greater integration or mainstreaming of gender equality into existing democracy initiatives, alongside new targeted programs.[8]

The expansion of gender mainstreaming within bilateral donor agencies and multilateral organizations helped advance this goal. As noted in Chapter 2, the Beijing Platform for Action endorsed gender mainstreaming as a core strategy for achieving gender equality change as early as 1995. Most donors subsequently adopted initial mainstreaming policies. Yet whereas several Scandinavian governments made progress in implementation, many others, including the European Union and the United States, lagged behind. USAID, for example, first introduced gender mainstreaming requirements under its 1996 Gender Plan of Action, but these remained weakly institutionalized.[9] It was not until the Obama administration came into office in 2008 and Hillary Clinton was appointed secretary of state that a new crop of leaders set into motion internal reforms aimed at strengthening the agency's work on gender equality, such as mandatory gender training for all aid officials, a newly empowered Office of Gender Equality and Women's Empowerment, and new requirements to integrate gender analysis into USAID's program cycle.[10]

As a result of these bureaucratic changes, USAID missions started conducting gender analyses as part of their country strategy development process, which ensured that more democracy programs included clear gender-related objectives and indicators.[11] A new Gender Equality and Female Empowerment Policy (2012), a new USAID Strategy on Democracy, Human Rights and Governance (2013), and the United States' first-ever Action Plan for Women, Peace and Security (2011) further strengthened the policy framework for integrating gender into democracy aid. Finally, advocates within the agency also pushed for dedicated gender experts within the Center for Democracy, Human Rights, and Governance to support USAID missions in their work on gender and politics, and in 2012–2013, USAID established new incentive funds to encourage USAID missions to work on women's political leadership.[12]

Other multilateral and bilateral donors as well as implementing organizations underwent a similar evolution. In 2013, for example, the UN Electoral Assistance Division (UNEAD) adopted a specific policy directive defining women's electoral and political participation as a key principle of UN electoral assistance and integrated a stronger focus on gender equality into its directives on electoral system design, electoral management, and electoral needs assessment missions.[13] As a result, all missions must now complete a checklist with gender-specific considerations, which helps inform their recommendations for action. UN electoral assistance programs today are therefore significantly more likely to include gender components than similar efforts in the past.[14] Within the wider circle of democracy assistance organizations, practitioners who had been pushing for a more holistic focus on gender equality could draw on shifting donor practices to expand their work.[15] Internal reviews and evaluations of past programs amplified their message by highlighting the limitations of ad hoc initiatives. Although investments in gender expertise varied across organizations, an increasing focus on gender integration is evident in many organizations' strategic plans, as well as in the proliferation of new programming tools and guidelines aimed at integrating a gender lens across different areas of democracy support.[16]

Together, the turn toward more holistic approaches to women's political empowerment and the increasing focus on gender mainstreaming significantly expanded the toolbox of aid interventions (see Table 5.2). From its early focus on legal and constitutional reform, capacity-building, and civic education, the field has evolved to include new initiatives aimed at transforming institutional cultures and practices, advancing gender-sensitive governance, building reform coalitions, and shifting social norms.

Table 5.2 **The Expanded Toolbox**

Civil Society	Leadership training and capacity-building for women's organizations
	Support for advocacy, networking, and other activities
	Support to women journalists and gender training for media outlets
Elections	Voter education and registration campaigns targeting women
	Gender mainstreaming in election management bodies
	Technical assistance for electoral regulation and reform
	Legal and policy measures against violence against women in elections, including training for law enforcement and judicial personnel
	Gender integration in international and domestic election observation
Parties	Training and mentoring women candidates and party members
	Funding mechanisms for women candidates
	Support for women's wings within parties
	Cross-party women's networks and dialogues
	Research and advocacy targeting internal party rules and processes
	Political party regulation and oversight through legal reform
Parliament	Technical assistance for gender-related legislative and constitutional reforms
	Training, mentorship, and exchanges for female elected officials and parliamentary staff
	Support for women's caucuses and gender committees and for coalitions between women parliamentarians and women in civil society
	Gender mainstreaming in parliamentary structures and processes, including support for gender audits and gender-sensitive budgeting

There are, of course, substantial areas of continuity. In many countries, legal and electoral reforms targeting women's political participation remain an important priority, and training for women candidates and politicians remains one of the most dominant programming models, particularly in the lead-up to elections. Donors also continue to partner with politically oriented women's organizations for advocacy, awareness-raising, and training initiatives. However, even within these continuing areas of engagement, an evolution has taken place: from passing quota reforms to strengthening and enforcing these legal measures, and from short-term, superficial training to more contextually attuned capacity-building approaches (for a discussion of the latter, see Chapter 6).

Moreover, rather than being implemented in isolation, these earlier approaches are increasingly complemented by new efforts to make political institutions more gender-sensitive, bolster women's political influence, and challenge discriminatory norms and violence against women in politics. In the next part of this chapter, we review the characteristics of second-generation approaches in greater detail, focusing on four core domains of international democracy support: electoral institutions and processes, political parties, parliaments, and the cross-cutting domain of social norms. Our goal is not to provide a comprehensive assessment of these approaches, but instead to illustrate the primary areas of learning and change. We return to questions about different models' effectiveness in the three chapters that follow.

Engendering elections

Over the past decade, many democracy aid providers have expanded their early support for gender-sensitive electoral reforms to a broader focus on gender equality throughout the entire electoral cycle. International actors have been deeply involved in helping new or developing democracies organize elections since the late 1980s, offering a mix of capacity-building, technical assistance, and support for international and domestic election observers. Yet in the 1990s and early 2000s, these efforts rarely included a systematic gender lens. Although first-generation approaches to women's political empowerment sought to improve the legal frameworks governing gender equality in elections, few initiatives integrated gender concerns into the *management and administration* of elections. For example, a 2014 UNDP study examining lessons learned in international electoral support concluded that "the attention given to the empowerment of women across the electoral cycle has generally been *ad hoc* and kept separate from the broader ('mainstream') electoral assistance programme."[17]

But across many parts of the world, gender inequities in electoral participation persist despite the adoption of progressive legal frameworks. Women in culturally conservative societies face barriers in registering to vote, due to restrictions on their mobility, high rates of illiteracy, a lack of documentation, or physical insecurity. In rural parts of Kenya, for instance, voter registration centers are sometimes located too far away for women to reach on foot, particularly since their domestic responsibilities prevent them from spending extended periods of time away from home.[18] Insecurity around election day can also deter women from voting: during Kenya's 2017 election, the Kenyan Human Rights Council documented 201 cases of election-related sexual and gender-based violence.[19] In Nepal, on the other hand, low literacy rates make it difficult for many women to access information about elections, voting rights, and other forms of political participation.[20]

Recognizing these challenges, major election aid providers—including UNDP, UN Women, International IDEA, and IFES—have developed new initiatives to tackle gender inequities at different stages of the electoral process, from voter registration to postelection data analyses.[21] Their efforts generally follow three main models. A first set of activities focuses on gender mainstreaming within electoral management bodies (EMBs) tasked with organizing elections. These efforts aim to ensure that women's interests and needs are considered at each stage of the election process and to increase women's representation in electoral institutions themselves. To this end, aid providers often support early-stage gender assessments to identify areas for action. These are followed by a standard menu of organizational reforms: setting up gender units within EMBs, designating gender focal points, developing an internal gender policy and action plan, instituting systems for collecting sex-disaggregated data, and conducting gender training for staff. The international BRIDGE program, a joint venture by the Australian Electoral Commission, the UNEAD, International IDEA, IFES, and UNDP, has emerged as a particularly important conduit for such training, providing targeted courses on gender, elections, and women's participation for electoral commissions and other relevant stakeholders.

A brief snapshot from Nepal illustrates this approach. Since 2008, UNDP has played a central role in providing electoral support in the country, with financial support from the EU, the UK, Denmark, and Norway. In the initial project phase, UNDP partnered with IFES to support the Electoral Commission of Nepal (ECN) in carrying out a "gender mapping" to analyze the existing institutional framework, identify barriers to women's political participation, and study women's status within the commission.[22] UNDP then worked with the commission to implement the recommendations that emerged. This led the ECN to adopt a Gender and Inclusion Policy and action plan and set up an internal gender unit in 2014.[23] UNDP and IFES also helped the commission integrate a gender lens into its voter outreach. For instance, in the run up to the 2017 elections, international partners supported the ECN to carry out roughly eight thousand voter education events across twenty-nine districts, most of which targeted women and citizens from marginalized communities.[24]

A second set of initiatives works with EMBs, civil society organizations, and other stakeholders to implement more targeted initiatives, such as establishing women-only voter registration campaigns or polling stations. These targeted programs often emerge in response to specific challenges, such as large gender gaps in voter registration. Lastly, international organizations have also increasingly integrated gender considerations into election observation missions to better document previously hidden barriers to equal political participation. The Organization for Security and Co-operation in Europe (OSCE) and the Organization of American States (OAS), for instance, have developed detailed methodologies that international monitors can use to assess gender equality in elections.[25] NDI, on the other hand, has invested in training local civil society groups in gender-sensitive election observation practices.[26] In Myanmar, for example, NDI—with funding from the UK Department for International

Development, now Foreign, Commonwealth & Development Office (FCDO)—partnered with the People's Alliance for Credible Elections to monitor the 2015 national elections and 2019 Yangon municipal elections and supported them in integrating a gender lens into their work.[27] In sum, gender integration in electoral assistance has progressed in recent years, helped by aid organizations' ability to find willing partners among technical experts working in electoral institutions and among civil society groups.

Engaging political parties

Beyond electoral institutions, a growing number of initiatives have also tackled gender inequities in political parties, based on the recognition that parties control candidate selection and thus serve as critical gatekeepers to women's political participation and representation. Early assistance efforts sought to bolster women's position within political parties by training women party members and supporting dedicated women's wings. Yet these strategies were often insufficient to improve women's collective influence within party structures. "There was an election in Zambia where we trained 120 women, and none of them won," recalls one gender expert at a major democracy organization. "We started to recognize that all of this capacity-building isn't changing anything. [. . .] How do you instead design political party programs so that the environment, and the party, and the organizational structure is one that enables women to operate?"[28]

Responding to this problem, several democracy assistance organizations launched new initiatives aimed at systematically documenting women's exclusion within political parties. Between 2010 and 2013, International IDEA carried out various research projects along these lines, including an analysis of party-level gender equality policies across thirty-three countries in Africa.[29] The organization then convened conferences and party dialogues in Malawi, Tanzania, Liberia, and elsewhere to share their findings with party leaders and discuss potential remedial actions. These efforts ultimately fed into the development of IDEA's "Framework for Developing Gender Policies for Political Parties," which was published in 2016 and used in subsequent advocacy initiatives.[30] UNDP and NDI similarly joined forces to study the various activities political parties had taken to promote women in political life and used their findings to develop a guidebook on gender-sensitive party reforms.[31]

These research initiatives have given rise to new aid programs that focus on advancing gender equality reforms within political parties as well as new efforts to integrate a gender lens into existing political party engagement. For example, in 2014, NIMD and International IDEA launched a three-year-long "Respect for Women's Political Rights Programme," which used research, advocacy, and convenings to encourage internal organizational changes among political parties in Kenya, Tunisia, and Colombia. Other democracy assistance organizations specialized in working with political parties have also expanded their programming on gender inclusion, typically through a combination of mentorship and exchanges, multiparty dialogues, and technical assistance. Fewer organizations have directly taken on the sensitive issue of political finance, although some have documented the gendered barriers to election funding across different countries and convened party leaders, government stakeholders, and advocates to discuss potential policy responses.[32]

In many ways, these approaches mirror the evolution of the electoral assistance field. International organizations have started mapping gender-specific barriers within political parties, engaged women party members and party leaders on potential reform options, and offered training and technical assistance to support remedial measures. Yet working with political parties presents a fundamentally different set of challenges than assisting electoral commissions, which tend to be staffed by nonpartisan bureaucrats. Engaging parties can be politically sensitive, particularly for large international organizations and donor governments that want to avoid accusations of interference and partisanship. Furthermore, party leaders themselves are not always interested in reform, particularly if the status quo serves their political interests. We return to these challenges and the track record of existing party aid initiatives in more detail in Chapter 7.

Bolstering women's influence

Another important characteristic of second-generation approaches has been a stronger focus on women's *influence* once they enter political office, as well as on gender-sensitive governance more broadly. As early as 1998, International IDEA's influential handbook titled *Women in Parliament: Beyond the Numbers* stressed the need for women's political representation to go "beyond numbers," and examined the factors that shape women's ability to affect political decision-making once in power.[33] Early aid programs sought to advance this goal through capacity-building initiatives for women politicians as well as international learning exchanges. Such initiatives have continued in many countries, especially in contexts where many women are accessing political office for the first time. However, as quotas have increased women's descriptive representation, the question of influence has become ever more pressing. Newly elected women often find themselves institutionally sidelined. Lacking political seniority, insider networks, and majority status, they struggle to influence legislative outcomes. Partisan constraints and political divisions can further limit their ability and willingness to engage on behalf of gender equality, underscoring the risks of relying on individual women legislators operating in inhospitable environments to act as the primary drivers of reform.

International organizations and their local partners have therefore gradually strengthened their focus on transforming legislatures *as institutions*, both to bolster the power of women parliamentarians and to strengthen parliaments' overall capacity and commitment to gender equality. The IPU has served as a pioneer in this domain. Through a landmark 2011 study, it developed the concept of "gender-sensitive parliaments," which it describes as legislatures that respond to the "needs and interests of both men and women in its structures, operations, methods and in its work."[34] Over the past decade, the organization has used this framework to conduct internal gender assessments of parliaments in Bangladesh, Chile, Rwanda, Turkey, Uganda, and elsewhere and to identify areas for reform.[35] Other international organizations, including the OSCE and UNDP, have taken a similar approach.[36]

Women's caucuses, networks, and parliamentary committees focused on gender equality have emerged as common partners in these parliamentary reform initiatives. Globally, forty-eight gender caucuses were created between 2005 and 2013 alone, in many cases with significant international backing.[37] In some cases, international actors provided the impetus for caucus formation by bringing together women parliamentarians and sharing comparative experiences with caucus design. In other countries, they offered logistical and technical support to existing coalitions. In Morocco, for example, UN Women and the Westminster Foundation for Democracy have supported the institutionalization of a Thematic Working Group for Equality and Parity in the House of Representatives, which convenes representatives of different parliamentary groups to deliberate on gender equality reforms and advance gender parity commitments within the institution.[38]

Another important and growing trend has been international actors' support for women's influence at the subnational level. In Nepal, Kenya, Morocco, and elsewhere, decentralization processes implemented over the past decade have opened up new spaces for women's political inclusion, through women's representation in local government as well as through new participatory governance processes. In these contexts, aid providers have responded by launching new capacity-building programs for women local officials, who often lack the political experience of their national-level counterparts.[39] Other efforts have focused on gender mainstreaming in subnational governance to make local governments more responsive to the needs of women citizens. In Morocco, UN Women has complemented its national-level parliamentary support by working with the Ministry of Interior to mainstream gender into the General Directorate of Local Governments, including by establishing a gender unit and organizing regional conferences targeting women local officials.[40] In short, donors and their implementing partners have increasingly worked to advance women's substantive representation in national and subnational political institutions, both by promoting gender-sensitive governance and offering direct support to women politicians and gender-focused parliamentary bodies (see Chapter 8).

Countering resistance and violence

Lastly, initiatives that seek to tackle entrenched sociocultural barriers to women's political empowerment have gained increasing traction, with new initiatives spanning the global, regional, and country levels. As advocates have successfully pushed for progressive legal and institutional reforms, they have found that sociocultural norms and attitudes about women's leadership tend to lag behind, creating a growing gap between legal frameworks and women's lived realities. Traditional gender norms that associate political leadership with men and masculinity—and women with domesticity and subservience—still prevent many women from engaging in politics and lead voters and male gatekeepers to assess women politicians' competency differently from men's. They also fuel violence and backlash against women who seek out political roles that have traditionally been coded as "masculine." In Kenya, for instance, women politicians recount how their male competitors weaponize traditional gender norms against them on the campaign trail in order to paint them as promiscuous and immoral, especially in conservative rural areas.[41]

Several areas of action have crystallized in response to these challenges. First, democracy assistance organizations have focused on the media as an important entry point for challenging negative stereotypes and normalizing women's political leadership. Although media outlets play an important role in shaping public perceptions of gender norms, they often fail to cover women's political work or perpetuate gendered assumptions about women politicians, by centering their appearance and private lives rather than their campaign platforms. To correct these biases, international actors have supported training on gender-sensitive reporting for women journalists and other media professionals and funded radio and television shows that showcase women in leadership roles.

Exemplifying this approach, UN Women in Nepal has partnered with the women's media organization Sancharika Samuha to launch media campaigns highlighting women's political participation through newspaper interviews and articles on gender equality in elections. Ahead of the 2017 elections, UNDP and UN Women also worked with the organization to organize targeted trainings for women journalists and build relationships between the participants and women politicians.[42] "The female politicians told us that they didn't even know that there were female journalists writing about the elections and the political process," shared one of the women involved in organizing the program. "Bridging that gap between women journalists and politicians was helpful, because women politicians often only talk to male journalists about their experiences in parliament since [men] tend to have more access."[43]

Second, a newer set of initiatives focuses on tackling resistance and violence against women in politics. Until recently, international efforts to promote women's political inclusion largely ignored the risks of patriarchal backlash, whether targeted at women individually or collectively. Yet as women's political participation has increased in many countries, male resistance against their leadership has become more apparent. Women politicians report widespread and targeted harassment, intimidation, and violence within their own homes, within political institutions, and increasingly online—while men in political power continue to downplay such experiences as merely the "cost" of doing politics.

This phenomenon has attracted increasing international attention, primarily in response to the advocacy efforts of women politicians and gender equality advocates. Bolivian women's networks were at the forefront of these efforts in the 1990s and early 2000s, spearheading an influential (and ultimately successful) campaign to criminalize violence against women in politics as a distinct offense. Multiple cross-national data collection efforts have followed since. As we discuss in Chapter 9, these initiatives have set the groundwork for new norm-building and advocacy initiatives, ranging from NDI's global #NotTheCost campaign to local security training efforts. At the same time, activists and their partners are also grappling with difficult new challenges, including heightened attacks on women rights defenders in contexts of democratic erosion and the increasing use of gendered disinformation campaigns online.

An incomplete evolution

Over the past decade, international aid targeting women's political empowerment has evolved. An initial focus on building women's capacity and reforming national legal frameworks has given way to a more sophisticated toolbox of reforms and interventions, including new efforts to dismantle entrenched institutional barriers to women's political representation and challenge discriminatory gender norms. Many policy documents now emphasize the importance of holistic strategies that target formal legal frameworks, organizational practices, and sociocultural norms, alongside a continued focus on building women's confidence and political skills. Most donors and international implementing organizations have also made progress in integrating gender considerations into different areas of democracy support, rather than treating women's political participation as a niche, stand-alone area.

Despite these advances, however, the shift to an "ecosystem approach" to women's political empowerment remains ongoing, and aid practices are still catching up with rapid changes in thinking and policy frameworks. The next section introduces several recurring constraints and sets the stage for the new frontiers explored in greater depth in the third part of this book.

Nascent engagement with informal rules and norms

Even as donors and implementing organizations have moved toward a more systemic understanding of women's political empowerment, their approach remains narrow in important ways. For one, many assistance providers still fall back on traditional training interventions targeting women candidates and parliamentarians as well as technical assistance focused on formal institutional and legislative reforms. Across different types of programs, theories of change continue to rely on injections of external technical knowledge, and pay less attention to the norms and incentives guiding the actions of powerholders. Meanwhile, more ambitious efforts to tackle discriminatory gender norms and informal institutions that operate in parallel to formal processes are more incipient, smaller in scale, and backed by less evidence.[44] "[T]he problem that we haven't solved is social norm change," a gender advisor at a US democracy aid organization emphasized. "There's no approach. There are no assessment tools. The organizations that are doing [democracy and governance work] are very focused on the process: let's make sure the rules look good, build capacity. But ultimately, it's about addressing the elephant in the room: how politics operates is always based on norms, some of which are codified, some of which are not. It's new and cutting edge."[45] Most second-generation approaches also continue to center women as the primary targets and drivers of gender equality reform, rather than treating male politicians, powerholders, and relatives as critical allies and agents of change (see Chapter 9).[46] To return to Krook's framework introduced at the beginning of this chapter: there is still a tendency to focus on formal rules rather than their interaction with social norms and informal institutions and practices.

This interaction is crucial, however, because entrenched discriminatory norms and informal practices that perpetuate men's political dominance are among the most deeply rooted barriers to women's equal political power. Across our four cases, we encountered numerous examples of male powerholders covertly subverting quota measures or excluding women from political negotiations and networks, while simultaneously engaging in and defending informal practices that disadvantage women candidates and other political newcomers, such as vote-buying and violent electoral intimidation. Family and community attitudes also act as critical obstacles to women's political participation, with women candidates' spouses and male family members often opposing their political engagement.

In some ways, assistance providers' difficulties in broaching these barriers are not surprising: informal norms, rules, and power relations fall outside the traditional comfort zone of democracy support organizations, which have specialized in aiding formal institutional and organizational reforms and providing technical assistance to local counterparts. Challenging informal norms and transforming political cultures is also more difficult than changing formal policies and rules: the entry points are less obvious, political pushback is likely, and positive change can be difficult to measure. These approaches demand longer time horizons and greater flexibility than short-term projects allow. Yet without more concerted efforts to upend vested interests and shift gendered power relations, institutional reforms remain superficial.

Insufficient strategic differentiation

A related challenge is the lack of strategic differentiation in current assistance approaches. Although aid providers have developed a growing body of best practices and a more diverse set of programmatic tools, they have made less progress in adapting their strategies to distinct political contexts, particularly those marked by profound societal and political cleavages between women or those experiencing democratic erosion. For instance, many aid actors still cling to the assumption that women's political inclusion, democratic progress, and broader social justice goals go hand-in-hand. Consequently, they have not always recognized and addressed the ways in which women's political leadership can sometimes come at the expense of other marginalized groups, or how women politicians themselves can be complicit in exclusionary and undemocratic policies and practices.[47]

These tensions are particularly acute in contexts of democratic backsliding and rising illiberalism. International actors often emphasize that women's political inclusion is central to stemming the global antidemocratic tide. And indeed, the authoritarian resurgence in many countries has been driven by male politicians and male-dominated movements advancing explicitly antifeminist agendas and pushing back against women leaders.[48] It is no coincidence that Hungary, which has undergone a major democratic reversal over the past decade, has the lowest rates of women's political representation in Europe. Yet in other contexts, authoritarian and semiauthoritarian regimes have actively promoted women's political inclusion as a strategy to garner legitimacy and consolidate political power. It is not always clear whether or in which contexts women's political inclusion has democratizing potential—as opposed to serving as a smokescreen for political repression.

This dilemma raises important questions not only about women's roles in co-opted political processes and institutions but also about international actors' responsibilities in these settings. If access to political office in a given country is determined by money and patronage, should women be supported to play the political game as it exists, even if doing so risks sidelining other women and men with more politically transformative agendas? In sum, even as the "toolbox" of interventions has expanded, aid organizations still have limited guidance on how to deploy these strategies in places where gender equality objectives and parallel struggles for democracy and social justice come into conflict (see Chapter 10).

Weaknesses in assistance models

A third challenge is more bureaucratic in nature: current assistance modalities are not well suited to an ecosystem approach. A key insight informing second-generation efforts is the need for multidimensional approaches that simultaneously tackle the various obstacles to gender equality change—such as mentoring for women candidates and political officials alongside advocacy for reforms to the broader rules of the political game that perpetuate men's overrepresentation at different stages of the political process. Yet in practice, funding for targeted women's political empowerment programs is often too limited for democracy support organizations and their local partners to design and implement multiyear and multilevel strategies. Particularly for women's rights activists at the forefront of gender equality struggles, most international funding is too short-term, thematically siloed, and inflexible to allow them to build stronger movements for change.

In some ways, advocates' push for gender mainstreaming was intended to solve this problem. And indeed, there have been some important advances in integrating a gender lens into broader and better-funded democracy assistance initiatives. At the same time, however, gender perspectives are frequently still missing from younger areas of democracy support, including emerging efforts to counter online disinformation and digital authoritarianism. Moreover, gender experts working on democracy issues worry that gender mainstreaming tends to be executed superficially. Rather than serving as a tool to analyze and mitigate the exclusionary effects of political institutions and processes, it is reduced to including or counting women in more traditional interventions.[49] In some "mainstreamed" projects, it is unclear what specific gender-related outcomes are being sought and what theories of change undergird them, and there are rarely systematic efforts to measure what has been achieved.[50]

To some degree, these problems are rooted in tensions embedded in the overall mainstreaming framework. Although donor governments, UN agencies, and international and regional organizations have adopted the language of gender mainstreaming and put the requisite internal policies in place, many scholars have documented that implementation problems abound. These shortcomings are rooted in a profound disconnect between the concept's highly ambitious goals of transforming gendered power relations and its procedural application by aid organizations. This misalignment fuels tensions between gender equality advocates, who inevitably observe dilution, and the staff of aid agencies, who treat gender mainstreaming as a technical process and are concerned with checklists, guidelines, and numerical targets.[51]

The persistence of small-scale interventions and gender mainstreaming "lite" are also symptoms of a more fundamental challenge: democracy actors' reluctance to fully commit to gender-transformative aid approaches. Practitioners in donor agencies and international democracy aid organizations observe that programming around women's political empowerment (and effective gender integration) still depends on the interests and commitment of individual aid officials within embassies or country offices, rather than being considered a critical cross-cutting priority by all. Some gender advisers note that weak commitments are rooted in institutional gender biases and patriarchal norms operating within donor governments and aid organizations themselves. "It remains a very difficult task to convince leadership and those working on the broader democracy promotion portfolio to prioritize women's rights work," one US aid official told us. "Even though women's leadership is now a recognized part of the democracy promotion agenda, this appearance or policies that underscore it are not translating into equal attention and funding or staffing."[52] Yet developing and supporting more holistic and differentiated approaches to women's political empowerment requires investing in staff with the necessary expertise and commitment, and taking new risks in designing more equitable funding models and partnerships with those at the frontlines of gender equality change (see Chapter 11).

The question of learning

A final cross-cutting limitation concerns evidence gathering and learning. The professionalization of democracy aid over the past two decades has fueled increasing pressure on policymakers and practitioners to demonstrate that their work is making a difference. Donor agencies understandably want to show what they refer to as "value for money" by demonstrating that their investments are producing positive results. Initiatives that seek to bolster women's political empowerment are not immune from this trend. Yet aid organizations face well-established challenges in measuring the impact of democracy assistance. Causal identification and attribution are difficult for interventions targeting complex and nonlinear processes of sociopolitical change.[53] This problem is particularly acute with respect to gender equality change in politics, which rarely unfolds overnight, and suffers from resistance and reversals. Over time, there has nevertheless been a diversification in the evaluation frameworks used, which now range from randomized control trials to participatory analyses involving visual storytelling. Some aid organizations have replaced narrow log frames, indicators, and traditional mid- and end-term evaluations with more continuous learning efforts or outcome-harvesting methodologies.[54]

However, with respect to women's political empowerment, the evidence base underlying different intervention models remains thin. Program evaluations, if they are made public, routinely call out weaknesses in evaluation frameworks, from missing baseline data to inconsistent reporting of project results. There is still a tendency to focus on the activities that are implemented, such as the number of women trained or meetings held, rather than their *outcomes*. When organizations *do* measure outcomes, they tend to foreground the number of women elected and the number of policies or reforms adopted, rather than changes in attitudes, norms, and influence that are more labor- and time-intensive to measure.[55] "If you take a women's political empowerment project, you have log frames, and indicators like 'three hundred women's cooperative committees formed in two years,' and you count how many meetings they held and that sort of thing," says an aid official working in Nepal. "But you don't go into: did they have the agency to do what they wanted to do, and the money? What influence did they have in decision-making processes?"[56]

Moreover, democracy organizations rarely receive dedicated funding to test the impact of one intervention model across different contexts and over time, which limits their ability to evaluate how contextual constraints impact their theories of change. For example, do awareness-raising initiatives change community norms about women in politics, and if so, in what ways does it depend on the context, the messenger, and the format? Or does integrating modules on women's political participation into training for male political leaders change how they view and treat their female colleagues? Even though the field is increasingly engaging with questions of norms, the wider community of practice still lacks evidence in these and other critical areas.

Conclusion

Over the course of the past decade, international support for women's political empowerment has undergone a substantial evolution. As women's descriptive representation has increased in many countries, practitioners' and advocates' attention has increasingly shifted toward the broader political ecosystem that limits their equal participation and influence. Both donors and implementing organizations today recognize the need for more holistic strategies that target not only women's capacity but also structural and sociocultural barriers. To this end, they have not only developed new research, advocacy campaigns, and programming models, but also devoted greater attention to gender equality across different areas of democracy support.

However, this evolution in many ways remains ongoing, and important new frontiers are emerging. Despite aid actors' stronger focus on structural and systemic barriers to women's political power, their work remains centered on women's access to and role in formal institutions, whereas efforts targeting informal barriers, such as gender norms and power relations and challenges of violence and patriarchal backlash, are more incipient. Additionally, as democratic institutions around the world have come under increasing stress, the uncertain relationship between women's formal political leadership and other forms of inclusion also raises new policy and programmatic challenges. Finally, current assistance models are not necessarily suited to an ecosystem approach. Targeted funding for women's political empowerment is often too short-term, small-scale, and inflexible to support local movement-building, whereas the push for mainstreaming has created new challenges of dilution and deprioritization.

Before we turn to these new frontiers and uncertainties facing the field, however, we take a closer look at the track record of established approaches. Focusing on capacity building, party assistance, and parliamentary support aimed at advancing women's political empowerment, the next three chapters tackle the critical question: what have we learned about what works?

6

The Limits of Candidate Training

On a Thursday morning in February 2022, a few hours before the full heat of the day had fully arrived, fifteen women leaders assembled around a hotel conference table in a Kenyan town known for its pristine beaches. Most of the women already knew each other from prior gatherings and greeted each other warmly as they trickled into the room. Among them were sitting members of the local county assembly with ambitions of progressing to national political office, women leaders and party activists who had run in previous elections and were hoping to try their luck once again, and one or two political newcomers. Six months before the Kenyan elections, they had been convened by a local human rights organization, funded by a Western embassy in Nairobi, for a capacity-building workshop aimed at bolstering their electoral campaigns. Over the next two days, the women would participate in a series of discussions and workshops, covering issues from personal branding to navigating the country's electoral regulations.

This convening in coastal Kenya was one of countless capacity-building workshops targeting women political leaders that take place around the world every year, from Mexico to Mongolia to the Solomon Islands. As international aid targeting women's political empowerment has evolved and grown over the past two decades, training programs for women aspirants and candidates have emerged as one of the most common interventions. By targeting women candidates' political knowledge and self-confidence, these programs seek to encourage more women to enter the political fray and help them run successful campaigns. In doing so, they hope to challenge the narrative that there are simply not enough qualified women competing for political positions.

Training interventions were a key part of the first generation of women's political empowerment aid, and they remain ubiquitous today. This chapter takes a closer empirical look at their design and underlying assumptions. Our research tells a complicated story about the role of training for women in politics.

Aiding Empowerment. Saskia Brechenmacher and Katherine Mann, Oxford University Press.
© Oxford University Press 2024. DOI: 10.1093/oso/9780197694275.003.0006

Capacity-building can be a powerful tool: it can provide crucial information and help women build stronger political networks and persevere in hostile environments. Whether or not training initiatives achieve these goals, however, depends on their design. To date, programs often still rely on one-off workshops that use standard training templates, target women participants in isolation from their families and communities, and neglect the practical challenges they face on the campaign trail. Yet some aid providers have also pioneered more innovative models, reflecting the shift toward second-generation approaches that pay closer attention to the broader political ecosystem shaping women's political participation. At a deeper level, however, the heavy reliance on training initiatives overemphasizes women's role in overcoming their own political exclusion and overlooks the role of systemic obstacles. Women's reluctance to enter politics is not only the product of gendered socialization processes or a lack of capacity. Instead, it is often a rational response to patriarchal political structures and institutions that training alone cannot address.

We begin by outlining the basic model of gender equality change guiding these interventions and the hurdles to measuring their success. Drawing on interviews with women politicians and practitioners across our four cases, as well as evaluations of programs in other contexts, we then explore recurring pitfalls in program design and describe promising alternative models. The final part of the chapter turns to the broader limitations of candidate training. By centering women's political ambition and capacity, these initiatives neglect the institutional and structural hurdles that create a profoundly unequal playing field for women aspirants and candidates. They help women navigate the gendered barriers they may encounter along their political journeys without removing these hurdles.

A supply-side model

Over the past two and a half decades, training initiatives for women in politics have proliferated around the world. In most cases, they take the form of time-bound projects funded by bilateral and multilateral donors and implemented by local or international civil society organizations in the lead-up to elections. Most initiatives consist of one-off workshops, although some also accompany a core group of women over several months. They typically target women who are already active in political parties, bringing them together in cross-party or single-party meetings, or women who are not yet active in party politics but are interested in running for office. Some programs also try to broaden their reach by using a "training of trainers" model, which consists of training a small group of women to then conduct workshops in their own communities or their respective political parties. Finally, some interventions include a mentorship component that links female political newcomers with senior women leaders to share experiences and offer support.

These programs respond to the pervasive claim that there are not enough women who are interested in political leadership. They seek to address this imbalance by encouraging more women to put themselves forward and equipping them with the confidence and skills they need to succeed in politics, thereby bolstering the overall "supply" of qualified women candidates. A training manual produced by the Konrad-Adenauer-Stiftung ahead of Kenya's 2022 elections epitomizes this logic. "For better performance in future elections with the latest being 2022, women aspirants need to be equipped with the right skill set to effectively campaign," it notes. "The goal [. . .] of this training manual is to provide a framework that can be used to enhance the knowledge and skills of women aspirants to become more strategic in their campaigns and increase their chances to win elections in 2022/future."[1] Implicit in these statements are two core assumptions: first, that women's political underrepresentation is primarily explained by capacity gaps on the side of women; and, second, that training interventions can successfully close these gaps—while also signaling the candidates' preparedness to party leaders and voters.[2]

Our review of program descriptions underscores that most training activities cover a fairly standard set of topics, ranging from information about electoral rules and the value of women's political participation to more specific political skills, including policy development, communication, and fundraising. For example, ahead of the 2013 Constituent Assembly elections in Nepal, NDI conducted training sessions in Kathmandu and Pokhara that focused on leadership skills and effective campaign tactics, such as recruiting volunteers and mobilizing women and youth voters. NDI repeated a similar initiative ahead of the country's first local elections in 2017, training women candidates on fundraising, network-building, and political messaging and outreach.[3] Over the past several years, some organizations have also incorporated newer issues into their training curricula, such as using social media platforms for campaigning and navigating harassment both online and offline.

The challenge of measuring success

Even though candidate training has emerged as one of the most common approaches to bolstering women's political empowerment around the world, the evidence base guiding this work remains weak. There currently are no studies that systematically compare the political trajectories of women who have participated in such training initiatives with those who have not or test the effectiveness of different training curricula. This is partly because few democracy assistance organizations receive funding for such time- and resource-intensive evaluation efforts.

However, most collect some data on the outcomes of their training activities, often in the form of participant surveys and qualitative interviews. Many also record the number of program participants who end up running for political office and getting elected. Yet proving a causal link between a single training intervention and election outcomes is almost always impossible, a problem that most practitioners are keenly aware of. After all, it is likely that women who opt into training programs are those who are most ambitious and eager to win, which complicates efforts to compare their trajectories to those of nonparticipants. Moreover, women candidates sometimes participate in many different types of training in parallel, which makes it difficult to isolate the impact of any one program.

Defining a threshold for success is equally difficult. Say one initiative reached two hundred women, and twenty were subsequently elected to office. Should we consider this number a success? The answer would depend on the wider political context and the hurdles it poses for women candidates. In addition, focusing only on election outcomes obscures other positive effects that a training program may have. Even if the participating women are not elected, they may gain new skills and networks that they can draw on in their future endeavors. Current evaluation approaches rarely track these longer-term outcomes, since most organizations lack the resources to follow up with all their program participants one or two years after a program concludes.[4]

However, despite these evidence gaps, it is possible to draw some conclusions about the strengths and limitations of existing program strategies. Donor evaluations, academic studies, and our interviews with practitioners and women politicians underscore one recurring finding: training initiatives often play a valuable role in bringing women together to share their experiences and build stronger political networks.[5] Conferences or workshops offer the chance to mingle over coffee or lunch, share the highs and lows of campaigning, and forge new connections and friendships. Given that women are often excluded from male-dominated networks, these spaces of solidarity can be a lifeline. In the lead-up to the 2017 elections in Kenya, for example, the women's organization Center for Rights Education and Awareness (CREAW) organized training seminars for women running for county-level positions around the country. "It was a helpful gathering and enlightening," recalls one of the participants from Nyeri county, who was running for political office for the first time. "It's not all the time that we have that platform to come and share our downs, our ups, what we have been going through, what we are planning. [...] That sharing is important."[6]

Beyond fostering solidarity, the stated objective of most capacity-building programs is to impart practical campaigning skills. Many political parties invest few resources in recruiting and supporting women members. Women also tend to be underrepresented in organizations that serve as traditional forums for "political apprenticeship" and pathways to elective office, such as political organizations at universities, professional associations, and trade unions.[7] Particularly for women venturing into politics for the first time, training workshops thus have the potential to fill important gaps in knowledge, dispel myths about electoral politics, and offer practical guidance, especially for political newcomers.[8] How useful these efforts are, however, depends heavily on their design and local relevance. Across our cases, women candidates, politicians, and practitioners we interviewed noted that training programs often repeat similar mistakes: they are too short-term and too distanced from women's campaign experiences, and they insufficiently focus on male family members and gatekeepers. In the next section, we explore these recurring pitfalls and identify more innovative programming models (for an overview, see Table 6.1).

Table 6.1 **Candidate Training: Recurring Pitfalls and Innovative Practices**

Recurring Pitfalls	*Innovative Practices*
Short-term or one-off training before elections	Long-term support focused on accompaniment, network-building, and mentorship, especially prior to candidate selection processes
Use of standard templates and external consultants	Training designed based on local needs assessments, adapted based on participants' ongoing feedback, and carried out by local experts
Classroom teaching of technical knowledge and skills	Applied support focused on bolstering women's public profile and addressing context-specific problems
Training designed to reach as many women as possible	Context-specific targeting, including in-depth support to smaller groups of women or tiered training approaches
Training women in isolation	Providing relational support to women with their spouses/families and communities
Targeting only candidates for political office	Building women's leadership across formal and informal political institutions and at multiple levels of governance

The drawbacks of one-off initiatives

One of the most common critiques of candidate training programs is that they come too late in the election cycle. From Kenya to Nepal, training often takes the form of one-off or short-term workshops rolled out four to six months before a country goes to the polls. Yet preparations for a political campaign sometimes begin several years before an election: this is the time when prospective aspirants have to begin saving money, get involved in party activities and community work, and build their political visibility and connections.[9] Making it through party-internal candidate selection processes, which typically take place months before the general election, also requires early planning.

In Kenya, for instance, many parties use decentralized party primaries to select their candidates, especially in their political strongholds. In these areas, succeeding at the primary stage requires having a public profile, significant financial resources, as well as a track record of delivering for the community.[10] In Nepal and Morocco, on the other hand, most parties select their candidates internally, based on the recommendations of local branch offices and the decisions of senior party leaders.[11] As a result, candidates benefit from insider networks in their respective parties. In either context, training workshops held several weeks before party nominations are unlikely to make a significant difference. "The year of elections, donors will come up with money and begin trying to get institutions to run with all of these ideas, but it's too late because men are already entrenched in the communities," Jennifer Riria, a Kenyan businesswoman and women's rights advocate, told us. "So, we need to begin now, two years before the election, and work with women and help them start initiatives on the ground!"[12]

A second and closely related weakness of training interventions is the widespread reliance on standard training templates that emphasize technical knowledge at the expense of tailored campaign support. In the worst case scenario, capacity-building curricula are adapted from templates designed at INGO headquarters in London, Stockholm, or Washington, DC, with only limited input from local organizations or from women candidates themselves. As a result, they risk emphasizing skills or tactics that do not fit local political realities. But even locally designed courses often emphasize standard technical knowledge over context-specific and practical support.[13] For instance, during the training workshop in coastal Kenya introduced at the beginning of this chapter, participants learned about the different types of electoral offenses under Kenyan law. However, the workshop did not touch on concrete steps women could take to protect their votes from election rigging, or how they should respond if faced with intimidation by their party colleagues and opponents. The facilitator further urged the participants to build a personal brand, but never asked them to articulate their campaign priorities to an audience or to practice negotiating with party leaders. The women were, in short, treated primarily as passive recipients of information, and the seminar was not designed to mentor them through specific challenges or help them practice concrete skills.

Donors' and implementers' use of standardized curricula and top-down teaching methods ignores the fact that women candidates have varying levels of resources and political experience. They also face different hurdles depending on their socioeconomic, ethnic, religious, and regional backgrounds. Some have no prior political experience and limited formal education, and therefore benefit from basic information about electoral rules, confidence-building, and training in campaign tactics and public speaking. Others may be prominent business leaders, civil society activists, or experienced incumbents running their third or fourth political campaign, whose support needs are likely to be more specific (or who may not need training at all). In Kenya, for instance, many women competing in national elections have previous leadership experience and substantial political networks. Rather than sitting through yet another "skills" training in a Nairobi hotel, many impatiently underscore their need for more financial support and national media coverage.[14] In both Myanmar and Nepal, the barriers facing ethnic minority women in rural areas differ significantly from those facing higher-status women in cities. "The level of confidence, the level of psychosocial trauma, the level of exposure—it's totally different," remarked an activist at an organization supporting women's grassroots leadership in Nepal. "You need to be able to respond to the specific needs of these women when you work with them. One size does not fit all."[15] Short-term training workshops in urban centers are ill-equipped to account for these differences, and thus often do not reach the most politically and economically marginalized communities.

Investing in long-term accompaniment

Recognizing these limitations, some organizations have started using longer-term accompaniment to better support women's political journeys on the ground. They are advocating for initiatives that begin several years prior to an election and offer ongoing training and mentorship to a core group of women. This approach allows implementing organizations to adjust their activities based on participants' feedback and their changing needs throughout the electoral cycle, from the initial decision to run to the candidate selection stage up to the final election. Ongoing mentorship and coaching initiatives also create more space for women to experiment with different tactics and report back on their experiences, receive encouragement during the most difficult moments, and build stronger networks with other women politicians.[16]

Following this model, the International Women's Development Agency's (IWDA) developed a campaign coaching program for women candidates ahead of the 2020 election in Myanmar. Hoping to avoid the last-minute nature of many candidate training initiatives, it partnered with a Burmese feminist civil society organization called "Women's Initiative Platform" to provide one-on-one coaching and campaign strategy support for women candidates two years before the election. "We were trying to push the idea that if you are going to be pre-selectable and electable, you can't develop that a month before the election," Jen Clark, a program manager working with IWDA, explained. "It's all about building a profile in your community and getting your name out there, which takes a long time."[17] The program helped participating women devise strategies to navigate party-internal candidate selection processes and campaign plans, in case they were selected. This approach proved largely successful: many of the participants were nominated as candidates by their respective parties, especially if they had already been active party members.[18] However, IWDA's model of starting program activities early in the election cycle and coaching women through the candidate selection stage remains relatively rare.

Given the importance of building a strong public profile, women candidates and practitioners often welcome programs that go beyond classroom discussions to integrate practical, hands-on support.[19] Some organizations integrate applied learning into their training curricula, by helping participants practice their public speaking skills, facilitating political economy analyses of their electoral districts, and giving them practical tasks to implement between training seminars. In Myanmar, the *She Leads* grassroots leadership program (implemented by IFES in partnership with local NGO Yaung Chi Thit between 2015 and 2020) asked participating women to apply the skills they learned throughout the program by carrying out small-scale projects within their communities. For IFES staff involved in running the program, these "assignments" became one of its strongest aspects: participants built experience engaging with male community leaders and cultivating local allies, and they often returned to future training sessions eager to share what they had achieved.[20] Other organizations have gone even further to provide participants with tangible resources, ranging from professional headshots and other promotional materials to civic education and community forums that allow women to interact with voters, party officials, and media outlets.[21]

Of course, offering sustained accompaniment and practical support comes with significant investments of resources, time, and expertise. As a result, these types of initiatives require implementing organizations to be more selective about the participants they recruit, rather than casting a wider net. Such an approach clashes with the pressure many organizations feel to demonstrate quick results, often by reaching as many women as possible. But if the ultimate goal is to get more women elected, past experience indicates that careful targeting can be more effective. For example, observing declining rates of women's parliamentary representation in Kenya, NDI sought to encourage as many women as possible to run for office in 2017. In the lead-up to the elections, the organization and its partners trained five thousand prospective women aspirants across the country. Yet the ambitious scale of the project came at the expense of both targeting and in-depth support. Many of the participants were weakly committed to running for office, and only about 30 percent declared their candidacies.[22] By contrast, IWDA's coaching program in Myanmar used a considerably more selective approach, relying on local women's organizations to recruit participants who had already graduated from other women's leadership programs or who were actively involved in political parties.

In the end, finding the right balance between breadth and depth depends on the political context and the goals of the program. In countries where many women are entering electoral politics for the first time—such as in Myanmar in 2015 or after the implementation of the subnational gender quota in Nepal in 2017—initiatives targeting a wide range of potential aspirants and candidates may play a useful role, especially if they are guided by locally identified needs. In these contexts, the objective may not only be to increase women's political representation, but also to familiarize women with the election process, connect them with political parties, and build their political networks.[23] In contexts like Kenya, on the other hand, where organizations have been training women candidates for decades, many activists and women politicians express their frustration with poorly targeted and superficial programs that may provide women candidates with encouragement and networks but have done little to increase the number of women contesting and winning elections.[24] Moreover, in parties where candidacies are largely determined by patronage networks, as is the case in Morocco, identifying and targeting women aspirants who are mostly likely to be selected may be impossible. In such contexts, the women with the greatest odds of being chosen as candidates may be those with close ties to local or national powerholders, rather than women with the strongest campaigns or leadership experience.[25] We return to these institutional and political constraints in the second half of the chapter.

Broadening the scope

Beyond pushing for more targeted, longer-term accompaniment, many of the advocates and practitioners we interviewed also stressed the importance of expanding the traditionally narrow focus of capacity-building programs. For one, most programs target women aspirants and candidates in isolation from their families and communities. The underlying assumption is, once again, that capacity and confidence gaps *on the side of women* are the primary barrier to address, and that *women* need to be given new tools to navigate gendered barriers they encounter. This approach ignores the critical role played by family members, particularly spouses, who usually must sacrifice time, money, and privacy to support their partner's or relative's political ambitions. For many women aspiring to political work, family resistance is a high barrier to participation: traditional gender norms, such as those depicting men as heads of households and women as domestic caretakers, can lead spouses to withhold their support. Resistance from male community leaders and locally influential authority figures can present additional hurdles, as their endorsement and networks are often essential to garnering local voter support.

In Nepal and Kenya, women politicians we interviewed described marital discord fueled by their political ambitions. Husbands feared being overshadowed by their wives or having their families' reputation tarnished. In some communities, men also control household assets, which makes it difficult for women to run for office without their explicit support.[26] "Men can just go and sell a plot of land to fund their campaigns," one woman politician running for a parliamentary position in Western Kenya noted. "For women, that's often impossible. They need to go to their husbands and ask for permission, which may not be granted."[27] Social expectations about women's domestic duties can create additional hurdles, if women candidates are expected to return home in the evenings to care for their children and husbands (while their male competitors continue campaigning). Not surprisingly, some evidence suggests that women politicians in countries with higher levels of gender inequality are still more likely to be unmarried and childless compared to their male counterparts. In Zambia, for instance, women MPs were 42 percent less likely to be married than their male colleagues in 2016.[28] Candidate-training programs that focus solely on women—even though their decision to go into politics is inherently relational—therefore miss an important barrier to women's political participation.

Yet to date, few programs support women by working with male relatives and gatekeepers or by carrying out broader civic education initiatives targeting women's local constituencies. A rare example from our research involved a grassroots leadership program run by Oxfam in Myanmar's Rakhine State, which intentionally included discussions with the husbands of women participants to address their potential concerns and questions. The program also organized activities targeting local male leaders, including IDP camp managers and religious leaders, to help prevent patriarchal backlash against women participants who were being encouraged to take on new leadership roles.[29] In some cases, the involvement of male gatekeepers has also happened more informally. In Nepal, for instance, UN Women officials recognized that women participating in their economic and political empowerment programs often faced a difficult environment at home and in their communities. In response, they began speaking to women's spouses, parents-in-law, and local male leaders, in addition to mentoring women participants to initiate a dialogue with their husbands.[30] However, most donor-funded training programs still fail to integrate family and community engagement as a core dimension of women's political participation.

In addition to targeting family members and male community leaders, broadening the scope of training initiatives can also involve advancing women's political participation beyond formal electoral politics, with the goal of building a longer-term pipeline of female political leaders and activists. In contexts where entrenched structural barriers and cultural norms inhibit many women from running for office, or where women struggle to make headway in rigid and undemocratic party hierarchies, cultivating alternative spaces for political apprenticeship is particularly important. Such spaces can range from trade unions and professional associations to local governance committees, school boards, and community associations. These institutions not only serve as training grounds for electoral politics, but also provide direct and meaningful opportunities to advance substantive policy and rights issues. Cultivating alternative pathways to leadership can also be a strategy for reaching women who may be left behind by a narrow focus on election campaigns, which are often less accessible to marginalized communities.

In Kenya, for example, the Heinrich-Böll-Stiftung has moved away from training women for political office and focuses instead on amplifying the work that women leaders are already doing in their communities. One initiative established county-level committees staffed by elected women politicians and civil society advocates to tackle gender-based violence. The program also supported the same advocates in cultivating downward ties to the village leaders in charge of handling and reporting cases of gendered violence when they arise. As a result of the program, women activists were able to access new leadership positions— not necessarily in national politics, but in ministerial committees in which they work directly with elected leaders.[31] By advancing women's political participation in relation to the issues that women are already working on in their communities, the program hopes to build a pipeline of influential leaders who can hold politicians accountable and eventually make the transition into political and state institutions.

IFES's She Leads program in Myanmar adopted a similarly wide scope in a very different context. When the program was set up in 2015, an exclusive focus on getting women elected seemed unproductive: in many parts of the country, women were not even registered to vote and had little to no education about politics and elections. As a result, the program trained women to register voters, learn about the electoral process, and educate their own communities. After the elections, the focus shifted toward bringing women into progressively higher leadership roles, including in local councils and civil society organizations.[32] Given that the program ran for multiple years, its model could be adapted to reach different groups of women, including women in conflict-affected regions who were almost entirely excluded from mainstream politics and had never before been reached by candidate training programs.[33] These types of initiatives may not produce immediate electoral gains. Yet they can contribute to a gradual process of incubating women leaders and create new spaces for political learning, particularly among those most excluded from existing political processes.

A limited approach

At their core, capacity-building interventions are designed to help women navigate gendered barriers to political success. As individual-level interventions, they can (if they are well designed and contextually appropriate) encourage more women to run and bolster their campaigns, particularly in contexts where many women are entering electoral politics for the first time and lack other forms of mentorship and support. However, they are not set up to transform political processes and institutions that systematically disadvantage women and other marginalized groups. As such, they remain an inherently limited tool for sociopolitical change.

In fact, a one-dimensional focus on "supporting women" can play into the narrative, often espoused by male party leaders, that men's political overrepresentation stems from shortcomings on the side of women, rather than from discriminatory and sexist practices and institutions.[34] In the words of one Moroccan rights activist, training interventions implicitly assume that something is "wrong" with women: "She doesn't know how to speak in public. She doesn't have self-esteem. She needs to build her self-confidence."[35] Not surprisingly, capacity-building programs for women politicians are often popular with political party leaders who otherwise show little interest in promoting gender equality. It is easier to agree that women need additional training and confidence than to acknowledge that existing party processes perpetuate women's exclusion. Yet no amount of training can level a profoundly unequal playing field. In the next sections, we turn to two critical barriers to women's inclusion that these interventions cannot address: exclusionary and discriminatory candidate selection processes and resource constraints that are rooted in women's structural marginalization.

Exclusionary candidate selection processes

In most countries, women and men aspirants have to make it through party-internal selection processes in order to become candidates. This step in the electoral process grants parties significant control over women's access to political office: parties determine who makes it onto the final election ballot, and they can hinder or promote a candidate through their endorsements and support. Parties use different strategies to choose their flag bearers, ranging from centralized decisions by party leaders to decentralized party primaries.

In Nepal, as noted earlier in this chapter, candidates are typically identified and ranked by local committees; the final decisions rests with party officials at the district or national level.[36] In Myanmar (prior to the 2021 coup) and in Morocco, candidate selection processes similarly take place internally, based on the recommendations of local and regional commissions and the decisions of higher-level leaders.[37] In Kenya, on the other hand, selection processes have traditionally varied across parties, with some of the country's larger parties holding open primary votes at the local level, and smaller, less institutionalized parties selecting candidates internally.[38] In the best-case scenario, training initiatives can help women understand and prepare for these processes and signal their qualifications to the relevant selectorate, whether the latter includes local party officials, senior party leaders, or party members in their electoral districts. However, a growing body of research suggests that "leaning in" is rarely enough. Instead, women aspirants face both direct discrimination and more subtle forms of exclusion on the side of mostly male party gatekeepers.[39]

The fact that the inner circles of power in most political parties predominantly consist of men automatically lends women a clear "outsider" status and reduces their visibility as potential candidates. In Nepal, a recent survey of 30,000 politicians across eleven districts found that 91 percent of political parties' local-level selection committee members were men, and that these members were slower to associate women with leadership qualities.[40] Research in other contexts has also found that male selectors often prefer male candidates over female competitors with similar profiles, due to a combination of ingrained gender biases and gendered assumptions about the traits and qualifications needed to succeed as candidates.[41] For instance, if party selectors reward incumbency and years served in the party, they will disadvantage political newcomers, who are often more likely to be women. In weakly institutionalized and personalized parties, insider ties become even more critical. Whether or not a woman is locally popular may not be relevant in these contexts. Instead, rewarding coalition partners, financiers, and local political brokers or balancing between different ethnic factions may be the bigger priority.[42]

Quota rules that require parties to select a certain percentage of women candidates can help counteract these biases. However, male party leaders are often skilled at circumventing or manipulating quota mechanisms. Common tactics range from simply violating formal rules to applying them in a minimalist fashion, for example by nominating women in unwinnable districts or selecting them for less politically desirable positions. In Nepal, the existing legal framework mandates political parties to nominate women for either the mayor or the deputy mayor position, and to nominate at least two women (one of whom is Dalit) to local ward committees. In practice, however, parties have responded by disproportionately assigning women to deputy mayor positions, while reserving both the more powerful mayoral spot and the position of ward chair for men. They have also relied on alliance politics to circumvent the quota measure entirely: by sharing the mayor and deputy mayor positions between two parties, they can each put forward a male candidate.[43] Leaders thereby strategically limit the impact of gender quotas on women's political representation and power.

On paper, decentralized party selection processes that allow voters to choose their own candidates may seem like a potential solution to these challenges. Although primaries make it harder to implement quota rules, women with name recognition and grassroots support may stand a greater chance of winning in open elections than through opaque party processes.[44] In emerging democracies, however, disorganized and sometimes violent party primaries can create a different set of hurdles. In Kenya, party organizations are relatively weak, and primary elections have repeatedly been marred by logistical problems and allegations of rigging and intimidation. For example, during the 2017 primaries, wealthy candidates were able to purchase party membership cards and distribute them to their supporters before others could access them, thereby rigging the vote in their favor. Others hired young men to intimidate women candidates, bribed returning officers, or paid voters from other districts and wards to come vote for them.[45] Fear of violence discouraged many women from entering the primaries in the first place, and those who competed often lacked the political and financial capital to win against better-connected and better-resourced male competitors.[46] "One thing we've constantly struggled with in Kenya is that you may have good candidates, who have social capital, but the challenge is within the political parties," a women's rights advocate in Kenya told us. "There's a political leader that the party has been formed around, so they are not democratic in terms of how they run their party primaries or how they select who they will back for particular positions. You can have a female candidate who is extremely popular in the community, well-intentioned, and has a good strategy for leadership after the election, but the party leadership does not want her, or her opponent is able to purchase their candidature."[47]

In sum, whether parties select their candidates internally or through more decentralized primary processes, women's personal qualifications, campaign strategies, and confidence are not the only factors shaping their success. Instead, they encounter barriers rooted in the gendered structure and practices of political parties, which tend to favor male political insiders or political actors with independent resources, connections, and political networks.

Resource constraints

The experiences of women candidates in Kenyan party primaries illustrate an important additional hurdle women face in electoral politics, namely the role of personal resources. Aspirants in many countries have to pay hefty fees to participate in party nominations. Building a public profile and attracting the attention of party gatekeepers also requires money, particularly in clientelistic political systems in which voters expect cash handouts or personal assistance from politicians (and parties expect candidates to bring resources into the party). Women often spend significantly more time on unpaid domestic work and caregiving than men, which leaves them with less disposable income to invest in political work. In patriarchal societies, structural discrimination in inheritance and property ownership further deepens these financial disadvantages. Moreover, running for office also requires various nonfinancial resources that women, on average, have less access to than men, such as the ability to leave home and domestic responsibilities for days or weeks at a time.

In our research, financial resources emerged as particularly high barriers to women's participation in Nepal and in Kenya. In Nepal, for instance, only 20 percent of women own land, and most are employed in the agricultural or informal sectors, often in precarious and underpaid positions. They are also much less likely than men to have access to other financial assets that can help them fund their campaigns.[48] Yet Nepali elections have become increasingly expensive.[49] Candidates are responsible for raising their own funds for campaigns through donations and loans, and have to spend money on mobilizing party cadres, paying for transportation, publicity, mass rallies, and door-to-door campaigns. A study conducted by the Election Observation Committee Nepal in 2017 also found that some candidates bought their party tickets, and that vote-buying remained a commonly accepted practice.[50]

These patterns pose high hurdles for most women interested in entering politics. "In Nepal, economic and political empowerment are interrelated," a women's rights advocate in Nepal told us. "If women don't have economic control and have to rely on their husbands or families, they cannot lead in politics. Families often cannot economically support women's political ambitions in the

Nepali context."[51] Financial disadvantages help explain why Nepali women have struggled to compete in first-past-the-post electoral races, which are particularly expensive for candidates. In the 2022 parliamentary elections, only 9 women were elected to a total of 165 constituency seats.[52]

In Kenya, women candidates and politicians similarly stress that money remains one of the most significant barriers to women's political empowerment. A 2021 report by the Westminster Foundation for Democracy and NIMD found that it is not unusual for candidates in parliamentary and senatorial races to spend several million Kenyan shillings (sometimes over the equivalent of US$150,000) on their campaigns, with handouts for voters making up a significant share of campaign costs.[53] These expenses automatically exclude many people who are not independently wealthy or connected to political funding networks. For women candidates, the challenge is even greater: despite spending *more* on average than their male competitors, they remain less likely to win.[54] Our interviews with Kenyan women candidates also underscore that they often incur expenses that men can forego, including heightened costs for their personal security.

Despite these resource constraints, most donor-funded capacity-building initiatives do not provide funding to women participants, as development actors seek to avoid accusations of political interference and partisanship (a problem we return to in the next chapter). In Kenya, the result is a profound mismatch between training programs' emphasis on individual skills and the realities of highly financialized, resource-intensive political campaigns. "When [women candidates] realize that they don't get any money out of [a training program], then they don't come," Dr. Regina Mwatha, a Kenyan scholar and women's rights advocate, told us. "They say, as a woman, one of the greatest weaknesses for me is the lack of financing. When I'm coming, it's just a waste of time if I don't get financing."[55] A Kenyan employee of a Western democracy aid organization echoed the same sentiment. "They will tell you: we have attended these seminars for many years; NDI is doing it, the Centre for Multiparty Democracy is doing it; UN Women is doing it. What we need now is to get money to brand ourselves. That's a gap in terms of programming [...] There is a gap between what they need to campaign and what we offer."[56]

Conclusion

Over the past two decades, countless civil society initiatives and donor programs have focused on building women's individual capacity as aspirants and candidates. By "leaning in" with confidence and skill, the theory goes, women can gradually make their way into male-dominated political institutions. In many contexts, these initiatives have been welcomed by women political leaders. They provide spaces for building networks, sharing experiences, and acquiring knowledge that women may otherwise struggle to access, particularly if they are relative political newcomers or come from marginalized social groups. Both practitioners and women candidates underscore the value of locally designed programs that begin several years before an election, offer sustained mentorship and accompaniment, and focus on tackling practical challenges women may face—from navigating party-internal candidate-selection processes to building political capital in their constituencies. In contexts where many women face entrenched sociocultural hurdles that prevent them from engaging in electoral politics, capacity-building focused on accessing local leadership roles can further contribute to building a long-term pipeline of politically engaged women leaders and advocates.

Yet advocates, practitioners, and women politicians also repeatedly confront the limits of candidate training as a mechanism for overcoming women's political exclusion. A polished campaign platform is unlikely to take women far in contexts where political campaigns are powered by candidates' financial muscle or their connections to party elites. Policy ideas and years of grassroots service will not translate into influence if political parties and legislatures remain dominated by "old boys networks" that lash out against women who threaten their hold on power. In short, even the most knowledgeable, experienced, and confident women politicians run up against institutions that are largely designed by and for elite men, who are rarely held to the same standards of competence.

7

Confronting the Gatekeepers

If training initiatives are limited tools to confront an unequal political playing field, the question arises: what other mechanisms or entry points exist to bolster women's access to decision-making? For many practitioners, advocates and researchers, the answer is clear: political parties have to change. By choosing who benefits from their resources and platforms and competes in elections, parties act as powerful gatekeepers to women's political participation and representation, from their initial recruitment as candidates up to their election into office and political work thereafter. Yet parties are rarely gender-inclusive organizations. Across Kenya, Nepal, Morocco, and Myanmar, women politicians and advocates identified parties as critical bottlenecks marked by sexism, cronyism, and entrenched hierarchies. "Parties are the premier gateway to political leadership, but their structures are completely unresponsive to women," one women's rights advocate in Kenya told us.[1] They are "corrupt, malfunctioning, and undemocratic," a Nepali civil society leader echoed. "These are all male-dominated structures. They are for men, not for women. When you try to fit into that structure, it is not comfortable."[2]

Recognizing these challenges, international democracy aid actors have begun integrating a more systematic focus on gender inclusion into their support for and engagement with party leaders and organizations, often as part of broader party assistance initiatives. At the heart of this work lie several puzzles. How can assistance providers convince party leaders who benefit from the status quo to redistribute power to underrepresented groups? And how can they reconcile the goal of promoting women's participation and influence within political parties with their preference to remain nonpartisan and avoid perceptions of political interference?

This chapter draws on our four cases to examine these questions in greater depth. We begin by illustrating the most daunting hurdles women face within political parties and how these interact with the broader political system. We then review the standard methods party assistance providers have used to

Aiding Empowerment. Saskia Brechenmacher and Katherine Mann, Oxford University Press.
© Oxford University Press 2024. DOI: 10.1093/oso/9780197694275.003.0007

advance women's inclusion and examine their track record. Practitioners generally acknowledge that neither capacity-building for women party members nor separate women's wings are enough to transform party practices: instead, systemic and organizational reforms are also necessary. To this end, aid organizations have fostered cross-party reform coalitions between women leaders and worked with party executives to assess barriers to inclusion and develop gender equality action plans. These efforts have borne some fruit, triggering a number of legislative and party-internal reforms. But progress has been uneven across parties and countries, and formal commitments and policy changes are not always implemented or sustained. Limited leadership commitment, low party institutionalization, and the pernicious role of money in politics all pose enduring challenges.

Gender biases in political parties

Political parties are deeply gendered organizations. While the number of women members and leaders varies across parties, their decision-making structures are almost always dominated by men.[3] This pattern is evident across our four cases. Prior to the 2021 coup, men held nearly all senior central executive committee positions in Myanmar's political parties; some parties excluded women from leadership altogether. Even the NLD, with Aung San Suu Kyi at its helm, was led by a small circle of older men from the Bamar ethnic group.[4] In Kenya, most political parties remain weakly institutionalized and structured around individual leaders, very few of whom are women. When women are promoted into senior party positions, they often find themselves pushed into deputy roles and excluded from backroom negotiations and informal decision-making networks.[5] In Morocco and Nepal, party ranks are similarly dominated by men.[6] These patterns of male overrepresentation create various challenges for women, ranging from hostile organizational cultures to exclusionary informal practices, such as late-night meetings, that disadvantage their equal participation. Cross-national research also shows that parties with few women in leadership are less likely to promote women in politics and adopt quota policies.[7]

Yet gender exclusion in parties runs deeper than women's exclusion from leadership. Gender hierarchies and gendered divisions of labor tend to permeate all party structures. Men often benefit from stronger in-group networks and norms that reward traditionally masculine traits and characteristics, which advantages them in candidate selection and promotion processes. Perceived as relative outsiders and confronted with gender biases, women, on the other hand, struggle to rise through the ranks, and get sidelined from "winnable" electoral districts or top party list positions.[8]

Unfair or biased candidate selection processes were a recurring theme across our four cases. Ahead of the 2020 election in Myanmar, for example, parties selected their candidates through internal selection committees, most of which had no women members. As a result, many female candidates felt that they were intentionally sidelined and assigned to constituencies where their party had little chance of winning.[9] In Nepal, women have struggled to secure party tickets in the country's 165 single-member constituency districts, with local party committees often excluding qualified women from the list of names they send to senior leaders. This pattern persists even though women perform well in elections: in the 2022 local elections, they made up 37.8 percent of candidates, and won 41.2 percent of seats.[10]

Globally, discrimination by party gatekeepers is often exacerbated by an unfavorable electoral system, weak enforcement of formal rules, and clientelistic political practices. A large body of research shows that women candidates perform better in electoral systems with proportional representation and large district and party magnitudes, since parties in these contexts are incentivized to balance their tickets with diverse candidates. In electoral systems in which parties win only one seat per district, on the other hand, party leaders have to exclude a male candidate in order to nominate a woman—which most parties choose not to do.[11] Mirroring this pattern, in Kenya's majoritarian electoral system women candidates have struggled to secure nominations in parties' traditional strongholds. Doing so requires insider networks, political capital, and financial resources to influence informal political negotiations, all of which women politicians, on average, are less likely to have. Even when parties hold primaries, many women perceive these contests to be rigged in favor of wealthier male candidates, who can offer handouts to voters and bribe party officials.[12] Moreover, formal candidate selection rules are poorly enforced and easily circumvented by powerful players.[13] In short, patriarchal norms interact with winner-takes-all dynamics, expensive elections, and high levels of informality to create a particularly difficult political environment for women.

In Morocco, patronage politics paired with an unfavorable electoral system act as a major hurdle. Many pro-palace parties rely on rural elites, so-called notables, to gain the support of rural voters. In return, these notables often receive priority access to party tickets or exert influence over the selection of candidates.[14] "Politics is about exchanges," one women's rights advocate explained. "I support you to go to parliament, and in return, we support your brother, who will be the president of the region, and I get to be head of the city council, or something similar. We will all support your campaign, but in exchange for favors. And women don't really have a place in all of this."[15] The Moroccan electoral system reinforces this challenge. Because of the small size of electoral districts and the high number of parties, most parties struggle to win more than one seat in each constituency. As a result, obtaining the first position on parties' candidate lists is paramount for getting elected, and women are almost never ranked first.[16]

Quotas can help address these dynamics, but they are no panacea. In fact, parties can be astute at circumventing such measures or applying them in a highly minimalist fashion. In Nepal, for instance, parties are legally mandated to reserve one-third of party committee positions for women. Yet many parties violate this rule, claiming that they lack qualified women to fill these roles.[17] As for quotas targeting candidate selection or reserved seats for women in parliament, women's rights advocates and practitioners across Nepal, Kenya, and Morocco criticize male party officials for placing female relatives onto party lists while sidelining women with serious political ambitions.[18] Although it is unclear just how widespread this practice is, it undermines women politicians' credibility and legitimacy.

Of course, these dynamics are not universal. Globally, there is significant variation in women's inclusion and participation across political parties, depending in part on parties' origins, ideological orientation, and the wider sociocultural context. The broader political environment also plays a role. For instance, financial barriers appear to have been lower barriers for women aspirants and candidates running in Myanmar's 2015 and 2020 elections than they have been in Kenya, where party primaries and general elections have become notoriously expensive. Nevertheless, gender exclusionary dynamics persists across most political parties and political contexts.

From training to organizational change

Over the past two decades, international support for political party reform has grown from a niche endeavor to a more significant component of global democracy aid. Today, the group of international actors working directly with parties ranges from large US democracy organizations, such as NDI and IRI, to the German political *Stiftungen* and various European multiparty institutes and foundations, including the Westminster Foundation for Democracy, NIMD, Demo Finland, and DIPD. Most of these organizations provide training and technical support to improve parties' internal capacity and democratic functioning. To elude accusations of partisanship, they typically work with parties across the political spectrum, though some also offer "sister party" support to ideologically aligned parties. Newer approaches to party aid also target the party system, in the hopes of strengthening trust and dialogue *between* parties and improving the regulatory frameworks governing multiparty competition.[19] International actors carrying out this work usually cooperate with local civil society groups; in some countries, they have also helped establish local multiparty platforms—such as the Center for Multiparty Democracy in Kenya (CMD-Kenya)—that serve as partners and implementers.

As party assistance has grown over time, so too has international actors' engagement with gender inclusion in political parties, as either a main programmatic objective or more often as a cross-cutting priority. Activities in this area typically share three overarching goals: strengthening women's representation and influence within party structures, increasing their selection as candidates, and making parties more responsive to women's interests and perspectives. While these objectives have stayed relatively constant, our research suggests a gradual shift in assistance models over time, from an initial focus on working with women party members and women's wings to a stronger emphasis on transforming parties' internal organizational structures and policies as well as the broader party system (see Table 7.1).

Bolstering the capacity of women party members through training, mentorship, and exchanges remains a common programmatic entry point. Having reviewed the strengths and limitations of training initiatives in Chapter 6, we will not expand on them here. The underlying theory of change is largely the same, albeit with a greater focus on promoting women's influence and advancement *within party structures*. In Morocco, for example, the Konrad-Adenauer-Stiftung recently implemented an EU-funded project on gender inclusion in political parties that focused in part on nurturing mentorship between senior women leaders and young female party members.[20] Few aid providers would argue that such initiatives are sufficient on their own to change gender relations within political parties. Instead, most view them as one element of a broader strategy that also includes advocacy, awareness-raising, and policy reform.

A second, well-established tactic consists of supporting women's wings in political parties to strengthen women's collective voice in internal decision-making. Following Nepal's political transition in the mid-2000s, for example, NDI worked with women's wings in the country's main political parties to develop a shared advocacy agenda.[21] Yet research on and practitioner experiences with women's wings reveal a mixed track record. In some countries, these bodies have served as important drivers of reform, successfully advocating for internal party quotas, recruitment targets, and other gender equality measures. International actors have had some success in strengthening their political influence by encouraging party leaders to grant women's structures greater autonomy, resources, and representation in party executive committees. In other countries, however, women's wings serve as auxiliary structures that marginalize women from core decision-making processes and act as vehicles for voter mobilization rather than catalysts for gender equality change.[22] In both Morocco and Kenya, for instance, advocates and practitioners expressed doubt about the transformative potential of women's wings. "If you [work] separately with women, and you

Table 7.1 **Political Party Aid Targeting Women's Participation**

Level of Change	Model	Activities	Target Group(s)
Individual	Capacity-building and mentorship for women party members Training for women and men party members on gender equality issues	Training workshops Training manuals Exchanges	Women and men in parties
Organizational	Support for women's wings Support for cross-party women's alliances	Training workshops Financial support Knowledge-sharing Dialogue sessions Exchanges	Women in parties
Organizational	Advocacy for changes in party processes, practices, and rules to make parties more gender-sensitive	Training workshops Multiparty dialogues Technical assistance and knowledge-sharing Support for civil society advocacy	Party leaders Party members Women's organizations
Systemic	Integrating gender equality provisions into party laws and regulations and campaign finance reforms	Multistakeholder meetings Multiparty dialogues Technical assistance and knowledge-sharing Support for civil society advocacy	Party leaders Women politicians Women's organizations Media outlets Electoral management bodies Relevant ministries

don't mainstream it into the party processes, it doesn't work," one NDI representative in Kenya told us. "Working with the elected women, targeting them separately, has not been very effective. We realized we would have had more impact if we had roped in the parties from the start."[23]

Given these risks of "ghettoizing" women within party structures, democracy support actors have increasingly explored alternative entry points. One strategy has been to foster cross-party women's networks, with the hope that broad-based

Confronting the Gatekeepers 121

coalitions are better positioned to advocate for systemic reforms than isolated women's wings.[24] One such initiative is the IPWA in Nepal, which has served as a cross-party platform to articulate and advance joint reform priorities.[25] Similar networks have been supported in other countries, including in Zambia, Tanzania, Colombia, and Georgia.[26]

Another strategy targets party leaders to advance broader organizational and policy changes that benefit women. Many programs begin by documenting the barriers women face within individual parties or encouraging parties to carry out a self-assessment. For example, NDI has developed a "Win with Women" tool to evaluate women's influence within party structures and to advocate for organizational reform. Ideally, these efforts increase the political salience of women's marginalization and offer "ammunition" to reform-oriented actors within parties.[27] Some programs then use these assessments to help parties develop internal gender action plans. In other cases, international actors have integrated debates about women's political inclusion into their high-level exchanges with party leaders, covered the issue in training workshops with lower-level party members, or leveraged multiparty dialogue to share reform options and create peer pressure between parties.

The "Women's Political Rights" (WPR) program implemented by NIMD and its partners in Kenya (as well as in Tunisia and Colombia) represents a rare example of a gender-focused party program that pursued change at multiple levels. In Kenya, the program kicked off with bilateral gender assessments of eleven participating parties, facilitated by the CMD-Kenya. The organization then encouraged these parties to develop their own gender equality plans and share their progress with implementation. In parallel, the program supported advocacy for a national gender quota and media campaigns promoting women's political leadership.[28] DIPD relied on a similar approach in Myanmar, first mapping the situation of women across different political parties and then using a multiparty dialogue platform to help parties develop reform proposals and discuss them with women's organizations.[29] Meanwhile, IWDA supported local women's organizations in Myanmar in lobbying party leaders for reform, and Demo Finland and NIMD facilitated advocacy meetings and cross-party discussions to promote gender-sensitive party reforms through the Myanmar School of Politics.[30]

Finally, some party-focused initiatives attempt to influence the broader legal and political environment that governs gender equality in elections, campaign finance, and political parties. As we describe in Chapter 4, the most common entry point has been the promotion of mandatory gender quotas. But some aid providers have also focused on integrating gender equality provisions into political party laws and campaign finance regulations and worked with electoral institutions to increase their oversight over party practices. In sum, there is greater recognition today that promoting gender equality within political parties requires a combination of system-, organization- and individual-level changes, and aid actors have developed a range of programmatic tools to encourage and support such reforms.

Fostering cross-party linkages

What has been the impact of these varied party reform initiatives? Many of the measurement challenges that afflict candidate training also apply to political party aid. Practitioners can assess whether their engagement prompts changes in policies and rules or boosts women's capacity and self-confidence. They can also measure increases in the number of women selected as candidates or promoted into positions of leadership. However, these outcomes are almost always difficult to attribute to specific interventions. For instance, program activities that produce positive changes in organizational norms and practices are sometimes negated by broader political developments, such as party mergers or dissolutions. In other cases, the fruits of sustained advocacy and dialogue may not be visible until after several years of engagement.

Keeping these caveats in mind, several themes emerged from our review of program evaluations and interviews with practitioners, women politicians, and women's rights organizations. First, there have been some successes in fostering cross-party dialogue among women party leaders to generate reform momentum and advance women's policy priorities. In Nepal, NDI and other actors helped the IPWA become a platform for women to build relationships, gain greater visibility, and articulate joint reform priorities during the country's transition process. As the constitutional negotiations continued, the network kept gender equality demands on the political agenda, reinforcing the mobilization of women in civil society and female politicians in the Constituent Assembly. For instance, the IPWA helped organize public protests insisting on the fair representation of women in the Interim Constitution Drafting Committee in 2007, leading to the appointment of four women to the committee. Alongside other actors, the alliance also contributed to anchoring the 33 percent gender quota in the final constitutional draft.[31] Below the national level, the IPWA formed district-level subcommittees to educate citizens about gender equality in the constitutional reform process and to recruit more women into political positions. In some areas, the platform also successfully increased funds earmarked for women.[32] Together, these findings mirror existing research on women's participation in political transitions, which underscores the importance of women mobilizing *within* and *outside* of political institutions and across political cleavages to influence constitutional negotiations.[33]

Looking beyond our four cases, a similar cross-party initiative in Zambia has also had some success. Demo Finland and its partner organization, the Zambian National Women's Lobby, have established a national cross-party forum platform called the National Women in Politics Platform that has served as a neutral space for women politicians to meet and exchange their experiences, even during moments of heightened political polarization. Women have used the platform to make joint statements on gender-related policy issues, carry out community development initiatives, and advocate for themselves within their own parties.[34]

Whether or not cross-party coalitions can serve as an effective entry point in other contexts is likely to depend first and foremost on the interests of local women leaders. In places where one party is politically dominant, for instance, women in opposition parties may have little interest in cross-party action. In countries where senior party leaders oppose women's cross-party cooperation altogether, more informal and unstructured dialogue may be more beneficial. Moreover, it remains unclear whether or under which conditions such cross-party initiatives can catalyze organizational reforms within individual parties. In Zambia, the National Women in Politics Platform has created channels for dialogue, solidarity, and advocacy. Members of the platform have also gained new positions within their parties. But the project has made less headway influencing parties' practices with respect to candidate selection or advancing the implementation of gender action plans.[35]

In Nepal, the IPWA has helped shape gender-inclusive legal frameworks at the national level. Yet the dominant political parties largely retained their centralized and hierarchical command structures, and promotions and candidate selection are still heavily influenced by personal ties to senior leaders.[36] The network has also struggled to retain its political influence over time, in part due to women's weak status in their own political parties. Some of its local chapters have become inactive in the face of continued patriarchal resistance and interference.[37] At critical junctures, including an instance in 2020 when the female acting speaker of the lower house of parliament was forced to forfeit her position to a male colleague, IPWA leaders did not speak out publicly. Given these challenges, some practitioners now view the alliance as an ineffective forum for advancing women's political interests.[38]

Incremental reforms

Efforts to advance systemwide and party-level organizational reforms through advocacy and political dialogue have also had a mixed track record. On the one hand, there have been clear successes reforming broader legislative frameworks. The widespread adoption and gradual strengthening of national-level gender quotas is a case in point (see Chapter 5), but international actors have also influenced other laws that touch on parties' operations, including campaign finance and party primary regulation. Multilateral actors play important roles in this area since they are well positioned to convene various electoral stakeholders and share transnational legal expertise and reform options.

In Kenya, for example, UN Women has helped ensure that the gender equality principles codified in the 2010 constitution are also reflected in other legal and electoral reforms. The organization supported a 2011 gender audit of the draft Political Parties Bill that convinced the electoral commission to add several important gender-responsive provisions to the law. The law now stipulates that parties must have no more than two-thirds of any gender in their governing bodies.[39] More recently, UN Women also worked with the Office of the Registrar of Political Parties (ORPP) to mainstream gender considerations into amendments to the Political Parties Act in order to ensure that party nominations are regulated in a more gender-inclusive manner.[40]

Of course, getting a policy or law in place is only the first step in a long and often challenging process. In Kenya, neither the electoral commission nor the ORPP have the resources or the "teeth" to ensure that parties comply with existing laws. Although both institutions have advanced gender-related policies, they have struggled to consistently enforce them. In some areas, they have been met with significant pushback, including legal challenges initiated by parties.[41] International actors and women's rights advocates also emphasize that existing laws and regulations still do not go far enough. They are therefore continuing to push for legislation to better regulate party primaries, reign in campaign spending, and limit the formation of briefcase parties. They also emphasize the need to improve dispute resolution processes by making them more accessible and responsive to women candidates.[42] The Kenyan experience underscores that regulatory and legal reform is an iterative process that requires long-term engagement and advocacy to incrementally improve formal legal frameworks and prevent backsliding.

With respect to reforming political parties *internally*, international actors have had some success in getting party leaders to participate in gender assessments, develop action plans, and, in some cases, implement voluntary internal quotas. In Myanmar, for example, the Shan Nationalities League for Democracy (SNLD), an ethnically affiliated party in Shan State, agreed to implement a 30 percent gender quota ahead of the 2020 election, a target the party nearly reached.[43] Party officials also ensured that women made up at least one-third of membership in nearly all the party's township-level Executive Committees.[44] IWDA partially attributed the success of this reform to the advocacy of its local partner organization, the Shan Women's Action Network. "This shows exactly where we as donor-funded programming needs to be: supporting women's rights organizations to do informal advocacy with parties to take on gender equality change," one IWDA staff member told us.[45] DIPD and Demo Finland/NIMD also reported positive results from their party engagement in Myanmar, including better links between some parties and women's rights organizations.[46] For example, DIPD's work encouraged several parties to agree to a joint gender equality action plan; two partner parties also adopted new gender policies and the NLD reinstated its women's wings (before these activities were disrupted by the military coup).[47] In Kenya, the WPR program motivated eleven parties to adopt new gender plans.[48] Beyond our cases, parties have developed similar gender equality action plans in Tunisia, Georgia, Zambia, and Sri Lanka.

Stubborn stumbling blocks

These examples suggest that dialogue and sustained advocacy can contribute to incremental positive change. Yet progress has also been highly uneven across parties and countries. In some cases, years of advocacy have amounted to relatively little reform. In Myanmar, for instance, international and civil society pressure effectively promoted women's status in the SNLD but had much less success with the (politically more significant) NLD. Although reforms undertaken by some of the country's ethnic parties put pressure on the NLD to follow suit, the party continued rejecting quotas or reforms to the country's majoritarian electoral system.[49] Similarly, in Zambia, Demo Finland has spent several years helping parties create internal gender equality plans, yet with more limited success in implementation.[50]

Even when parties do take action, it can be difficult to differentiate between gradual building blocks toward broader change processes and superficial gestures that maintain existing distributions of power. For instance, one practitioner we spoke with in Myanmar felt that getting party leaders to even discuss a gender policy was a sign of success, particularly if those leaders had previously refused to acknowledge the need for internal party reforms.[51] On the other hand, practitioners and advocates have also observed a persistent disconnect between parties' rhetorical commitments and their actual practices. In Kenya, for example, parties have repeatedly promised to improve their nomination processes but still resort to selecting men in their most competitive districts.[52] Ahead of the 2022 elections, several major political parties also challenged (and ultimately blocked) a previous court ruling requiring them to nominate more women candidates. In both public and private, they argued that they could not "impose" women candidates on their voters.[53]

Although parties have sometimes adopted tangible reforms, such internal quotas, it is less clear that changes in policies, party constitutions, or action plans alone significantly reshape party activities. This problem is particularly acute if parties are weakly institutionalized and operate through informal networks and practices rather than formal rules and procedures. In Nepal, for instance, the "Making Politics Work with Women" project led by UN Women between 2007 and 2012 included a participatory gender audit of eleven parties' constitutions. This process also generated various recommendations to address the identified problems. Yet the program's evaluation found that most parties "were not yet ready to fully practice the gender and social inclusion policies" needed to bolster women's participation. The initiative did not increase the number of women candidates winning elections or women's representation in parties' executive organs.[54]

In Kenya, there is also little evidence that past gender equality action plans have substantially altered parties' candidate selection processes, particularly since many of the parties that existed a decade ago have since disbanded and re-formed in new constellations. Highly fluid coalition politics also complicate the role of party-internal policies and commitments: over the past several election cycles, women have been sidelined in informal negotiations that happen *between* parties to distribute various political posts. Even when women have formally obtained party tickets, they have sometimes been pushed aside in these backroom deals.[55]

Democracy aid organizations to date have insufficiently documented these longer-term outcomes of their party reform initiatives. Evaluations often highlight (and practitioners point to) the adoption of gender plans and policies or the establishment of women's wings as successful outcomes. However, they provide much less detail about the implementation of these reforms and how they affect women's influence within their parties or their selection as candidates over subsequent election cycles. As a result, there is little accumulated or shared learning about stumbling blocks in reform and implementation processes that could inform subsequent interventions.

A closer look at current programming models shows that aid providers rely heavily on *identifying* gendered barriers within political parties, with the assumption that a combination of greater awareness, peer pressure, and technical assistance will lead parties to address them. Not surprisingly, this strategy is most likely to work in political parties where there is already some internal reform momentum, where women leaders and women's wings wield some amount of influence, or where party leaders are ideologically or strategically committed to promoting gender equality. It is less clear, however, how this approach motivates action if party leaders believe that selecting women as candidates will hurt their electoral prospects, drive resistance and defection from lower-level male party cadres, or lead them to lose powerful financiers and allies. Evidence that voters do in fact support women candidates may be helpful in some cases, but it may fail to produce action if party leaders can keep winning elections, join ruling coalitions, or get lucrative political positions without undertaking reform. In these cases, international actors' commitment to building trust with party counterparts, honoring local ownership, and avoiding confrontational approaches comes into tension with the reality that deeper gender equality change requires a significant redistribution of power, which usually engenders resistance.[56]

In addition to generating political will, aid providers must also navigate political parties' internal capacity and political continuity—or lack thereof. By prioritizing reforms to formal rules, policies, and procedures, programs often assume a degree of organizational coherence that does not exist. Where parties lack high levels of institutionalization, internal reformers struggle to gain traction: they may invest resources in building an internal structure or policy only to have their progress reversed by a political split or sudden change in senior leadership. Moreover, when working with fluid and weakly institutionalized parties, international actors and local advocates frequently struggle to build the relationships with party leaders needed to accompany and monitor reform processes over time, or to maintain past gains as parties reconfigure. In Kenya, for example, most parties operate as loose electoral coalitions that fragment as political alliances shift. Many of the parties that once participated in NIMD's WPR program no longer exist in the same form today. The program encountered a similar challenge in Tunisia: high levels of political instability left parties without "the time and sometimes the will to structure themselves in terms of activists' database, organization, platforms, internal rules and strategies."[57] In Morocco, one aid official summed up the problem as follows: "As soon as you go one level down [in the party], you have this chaotic, non-defined mix of responsibilities and people who claim they're in charge or that you should work with them. [. . .] It never works and it's very complicated."[58] In sum, altering the internal practices of political parties requires an alignment of variables that often lie beyond international actors' control: political commitment by leadership, accountability mechanisms to ensure implementation, and party organizations that are already somewhat conducive to change.

Confronting the cost of politics

A final roadblock is the pernicious role of money in politics, which is closely intertwined with parties' candidate recruitment and selection practices. Even as efforts to tackle gender inclusion in parties have multiplied, many international actors still shy away from campaign finance issues—a politically sensitive topic in an already sensitive area of assistance. Across our four case studies, we encountered a handful of donor-funded efforts to document the gendered financial constraints women experience. Most prominently, the Westminster Foundation for Democracy and NIMD have jointly commissioned a range of country case studies investigating the high cost of engaging in politics and assessing gaps between formal rules and actual practices, including in Kenya.[59] These documentation efforts are critical, as they shed light on an area that can be shrouded in secrecy. But many practitioners we interviewed emphasized that there have been few additional programmatic initiatives to tackle the financial barriers that disproportionately affect women in politics.[60]

Depending on the political context, these barriers can be exceptionally high, and they are closely tied to women's status within political parties. As we previously described, women candidates in Kenya and Nepal incur high financial costs, which discourages many from entering politics in the first place. But the problem is not just one of campaign costs: in clientelistic political systems, candidates' influence in informal political negotiations is heavily shaped by their access to resources. At the local level in Kenya, some women candidates described their competitors bribing party officials to get party tickets, paying young men to intimidate their opponents, and using their resources to ferry voters across districts and polling stations.[61] Meanwhile, at the highest levels of leadership, independent wealth is even more critical to politicians' electoral credibility and their ability to build and maintain political coalitions. Lacking the requisite resources, prominent women leaders such as Martha Karua have struggled to compete with the "big men" who still dominate the political scene.[62]

Despite these pervasive challenges, international democracy support actors have been reluctant to engage on gendered campaign finance issues. As noted in Chapter 6, most donors are wary of directly funding women candidates, because they do not want to be seen as interfering with local political campaigns or fueling corrupt electoral practices.[63] They have, in some cases, provided in-kind support to cover campaign expenses, by purchasing campaign materials or paying for women candidates' transport costs. They have also integrated information on fundraising strategies into training curricula. While helpful, these tactics are typically small in scale, temporary, and unsatisfying to women candidates who face much wealthier and better-connected male competitors.[64]

Existing research suggests that more targeted financial support could make a difference, though such measures are not necessarily sufficient to alter the playing field for women candidates. Ahead of Malawi's 2009 election, for example, several international donors partnered with the Ministry of Women and a network of women's civil society organizations in a "50–50 campaign" to support women through the resource-intensive party nomination stage. The initiative offered every woman seeking a party nomination the equivalent of US$231 in campaign funding and provided t-shirts and posters to the one hundred women selected as candidates for the general election. Yet although the election resulted in a 9.3 percent increase in the number of women in parliament, a study by Kayuni and Muriaas (2014) finds little evidence that the campaign increased the attractiveness of women candidates to parties' selectorates. Even with financial assistance, most female candidates did not have enough resources to compete with candidates who engaged in vote-buying and other illicit practices.[65] In Kenya, on the other hand, CMD-Kenya and other democracy aid organizations have successfully convinced parties to lower or waive their nomination fees for women and other underrepresented groups, thereby making it easier for women to declare their candidacies.[66] However, in both Kenya and Ghana, such fee reductions have proven insufficient to bolster women's electoral chances, as party fees represent only a small fraction of the total cost of winning elections.[67]

These limitations point to the need for more systemic reforms, including mechanisms to disclose and regulate the flow of money in elections and crack down on corrupt electoral practices. In recent years, organizations such as IFES and International IDEA have documented various political finance rules used around the world, including those at the intersection of gender and political finance. For example, they have collected information about gendered electoral financing schemes that condition parties' receipt of public funding on the share of women who are nominated or elected, or regulations that allocate a certain proportion of public funding specifically for party activities related to gender equality.[68]

Yet it is not always clear which reforms are most appropriate for different contexts, and researchers have only recently begun investigating the effectiveness of such measures in bolstering women's political representation. Early findings suggest a complicated picture: different schemes can work under various conditions, although the number of women already in political office and effective enforcement and oversight mechanisms appear to play important roles.[69] The case of Kenya underscores this last issue. Current laws oblige publicly funded parties to earmark 30 percent of state resources for "special interest groups" (women, youth, minorities, and people with disabilities), yet there is little transparency around how parties spend this money.[70] Since gendered electoral financing schemes can potentially serve as a powerful complement to gender quotas (or an alternative avenue for reform where quotas prove difficult to implement), international actors could expand the existing evidence base by systematically investigating the effects of different reform strategies across their interventions and across contexts.

Incentivizing government counterparts to enact campaign finance reforms represents another challenge. Not surprisingly, it is difficult to convince politicians who benefit from weak political finance rules to improve regulation and oversight. To return to the Kenyan example: although the country has passed an Election Campaign Financing Act, its implementation and strengthening have been repeatedly blocked and delayed by politicians.[71] Adding to the problem is the fact that many established democracies also struggle to regulate the role of money in politics, which can limit donor governments' credibility when lobbying foreign counterparts to pass reforms. Multilateral organizations, on the other hand, often pursue technical approaches to electoral assistance and are hesitant to challenge governments on issues of political corruption.

The need for pragmatism

Together, these hurdles help explain why many democracy aid providers still view party assistance and political finance reform as a difficult political terrain. Some donor officials we interviewed emphasized parties' outsized role in hindering women's political representation, but expressed doubts about the prospects of change through international aid. Some noted that they had engaged parties again and again, only to see them backtrack on their commitments.[72] Women's rights advocates and staff at international democracy aid organizations, on the other hand, almost unanimously criticized donors' lack of engagement and funding in this area. In their view, parties represented too big of a hurdle to ignore.[73]

What should we make of these competing perspectives? Our analysis suggests that there is value in continued party engagement on women's political inclusion. In some cases, advocacy, training, and dialogue have contributed to incremental changes within parties, and moments of political opening have brought about broader legislative and regulatory reforms. At the same time, both local advocates and their international supporters need to be pragmatic about their goals and expectations. Parties are complex organizations that are difficult to transform. They respond to multiple internal and external incentives, not all of which can easily be influenced by reform-oriented actors or within a one- or two-year timespan. Multiyear engagement is therefore critical. Practitioners and their partners also need time to build trust with their interlocutors within parties to be able to act as convenors when reform opportunities arise.[74]

But even longer-term programs are not guaranteed to succeed. For one, the scale of international support for any given political party will usually be small compared to the wider political environment shaping politicians' incentives. In Kenya, international actors have repeatedly engaged parties on reforms, only to see the same parties disintegrate as electoral coalitions split. Myanmar represents an even more extreme example of reversal. Several international organizations observed positive changes among their partner parties, particularly at the subnational level. But these activities were put to a halt after the 2021 military coup. In the best-case scenario, the norms and relationships built through international and civil society engagement will outlast the programs themselves and create the basis for other forms of political action. Yet these longer-term, intangible impacts are difficult to assess.

Second, because gender equality change within parties is about redistributing power, efforts in this vein are likely to elicit active and passive internal resistance. In practice, this means that reform-minded parties (or parties with an electoral interest in attracting women) will often be faster to change than those that are status quo oriented, such as dominant parties. Research by feminist institutionalist scholars and practitioner experiences across our four cases also underscore that formal policies, rules, and commitments will likely be easier to reform than those areas where male privilege is more normalized, invisible, and entrenched.[75] Moreover, informal rules within institutions often preserve the status quo even in the face of progressive reform. For example, policy changes to promote women's representation in executive bodies sometimes result in meaningful decision-making moving into male-dominated informal spaces and networks.[76]

These risks of reversal and resistance do not mean that party-focused assistance is not a worthwhile endeavor, but both should be factored into international actors' and local advocates' strategies. In practical terms, party-focused interventions should be more explicitly rooted in gendered political economy analyses that go beyond assessing formal rules and women's status within parties. Instead, they should also explore how parties' organizational characteristics (such as their candidate selection practices and the role of informal networks) influence internal gender relations and analyze the reform incentives of and constraints on different party actors. In places marked by high party volatility and unstable electoral coalitions, such as Kenya, investing in party-level organizational reforms may not be the most effective entry point. Alternative strategies may include advocacy for stronger party regulation and support for oversight agencies, dispute resolution bodies, and citizen-led election observation during party primaries.

A revamped theory of change would start with the recognition that gender equality change is a power struggle between change agents and those who benefit from the status quo.[77] Democracy support actors and their local partners can maximize their chances of success when they layer different tactics to expand the resources available to change agents, which may include bottom-up mentoring for women party members, coalition-building among reform-minded party officials and civil society actors, and support for external regulation and oversight. The same logic applies to initiatives focused on gendered financial barriers in politics, which cannot be overcome with a simple policy fix. In both areas, formal policies, action plans, or even legal reforms should not be viewed as end points, but rather as incremental steps that give rise to new forms of contestation over implementation and enforcement.

Conclusion

Initiatives promoting gender equality in political parties and mitigating gendered financial barriers attempt to move beyond the "lean in" approach to women's political empowerment embedded in traditional capacity-building interventions. They accurately identify political parties as key gatekeepers reproducing men's political dominance. In recent years, some democracy support organizations have confronted this challenge by developing more sophisticated assistance models, often combining mentorship and training for women party members with higher-level dialogue and advocacy for organizational and systemwide change. In some countries, they have facilitated cross-party women's alliances that have served as spaces for building solidarity and pursuing joint gender equality advocacy. Assistance efforts have sometimes spurred incremental reforms to national party laws and party-internal action plans and policies .

But these aid initiatives also encounter recurring stumbling blocks. In some cases, advocacy for reform has stalled or failed to get off the ground because party leaders proved uninterested in gender equality reform. In others, successfully adopted action plans and rhetorical commitments have been implemented inconsistently, with parties' weak institutionalization presenting a difficult challenge. The gendered effects of money in politics have compounded these obstacles. The most direct entry point, namely channeling resources to women candidates, unsettles aid providers' commitment to political neutrality and cannot dismantle broader systemic hurdles, including clientelistic and in some cases illicit electoral practices.

In light of these challenges, it may be tempting to conclude that gender inequities in political parties are impossible for external actors to influence: parties are sometimes too volatile, sometimes too atrophied and hierarchical, and generally deeply embedded in patriarchal structures. Yet many women politicians and activists emphasize that parties exert too much influence on political processes to sidestep them entirely. Instead, democracy support actors and their local partners face the task of formulating pragmatic goals that are rooted in clear assessments of party actors' incentives and capabilities. Specifically, they could strengthen current assistance models—such as action plans, training, dialogues, and advocacy—by building theories of change that explicitly consider how these tactics can bolster the resources and influence of change agents within parties and what types of resistance they are likely to encounter. Where parties lack the core features needed to make reforms stick, aid providers and advocates may need to search for alternative entry points, including party regulation and oversight alongside greater civic education and bottom-up pressure from civil society.

Yet the challenges of patriarchal exclusion and discrimination do not end once women make it through party selection processes and elections. Instead, they often continue once women reach elected office. In the next chapter, we therefore turn to the problem of translating women's presence in parliaments and local governments into meaningful political influence.

8

From Presence to Power

Like thousands of women in Nepal, Sita was elected to local government for the first time in 2017.[1] At the time, she saw running for office as an opportunity to solve the many challenges facing her rural community. But three years into her tenure as vice-chairperson, her views of the role had changed. "The mayor is male. When there is a debate, even though I may have a logical argument, my voice is not heard properly. His decision is taken forward," she told us when we reached her by video call in November 2020. "The same mentality is adopted by our staff members. Even when I am right, my voice is not heard." Feeling powerless, Sita had set her eyes on becoming the mayor. But her party shot down her ambitions. "They told me that the men have invested a lot of time, money, and resources to come to this position. And [women] have just started and haven't invested as much. So for now, they only want to give us the ticket for deputy mayor, not the mayor. Even though we are definitely capable enough."[2]

The same dynamic has played out in other parts of the country. Even as Nepal's gender quota has bolstered women's presence in national and subnational government, the most influential political positions are still occupied by men. In 2017, women won 40.9 percent of 35,041 local-level positions across the country.[3] Yet many of these women councilors have struggled to make themselves heard in male-dominated decision-making processes. An Asia Foundation study conducted between 2017 and 2018 found that male politicians openly questioned their female counterparts' competence and qualifications.[4] Women representatives have also faced considerable pressure from voters. "People have started to say: Okay, now women have 33 percent [of political seats] [. . .] But what are you women doing?" noted a gender equality advocate in Nepal. "You put them [into political seats], but their hands and legs are all tied up."[5]

Around the world, women's numerical gains in political institutions have surfaced new questions and doubts about the meaning of democratic representation. Has women's growing political inclusion increased their actual influence over decision-making processes? To what extent have these changes addressed

Aiding Empowerment. Saskia Brechenmacher and Katherine Mann, Oxford University Press.
© Oxford University Press 2024. DOI: 10.1093/oso/9780197694275.003.0008

what Celis and Childs (2020) refer to as the "poverty of women's political representation?"[6] In the eyes of many feminist advocates, women's high-level leadership has not had the transformative impact that they once hoped for. In some cases, women with access to positions of political power have proven to be unreliable allies to feminist movements. Women politicians also face profound institutional and political obstacles that inhibit their influence, ranging from subtle sidelining and marginalization to overt sexism, harassment, and resistance. Across the board, women legislators are rarely equal in numbers or political seniority to their male counterparts. Nonetheless, they continue to be held to higher standards of performance and are expected to demonstrate their "added value" in ways that male politicians are not.

These patterns have spurred new aid initiatives that seek to reinforce the influence of women elected officials and, by extension, the representation of women's diverse political interests.[7] This chapter analyzes these assistance efforts, examining initiatives targeting national parliaments as well as the growing range of activities targeting subnational assemblies and councils. In the first part of the chapter, we discuss aid providers' traditional focus on strengthening women's legislative effectiveness through individual-level training and support for women's networks and caucuses. Drawing on examples across our cases, we argue that these efforts can help newly elected women adapt to their roles, assert their rights, and advance joint legislative priorities. At the same time, these interventions suffer from two central limitations: by targeting women legislators' skills and capacities, they miss opportunities to amplify important alternative drivers of women's substantive representation and struggle to overcome gendered institutional constraints.

The second part of the chapter turns to several complementary entry points that emerge from our cases, including bolstering reform-oriented "critical actors" within parliaments, fostering stronger links between elected officials and women's movements, and reforming internal parliamentary structures and processes. Our analysis underscores that assistance providers could improve their support by clearly distinguishing between individual women's political influence and the substantive representation of women as a diverse group of citizens, and by supporting the multiple sites, actors, and channels involved in claim-making on behalf of gender-transformative change.

An indirect link

Over the past decade, gender equality has become an important component of parliamentary aid programs, which offer training and technical support to legislatures on issues that range from legislative drafting to constituency outreach and budgeting.[8] These programs primarily aim to strengthen women legislators' political efficacy and influence, not least to demonstrate the value of women's leadership and encourage other women to become politically engaged. Yet many interventions also have a second objective: improving women's *substantive* representation, defined as the political representation of the interests, perspectives, and needs of women in society.[9]

These dual goals mirror the objectives of gender equality advocates. For many feminist activists, promoting gender parity in politics is first and foremost a matter of justice. Women's equal presence in political institutions reinforces those institutions' legitimacy and helps build citizens' institutional trust.[10] Their continued exclusion, on the other hand, signals worrisome deficits in societal fairness and inclusion. Without sharing political decision-making power, the argument goes, "women cannot reasonably be considered the political equals of men."[11] Yet in most cases, those pushing for women's political representation have additional expectations for change. They argue that women, once they are in positions of political leadership, will bring different priorities and perspectives to the table, thereby changing both legislative processes and outcomes and deepening the quality of democracy.

A large body of empirical evidence supports these claims. Across different regions, studies have shown that women legislators speak up more often on women's rights and introduce more bills on issues impacting women, from gender-based violence to childcare.[12] Women's presence in legislatures also influences political outcomes. For instance, higher proportions of women legislators are correlated with lower defense spending and greater prioritization of social welfare and healthcare spending, as well as the implementation of more family-friendly policies.[13] At the same time, the presence of women alone does not automatically ensure women's substantive representation. Instead, the relationship between women's presence and changes in outcomes is complex, mediated by several political and institutional factors.

For one, determining whether women legislators act on behalf of women citizens first requires us to define what women's political interests are, which is a difficult task. Women are a heterogeneous group, and simplistic assumptions about women's interests imply shared experiences where they do not exist.[14] Some scholars have attempted to resolve this dilemma by taking a narrow approach, arguing that women's substantive representation should be understood as action on behalf of gender equality. Others have argued that this approach sidesteps the role of conservative women representatives, who also make claims on behalf of women but generally do not subscribe to feminist demands for gender-transformative change.[15] A third perspective—and the one we adopt—tries to reconcile these two stances, suggesting that women's substantive representation, and indeed, democracy, is enhanced if women's diverse and conflicting views are fully represented in the political process.[16] These debates matter for practice: any assistance program that seeks to make political processes more responsive to women's interests needs to grapple with how to define these interests and their representation in politics.

Second, no matter which political interests women represent, they almost always face institutional constraints that limit their power. In many contexts, women who enter male-dominated parliaments find themselves not only in the numerical minority but also marginalized from powerful committees and informal decision-making spaces. They frequently encounter implicit biases and outright resistance from their male counterparts, who may feel threatened by women's increasing political voice. In concert, these factors can substantially limit women's influence over legislative outcomes, even as their numbers in political bodies increase.[17] Adding to these institutional barriers is the fact that women politicians vary in their individual capacity and desire to advance women's interests, however broadly or narrowly defined. They may be constrained by their political party's agenda, worry about stigmatization and pushback, or come from elite circles far removed from most women's everyday experiences and needs. In sum, while women representatives often diversify the legislative agenda, the connection between the "politics of presence" and the "politics of ideas" is not direct.[18]

For assistance providers, these complexities underscore the importance of clearly stating their programmatic objectives and theories of change, as well as distinguishing between elected women's political efficacy and power, the effective representation of diverse women's political interests, and the successful adoption of feminist policies. They also highlight the need for practitioners to consider the various constraints on women's substantive representation. In the next part of the chapter, we turn to our case studies to examine how assistance approaches grapple with these questions and place them in conversation with existing gender and politics scholarship.

Learning the rules of the game

Globally, aid providers have focused primarily on building the skills and capacities of elected women representatives through training and mentoring initiatives. These efforts are based on the recognition that women often enter parliaments as relative political newcomers, particularly in countries where gender quotas have required parties to rapidly increase their recruitment of women candidates. The implication is not that women are less qualified or "deserving": they may have long track records of community activism and leadership but lack familiarity with parliamentary skills and procedures. In Myanmar, for instance, women parliamentarians who entered political office in 2015 on average had *more* formal education than their male counterparts. Nevertheless, many described themselves as lacking the experience and self-confidence needed to introduce legislation or speak up in parliament.[19] Training workshops try to fill these gaps in experience by coaching women in legislative skills, communication, and leadership, while also providing guidance in substantive policy areas.[20]

In Nepal, women's political representation first jumped in 2008 following the establishment of the CA and the implementation of a 33 percent gender quota. Given that many women entered the CA as grassroots leaders, organizations such as UN Women, NDI, and the Asia Foundation initially provided newly elected female delegates training in the basic literacy and public-speaking skills needed to participate in assembly debates, particularly since many women felt that their contributions were intensely scrutinized. Over time, various organizations also organized training workshops focused on educating women representatives about international women's rights frameworks and constitutional reform issues. These workshops also sought to connect women representatives to international experts and relevant local stakeholders.[21] NDI, for example, launched a "Women's Leadership Academy," which offered workshops to more than one hundred women CA members alongside political party leaders, government officials, and activists.[22]

After Nepal's 2015 constitution decentralized the country's political system, several international organizations launched further initiatives to support the more than fourteen thousand female local officials who were elected in 2017. Once again, many of these women were political newcomers who reported not being heard or respected in their new roles, or who felt that they lacked the technical skills to influence local decision-making.[23] To counter these challenges, IFES and the Center for Dalit Women Nepal jointly launched the "She Leads Nepal" program, a US$1.4 million initiative aimed at building the confidence, networks, and skills of hundreds of female ward members across five districts.[24] Over time, the program also supported these women's 2022 re-election campaigns and engaged their family members as allies for women in politics. NDI, the Asia Foundation, and UN Women have run similar mentorship and training programs for women in local government in Nepal, especially for female deputy mayors. Meanwhile, UNDP has supported capacity-building for Nepali women parliamentarians at the federal and provincial levels as part of a long-standing parliamentary support program.[25]

Some programs also connect women legislators with counterparts in other countries or provide them with practical resources to support their work, such as research support and resources for constituency offices and visits. In Myanmar, the Dutch-funded "Women's Action for Voice and Empowerment" (WAVE) program—designed and implemented by IWDA and the local women's organization Akhaya—paired six women parliamentarians from different political parties with experienced Australian women politicians.[26] The program also helped women MPs organize events in their constituencies and build their public profiles. These activities sought to develop participants' leadership skills while also encouraging them to become stronger gender equality advocates.[27]

Most evaluations of these initiatives rely on self-assessments by women participants, who often welcome targeted support. In Nepal, provincial women legislators who participated in UNDP's parliamentary support program noted that the training helped them better understand their legislative roles, provided new insights into gender equality issues, and strengthened their ability to participate in assembly sessions and committee meetings.[28] Earlier training efforts targeting women in the CA similarly helped strengthen women's voices in assembly debates and offered spaces to learn from international best practices and domestic gender experts.[29] Anecdotal evidence from Nepal and Kenya suggests similar benefits for newly elected women in local government, who were better equipped to understand their legislative roles and push back against overt instances of discrimination.[30] In Myanmar, an evaluation of WAVE's mentorship initiative found that the program also provided women MPs with valuable psychosocial support and a sense of cross-national solidarity.[31]

At the same time, the impact of training initiatives depends on their alignment with women's varying needs and the local institutional context. For instance, after Myanmar's initial opening to international aid, practitioners observed that women parliamentarians quickly became overwhelmed with requests to participate in ad hoc and sometimes poorly designed activities, which ultimately imposed additional burdens on them rather than easing their work.[32] Following Kenya's 2013 elections, by contrast, donor-funded training for women county assembly members quickly became part of the local political economy: many women politicians would only participate if they received financial compensation, leading advocates to question whether they were genuinely interested in enacting change.[33] Doubting the benefits of technical training, some aid providers therefore shifted their focus toward nurturing women's political activities on the ground, for example by connecting them with constituents and helping them carry out social audits of government-funded projects.[34] This example from Kenya underscores a broader challenge, namely that most aid programs inadequately measure whether efforts to strengthen women politicians' capacity translate into tangible changes in their legislative *behavior* and *influence* on political processes and outcomes—and if not, what may be causing this disconnect.

A narrow focus on capacity also obscures the significant institutional and political constraints that hinder women's political influence, and sidesteps the question of *male* politicians' capacity, attitudes, and practices. An evaluation of the WAVE program in Myanmar, for example, found that it succeeded in strengthening women MPs' skills and increased their interest in gender equality issues. But the program was not designed to address the many hurdles Burmese women legislators faced in their everyday work, such as insufficient support staff, challenges balancing their political work with care responsibilities, gendered security risks, and political pushback against women's leadership.[35] In Nepal's CA, training similarly did not prevent women from being sidelined from high-level decision-making spaces within parties and informal negotiations between male leaders, a problem that worsened as constitutional negotiations became more polarized.[36]

In our research, women's exclusion from informal decision-making networks and patriarchal resistance against women's political influence emerged as particularly critical challenges that cannot be resolved by strengthening women's skills and confidence. When women ward members in Nepal have tried to exercise political agency, for instance by allocating a greater share of local budgets to programs targeting women, they have routinely faced pushback from male ward chairs and mayors, who tend to prioritize infrastructure projects that offer more opportunities for kickbacks.[37] In some cases, men in mayoral positions have relied on informal networks linking them to men serving as ward chairs to bypass women deputy mayors in decision-making.[38] In Kenya, women county assembly members who have proposed their own legislative initiatives have had similar experiences. Assembly leaders have refused to put gender-related proposals on the agenda or have told quota-nominated women representatives that they lack the legitimacy to introduce legislation. In fact, some women representatives note that becoming more vocal about their ideas and critical of their assembly leadership has made them *more* vulnerable to backlash and exclusion—a risk that training initiatives rarely acknowledge or address.[39]

Collective power through women's caucuses

For international actors, one strategy to prevent male politicians from sidelining women legislators has been to invest in women's collective power, typically by supporting parliamentary caucuses and networks. The rationale behind these initiatives is simple: whereas individual women are vulnerable to marginalization, women's collective demands are more difficult to ignore. In Kenya, USAID funded NDI and the State University of New York to support the National Assembly's gender caucus, the Kenyan Women Parliamentary Association (KEWOPA), with research, financial grants, and training.[40] In Nepal, UN Women and International IDEA helped establish an informal women's caucus in the first CA and offered support for its advocacy on gender-sensitive constitutional provisions.[41] An NDI initiative in Myanmar convened women MPs in an informal working group to coordinate joint policy initiatives, whereas the Asia Foundation organized forums bringing together state-level women legislators.[42] Meanwhile, in Morocco, the EU and UN Women have supported the Arab Women Parliamentarians Network for Equality, a regional network of women parliamentarians that advocates for gender equality in the Arab region.[43]

These coalition-building initiatives have, first and foremost, provided spaces for women parliamentarians to share their experiences and learn from each other. They have also, in some cases, helped advance gender equality reforms. In Kenya, for example, KEWOPA has taught newly elected women parliamentarians the "unwritten rules of parliament" and helped them successfully advocate for maternity leave and greater access to parliamentary leadership positions.[44] It has also served as a platform for women to study legislative bills, define joint positions, and collaborate with women in civil society. These efforts have contributed to several important pieces of gender equality legislation, including the 2006 Sexual Offenses Act, the 2011 Prohibition of Female Genital Mutilation Act, the 2013 Matrimonial Property Act, and the 2015 Protection Against Domestic Violence Act.[45] For example, before the Sexual Offenses Act was passed, KEWOPA members lobbied male parliamentarians and their spouses, convinced male MPs to cosponsor the bill, and participated in joint advocacy workshops with civil society.[46] Empirical studies of women's caucuses in other countries, including in Uganda, Uruguay, and Timor-Leste, similarly credit these bodies with sponsoring and advancing gender equality bills and gender mainstreaming guidelines.[47]

Yet women politicians' and practitioners' experiences across our four cases underscore that it is not enough to simply bring women parliamentarians together and assume that good things will happen. For one, the activities and influence of women's caucuses are sometimes hampered by a lack of institutional support. In both Myanmar and Nepal, women's demands for formally recognized caucuses were rejected by political leaders who feared that recognition would elicit similar claims from other underrepresented groups.[48] As a result, women had to collaborate informally and, in Nepal's case, the caucus was eventually banned entirely. In Kenya, KEWOPA has tried to establish parallel caucuses in the country's forty-seven subnational county assemblies. However, these bodies have similarly struggled to gain recognition as permanent bodies with formal mandates and dedicated funding. Given that Kenyan Members of County Assemblies (MCAs) face significant pressure to provide direct services and implement development projects in their communities, women MCAs note that resource-deprived caucuses have been of limited political use beyond offering platforms for training.[49] Although weak institutional backing does not necessarily prevent coordination and knowledge-sharing, our case studies suggest that it can make caucus activities more dependent on external support and thus less sustainable over time—particularly if there is limited momentum coming from women politicians themselves. It also limits caucuses' legislative role: in contrast to standing gender equality committees, for instance, caucuses typically do not have a mandate to scrutinize budgets and legislation or organize hearings.

Political and ideological divisions can further limit women's ability to work together.[50] Existing research highlights that this constraint is particularly strong in proportional representation (PR) systems with high levels of party discipline.[51] Reflecting this pattern, women politicians in Nepal's CA at times found themselves divided along party lines, and some representatives elected to PR seats placed partisan loyalty over cross-party mobilization for women's interests.[52] These constraints were exacerbated by other social cleavages. Women belonging to Dalit, Janajati, and Madhesi groups sometimes prioritized mobilizing around caste-based and linguistic discrimination over advancing a unified women's agenda, and particularly contentious issues like women's citizenship rights were not conducive to consensus.[53]

However, partisan constraints and divisions can also hinder cooperation in non-PR contexts. In Kenya's county assemblies, for instance, most women representatives are nominated by their political parties rather than directly elected by constituents. This pattern creates pressure on women to align their political work with the interests of their party factions to avoid losing their committee positions or other institutional perks, which complicates women's ability to work across political lines. In some instances, leaders have purposefully de-whipped vocal women representatives from their committees while promoting those who demonstrate party loyalty, thereby heightening divisions among women representatives.[54] Meanwhile, in Myanmar, strict party hierarchies limited the space for sustained cross-party collaboration even before the return of military rule, despite the country's majoritarian electoral system.[55] A 2017 survey of national-level women legislators revealed that almost half thought that they could only address women's issues if their parties had policies directing them to do so.[56]

Of course, these challenges are not insurmountable. Research in other countries indicates that women legislators sometimes overcome divisions by focusing on a narrow set of issues they can all agree on, or by formally sharing caucus leadership positions between representatives from different parties.[57] Women leaders in Nepal's CA used this strategy to unite around several core gender equality demands.[58] Yet the overarching takeaway that emerges from our cases is that sustained coalition-building tends to be labor-intensive and requires careful strategizing to ensure that collaboration does not harm women politically. This is particularly important in divided societies and highly masculinized institutions in which women's political advancement is largely controlled by powerful men.

In sum, well-tailored training interventions and support for women's caucuses can effectively build women's confidence, shore up their political knowledge, and nurture cross-partisan solidarity. However, they are often insufficient to advance broader institutional reforms and ensure women's substantive representation in the legislative process. For one, strengthening women politicians' individual and collective capacity does not necessarily shift their political *incentives* and *preferences* toward lobbying for gender equality or other issues of concern to women. Some women legislators may be constrained by their parties or choose to prioritize other policies over advocacy for gender issues.[59]

Second, even when women's capacity and preferences are aligned, neither intervention on its own is sufficient to transform the broader opportunity space that shapes gender equality outcomes within legislatures, which includes both the institutional environment and the actions and attitudes of male powerholders. Reflecting on her organization's efforts to foster subnational coalition-building between women MPs in Myanmar, one INGO official told us:

> [These MP forums] have been helpful when it comes to the more basic and human part of not feeling alone and knowing that there are others facing similar challenges and seeing them as structural challenges rather than individual deficiencies that impact confidence. But there is a limit to the change one can make just by working with women. There were barriers they were facing from the parties and the parliamentary sessions. There is only so much that can be done by bringing women together.[60]

Critical actors: A missing piece?

Considering these limitations, some scholars of gender and politics have argued that we "are looking in the wrong place" if we link women's substantive representation to women legislators alone.[61] While acknowledging that women's presence in political institutions matters, they have called for more serious consideration of alternative channels and forms of representation. Instead of asking 'what do women representatives do?' they ask: 'Who acts on behalf of women, and why? How and why does women's substantive representation in the legislative arena occur?'[62]

One important finding that emerges from this line of research is that women's substantive representation often occurs due to the efforts of "critical actors": reform champions who initiate policy proposals and embolden others to enact change.[63] In many cases, these actors are women parliamentarians with strong commitments to gender equality, ties to women's organizations, and political capital within their institutions. These attributes allow them to champion explicitly feminist reform proposals, regardless of the total number of women representatives (and regardless of their parties' official stance). In a comparative study of women's caucuses in Uganda and Uruguay, for example, Johnson and Josefsson (2016) find that it was not the number of women legislators that determined whether women organized collectively, but the presence of parliamentarians committed to promoting *women's interests*. These critical actors mobilized others behind their goals, relying on the institutional space provided by caucuses.[64] Importantly, however, critical actors are not always women. They can also be more "unusual" allies, such as male legislators with progressive political commitments.[65]

Various examples from our cases support Johnson and Josefsson's findings and illustrate the crucial role that feminist critical actors play in driving gender equality change. In Myanmar, for example, both international organizations and domestic women's rights groups noted the political importance of Daw Tin Ei, the female parliamentary speaker of the Mon State parliament, in pushing forward gender equality change.[66] She leveraged her position to create a committee dedicated to women and children, which facilitated cooperation between women legislators and women in civil society and offered them a formal platform to voice gender equality issues. In the Yangon parliament, by comparison, women's representation was significantly higher—yet the male leadership blocked women MPs' demand for a caucus, making cooperation more difficult.[67] In Nepal's CA, it was also a small group of outspoken representatives who took a strong stance on gender equality issues against the wishes of their own parties.[68] Meanwhile, in Kenya, KEWOPA has served as a critical actor in its own right, while also developing partnerships with other critical actors—namely progressive male legislators—to cosponsor and support legislation subject to patriarchal resistance.[69]

To date, the concept of "critical actors" rarely appears in international assistance organizations' strategies and theories of change. Yet these findings have several important implications for implementers and advocates seeking to advance *substantive* gender equality reforms. For one, they underscore the need to explicitly identify, recruit, and support gender champions, whether through mentorship, exchanges, or issue-based networks and working groups. Doing so might also entail a more intentional focus on the role of male legislators in advancing—or in some cases, blocking—gender equality change. While parliamentary support programs offering gender-related training to both women and men politicians have become more common, efforts to cultivate male allies are far from the norm (for more on engaging men, see Chapter 10).

A focus on gender champions might also change how organizations approach candidate training. Across our four cases, both international and domestic women's organizations supporting women candidates usually took an explicitly nonpartisan stance, aiming to increase the number of women elected regardless of their political orientation. However, this strategy does not necessarily promote elected officials with strong commitments to gender justice and ties to grassroots women's movements. In Kenya, for example, some gender equality advocates criticize elected women politicians for going into politics to advance their own financial interests—just like their male counterparts. Leaders with strong feminist commitments, on the other hand, tend to shy away from electoral politics, perceiving the space as violent and corrupt.[70] In this context, advocates seeking to advance *feminist* policy change may need to intentionally recruit, cultivate, and support candidates with links to women's movements and experiences with feminist advocacy—a priority that can conflict with international donors' commitment to nonpartisanship.

Perhaps more radically, a focus on critical actors pushes practitioners and advocates to rethink the value of quota designs that increase the number of women legislators but place them in institutionally disadvantaged positions. For instance, in Morocco, the gradual expansion of reserved seats for women has undoubtedly brought more women into office: in the 2021 election, 90 out of 96 women representatives entered the Moroccan House of Representatives through regional, women-only closed party lists.[71] At the same time, the design of the quota system has hindered women legislators' ability to exercise political influence. Those elected through the quota can only serve one term and, given the difficulty of transitioning to nonquota seats, are regularly pushed out of office before they gain enough political seniority to shape the legislative agenda. Moroccan parties have also used the quota system as a patronage tool, granting list positions to women connected to powerful families in exchange for their political support. As a result, many women legislators have relatively weak linkages to the Moroccan women's movement, and they have not necessarily been at the forefront of pushing for gender equality change.[72]

A similar pattern is evident in Kenya, where quota-nominated women legislators at the national and subnational levels are systematically sidelined from institutional leadership roles. Here too, senior male leaders exert significant discretion over the nomination process, fueling widespread perceptions of corruption and patronage. Women who are politically ambitious and involved in grassroots organizing often feel that they are purposefully overlooked in favor of more politically compliant candidates.[73] In light of these dynamics, both Moroccan and Kenyan women's organizations have pushed for reforms to their respective quota systems, and emphasize the importance of helping women make the transition from quota to nonquota seats.[74] At the same time, opening hard-fought quota reforms up for political debate carries significant risks and can play into the narratives of status quo–oriented actors who have always opposed and undermined such reforms. A critical actor lens nevertheless underscores that it matters which women make it into political office, whether reform-oriented actors attain positions of influence, and what types of alliances these actors are able to forge with male allies and other partners.

Building cooperative constellations for change

The role of critical actors in forging reform coalitions highlights a second (and related) channel for advancing women's substantive representation, namely the formation of "cooperative constellations" between reform-minded actors within parliaments, relevant state institutions, and feminist advocates in civil society.[75] A large body of research underscores the important role of strong, autonomous feminist movements in advancing gender equality change. In areas ranging from violence against women to women's reproductive rights, movements have shifted social norms, pushed new issues onto the political agenda, and lobbied for legal reforms.[76]

Women's collective mobilization has also helped advance women's political leadership in many countries, by offering spaces where women can articulate and contest their collective interests and build their political capital. Women's movements and organizations have played critical roles in lobbying for gender quotas, pushing for gender-sensitive constitutional reforms, and raising awareness of violence against women in politics.[77] Some scholars therefore view women's movements as important alternative channels for women's substantive representation, beyond individual women's high-level leadership.[78] But the role of women's collective mobilization in civil society does not make parliamentary spaces irrelevant. While movements use a wide range of tactics to achieve their objectives, from street protests to public awareness-raising campaigns, they often rely on informal coalitions with reform-oriented parliamentarians (and bureaucrats) to shape legislative and policy action.[79]

One promising avenue for international support has therefore been to facilitate local, national, and regional spaces for *issue-based* exchanges of information and network-building between women legislators, bureaucrats, and activists, both to bring new perspectives and ideas to the attention of women politicians and to strengthen the bargaining power of critical actors in parliaments through external mobilization and monitoring. In Myanmar, for example, the WAVE program successfully brought women MPs participating in their mentoring initiative into dialogue with feminist groups in civil society.[80] In the end, these relationships with local civil society advocates had a more significant impact on their parliamentary work than the exchanges with Australian women parliamentarians. Women's organizations were able to leverage the informal interactions facilitated by the program to connect women MPs with their constituents and provided research and expertise on the various policy issues that came up in parliament.[81] As a result, MPs who previously lacked strong ties to the women's movement became more solid advocates for gender equality reforms.[82] It also became easier for women's rights advocates to advance their legislative ideas. For instance, WAVE's civil society partner Akhaya successfully advocated for greater civil society input into the drafting of the Prevention and Protection of Violence Against Women Bill by collaborating with two women MPs on the Upper House Women and Child Rights Committee.[83]

Whether or not such coalitions are locally appropriate depends on the civic space available to feminist organizations and the emphasis they place on high-level reform. In Morocco, there have been numerous coalition-building initiatives between women politicians and reform-oriented actors in civil society, including an ongoing national campaign to achieve constitutional parity by 2030 (supported by the German Friedrich-Ebert-Stiftung).[84] At the same time, some women's rights organizations have become skeptical of engaging parliamentarians at the national level, disillusioned by high turnover rates and women legislators' weak engagement on key gender equality issues. Some activists have experienced greater success at the grassroots level, where women's organizations have engaged with locally elected officials on gender-based violence and other women's rights concerns.[85] Furthermore, in countries where antifeminist parties and actors have taken hold of power within parliaments and state institutions, feminist organizations may also prefer more oppositional, disruptive, or grassroots-oriented strategies rather than focusing on high-level policy engagement.[86]

No matter whether feminist and women's rights organizations prioritize insider or outsider strategies, however, their strength tends to lie in their ability to unite across regional, political, and social divisions. Across our four cases, there were many examples of international donors funding women's organizations or networks that include women from civil society. To date, however, international aid programs rarely treat movement-building or strengthening as a goal in and of itself, or as a complementary avenue to strengthening women's descriptive and substantive representation in the political process. One exception is IWDA's WAVE program, which—beyond its activities in Myanmar—also partnered with women's organizations in Cambodia, Timor-Leste, Papua New Guinea, and Solomon Islands. In addition to bolstering women's individual leadership and advancing political and legal reform, the program encouraged feminist movement-building by offering long-term flexible and core funding to women's organizations, providing spaces and tools for local and regional convenings and alliance-building, and nurturing a "movement mindset" among program partners.[87] The initiative exemplifies a more collective approach to women's political representation that can counteract the distortions inherent in flawed and exclusionary political institutions—a theme we return to in Chapters 10 and 11.

Transforming parliamentary institutions

Although efforts to support gender champions and reform constellations move away from a singular focus on women legislators, they still prioritize the activities of *political actors*. Yet as we noted earlier in this chapter, reformers who seek to strengthen women legislators' political influence or advance women's substantive representation also have to contend with significant institutional hurdles. Nearly all parliaments are male-dominated bodies, and heteronormative masculinities are deeply embedded into their structures, procedures, and operations.[88] These cultural norms and practices are often presented as gender-neutral, even when they actively work against the advancement of gender equality. Over the past decade, this insight has given rise to new initiatives that seek to transform parliaments *as institutions* and make them more responsive to gender equality concerns. Internally, such efforts typically seek to ensure more inclusive working arrangements for women parliamentarians and staff, for example by reforming sitting times, codes of conduct, mechanisms for leadership selection, and parental leave and childcare policies. Externally, the goal is to ensure that a gender lens is integrated into all aspects of parliamentary work, including budgeting, legislative development, and oversight.[89]

As noted in Chapter 5, the IPU has acted as a pioneer in this domain, by coining the term "gender-sensitive parliaments" (GSPs), collecting best practices from around the world, and designing self-assessment tools that parliaments can use to evaluate their own reform progress. Other international organizations, including the OSCE, UNDP, and the Commonwealth Parliamentary Association, have built on this framework and developed their own guidelines and tools, drawing on research by gender and politics scholars.[90] Their efforts have helped establish gender-sensitive parliaments as an international democratic norm and drawn greater attention to violence and harassment targeting women in parliaments. In some countries, international organizations have assisted national parliaments with implementing concrete reforms, for example by facilitating gender audits and supporting the implementation of targeted gender equality action plans. Although there have been few studies of the longer-term effects of these efforts, they have had some success in triggering change: Ecuador, Belgium, Georgia, Djibouti, North Macedonia, and Montenegro are among the countries that have revised their parliamentary practices or policies.[91] In Montenegro, for instance, an OSCE-assisted gender action plan prompted amendments to the parliamentary rules of procedure in order to improve women's representation in parliamentary leadership.[92] In 2016, the Kenyan parliament also used the IPU toolkit to carry out a self-assessment, which then informed the country's first gender training for parliamentary staff—though the parliament has yet to institute mechanisms to sensitize male parliamentarians on gender issues.[93]

Even as the concept of a gender-sensitive parliament has gained popularity, programs that support reforms in this vein remain relatively rare. "We have many more tools now than in the past," noted one expert working on women's political empowerment in a European regional organization. "But what has moved more slowly is the *application* of these concepts and tools within parliaments" (emphasis added).[94] A 2018 evaluation of UN Women's work on women's political participation found few examples of interventions that supported gender-sensitive reforms of parliamentary culture and norms; a UNDP review similarly revealed that few country offices had undertaken parliamentary gender audits or assessments.[95] Resource availability is a key obstacle to providing more robust support in this area. The IPU, for instance, does not have regional field offices, and the organization's gender team is small. Other organizations, such as the European Institute for Gender Equality, measure the gender-sensitivity of parliaments within the European Union, but do not provide technical assistance to help resolve the gender inequities that these assessments uncover.[96] Another challenge is the continued tendency of some donors and organizations working with parliaments to view gender equality as a "women's issue," rather than as an issue of institutional reform.[97]

Data from our four cases echo this broader pattern, as we encountered few programs that fully incorporated the GSP framework. However, various programs adopted elements of the approach into their work. In Kenya, UN Women has funded the Society of Clerks at the Table (SOCATT) to train staff members working in county assemblies on gender-responsive budgeting, planning, and reporting, with the hope that they become gender equality advocates and guardians of institutional knowledge.[98] Since 2012, UN Women has also partnered with the Parliamentarians' Working Group for Equality and Parity in Morocco to help its members monitor and harmonize new laws with the country's international commitments on women's rights.[99] The group has successfully integrated gender considerations into the parliament's internal regulations and several pieces of legislation, though it has yet to attain the status of a permanent commission.[100] Finally, in Nepal, UNDP's Parliamentary Support Project has tried to mainstream gender throughout its work, for example by supporting the Women and Social Development Committee in the federal parliament, conducting training sessions on gender-sensitive budgeting, reforming internal parliamentary practices, and helping various committees review legislation through a gender and inclusion lens. The project's final evaluation noted some successes, but its brief and technical discussion of gender issues makes it difficult to assess whether lasting progress was made.[101] A recent study on gender norms in Nepal's parliament found that women parliamentarians still experience significant patriarchal discrimination and exclusion from decision-making processes.[102]

In general, practitioner experiences and research on gender-sensitive parliaments highlight several factors that facilitate lasting reforms. First, changing parliamentary processes typically requires feminist critical actors—such as individual MPs, clerks, or gender equality committees—who encourage international engagement and drive action internally. Just like in political parties, attempts to transform power relations in parliaments tend to trigger resistance, and it is difficult to sustain momentum without the dedication of internal champions.[103] Second, moments of political transition can be important windows of opportunity. These periods come with greater openness to institutional innovation, which can make it easier to establish new ways of working, even if old norms and ideas tend to reassert themselves.[104] Finally, gender audits and similar exercises are only useful to the extent that they come with targeted recommendations that are then institutionalized.[105] Accompaniment and mentoring are often essential to increasing institutional buy-in, given the misunderstandings that surround terms such as "gender analysis." In the long run, parliaments therefore benefit from establishing dedicated gender equality bodies that are adequately empowered and resourced to work with civil society, hold hearings, and scrutinize legislation in order to enable continuous monitoring and reform.[106]

However, some obstacles to parliamentary reform are structural and therefore more difficult to dismantle. In many new democracies, parliaments hold weak institutional power relative to the executive. They sometimes play only limited roles in introducing legislation and exercise little oversight over budgeting and spending. In these institutional contexts, aid providers seeking to promote gender-sensitive budgeting and similar reforms must confront the fact that parliamentarians likely lack access to sex-disaggregated data or may not be empowered to question the decisions and allocations of the executive branch.[107] For international actors and their local partners, this challenge underscores the need to anchor their work in a detailed political economy analysis that identifies the constraints on and incentives for parliamentary action.[108]

The challenge of limited legislative independence also raises bigger strategic questions. The GSP framework sets out a more holistic approach to women's descriptive and substantive representation, one that moves away from an exclusive focus on women legislators toward institutional and sociocultural levers for change. To date, however, programmatic tools and resources on gender equality in parliaments have only weakly engaged with problems of democratic erosion or autocratic co-optation. What does it mean to support gender-sensitive parliaments in contexts that are not fully democratic? How should reformers work with parliaments that seek to implement gender-sensitive reforms while falling short on other measures of representation and inclusion? These questions point toward new areas for research and reflection, for scholars of gender and politics and for practitioners alike.

Conclusion

Around the world, women's parliamentary gains have given rise to new aid initiatives aimed at translating their legislative presence into meaningful political power. Guiding this work are two related goals: first, to ensure that women legislators have the knowledge and capacity to fulfill their roles and, second, to better integrate women's interests and perspectives into political decision-making. For many international actors, the starting point has been to fund and implement capacity-building interventions for women representatives or to support the creation and activities of women's caucuses. Evidence from across our cases suggests that such efforts can indeed be effective at bolstering women's skills, knowledge, and engagement for gender equality, especially if they center women's self-identified needs. In Kenya, Nepal, and Myanmar, formal and informal caucuses have also served as platforms for training, coordination, and information-sharing; in some cases, they have successfully advanced legislative reforms focused on gender equality.

Yet these approaches are rarely sufficient to ensure women's equal political power and integrate gender perspectives into the legislative process. Women legislators are not always capable or willing to advocate for gender equality reforms, nor are they necessarily representative of women's diverse perspectives and experiences. Moreover, the institutional context often limits their ability to exercise political influence. This chapter, therefore, explored several complementary approaches that have received less attention from assistance providers, including a focus on nurturing critical actors, support for women's movements and feminist coalition-building, and activities that promote gender-sensitive parliamentary reforms. These models represent promising innovations, but they currently make up only a small fraction of aid initiatives targeting parliaments and local governments.

PART III

NEW FRONTIERS

‖ 9 ‖

Tackling Patriarchal Gender Norms

When Rose decided to run for a seat in her county assembly in Western Kenya, she was a young woman who lacked any links to the senior leaders of her political party, the Orange Democratic Movement. After launching her campaign, she quickly learned that she was not the local powerholders' preferred candidate. "I was threatened so much," she recalls. "Some people actually threatened to send gangs to come and rape me, so that I would forget about all this nonsense about vying." Even though Kenya's Electoral Code of Conduct bans political parties from engaging in violence, Rose faced a wave of threats.[1] Her campaign team advised her to go to the police, but she refused. "Even if I do go, what am I reporting and who am I reporting? Do I have evidence that this was even said? They are not going to act."[2]

Rose's experience is common among female candidates, activists, and politicians in Kenya and elsewhere. For women, particularly those from historically marginalized groups, politics can be a hostile and even violent space. By entering a domain that has traditionally been reserved for men, they challenge entrenched gender norms that associate public leadership with masculinity, which triggers both overt and covert patriarchal resistance. Although such backlash against women's political participation is not new, it has become more visible as more women have entered the political sphere. Across different political and cultural contexts, women politicians, candidates, and voters report being targeted with intimidation, rumors, and attacks that are often explicitly sexual and gendered in nature.[3] They also encounter more subtle forms of marginalization and exclusion, including political elites who subvert or circumvent gender equality reforms in order to preserve their dominant status.[4]

For practitioners designing interventions to advance women's political empowerment, these varied forms of resistance have raised new and difficult challenges. As described in the previous chapters, international assistance to date has primarily focused on bolstering women's individual capacity and encouraging institutional reforms within political parties, electoral bodies, and

Aiding Empowerment. Saskia Brechenmacher and Katherine Mann, Oxford University Press.
© Oxford University Press 2024. DOI: 10.1093/oso/9780197694275.003.0009

parliaments. Recognizing that gender norms are slow to transform, many advocates and practitioners put their faith in legal and institutional change and in the symbolic power of women's political leadership. They hoped that women, once in positions of authority, would challenge existing gender stereotypes and gradually transform the attitudes of resistant voters and powerholders.

Yet as women's political participation around the world has increased, it has become clear that democracy-support practitioners and local gender equality advocates have sometimes underestimated the strong headwinds of patriarchal resistance.[5] Time and again, their efforts to reform institutions have been stymied by male gatekeepers' weak reform commitment, by the persistence of informal male political networks, and, in some cases, by outright pushback, including within women's own families and communities. In the face of stunted progress, the obstacles posed by male resistance, sexism, and violence have come into much sharper focus than in the past.

In this chapter, we turn to two areas of research, advocacy, and programming that have emerged as entry points to address these challenges: on the one hand, new initiatives that engage men in dismantling patriarchal norms and institutions and, on the other, a growing range of transnational, regional, and local efforts to counter violence and harassment against women in politics. These approaches seek to tackle discriminatory gender norms from two different angles—by altering the attitudes and behaviors of male powerholders, and by strengthening accountability for harassment and abuse. Together, they represent a strategy to overcome gendered power imbalances in politics that recognizes men as important agents of change. Yet they also push democracy aid providers into unfamiliar and difficult territory, marked by uncertainty about which approaches work in different settings and how to measure success.

The long shadow of patriarchal norms

All societies are shaped by culturally entrenched gender norms, the "invisible guardrails" that set out how women and men are expected to behave.[6] Globally, one recurring pattern is a gendered division of roles that assigns women the primary responsibility for (unpaid) domestic labor, particularly cooking and childcare, and tasks men with leadership in the public sphere. Patriarchal gender norms also construct hierarchies that demand women's submission to male authority both within the household and in society, regulate women's sexuality and mobility in the name of preserving family honor, and restrict women's ability to make choices about their own lives.

These patterns produce lasting biases toward women's political leadership. According to the World Values Survey Wave 7, conducted across 100 countries between 2017 and 2022, only 52.8 percent of people agree that equal rights between men and women are an essential characteristic of democracy. Slightly more than one-third also agree or strongly agree that men make better leaders than women, though more men than women hold this view. In many parts of Asia, the Middle East, and North Africa, attitudes about gender equality and women's political leadership are significantly more conservative. In Myanmar, Pakistan, Egypt, and Tajikistan, for example, over 70 percent of people regard men as more capable leaders.[7] General attitudes about gender equality also vary widely and are not necessarily shifting in a more progressive direction. For example, over the past twelve years, support for gender equality and women's empowerment has grown in Germany, Singapore, New Zealand, and Japan; meanwhile, attitudes in Korea, Chile, Iraq, and Mexico have become more conservative.[8]

Discriminatory gender norms constrain women's political participation at multiple levels. For one, they perpetuate structural inequities that prevent women from engaging in politics in the first place, by leaving them with less time, education, and resources. They also shape who people think belongs in the political sphere. In places where norms that associate politics with masculinity remain strong, women may be less likely to consider a political career and those who seek out political roles must often contend with pushback.

Yet even in more gender-egalitarian societies, entrenched gender norms can have discriminatory effects and produce biased assessments of women leaders. In Kenya, Afrobarometer data shows that almost nine out of ten Kenyans say women should have the same chance as men of being elected to public office. Yet more than half also believe that women politicians are more likely to be criticized or harassed.[9] Research conducted in the United States similarly finds that male politicians are often rewarded for being ambitious and power-seeking, whereas women who display these same traits are seen as deviating from gender stereotypes that frame women as more "communal" and become targets of backlash.[10]

Finally, as noted in previous chapters, gender discriminatory norms are often "baked" into political institutions such as parties and parliaments. For instance, many parliaments around the world until now lack policies on sexual harassment, childcare facilities, or provisions for parental leave. Within parties, male party officials still often view men who resemble themselves as more capable political leaders than women. These biases are sometimes reinforced by institutional practices, such as late-night meetings, that make it difficult for women with household responsibilities to participate.[11]

These patterns raise an important question: how and when do norms about gender and politics change, and what can be done to accelerate this process? Existing research finds that gender norms tend to be sticky, lagging behind changes in the material circumstances of men's and women's lives.[12] Even as the world has witnessed dramatic increases in women's access to education, employment, and political office over the past quarter-century, the overall change in cultural attitudes about gender equality has been comparatively slow.[13] At the same time, discriminatory gender norms, including those about women's political leadership, are not immutable. Economic growth, prolonged conflict, and urbanization have all catalyzed changes in norms by pushing women into more socially valued roles, thereby shifting people's attitudes and beliefs over time.[14] Legal reforms, women's rights movements, government messaging, and media representations have also played important norm-changing roles in many societies, by altering people's perceptions of what *other people* think or do.

In the political sphere, some evidence suggests that increases in women's political representation fuel rising popular support for gender equality in leadership.[15] Yet this correlation is not universal, and evolving public attitudes are usually not sufficient to eliminate all forms of resistance or transform sexist organizational cultures. In some instances, the implementation of quotas and other gender equality measures can also produce a sense of group threat among male politicians and, in turn, fuel various forms of backlash.[16]

Democracy assistance actors have traditionally shied away from questions of gender norm change. Structural economic and political shifts are beyond the scope of typical democracy aid programs: two- to five-year timelines hardly lend themselves to gradual processes of social transformation. Moreover, aid organizations typically prefer activities with tangible "outputs" to demonstrate that their investments are making a difference. It is easier to document changes in laws and policies or the number of women participating in politics than it is to capture shifts in norms, whether among ordinary citizens or political elites. Social norms and practices are also sensitive areas for international involvement, as work on these issues can give rise to perceptions of cultural imperialism.

When democracy aid organizations have tried to influence societal norms and attitudes, they have often focused on political entry points to gender norm change. International standard-setting has been one important area of action, with organizations such as the IPU and UN Women working to shape global norms related to women's political inclusion.[17] At the country level, donors have also funded civic education initiatives, programs encouraging gender-sensitive media coverage, and campaigns that seek to normalize women's participation in politics. For example, USAID has sponsored fictional television series in Morocco (titled "Madam President") and Nepal (titled "Singha Durbar") that aim to normalize and promote women's leadership.[18] Similarly, in Kenya, the EU has funded a reality television show called "Ms President," in which women contestants showcase their leadership abilities.[19] But the impact of these media initiatives is hard to evaluate, as it is difficult to discern who is watching and how media portrayals of women in politics are affecting their beliefs.[20] Moreover, such programs do not directly address one of the most acute manifestations of patriarchal norms in politics: the discriminatory attitudes and behaviors of male gatekeepers who feel threatened by women's increased political engagement.

Engaging men as stakeholders

A recent set of interventions is trying to fill this gap by foregrounding men as agents of gender equality change in politics. When tackling the cultural barriers to women's political leadership, men are, by necessity, front and center. Married women in heterosexual partnerships often need their husbands' support to run a successful political campaign. In some traditional societies, they may also need male family members' permission or accompaniment to vote or participate in other political activities.[21] In Morocco, for example, a 2010 survey found that 62 percent of women felt restricted to leave their homes without the permission of either their husband or parents.[22] Beyond the household, men in cultural or religious leadership roles sometimes play important roles in selecting candidates. As we have explored in previous chapters, elite men also dominate leadership positions within political institutions and thus influence women's political advancement and access to decision-making.

The idea that men need to be involved in gender equality change is, of course, nothing new. Within the international development field, initiatives along these lines first took root in the 1980s and 1990s among feminist groups working to combat gender-based violence and prevent the spread of HIV/AIDS. These efforts have since expanded to new areas, including care work, education, and women's economic empowerment.[23] Until recently, however, few democracy assistance actors were familiar with this body of work. Interventions to advance women's political empowerment engaged men as targets of advocacy or to obtain their buy-in for a particular activity, but not as essential partners and allies.[24] As a result, there are few studies or programming strategies focused on transforming patriarchal gender norms within political organizations and institutions, in contrast to a much larger field of research and practice focused on norm change within households and local communities. Even as references to "engaging men and boys" and transforming masculinities have multiplied in policy documents, many actors in the democracy community are only now catching up with learning accumulated in public health, sociology, and other fields.[25]

Over the course of our research, this gap was particularly evident in Morocco, Myanmar, and Nepal. Women's rights advocates, women politicians, and practitioners in these countries underscored the importance of working with women's male relatives, community gatekeepers, and political actors. Yet while some described small-scale or ad hoc efforts along these lines, few had observed or participated in systematic interventions. Kenya presents a somewhat different picture: in recent years, several initiatives have targeted male community leaders to gain their support for women's political leadership.

Looking across our four cases and drawing on our review of programming tools and interviews with donors and aid practitioners, we identify three basic models of engagement that have emerged in recent years. We term these approaches the *awareness-raising* model, the *allyship* model, and the *norm transformation* model (see Table 9.1). The awareness-raising model is the most

Table 9.1 **Male Engagement: Three Intervention Models**

Model	*Theory of Change*	*Example*
Raising awareness	If male participants are aware of the challenges facing women politicians and recognize the value of gender equality, they will change their behaviors and foster a more enabling environment for women in politics	Training and engaging female and male party members on the value of women's political leadership
Cultivating male allies	If respected male leaders take action to support women's political participation, others in their communities will adjust their views and behaviors accordingly, creating a more enabling environment for women's political empowerment	Recruiting male leaders to speak out on behalf of female candidates and women's political leadership and condemn violence against women in politics
Transforming gender norms among men	If men recognize the harmful effects patriarchal gender norms have on themselves and their communities, they will be more likely to challenge these norms and adjust discriminatory behaviors, creating a more enabling environment for women politicians	Facilitating workshops with male political leaders that encourage them to reflect on and deconstruct their own gender biases, listen to and engage with women's political experiences, and develop action plans

common programming strategy. As the name suggests, it involves increasing the buy-in of male politicians, public officials, and voters by raising their awareness of gendered barriers in politics and highlighting the benefits of women's political inclusion. Common tactics include inviting male leaders to participate in events focused on women's political rights, discussing women's political leadership in bilateral exchanges with parties or in civic education campaigns, and offering gender equality training to both male and female politicians.

This model assumes that men are unaware of the challenges women face in politics or underappreciate the benefits of women's political inclusion, and that new information will change their attitudes and behavior. However, the underlying theory of change behind these efforts is rarely explicitly articulated, let alone empirically tested. For example, men may leave training seminars on gender topics still convinced that gender equality is "women's responsibility," particularly if there are no follow-up mechanisms to incentivize and measure behavioral or policy changes. As Cheema et al. (2022) argue in a study of a get-out-the-vote campaign in Pakistan, whether or not short-term awareness-raising interventions work may depend on how permissive or restrictive gender norms are to begin with. In contexts where male gatekeeping presents various logistical or other hurdles, interventions that share practical information and encourage men to take action may prove effective if norms are *already* permissive of women's political engagement. On the other hand, the same awareness-raising model may not work well in contexts or issue areas where gender norms are more restrictive.[26]

A second model—the allyship model—engages men as allies and advocates for women's political participation, thereby challenging the idea that "gender work" is done by, with, and for women. This approach leverages the power of role models to change community norms. If a prominent and well-respected male authority figure takes action to support women's political participation, others in the community may be more likely to adjust their own beliefs. In some cases, this form of coalition-building with male allies happens informally. For example, women's organizations and women politicians sometimes ask male legislators to sponsor gender equality legislation to cultivate broader support for their initiatives. Yet some programs also try to cultivate male gender champions in a more systematic manner, by training the spouses of women political leaders or recruiting traditional leaders and respected male community members to speak out on behalf of women's political participation.[27]

UN Women's global #HeforShe Campaign is one of the best-known illustrations of this approach. The campaign encourages male leaders to make specific commitments to gender equality.[28] At the grassroots level, GROOTS Kenya's Champions for Transformative Leadership program, which has received funding from UN Women, USAID, the European Union, and others, is another example.[29] Focusing on three Kenyan counties, the program recruited a network of 650 men, including the spouses of women leaders, to publicly support the constitutional provision for a mandatory gender quota and to provide direct support to women candidates during party primaries and general elections. These "male champions" lobbied elders, religious leaders, and other opinion leaders to change community perceptions, in addition to providing physical security to women candidates.[30]

Lastly, a newer (and related) set of programs focuses explicitly on transforming the patriarchal gender norms held by male political actors, most often through targeted dialogues and learning workshops. The norm transformation model encourages men and boys to question and dismantle their own beliefs about masculinity as well as behaviors that justify gender inequality, and then guides them to action in their own lives and organizations.[31] Although these initiatives place a stronger emphasis on individual-level change, they overlap with allyship interventions: for example, men who go through a process of norm transformation may become role models for gender equality change in their own communities. There are still relatively few examples of programs that apply this approach to the political sphere (as opposed to reproductive health, childcare, and gender-based violence). In the next section, we briefly describe two initiatives that have sought to fill this gap: the "Male Allies for Leadership Equality" program launched by IFES and the "Men, Power and Politics" approach developed by NDI.

Transforming masculinities

In the democracy assistance field, IFES was among the first actors to develop a programming strategy that focuses on men as agents of gender equality change. In 2015, the organization received funding from USAID to launch its "Male Allies for Leadership Equality" program, which works with male political leaders to foster greater collaboration between women and men in politics. The program was designed to accompany women's leadership initiatives, thereby complementing aid providers' traditional focus on building women's confidence and skills with activities targeting men.[32] This approach builds on an important lesson learned from past "male engagement" efforts, namely that gender-synchronized programs targeting both women and men (separately and together) are more effective than those working with each group in isolation.[33]

IFES's program is structured around a curriculum that covers topics ranging from communication to questions of power, gender bias, and household equality. Participants meet in single- and mixed-sex sessions to exchange their experiences and views, guided by an expert facilitator. The curriculum was initially designed based on focus group discussions conducted with women and men in Nigeria and Syria, though it has since been adapted to different cultural and institutional contexts.[34] In 2021, for example, the program was implemented as part of a women's leadership initiative in Pakistan. Women leaders were trained to promote women's voter registration in their community, whereas men in the same communities were trained to partner with and support them.[35] To date, however, IFES has lacked the resources to rigorously evaluate its approach, beyond pre- and postintervention tests of participants' knowledge and attitudes. As a result, it is difficult to assess whether or under what conditions the program has succeeded at shifting discriminatory gender norms and behaviors, particularly in the long run.[36]

Over the past several years, the Gender, Women and Democracy team at NDI has also expanded its work on engaging men as agents of gender equality change. The organization's "Men, Power and Politics" approach relies on a three-part theory of change: first, encourage male political actors to reflect on their personal experiences with gender norms; second, lead them to recognize how gender norms impact political structures; and third, help them devise specific strategies to enact change within their organizations.[37] The program is structured around a series of workshops with male political leaders that can be integrated into different types of democracy interventions, whether they target civil society, political parties, or other institutions. The strategy also involves women politicians and local women's groups who can hold male political leaders accountable to their commitments.

In 2019, NDI first piloted this approach in the Democratic Republic of the Congo (DRC). In partnership with the local organization COMEN, program staff recruited male party leaders from the country's five major political parties, which are heavily male-dominated organizations.[38] Early discussion sessions revealed that male participants were open to unpacking the gender norms shaping their personal lives, but they were less open to critically examining their political activities. To address this challenge, some of the male participants were invited to learn about the experiences of women within their respective parties, and then asked to educate other male party members about what they had learned and to develop action plans. This approach strengthened gender equitable attitudes among the participants, who reported participating more actively in domestic chores and care work at home. But it failed to significantly change their behavior within their parties, and women party members remained skeptical of male leaders' commitment to meaningful change.[39]

The need for learning

Despite the growing consensus that engaging men matters for gender equality change in politics, much remains unknown about which strategies are most effective across different institutional contexts. Building out this field of practice will require democracy aid providers to test new programming tools—such as NDI's Male, Power and Politics approach—in various settings and compare their findings. It will also require them to expand their skill set in measuring social norm change. In practice, shifts in awareness, norms, attitudes, and behaviors are often conflated: organizations may think they are contributing to norm change but lack the right tools to measure whether such shifts are taking place.[40]

Existing programs as well as learning in adjacent fields highlight some initial lessons for democracy aid organizations. First, recruiting male allies to serve as role models and advocates has proven to be a promising strategy, especially if these men exert high levels of influence in their communities. In Kenya, for example, women's rights activists note that engaging traditional leaders and community-level male champions has made a difference, particularly in rural communities characterized by conservative gender norms. In some cases, engagement efforts have triggered changes in attitudes among the male champions themselves, while also increasing community buy-in and allowing women to access spaces and meetings that have traditionally been closed to them.[41] At the national level, women legislators have also successfully advanced gender equality laws by nurturing alliances with male parliamentarians.[42]

However, developing allyship takes time, resources, and local networks, and it cannot be done as part of a short-term activity a few weeks before an election. Moreover, male allies must be carefully chosen. Allyship interventions always come with the risk that male leaders will leverage gender equality talking points to advance their own political agenda, while behaving in ways that hinder or undermine women's political empowerment. "Every single male politician in the country has said some very nice words about women in leadership," one Kenyan aid official told us. "But very few have gone to translate that into actual action on the ground."[43] In most cases, women's organizations with in-depth local knowledge are best positioned to identify individuals who are both genuinely committed *and* influential in their communities.

The risk of co-optation points to a broader tension: allyship interventions that rely on men as reform champions may inadvertently reinforce rather than challenge elite men's dominant status. Calling on male leaders to stand up for women's political empowerment can play into the narrative that men act as paternalistic protectors and valorize the masculinity of already dominant men, while excluding men in more marginalized positions or men who do not fit traditional gender binaries or conceptions of masculinity.[44] This problem highlights the need to pay close attention to status differentials among men, which may also impact their attitudes and behaviors toward women.

Aid providers and local partners also confront the reality that some male powerholders benefit from unequal power relations in politics. In the fields of public health or economic development, norm change interventions often incentivize men to participate by emphasizing the shared gains of gender equality change, such as better health outcomes or greater financial security.[45] In electoral politics, however, increasing women's political influence, particularly through quotas, inevitably results in greater political competition for men, especially for those lower down the political ladder. Although assistance providers can emphasize the potential organizational benefits of women's inclusion for parties and parliaments, such as greater democratic legitimacy, these rationales may not be convincing in all contexts.

Given these challenges, several decades of male engagement efforts in public health and other fields underscore that for allyship as well as norm transformation interventions, accountability to feminist movements and goals is essential.[46] Not surprisingly, as donor interest in uprooting patriarchal gender norms and transforming masculinities has skyrocketed, some women's rights advocates worry that women's interests will get sidelined in favor of poorly conceived male engagement programs, particularly given that feminist groups around the world still struggle to access resources. "We don't want to get to a point where all the gender equality money is going to funding men's programming and building the capacity of men," cautioned one US aid official.[47] Some women politicians are also wary of such initiatives: given the hostile political landscape that they must navigate, they mistrust men's intentions and fear exploitation. Common strategies for ensuring accountability to feminist goals include working in collaboration with local women's organizations, using gender-synchronized approaches that involve both women and men, and measuring tangible outcomes for women alongside changes in male attitudes.[48] The end goal of a program should not be that men espouse more gender-egalitarian attitudes, but that they take concrete actions that measurably improve women's political participation and influence.

Lastly, the field must grapple with questions about the scale and sustainability of norm change interventions. Existing evidence underscores that it can be difficult for small-scale activities to disrupt gender hierarchies. Take the example of another program implemented in the DRC, this one with the aim of reducing intimate partner violence. For four months, male participants participated in weekly discussion groups focused on promoting gender equality in household labor and questioning existing gender norms. Yet even though the participants were willing to change their quotidian practices and became more involved in household chores, the program's evaluation found that they were not willing to abandon the belief that men are natural household leaders or share power with their wives, perhaps out of fear of social sanction.[49] As noted above, NDI's intervention to influence gender norms within Congolese political parties similarly struggled to convince male party leaders to change their political practices.[50] These initial findings underscore that there are many open questions about whether and how individual-level changes translate into organizational or systemic transformation, and what time horizons are needed. Long-term interventions that advance gender equality change at multiple levels and carefully track changes in norms, behaviors, and outcomes over time are likely to be essential.

Fighting violence and backlash

A second area of action that has received increasing policy and aid attention addresses violence against women in politics. Violence is the most overt manifestation of patriarchal norms in politics. Whether they are serving as local councilors in rural Nepal or running for congressional office in the United States, women cite violence, harassment, and abuse from voters, colleagues, and competitors as pervasive challenges hindering their full and equal political participation. In the most egregious cases, violence takes the form of physical attacks, sexual assault, or the destruction of property. But women are also subject to a much wider and often less visible spectrum of abuse, ranging from threats, intimidation, and insults to false rumors that are spread both offline and online.[51] For instance, a survey of men and women on Kenyan university campuses conducted by NDI found that nearly a quarter of politically active women respondents had experienced online violence.[52] A practitioner working in Myanmar similarly described "endless stories of women [in politics] being attacked online, sexualized, their families are attacked [...]. It is still very difficult for women to declare political positions given online harassment."[53]

In the past, such violence has often been dismissed as the "cost of politics"—an unfortunate phenomenon, but one that simply comes with the territory of engaging in electoral politics. And indeed, existing research shows that male political actors also experience violence, threats, and abuse, particularly in contexts characterized by weaknesses in the rule of law.[54] Yet the experiences of men and women are not the same. A growing body of research underscores that women are targeted at much higher rates than their male counterparts, and often in explicitly gendered and sexualized ways. Studies conducted in the Maldives, Sri Lanka, Sweden, the United Kingdom, and the United States all show that women are more likely to face various forms of psychological abuse, and, in some cases, higher rates of physical intimidation, especially if they occupy highly visible political positions.[55] Moreover, acts of violence against women in politics tend to follow explicitly gendered scripts. Whereas men are attacked based on their political work and competence, perpetrators focus on and highlight women's bodies, sexuality, and their traditional social roles as mothers or wives. Women belonging to minority groups and those occupying highly visible positions are particularly vulnerable.[56] Implicit is the message that women or members of other marginalized groups do not belong in the political sphere *because of their identity.*[57]

This violence and intimidation can have profoundly negative effects on women's political participation. In India, Nepal, and Pakistan, for instance, between 60 and 70 percent of respondents in a UN Women–funded survey stated that "women do participate in politics because they are afraid of violence."[58] In Kenya, many of the women we interviewed also pointed to gendered violence and abuse as one of the main reasons why women are less interested in pursuing political careers, or opt to compete for appointed positions rather than elective posts that put them in direct competition with men. On the campaign trail, women candidates described taking additional measures to ensure their safety, including hiring male security agents, staying at relatives' houses, and avoiding certain types of political rallies.[59] Online violence takes an additional toll on women politicians' mental health and well-being, particularly since digital harassment and slur campaigns often spread quickly and make it difficult to distinguish between real and fake threats.[60]

International attention to these challenges was first raised by women politicians and activists giving voice to their own experiences. Starting in the late 1990s, women councilors in Bolivia began mobilizing against systematic efforts by male politicians to coerce them out of political office. They drew on international and domestic legal frameworks on gender-based violence and democracy to push for state action. Over time, their activism caught the attention of international organizations and democracy aid actors who heard similar stories of male resistance, violence, and backlash in other countries.[61] Given the widespread normalization of violence in political life, these organizations' initial response was to document the contours of the problem.[62] Noting that many conventional measures of political violence failed to capture women's experiences, they began collecting new data that could inform awareness-raising efforts and targeted policy responses.

Strengthening the evidence base has undoubtedly been one of the democracy aid community's most significant contributions to fighting violence against women in politics. Over the past six years, data collection efforts have multiplied. In 2011, IFES became one of the first organizations to document the gendered dimensions of electoral violence. The organization has since developed a formal framework for monitoring and measuring violence against women in elections, launched an analysis tool to capture online threats and abusive rhetoric targeting women political actors, and published assessments of violence against women in politics in Bangladesh, Papua New Guinea (and the autonomous region of Bougainville), Zimbabwe, and Haiti.[63] Meanwhile, NDI has collected cross-national data on violence against women politicians in political parties and online, and trained citizen election observation groups in various countries to monitor gendered violence during elections.[64] The IPU, on the other hand, has relied on its global network to conduct surveys about women parliamentarians' experiences of violence, and UN Women has convened international expert meetings in order to share and harmonize different data collection tools.[65] These research efforts have generated new guidance on policy responses, including best practices for political parties, for combating online violence against politically active women, and for preventing gendered violence in politics more generally.[66] In sum, policymakers and practitioners now have access to considerably more detailed information about the problem and its potential solutions, even as efforts to build comparable cross-national measures continue.

A multidimensional problem

New programmatic strategies have emerged in tandem with these evidence-gathering initiatives. However, translating evidence into action is far from straightforward in this area. Violence against women in politics is an inherently multidimensional problem, rooted in harmful gender norms and exacerbated by institutional and policy failures by political parties, election management bodies, judicial and law enforcement authorities, and social media platforms. It impacts women voters, candidates, elected officials, and civil society activists and journalists. Responses therefore involve many different actors and entry points, from grassroots activism to high-level legislative and normative change. Given this complexity, scholars and practitioners have identified three broad strategies that work in tandem to mitigate and prevent violent backlash: raising awareness of the problem, supporting legal and regulatory reforms and enforcement measures, and providing security training and support services to politically active women.[67]

For democracy support organizations, awareness-raising and advocacy has emerged as a particularly common area of action. Most prominently, NDI in 2016 launched its #NotTheCost campaign, a "global call to action" that outlines strategies for reform-minded governments and organizations and presses the UN and other international and regional organizations to prioritize the issue.[68] The fruits of this effort and other campaigns have been visible at the multilateral level, where advocates have successfully integrated the issue into existing normative frameworks and transnational mechanisms focused on gender equality and democracy. In October 2018, for instance, the UN Special Rapporteur on Violence against Women presented the first-ever thematic report on violence against women in politics to the UN General Assembly, which subsequently informed the first UN resolution calling on states to address the issue.[69] According to one UN official, "at the highest level of the UN, it has now been established in writing that this is a priority."[70]

At the regional level, efforts to strengthen international norms and create binding commitments are particularly advanced in Latin America. Most prominently, in 2015, the Conference of States Party to the Belém do Pará Convention adopted a Declaration on Political Harassment and Violence against Women. Building on this interstate commitment, the Committee of Experts of the Follow-up Mechanism to the Belém do Pará Convention (MESECVI) developed an Inter-American Model Law on the Prevention, Punishment and Eradication of Violence Against Women in Political Life to guide domestic legislative reforms.[71] These commitments have provided critical advocacy tools for activists and reformers, generated greater political awareness among governments, and fueled important legislative developments.[72]

Progress is more difficult to assess at the country level. The political salience of gendered political violence varies from country to country, and international actors have been more engaged on the issue in some places than in others. UN Women, in partnership with regional actors, has helped support legislative frameworks to criminalize different forms of violence and harassment against women in politics, drawing on its convening strength and technical expertise in electoral reform. Progress on this front has also been most pronounced in Latin America, where multiple countries—including Bolivia, Argentina, Ecuador, Peru, and Mexico—have either adopted stand-alone laws, incorporated gendered political violence into existing legislation, or passed new electoral regulations and protocols. Legal reforms have been more limited in other parts of the world.[73]

In Africa and elsewhere, however, both UNDP and UN Women have also trained election officials, law enforcement, and judicial actors to identify and respond to gendered political violence.[74] Other democracy support organizations have supported civil society advocacy and monitoring initiatives. In Colombia, for example, NIMD has collaborated with NDI, UN Women, and other organizations to form an Observatory on Violence Against Women in Politics that monitors and analyzes incidents and helps inform national legislation.[75]

We also observed considerable variation in international engagement on the issue across our four cases. International democracy support actors were more involved in funding and supporting activities focused on violence against women in politics in Kenya and Myanmar than in Morocco and Nepal. Yet this discrepancy does not necessarily mean that the issue is less severe in the latter two countries. In Nepal, for example, one women's rights activist described "rampant harassment and violence against women involved in politics [...] at home, in the community, institutions, and even in parliament."[76] Yet although international actors working in Nepal have supported data collection and research on the issue, there were no ongoing programs or initiatives focused gendered political violence at the time of our research.[77]

By contrast, in Kenya, high levels of sexual and gender-based violence during previous election cycles have fueled strong attention to the problem ahead of elections. Local advocates and international aid providers have identified weak responses by the Kenyan security forces as a key contributor to the problem: an analysis conducted after the 2017 polls found that law enforcement lacked sufficient capacity to adequately address sexual and gender-based violence targeting voters and candidates, and that many survivors lacked information about their reporting options.[78] In the lead-up to the 2022 elections, UN Women therefore prioritized convening police forces, rights advocates, election officials, and political parties to streamline their responses to gendered political violence.[79] With support from the Italian government, UN Women and the Office of the UN High Commissioner for Human Rights in Kenya also trained police commanders and officers working in four hotspot locations and supported human rights advocates to spread awareness about reporting options and referral pathways.[80] In the past, various international actors have also worked with electoral stakeholders to strengthen dispute resolution processes and established national gender-based violence hotlines to assist the tracking and referral of cases.

Have these initiatives made a difference? On the one hand, aid officials have observed some improvements in cooperation between law enforcement authorities and women's rights advocates, including during the 2022 election.[81] At the same time, gender-based political violence remains a substantial threat. Although the Independent Policing Oversight Authority announced that only one case of sexual and gender-based violence was reported to the police during the latest round of voting, a study commissioned by the Federation of Women Lawyers in Kenya identified 157 cases of violence against women in the seven days before and after election day alone.[82] Moreover, various forms of low-level violence and intimidation persist: our interviews with women aspirants and candidates across different parts of the country suggest that threats, defamation, and verbal attacks remain significant obstacles deterring women from joining competitive primary races.[83] This problem speaks in part to the continued failure of political parties to enforce strict codes of conduct among their members and candidates. Online harassment targeting female candidates and politicians has also emerged as a pressing and underaddressed policy issue, particularly since online incidents are rarely reported to authorities.[84]

Online violence targeting women political leaders was also a major challenge in Myanmar, in addition to attacks by political opponents, armed groups, and security forces.[85] A few democracy support organizations developed programmatic responses. For example, NDI integrated a gender lens into its support for citizen-led election monitoring to ensure that local groups had the tools to identify and report online and offline violence targeting female candidates. Some organizations also worked with Facebook to support the digital literacy and security of women politicians.[86] Yet the issue of online hate speech was politically sensitive, which complicated international action. Ahead of the 2020 elections, IFES planned an awareness-raising campaign about online violence targeting women candidates that ran into both local and international resistance. "People felt it was too hot of a topic," one person involved in the initiative told us. "It was the first time we ran up against something related to gender that was too hot to touch."[87] Other international actors acknowledged the severity of the problem but did not develop targeted responses. One staff member at an international democracy organization admitted that their programming "did not respond to [violence against women in politics] beyond acknowledging and identifying it as a barrier. In terms of a response, it was less beneficial."[88]

Adapting to new threats

To summarize, multilateral organizations, democracy aid actors, and women's rights advocates have made significant progress raising global awareness of the violence facing women in the political sphere. Their data collection and advocacy efforts have helped name and conceptualize the problem, influenced international and regional frameworks, and generated a large toolbox of policy and intervention options. In some countries, they have also trained law enforcement and electoral authorities, supported civil society advocacy and monitoring, and offered direct services and training to women leaders. All these efforts will likely remain important priorities in the coming years. Assisting with legal and regulatory reforms is a logical area for continued international support, given international organizations' capacity to convene multiple stakeholders, generate reform pressure, and share transnational expertise. In countries where new laws and protocols have already been passed, next steps should focus on generating more knowledge about their implementation in order for advocates to understand whether and how these new tools are impacting women's safety.

At the same time, new threats and challenges have emerged that demand more concerted international action. One pressing issue is the worrisome rise of online violence and abuse targeting women leaders—which manifests as routine sexist harassment and trolling as well as organized disinformation and hate speech used to silence women opponents and critics.[89] In Iran, China, and Russia, for example, state-sponsored entities have deployed false or misleading sexualized narratives against prominent women journalists, thereby unleashing waves of online abuse against them.[90] Another recent study uncovered similar campaigns in Poland and the Philippines, where women who opposed or criticized the state were targeted with sexualized and gendered narratives and attacks.[91]

State and state-aligned actors' use of online attacks to vilify women leaders underscores another global challenge: violence against women in politics appears to flourish in contexts of democratic erosion and heightened political extremism. In the United States and United Kingdom, for instance, rising political polarization has been correlated with increasing abuses targeting political figures, a pattern that disproportionately impacts women and minority groups.[92] In several authoritarian and backsliding countries, including in Russia, Turkey, Hungary, Brazil, and the Philippines, governments with explicitly antifeminist agendas have also intentionally *weakened* legal protections sanctioning gender-based violence and cracked down on women's rights activists who challenge their socially conservative ideals.[93] This form of backlash can facilitate violence against politically active women by encouraging sanctions against those who openly challenge patriarchal power structures.[94]

Many policymakers, practitioners, and women's rights advocates are still grappling with this new political environment. Research and policy responses to online disinformation and digital security challenges remain fragmented, and their gendered effects often go unacknowledged. Further complicating responses is the difficulty of bringing together both policymakers and technology companies, which have been slow to address gendered harassment and abuse on their platforms. Moreover, in flawed democracies or authoritarian contexts, partnering with government authorities is rarely an option, particularly if political leaders condone or are complicit in violence and harassment.

Despite these challenges, there are many useful measures that democracy aid providers and organizations can take to advance the field. They can use their convening power to act as conduits between social media platforms and gender experts and organizations in the Global South or bring together and train the relevant stakeholders in different countries to advance context-specific policy responses and government regulations. They can also share tools for self-protection and security with activists and organizations.[95] Finally, in places impacted by illiberalism and backsliding, they can support political coalitions that challenge antidemocratic and antifeminist political projects from the bottom up.

Creating a political environment that is safe for all women and marginalized communities also requires advocates and reformers to address the underlying socio-cultural norms and attitudes that drive and enable gendered and racialized violence. Short-term interventions to prevent and combat such violence can only get at a piece of the puzzle.[96] These efforts need to be accompanied by proactive and sustained investments to counter the social ills that breed toxicity and abuse: political polarization and social inequality, entrenched misogynistic and patriarchal norms, and overlapping systems of racial or ethnic exclusion. It is in this area that efforts to fight gendered political violence intersect with the need to transform harmful gender norms and engage men as allies. Both should be seen as building blocks toward a broader process of social transformation that requires patience and long-term commitments from funders and aid organizations.

Conclusion

If the first generation of international aid for women's political empowerment focused on "adding women," the second generation initially sought to transform patriarchal processes and institutions. As programs have evolved, donors, practitioners, and local advocates are increasingly grappling with entrenched patriarchal gender norms and practices that perpetuate women's exclusion and undermine formal institutional reforms. In response, two key areas of action have taken shape. First, recognizing that male gatekeepers often constrain women's political engagement in political organizations, the family, and society at large, new initiatives are engaging men as allies and challenging harmful forms of masculinity in politics. Second, aid providers and organizations are also paying much greater attention to violence, harassment, and resistance targeting women in political life.

Their efforts have produced important results. A small but growing number of democracy programs strategically involve men as stakeholders in gender equality reform, by relying on traditional awareness-raising strategies or recruiting male gatekeepers as allies and champions. A few organizations have also developed more elaborate norm-change strategies, applying best practices for transforming masculinities from other fields to the political sphere. By comparison, efforts to fight violence against women in politics are more advanced. International actors have invested significant resources into defining the problem, improving data collection, and raising awareness. Complementing the work of local women's rights advocates, they have strengthened international and regional norms on the issue, helped advance legislative reforms, trained electoral stakeholders and law enforcement, supported civil society advocacy, and offered direct security training and protective tools to women politicians.

Yet, despite these innovations, many initiatives are still new, and their effectiveness is uncertain. It will take time and experimentation for practitioners to test these approaches across different political contexts and hone their strategies accordingly. Their work is further complicated by new political developments that are poorly understood. Growing numbers of women politicians confront unprecedented levels of gendered and sexualized online abuse and coordinated disinformation campaigns. Efforts to combat this violence and transform discriminatory gender norms must also contend with a global trend of democratic erosion and transnational antigender mobilization. In some countries, political leaders, parties, and civil society organizations are actively pushing back against progressive gender norms, fueling social polarization and giving new platforms to extremist voices.

Beyond these immediate threats, however, aid providers and advocates are confronting a broader challenge. Gender norm change is a slow process that often unfolds over generations and involves far-reaching social, economic, and political transformations. Particularly in the face of resistance, it requires sustained mobilization by feminist and women's rights movements.[97] Not only is the democracy assistance field currently ill-equipped to measure changes in norms, attitudes, and beliefs but the incentive structures built into aid bureaucracies are also at odds with the patience and flexibility required for this work. We delve more deeply into these challenges in the remainder of the book. In the next chapter, we examine how international support for women's political empowerment intersects with other forms of injustice and oppression, including authoritarian efforts to consolidate power. We then turn our lens back to the aid ecosystem itself, analyzing recurring weaknesses in assistance models that weaken long-term gender equality change.

10

Widening the Lens

Laxmi grew up in a remote region of Nepal.[1] As a girl from the country's marginalized Dalit community, she learned early on that many fellow citizens saw her as undeserving of the full dignity accorded to higher-status groups. She set her mind on making a difference for women in her community. Yet after moving to Kathmandu to pursue her education, she repeatedly observed how Dalit women like her were left behind by the political changes sweeping the country. In the early 1990s, "marginalized women were not involved in the women's movement," she told us in November 2020. "Women from the higher-class, privileged groups were united in raising women's voices, but not the voices of marginalized women." Today, Laxmi has built a life as an activist fighting for Dalit women's rights. Despite the legal progress achieved by Nepali gender equality activists like herself over the past fifteen years, she still notices the same patterns. "My concern is that women from the privileged group, who have access to and who are related to the male leaders, have benefited most from the quotas for women [. . .] Indigenous women have not benefited properly. The worst condition is that of the Dalit women. They are always denied or excluded in the name of the women—the privileged women."[2]

Laxmi's frustration gives voice to the uneven progress experienced by countless women around the globe. Nowhere in the world are women a homogeneous group. Their experiences are shaped not only by discriminatory gender norms and expectations but also by cross-cutting economic, political, and social hierarchies that lend some women higher status and greater opportunities than others. As a result, women's hard-fought political gains of the past several decades have often accrued to women belonging to privileged social and political groups. Some women have gained access to elite circles of power, whereas others still struggle to exercise basic political rights. These inequities are sometimes the legacies of historical injustices. In other places, however, they are actively reproduced by exclusionary governance systems.[3] Many autocratic regimes, for example, have selectively promoted women's political leadership to bolster their

Aiding Empowerment. Saskia Brechenmacher and Katherine Mann, Oxford University Press.
© Oxford University Press 2024. DOI: 10.1093/oso/9780197694275.003.0010

international legitimacy while simultaneously cracking down on women's rights activists challenging the dominant political project.

This chapter examines whether and how democracy aid actors have grappled with these partial gains and cross-cutting inequities. The first part of the chapter explores how an explicitly intersectional lens might change assistance focused on women's political empowerment, and the difficulties that aid organizations have faced in translating the concept into practice. Some have attempted to overcome the traditional elite bias of past interventions by centering the political participation of marginalized women, yet this shift remains partial and inconsistent. Moreover, most interventions are still based on a narrow inclusionary logic, seeking to integrate more diverse women into formal political institutions rather than linking women's political empowerment to broader struggles for political, social, and economic transformation. The second part of the chapter examines the limits of these inclusionary approaches in countries experiencing democratic backsliding and closing civic and political space. Aid providers confront murky new waters as growing numbers of nondemocratic leaders lash out against women's activism, restrict international democracy assistance, or co-opt women's political leadership for illiberal ends. What does it mean to support women's political empowerment within undemocratic and exclusionary systems and institutions? How should international actors respond to gender quotas and similar measures adopted by nondemocratic governments? Although some organizations have begun tailoring their work to this changing global context, much more needs to be done to capture their learning and adapt existing approaches.

Reckoning with hierarchies

Efforts to promote women's political representation are generally premised on the idea that women's high-level leadership will strengthen women's everyday political and social rights. Women politicians, so the narrative goes, will promote gender equality reforms and signal to the public that women are capable political leaders, thereby encouraging other women to engage in politics. As noted in Chapter 8, these theories of substantive and symbolic representation are built on the assumption that women share certain experiences rooted in entrenched systems of gender discrimination and gendered divisions of labor. These experiences create a representational link between women voters and legislators, allowing women to see their lives and interests reflected in the political process.

Yet in countries marked by deep societal cleavages and inequities, women who advance in electoral politics are not necessarily representative of most women in society. Instead, political gains often accrue disproportionately to women from socially, politically, and economically privileged groups. In the most extreme cases, women heads of state have hailed from dynastic political families that insulate them from everyday realities of gender discrimination.[4] Yet even in places where political power is not concentrated in the hands of so few, women (and men) belonging to dominant groups tend to enjoy greater access to the resources, education, and social networks needed to effectively engage in politics. Women from marginalized communities, on the other hand, usually face significantly higher barriers to participation than both elite women *and* men who share their own backgrounds. These differences highlight that patriarchal gender norms alone are not responsible for women's political exclusion. Other systems of oppression interact with gender inequality to shape their political agency and opportunities.[5]

Scholars have examined these interlocking inequities through the concept of "intersectionality." Initially coined by legal academic Kimberlé Crenshaw to describe how Black women's experiences in the United States are shaped by *both* sex and race, the term has given rise to a rich and diverse field of study.[6] Linking these various bodies of scholarship is the recognition that individuals can simultaneously be privileged and disadvantaged or experience multiple forms of oppression at once. In Nepal, for instance, women politicians are routinely marginalized by entrenched patriarchal structures and norms. At the same time, women from higher-caste backgrounds benefit from social and economic privileges that are out of reach for Dalit women, who have historically been at the bottom of the country's social and political hierarchies. Yet even Dalit women are not a homogeneous group: the Madhesi Dalit community from the country's Terai region is far less represented in politics than Dalit women from the more urbanized Hill region.[7] An intersectional lens enables researchers, advocates, and practitioners to recognize these differences, thereby honoring the full social and political complexity of women's lives.[8]

These insights have important implications for practitioners (see Table 10.1). First, an intersectional lens can help practitioners examine whether the

Table 10.1 **Translating Intersectionality: Three Guiding Questions for Practitioners**

Reach	Which women are reached by existing interventions, and which are left behind?
Effects	Do interventions have the same effects across groups of women, or are some groups benefiting more than others?
Theory of Change	Are interventions targeting the varied causes and manifestations of women's political disempowerment, or do they privilege the barriers faced by elite women?

participants or beneficiaries of any given program are reflective of women in society, or whether their interventions primarily target women from elite backgrounds. Second, it allows them to assess whether the *effects* of any given policy or intervention empower some groups of women more than others. For example, cross-national research shows that women from minority ethnic, racial, and religious communities often benefit less from stand-alone gender quotas than women from the majority group in society.[9] When women from marginalized groups are given targeted political opportunities, on the other hand, their gains tend to come at the expense of other underrepresented groups.[10] In Nepal, for instance, a targeted quota measure has rapidly increased Dalit women's representation in local government, with more than six thousand Dalit women elected to local office in 2017. At the same time, the representation of Dalit men remains negligible.[11] The quota has also fueled new forms of competition between Dalit women and women belonging to other minority groups left out of the quota measure.[12] Meanwhile, upper-caste men continue to control the most powerful mayoral and chair positions, their dominant status remaining largely unchallenged.[13]

Finally, and perhaps most importantly, an intersectional lens can lead advocates and practitioners to more nuanced explanations for women's political disempowerment and, therefore, to different policy solutions and theories of change. If women are also disadvantaged by extreme poverty or ethnic discrimination, then, as Berry and Lake (2021) write, "a singular focus on their gendered exclusion is unlikely to alter the social structures that ensure women's continued subjugation and harm."[14] What emerges from this perspective is the need for more holistic approaches that address gender inequities together with interlinked systems of political, social, and economic domination.

Translating intersectionality into practice

Historically, international support for women's political empowerment has not been well-attuned to differences and hierarchies between women. Even as theories of intersectionality have traveled from activist and academic circles into the international development field, they have been slow to take hold among democracy assistance organizations. One obvious reason is the latter's traditional focus on formal political processes and institutions, which produces a strong bias toward the interests of political elites. By framing women's political empowerment in terms of their representation in political parties, parliaments, and government institutions, aid organizations have tended to work with women (and men) who are already within the broader orbit of electoral politics, whether as civil society advocates, political party members, or elected representatives.

Many of the field's standard programmatic tools also privilege citizens from relatively elite groups. For instance, training programs for women candidates and aspirants typically reach those who already enjoy the resources, education, and independence required to seriously consider a political career. Similarly, civil society support generally benefits professionalized organizations run by urban and educated staff rather than grassroots associations.

Over time, donors and implementing organizations have become more aware of these blind spots. After years of gender-focused policies and efforts to mainstream gender into interventions, they now feel greater pressure to take intersecting inequalities into account—not only in the form of separate human rights- or minority rights-focused policies and initiatives, but also as part of their gender equality work. For example, the European Union's Gender Action Plan III establishes intersectionality as one of three overarching principles guiding the EU's external engagement for gender equality, and mandates attention to the "most disadvantaged women" in all initiatives.[15] USAID's 2023 policy on gender equality and women's empowerment similarly calls for the application of an "intersectional gender lens" to address "the ways in which gender and other inequalities can limit certain people's access to, participation in, and benefit from development interventions."[16] Despite these policy commitments, however, democracy aid organizations have yet to develop practical guidelines for integrating intersectional approaches into their work.

Our cases indicate varying levels of engagement with questions of intersectionality among both international and local actors working on women's political empowerment. In Nepal, recent internal conflict and widespread caste-based discrimination have made differences between women more politically salient, leading many international actors to combine their work on gender equality with a broader focus on social inclusion (more on this below).[17] In Myanmar, ongoing ethnic conflict and persecution has similarly directed greater international attention to intersecting societal cleavages. In Morocco and Kenya, however, international donors and implementing organizations have engaged less explicitly with intersecting axes of oppression and marginalization. In Kenya, many gender equality advocates recognize that ethnically based political competition limits women's full political inclusion. To date, however, few interventions have foregrounded the relationship between gender and ethnicity, a pattern that advocates attribute to insufficient funding and to a lack of clarity on potential entry points.[18] In Morocco, on the other hand, class-based inequities emerged as the most salient cleavage in our conversations with local and international interlocutors, alongside divisions between urban women and women living in the country's vast rural areas, who participate in informal political spaces but remain marginalized from formal political institutions. Although international actors are aware of these divisions and have made some efforts to diversify their activities, most training seminars, conferences, and workshops remain concentrated in the country's urban centers.[19]

When international actors have incorporated an intersectional lens into their programming, their efforts have typically fallen into one of two categories. First, some organizations have adapted their existing programs to reach more diverse groups of women, including women from marginalized groups. Ahead of the 2015 communal and regional elections in Morocco, for instance, IRI shifted its work with political parties from party headquarters in Rabat to parties' local-level branches, partly to enable women from smaller cities and villages to attend campaign training activities.[20] A second approach consists of funding and implementing initiatives that intentionally target women from marginalized communities. The "Participation and Voice for Excluded Women" (PAVE) program in Nepal exemplifies this model. Funded by the Jo Cox Foundation and designed and implemented by three Nepali feminist organizations and Womankind Worldwide between 2019 and 2022, the program supported women leaders from marginalized communities in Province 7. Recognizing that elected women politicians from disadvantaged backgrounds face not only gender discrimination but also profound economic hurdles to their political careers, the program provided participants with entrepreneurship training and seed money for their businesses. It also brought together women's organizations with different areas of focus (such as Dalit women and widows), to help them learn from each other, bridge thematic silos, and rethink their ways of working.[21]

Programs like PAVE illustrate promising methods to center marginalized women's political empowerment. Nevertheless, donors, practitioners, and advocates underscore several practical challenges that hinder their work in this area. For one, obtaining detailed intersectional data is a challenge. Few governments collect and publish even basic sex-disaggregated data on citizens' political participation; systematic information on other identity categories, such as socioeconomic class, ethnicity, and sexual orientation, is even more difficult to access.[22] In Kenya, for example, the Afrobarometer survey provides data on women's turnout in elections, but practitioners generally lack insights into the socioeconomic backgrounds of women running for local and national office, or the political engagement of disabled and LGBTQ+ individuals. Collecting such data through survey research or other means can be politically sensitive and resource-intensive, particularly if funding for research is not built into donor grants.[23] Thus, while international organizations can do more to understand which women participate in their programs and activities, they struggle to unpack wider national and cross-national trends.

Engaging marginalized communities also demands logistical and resource commitments. In most cases, implementing organizations have established networks with long-standing local partners. Building similar ties in new localities or with different communities requires time and resources to ensure that planned interventions fit local capacities and needs. Aid organizations need to translate materials into local languages, train facilitators familiar with the specific context, and take additional steps to ensure their activities are accessible to marginalized groups. Partnering with grassroots organizations comes with further challenges. These groups struggle to fulfill donors' bureaucratic and financial requirements, and thus need targeted capacity-building and mentorship to be able to comply. None of these barriers are insurmountable, but they require time, funding, and expertise. If funders do not explicitly ask for the inclusion of marginalized communities in their calls for proposals and do not adjust timelines and budgets accordingly, it is easier for democracy support organizations to work with their traditional partners in urban centers.[24]

A depoliticized agenda?

Beyond these practical constraints, however, lie further quandaries. What does it mean to adopt a *truly* intersectional approach to women's political empowerment? Does an intersectional lens transform the objectives of international support and, if so, how? Although aid agencies and organizations increasingly use the term "intersectionality" in their policy statements and strategies, they often appear to equate it with "diversity among women" or the inclusion of marginalized women. As a 2016 Oxfam study notes, "it is now widely accepted [in the development sector] that in addition to gender, identities such as those related to socio-economic class, ethnicity, sexual preferences, age, physical ability, etc., shape our experience of discrimination and oppression."[25] It is less clear, however, that this recognition of difference is producing radically different ways of working, beyond efforts to diversify the participants or targets of aid interventions. Gender practitioners use intersectional analysis to understand how women might face varying advantages and disadvantages when engaging in politics. Yet they rarely ask how these experiences might alter the meaning of political empowerment itself.

Insights from intersectional feminist scholarship, however, pose fundamental challenges to existing assistance approaches, particularly in countries marked by profound social and political divisions. For one, taking the political lives of marginalized women seriously unsettles the boundaries between "political," "social," and "economic" empowerment, and those between gender justice and other struggles for emancipation. The existing aid architecture draws firm lines between policies and funding focused on socioeconomic rights and development, stabilization and peacebuilding, and democracy and governance—divisions that are mirrored in gender equality interventions. Initiatives intended to bridge these domains, as the PAVE program sought to do in Nepal, are rare. Yet these bureaucratic divisions rarely map onto women's lived realities. In both Nepal and Kenya, feminist advocates underscore that economic rights and financial autonomy are essential building blocks of poor women's political empowerment. Women require resources to advocate for themselves within their households, form political networks, run for local leadership positions, and sustain their political engagement over time. Meanwhile, elite men's *over*representation in political leadership is often enabled and sustained by systems of economic extraction and elite capture, which women's formal political inclusion alone cannot dismantle.[26]

Although it is impossible for a single organization or intervention to tackle all forms of exclusion at once, an intersectional lens underscores the importance of dismantling programmatic silos and eroding the informal power hierarchies that undergird exclusionary political institutions. In practical terms, aid providers might begin by deepening their understanding of marginalized women's experiences of politics and power. Supporting electoral commissions to improve women's voter registration rates in marginalized communities may be a worthwhile endeavor, but it misses the mark if women in these communities doubt that voting will alter their lived experiences of discrimination. In this case, electoral participation may not be a meaningful indicator of political empowerment, nor a locally defined priority for mobilization and reform. A more promising approach may be to nurture women-led or gender-inclusive coalitions across different struggles for equality and justice, moving from top-down theories of change toward a focus on building collective power among those left behind by the status quo. To date, very few democracy aid programs support such intersectional movement-building as a core element of women's political empowerment.

A second insight that emerges from intersectional scholarship is that women's inclusion in formal political institutions is not always the most effective entry point to social and political change. Most donor approaches are premised on a logic of inclusion: they seek to incorporate women into institutions in order to incrementally change these spaces for the better. However, a growing body of research demonstrates that quota reforms and other interventions implemented in the name of gender inclusion are sometimes instrumentalized by political actors pursuing exclusionary, ethnonationalist, and antidemocratic political projects.[27] For example, both Rwanda and Uganda have earned international praise for promoting women's representation in parliament, even as these countries' ruling regimes have consolidated their power through undemocratic political practices.[28] Similar dynamics play out in less authoritarian contexts. Political elites may agree to gender quotas to signal their reform-mindedness to international and domestic actors, but block other reforms that threaten political, caste, ethnic, or class hierarchies in more fundamental ways. The resulting system may enable important advancements for some women, but it is unlikely to lift those at the bottom of existing power hierarchies.

During Nepal's constitutional negotiations, for example, the legacy of internal conflict initially fueled widespread support for a political settlement inclusive of the country's diverse ethnic and religious groups. As the negotiations dragged on, however, upper-caste, Hindu elites gradually reasserted their power and began framing initiatives promoting power-sharing and decentralization as foreign meddling intended to fuel societal discord.[29] Government authorities asked the UN to drop references to "structural discrimination" from its development assistance framework and to replace specific ethnic and caste groups with a generic nod to "poor and disadvantaged communities."[30] They also pressured the UK's Department for International Development to end its partnership with the Nepal Federation of Indigenous Nationalities (NEFIN), an organization promoting ethnic federalism in the Nepali constitution. In this political environment, international donors shifted toward a focus on "gender and social inclusion" (GESI), which was deemed less politically sensitive than work on ethnicity, caste, and regional autonomy. Yet as development practitioner and researcher Lynn Bennet writes, "there is some danger that the very thing that made GESI broadly acceptable to government [. . .] may be what ends up limiting its ability to bring meaningful change for other groups."[31]

In brief, existing policy documents tend to frame intersectionality as another technical tool—a set of guidelines to implement in program planning and design. Yet the illustrations above highlight that taking the concept seriously requires entering highly politicized debates about the distribution of power in a society. In some countries, doing so may engender greater political pushback against international actors than focusing on gender equality alone. In these contexts, assistance providers have to navigate difficult decisions: whether to link gender equality to other issues of social and political justice, or how to balance collaboration with state institutions with bottom-up approaches. These questions are becoming even more pressing as growing numbers of countries experience democratic backsliding, which poses distinct barriers to gender equality and limits how much political agency women can exercise within formal institutions.

Confronting the global democratic recession

Aid for women's political empowerment emerged during a period of global democratic expansion. As we discussed in Chapter 4, processes of political liberalization that began during the 1980s and 1990s opened new spaces for women to engage in formal politics, even if multiparty elections initially produced limited gender equality gains. Unsurprisingly, the standard menu of assistance that emerged during this period relied in large part on an assumption of continued democratic progress. Getting more women to vote, encouraging them to run for office, and bolstering their capacity as legislators made sense in a context in which these institutions held the promise of political change: the goal was to *deepen* the quality of democracy by making political institutions more representative, inclusive, and responsive to the public. International actors also assumed they would be able to promote democratic reform across borders and support politically oriented women's organizations without restrictions or pushback from host governments.

Today, the global political landscape looks decidedly different. For over a decade, countries around the world have experienced a trend of gradual democratic decline. Although complete democratic breakdowns have been relatively rare, many countries have witnessed a creeping erosion of democratic institutions and basic civil and political rights.[32] Countries that democratized during the 1980s and 1990s have proven particularly vulnerable, as leaders and ruling regimes have capitalized on weak oversight institutions to concentrate power in the executive, weaken electoral processes, and restrict oppositional civil society actors. At the same time, several prominent authoritarian states—including China and Russia—have become more politically repressive and taken on more active roles in shaping political outcomes across borders and at the multilateral level. Scholars continue to debate the underlying drivers of these trends, though most agree that the phenomenon cannot be reduced to a single explanation. In some places, backsliding has been fueled by elected illiberal leaders who have tapped into social and political grievances to mobilize support. In other countries, ruling regimes have opportunistically weakened institutions to entrench themselves in power, or used undemocratic means to restore an authoritarian status quo.[33] Overall, more and more people around the world are now living in contexts of shrinking political and civic space, and international democracy assistance organizations have to operate in increasingly difficult political environments.[34]

Rising authoritarianism presents distinct threats to gender equality and fuels fear among women's rights advocates that past political gains are at risk. The concentration of power in the hands of a male-dominated and broadly unrepresentative ruling elite inevitably hardens patriarchal governance and exacerbates women's exclusion from decision-making roles. Moreover, whereas democracies allow women and other marginalized groups to mobilize in civil society and exert pressure on exclusionary political institutions from the bottom up, backsliding regimes tend to impose new legal and extralegal restrictions on autonomous civic activism, especially on organizations and movements that challenge their power.[35] Women's rights activists and movements that mobilize for equality, peace, and democratic inclusion thus find themselves particularly at risk.[36]

Furthermore, de-democratization in some regions has also been driven by right-wing populist and nationalist leaders who have made antifeminism an integral part of their legitimation strategies. Particularly in Europe and Latin America, illiberal leaders—such as Jair Bolsonaro in Brazil and Viktor Orbán in Hungary—have cast themselves as strongmen who are defending "traditional family values" from Western cultural imperialism, thereby aligning themselves with a growing transnational movement organizing against progressive gender norms.[37] Although their attacks have focused on liberal rights that challenge the patriarchal family model, such as women's reproductive rights, LGBTQ+ rights, and protections against gender-based violence, rising illiberalism also threatens women's political participation. At a basic level, policies and rhetoric that tie women's value to their childbearing and homemaking roles reinforce the structural and sociocultural barriers that confine women to the private sphere.[38] Antipluralist ideologies and political polarization have also fueled heightened vitriol and attacks against women who challenge traditional gender, ethnic, and political hierarchies, sometimes in the form of state-orchestrated disinformation campaigns.[39] Moreover, illiberal autocrats and their nonstate allies have cracked down on women's rights organizations and LGBTQ+ rights defenders who defy their political agenda, using strategies that range from policy sidelining, vilification, and surveillance to blacklisting, bureaucratic harassment, and physical violence.[40]

Among our four cases, Myanmar exemplifies an extreme case of democratic breakdown, with immediate and drastic consequences for women's political engagement. Since its partial liberalization in 2011, the country's democratic opening had always been fragile. Women's political rights remained heavily circumscribed by ongoing armed conflict and the military's outsized political influence, particularly for women belonging to the country's ethnic minority groups. At the same time, women's organizations benefited from new opportunities to influence the policy process, access international networks and resources, and challenge discriminatory legislation. They found allies among the rising numbers of women elected officials, who used their position to advocate for reform. The military coup in February 2021 abruptly reversed these gains, ushering in the return of a highly militarized, violent, and patriarchal political order. By declaring the results of the 2020 general election invalid and dissolving parliament, military authorities once again pushed most women out of formal politics. Government-led institutions and activities focused on advancing gender equality became defunct overnight. Over the subsequent weeks and months, the security forces unleashed a wave of brutal repression against any dissenting voices, including against the thousands of women politicians, activists, and journalists who took up frontline roles in the civil resistance against military rule.[41]

As in many backsliding regimes around the world, women in Myanmar have continued to resist authoritarian governance at significant personal risk. They have formed women's networks within the interim National Unity Consultative Council, an inclusive dialogue platform set up by various opposition groups. They have also successfully advocated for a 30 percent gender quota in the Federal Democracy Charter, a roadmap for democratic reform that was approved by a People's Assembly convened by the resistance movement in January 2022.[42] Activists have launched online advocacy campaigns like the Sisters2Sisters initiative, which seeks accountability for the military's abuses of power against women activists and protesters, and delivered urgent humanitarian services to communities in need.[43] Yet these forms of political mobilization are taking shape in a context of heightened surveillance, repression, and pervasive gender-based violence.[44]

Closing political space and rising hostility against women's rights and gender equality pose profound new challenges for international actors that seek to support women's political participation. In these contexts of democratic erosion, the conventional democracy aid toolbox, which is heavily reliant on partnerships with formal political institutions, is either unworkable or vulnerable to political capture; at the same time, international support for civil society also faces heightened restrictions.[45] Democracy assistance actors have operated in these settings by shifting from direct support for state institutions toward a greater focus on local governments, youth mobilization and civic engagement, and informal dialogue and coalitions, while side-stepping more confrontational or oppositional approaches.[46] A similar pattern is evident with respect to women's political empowerment interventions, with international actors sometimes moving more funding to women's organizations, supporting less overtly political gender equality initiatives, and seeking out local-level or regional entry points for gender equality reform.[47] However, these responses have unfolded in an ad hoc and reactive fashion, with little systematic guidance on what it means to support women's political empowerment across different backsliding contexts or in places characterized by state-endorsed antifeminism.

Our case studies illustrate the various ways aid actors have responded to democratic decline. In Nepal, international aid actors have faced growing government hostility toward international democracy support as well as new efforts to regulate their activities. At the same time, some organizations have found greater space to support women's political inclusion in local government, as part of the country's broader decentralization process.[48] After the military coup in Myanmar, by contrast, many international organizations initially halted their aid programs entirely. Over the past two years, some have redirected their gender equality funding toward women's civil society organizations or initiated new programs that focus on women's empowerment in local governance and conflict responses.[49] NIMD and Demo Finland have relaunched their previous work on democratic inclusion in political parties by organizing virtual training initiatives for youth and women from different ethnically based political parties.[50] However, donor governments have been wary of directly supporting the national resistance movement, including women's political mobilization against authoritarian rule.[51] Women's rights defenders in the country have criticized the lack of international support in the aftermath of the coup, particularly as international attention shifted away from Myanmar toward Afghanistan, Ukraine, and other crisis zones.[52] These gaps in support underscore a broader challenge: supporting women's prodemocratic mobilization in backsliding contexts requires international actors to engage more directly with contentious action and take greater political risks—a theme we return to at the end of this chapter.

Risks of autocratic co-optation

Despite these worrisome patterns of backlash, authoritarianism does not always go hand in hand with state hostility to women's rights. As noted earlier in this chapter, some authoritarian and semiauthoritarian regimes have actively promoted gender equality reforms and implemented measures to strengthen women's descriptive representation in politics. In fact, as Donno and Kreft (2018) note, "the average proportion of female legislators is now equal across democracies and dictatorships in the developing world," primarily due to the widespread adoption of gender quotas.[53] Nondemocratic regimes have also made progress on other gender equality fronts, for example by adopting legislation on gender-based violence, access to land and inheritance, and other women's rights issues.[54]

Existing research shows that nondemocratic regimes have various rationales for adopting such measures. In many cases, they seek to bolster their international legitimacy and prestige. Because democracy and gender equality have become "bundled norms" in the eyes of donor institutions and international organizations, leaders are incentivized to promote women's rights to signal their adherence to global democratic norms and reap reputational (and financial) rewards. This dynamic explains why aid-dependent electoral autocracies are particularly likely to implement such reforms.[55] Governments may also adopt quotas and other gender equality measures to appeal to domestic political audiences, such as women voters and rights advocates. Gender equality reforms are an attractive mechanism for building legitimacy because they give the appearance of greater inclusion but are less politically costly than liberalizing political competition or loosening restrictions on civil liberties. For instance, governments can implement quotas without threatening the ruling party's legislative control.[56]

Morocco exemplifies these patterns. King Mohammed VI has championed women's political leadership and women's status improvements as part of a successful strategy to bolster his international image as a reformist king, undercut hardline Islamist movements, and strengthen his support base among secular and reform-oriented citizens.[57] Moroccan women's organizations have also turned to the monarchy for support in the face of conservative resistance to their reform priorities. This collaborative relationship has brought about a series of significant legal reforms, including gender quotas that have substantially changed the composition of national and subnational legislatures. At the same time, these numerical gains have not redistributed political power away from male political elites or advanced the country's democratization process.[58] Moreover, the monarchy's liberal stance on women's political rights coexists with high levels of state hostility against civic actors that challenge the political rules of the game, including those that speak out against the state's rights abuses, the monarchy, or Morocco's occupation of Western Sahara.[59]

In more politically closed countries, this merging of state measures to promote women's rights and antidemocratic actions is even more pronounced. Rwanda is often cited in this respect. The country boasts the world's highest rate of women's parliamentary representation, but these gains have occurred in a context of hardening authoritarianism, state surveillance, and repression.[60] In Nicaragua, women similarly make up over half of all legislators, yet the ruling party under Daniel Ortega has increasingly cracked down on all forms of political opposition, including feminist movements and activists.[61]

For international democracy aid actors, regime co-optation raises different dilemmas than outright hostility against women's rights and inclusion. How should they engage with gender equality reforms adopted for antidemocratic ends? On the one hand, such reforms have sometimes been championed by domestic advocates and can bring about meaningful changes, even in nondemocratic contexts.[62] In Morocco, for instance, the women's movement has played a key role in mobilizing for legal reform, including quota measures. Research also shows that Moroccan deputies elected through gender quotas are more responsive to women constituents, thereby increasing the latter's access to services.[63] On the other hand, there is also a risk that top-down reforms enacted in politically restrictive contexts remain superficial. Without systemic efforts to challenge patriarchal norms and other forms of political and social exclusion, women's gains may remain "precariously dependent on the state," inaccessible to the most marginalized women and vulnerable to political backlash.[64] Even more problematically, such measures can easily become a form of "gender-washing," drawing international focus away from persistent or worsening abuses of political power.

To date, the democracy assistance community has insufficiently grappled with these patterns of co-optation. Donor governments' gender equality strategies and democracy policy frameworks generally do not acknowledge the tensions that can arise between promoting gender equality and supporting democratic governance, instead presenting both goals as intrinsically linked. Gender analyses that explicitly relate women's political empowerment to formal and informal power dynamics, democratic constraints, and powerholders' political incentives to enact reform are rare. Instead, there is still a tendency to equate gains in women's formal political representation with meaningful democratic change regardless of the political context. Exemplifying this pattern, a USAID gender analysis conducted in Egypt in 2020 briefly notes the government's increasing restrictions on civil society but discusses women's increased representation in the Egyptian cabinet and legislature without reference to the broader context of tightening authoritarian rule, noncompetitive elections, and violent crackdown on feminist activism in the country.[65] A similar analysis commissioned by USAID in Morocco the same year notes political parties' lack of political will as an ongoing barrier to gender parity in politics and emphasizes the need to "build the capacities of political parties." But the document does not discuss how women's marginalization from party politics is exacerbated by the country's clientelistic politics, including the monarchy's purposeful reliance on patronage ties to rural elites to maintain its political power.[66]

In practice, a lack of attention to underlying power relations can result in overly technical theories of change that are divorced from the deeper drivers of women's political exclusion. In Morocco, for instance, some international actors have continued to promote women's representation in the country's formal political institutions, based on the assumption that their presence in these bodies matters both substantively and symbolically—even in a context of broader democratic constraints. This approach also reflects the priorities of mainstream women's organizations in the country, which continue to mobilize for gender parity measures in politics. At the same time, the repeated and widespread reliance on capacity-building for women candidates and women elected officials appears out of sync with many of the core obstacles to women's meaningful political empowerment, including the country's weakly institutionalized political parties, women's exclusion from local power networks, and a quota system that pushes women into institutionally subordinate positions.[67] Few targeted interventions have explicitly sought out alternative entry points, such as promoting the political mobilization of and claim-making by economically marginalized women.

Neglecting how women's political empowerment relates to the broader democratic context not only makes interventions less effective but also puts international donors at risk of directly subsidizing exclusionary state institutions and political agendas, thereby deepening political and social inequities. In Morocco, the EU has provided extensive, multi-year budget support for the implementation of the government's Plan for Gender Equality, which includes specific objectives related to women's political representation and gender mainstreaming in public policies. Yet, over the same period, the country's track record on freedom of association and expression has steadily declined.[68] Although it is possible that these investments have produced tangible results for some Moroccan women, the same resources could likely have been allocated differently, with a greater focus on bolstering reform champions, supporting women's movements, or ensuring downward accountability to citizens.

The case of Egypt is even more striking. The EU has provided more than 20 million euros in funding for women's empowerment initiatives in the country since 2014, enabling the government to present itself as a champion of women's rights even as it has unleashed repressive measures against women activists who deviate from the official government line.[69] These examples are emblematic of a pattern that extends far beyond gender equality aid: in 2018 and 2019, just over 84 percent of external EU funding went to authoritarian and hybrid regimes, including in the form of budget support provided across a wide range of sectors.[70] Other donors, including the US government, have also come under fire for bankrolling autocratic practices, particularly through the provision of security sector assistance.[71] Within the gender equality sector, direct financial support to nondemocratic regimes exemplifies a segmented and narrow approach to women's empowerment that treats gender equality as divorced from other struggles for justice and inclusion. Although there may be instances where the benefits of collaborating with nondemocratic governments on gender equality outweigh the costs, the trade-offs and risks inherent in these decisions need to be carefully weighed, with a clear-eyed understanding that state-controlled women's rights reforms can be at odds with democratic accountability and inclusion.

Forging more politically informed approaches

These brief illustrations highlight several important challenges facing donors and practitioners who are supporting women's political empowerment in a context of global democratic backsliding. First and foremost, there is a need for much more systematic analysis of the relationship between gender, patriarchy, and democratic erosion. In some countries, autocratic regimes clearly use women's rights as a tool to mobilize and consolidate support and curry international favors. In other places, antifeminism has become a core driver of autocratic coalition-building. Across different regions, women are also at the forefront of democratic resistance movements and make such movements more likely to succeed.[72]

Even though the global democratic crisis has attracted significant policy attention in recent years, existing analyses and policy debates often ignore these important gendered dimensions. For instance, in the lead-up to the first Summit for Democracy organized by the Biden administration in 2021, gender equality advocates within the US government had to fight to integrate women's rights into the Summit agenda.[73] As governments design and implement new policies and initiatives aimed at tackling the various dimensions of democratic backsliding, insufficient attention to the gendered drivers and effects of authoritarianism risks resulting in incomplete diagnoses, less effective responses, and missed opportunities for action.

Currently, practitioners also lack practical guidelines to adapt existing programming approaches to varying political contexts, including to countries experiencing democratic erosion, internal polarization and conflict, or the co-optation of gender equality reform by autocratic actors. Over the past decade, international and multilateral organizations have produced a wide range of "technical" programming tools and best practice documents addressing different dimensions of women's political empowerment, from gender quotas and gender-sensitive electoral laws to gender-sensitive parliaments. Yet there is still little guidance for aligning these approaches to varying political contexts and a dearth of research examining which contextual variables are most likely to condition their effectiveness. Country-specific gender analyses often identify institutional and sociocultural barriers to women's inclusion, but they insufficiently investigate how the broader political economy produces, reinforces, or mitigates these hurdles and shapes potential entry points for action.[74]

By necessity, practitioners on the ground have had to adjust their strategies based on the political space available to both aid organizations and local civil society groups, as well as the government's interest in gender equality reform. Yet, to date, aid providers have rarely tracked or assessed the various approaches they employ in hostile political environments. For practitioners working on women's political empowerment and on democracy support more broadly, democratic stagnation or erosion could be an impetus to rethink standard approaches and to envision new ways of working that are more adaptive, flexible, and attuned to politics and power relations. Doing so requires a better understanding of how informal institutions and practices—from backroom deals to male-dominated patronage networks—shape women's political inclusion.

Although the most appropriate strategies in any given context will vary depending on the severity of government repression and hostility against gender equality, our research highlights several themes that are likely to apply across different contexts. First, the global trend of democratic backsliding further underscores the need to move beyond a narrow focus on women's leadership as a reliable indicator of women's political empowerment *or* democratization. Equating superficial gender equality wins, such as women's increased parliamentary representation or the adoption of a new law, with meaningful inclusion can play into the hands of autocratic regimes that leverage gender equality reforms to distract from other exclusionary practices. For democracy aid organizations working in hybrid political regimes and in electoral autocracies, the challenge is to carefully analyze the relationship between women's political rights and participation, their high-level representation and influence, and meaningful redistributions of political power, rather than assuming that all of these goals go hand-in-hand.

Second, in contexts of democratic reversal or erosion, effectively supporting women's political mobilization in civil society and in other nontraditional or informal spaces becomes particularly important. Over the past several years, one of the most striking global trends has been not only the rise in attacks on civic space and women's rights but also women's collective resistance against patriarchal authoritarianism and violence. Just as in Myanmar, women in Brazil, Poland, Belarus, China, Iran and elsewhere have taken to the streets in large numbers to push back against state abuse, sometimes directly linking the struggle for women's rights to the broader struggle for democracy. New research suggests that such mobilization is critical: Chenoweth and Marks (2022) find that globally, "mass movements in which women participated extensively on the frontlines have been much more likely to succeed than campaigns that marginalized or excluded women," and are also more likely to produce lasting democratic change.[75]

Even in the absence of broad-based popular resistance, feminist and women-led organizations working in contexts of shrinking civic space and backlash have pioneered new advocacy tactics, including digital activism and coalition-building with unusual allies, from trade unions to indigenous collectives.[76] They are challenging established modes of protest and civic activism by centering care and well-being as critical to long-term movement-building, and by forging new linkages between different struggles for justice. Yet their frontline participation in oppositional political movements also makes women vulnerable to repression and violence, particularly as governments update their counterprotest strategies to target new forms of mobilization and activist tactics.[77]

These patterns highlight the need for international democracy assistance actors to pay greater attention to women's *collective* rather than individual political leadership, particularly in countries where formal political institutions are captured, eroded, or politically stuck. They also underscore the limits of donors' traditional reliance on projectized, short-term civil society grants, echoing what scholars of the WPS agenda have also observed in conflict-affected societies.[78] In Myanmar, for instance, women's rights defenders have asked international actors for more flexible funding that would allow them to maintain their operations and better respond to rapidly changing political circumstances. In the aftermath of the coup, some donors allowed women's groups to keep their project-based grants but use them for other purposes; others have provided nonearmarked grants to simply allow organizations to survive. Yet these measures were small-scale crisis responses rather than a systematic shift in the field.[79] For an international democracy aid community that has prioritized low-risk, technical assistance and prized its impartial political stance, effectively supporting women's political mobilization in difficult political contexts will require significant changes in strategy and practice.

Conclusion

Aid for women's political empowerment emerged and grew during a period of relative democratic optimism, when women in many democratizing countries were mobilizing for greater political voice and representation. Assistance providers and local advocates alike hoped that advancements in women's political leadership would help deepen the quality of democracy for all citizens. Yet the past decades have shown that the relationship between women's political leadership and broader democratic inclusion is complex. In some countries, women's political gains have been unevenly distributed, as gender inequities persist alongside profound social, economic, and political cleavages. Undemocratic or illiberal political actors have sometimes used women's political leadership as a smoke screen, creating the appearance of reform while advancing exclusionary political projects. In recent years, other antidemocratic actors have been less restrained in their efforts to reinstate social hierarchies, leaning on explicitly antifeminist discourse and eroding women's social and political freedoms to garner public support.

Assistance providers are gradually adapting to these emergent threats. References to intersectionality in donor strategies have become more common, and a growing cohort of programs prioritizes the political empowerment of women from marginalized groups. Practitioners have also had to adjust their work to closing political and civic space, often by shifting their focus to women's local-level leadership or civil society participation. Yet these efforts have unfolded in an ad hoc and inconsistent fashion. There is remarkably little analytical and practical guidance on how to modify existing assistance models in contexts of entrenched structural violence and inequality, democratic erosion and polarization, and authoritarian co-optation of women's rights.

Going forward, these challenges necessitate aid providers and advocates to explore new avenues for strengthening reform actors in difficult political contexts. Doing so will require more comprehensive gender and power analyses that critically examine the relationship between women's high-level political leadership, women's everyday rights and empowerment, and intersecting axes of exclusion. It also involves looking beyond formal political institutions and processes to support women's autonomous political mobilization and facilitate links between different movements for justice and inclusion. Policymakers and aid providers will have to confront questions of political risk: supporting actors and groups who challenge patriarchal authoritarianism and entrenched social inequities will trigger resistance and pushback.

11

Toward a Different Assistance Model

"In my view, what international donors are doing is good, but it is limited. They organize workshops; they invite women from different political parties for two or three days. Some do follow-up activities [. . .] But some just organize something for two or three days and then it's goodbye. It's not enough. It is not enough to change people's mentalities, to build a culture of women's leadership in society."[1] These words, spoken by a Moroccan women's rights activist, exemplify a common view among the gender equality advocates we met over the course of our research. Although many underscored the importance of international resources for their work, they voiced doubts that current assistance *methods* were well suited to advancing gender-transformative change. Donor funding, in their experience, was often too short-term, too fragmented, too top-down, and too technical, and offered through project grants that hinder local groups from growing their constituencies and pursuing their advocacy priorities.

The concerns raised by women's rights leaders in Kenya, Morocco, Myanmar, and Nepal echo previous analyses of Western democracy assistance. Scholars have criticized foreign aid for its overreliance on technical and siloed approaches that do not challenge powerholders and for prioritizing short-term, measurable outputs over long-term investments in bottom-up mobilization.[2] Researchers assessing the WPS agenda similarly highlight donors' overreliance on short-term projects and their limited investments in grassroots organizations.[3] Over the past several years, some staff members of Western and multilateral donor agencies have started grappling more extensively with these recurring shortcomings. Particularly as their focus has shifted to challenging patriarchal gender norms, empowering marginalized women, and responding to democratic backsliding and antifeminist backlash, they emphasize the need to experiment with more flexible ways of working.

In this chapter, we examine how current assistance modalities and practices need to change to meet the challenges facing the field. We foreground the perspectives of local women's rights organizations across our four cases, which

Aiding Empowerment. Saskia Brechenmacher and Katherine Mann, Oxford University Press.
© Oxford University Press 2024. DOI: 10.1093/oso/9780197694275.003.0011

are often the final recipients and implementers of international aid and the actors at the forefront of gender equality struggles. We first delve into three core critiques of international assistance: donors' chronically short time horizons, persistent programmatic and thematic silos, and the lack of flexible and core support for local women's rights actors. We then turn to several models that seek to address these shortcomings, highlighting their transformative potential and current limitations. Some donor governments have established new funding mechanisms that channel more resources to women's organizations and movements. Others have adopted feminist foreign policies that prioritize gender equality objectives across their external relations. These reforms respond to civil society calls for more equitable partnerships, high-level diplomatic support, and greater policy and aid coordination. Yet they also remain vulnerable to bureaucratic roadblocks and political pushback.

Chronic short-termism

In 2016, UN Women convened a meeting of parliamentarians, women candidates, electoral officials, and other development organizations operating in the Indo-Pacific. The goal of the gathering was to assess the past decade of international efforts to support women's political participation in the region and reflect on both their successes and weaknesses. "What came out of the meeting was that we had short-term, limited interventions that did not result in significant change," recalls one of the international aid officials involved. "I still see this reflex to implement small, time-limited interventions that are relatively disconnected from any real analysis of what is stopping women's participation at the country level."[4]

Donors' and implementers' reliance on excessively short time frames remains a common critique of democracy assistance around the world.[5] After several decades of learning, most practitioners recognize that democratic reform unfolds in nonlinear and unpredictable ways, and they have moved away from overly rosy assumptions about the nature and pace of political change. At the same time, limited bilateral funding for democracy assistance, combined with donor pressure on international aid organizations to demonstrate measurable results, make it difficult to implement longer-term, open-ended interventions that move beyond narrow, predefined project templates. Although this problem affects the field as a whole, it is particularly pronounced for programs focused on women's political empowerment, which receive only a small share of overall democracy aid funding. As we laid out in Chapter 2, aid providers have increasingly integrated activities related to gender equality and women's participation into democracy support initiatives. Yet spending on *targeted* gender programs remains limited. A significant share of aid for women's political leadership still comes in the form of short-term funding made available in the lead-up to national elections, often as part of broader electoral assistance packages.[6] The result is a stark disconnect between rhetoric and practice. Policymakers and practitioners recognize that challenging male dominance in politics is a gradual and multidimensional process. But multiyear programs that allow international and local partner organizations to advance gender equality change in politics across multiple levels and institutions are rare.

Although this pattern hinders both international and local organizations, it is particularly challenging for local women's groups that are smaller than Western democracy aid organizations and depend heavily on international resources. In Kenya, for example, women's organizations have struggled to secure funding to advocate for women's leadership or recruit and support women candidates more than a year before an election. "Most of this funding comes very late, so you cannot start doing needs assessments, trying to understand where people are. You are really bound by time, so you have to do something within six months," one woman's rights advocate in Nairobi told us. "If we do not have the funding, it means we do not do the work. And if we have the funding, it means we have to go with the timelines that have been set by the funding institutions. We cannot really get into the details of what your needs are, or remove a chunk of the budget and use it to cover these needs, and then another chunk to do something else."[7] Due to these short-term disbursements, workshops for women aspirants and candidates, party officials, and community leaders often arrive too late in the campaign cycle for women to build a political constituency and strengthen their political party ties (see Chapter 6).

Women's organizations find it even more difficult to continue their work on women's political leadership after elections conclude and donors' election-related funding dries up. Instead of pursuing initiatives to build a strong pipeline of women candidates, advocate for institutional reforms, or transform local-level norms around women's political leadership, they are often forced to shift their programmatic focus to other issue areas, such as gender-based violence.[8] This problem is exacerbated by aid providers' insufficient focus on sustainability. Programs rarely include mechanisms to preserve positive changes that have been secured or to help local partners transition to alternative funding sources once project-related resources run out. "The donor community does a program once and forgets what happened," a gender equality advocate in Nepal noted. "There needs to be continuous support for programs. We need follow-up programs [...] Once a program is over, they don't care."[9] A staff member of a major US democracy assistance organization echoed this criticism. "A lot of the time people are siloed, and they are jumping from activity to activity. The focus and the investment of the donors is not necessarily on longevity. Even though the donor will be in the country for thirty years, our programs are often five years at best, and oftentimes two or three."[10]

Mainstreaming gender objectives into broader and better-funded democracy programs, such as large-scale electoral and parliamentary assistance initiatives, has not resolved these problems. For one, projects that include gender equality or women's participation as secondary rather than primary objectives rarely benefit feminist and women-led organizations directly and, therefore, do not address these actors' recurring funding shortfalls. In fact, mainstreaming can create additional pressure on these groups. They struggle to access funding that is *not* ear-marked for gender equality work, as donors and implementing organizations see them as specialized "women's rights actors" that have little to add to broader democratic reform agendas. At the same time, they increasingly compete with other democracy and human rights organizations for gender-related projects.[11]

Moreover, gender mainstreaming initiatives within the democracy aid sector vary widely in quality and depth (see Chapter 5). Within many donor agencies and multilateral organizations, there are simply too few staff members tasked with ensuring that all policies, initiatives, and calls for proposals include a thorough gender and power analysis and clear gender-related objectives and evaluation criteria.[12] Within USAID, for instance, only one staff person within the Democracy, Human Rights and Governance Center solely focuses on gender issues. USAID missions are similarly understaffed: in some missions, one person is designated as the gender focal point on top of their many other responsibilities. As a result, donors do not always hold implementing organizations to high standards for integrating gender equality into their theories of change, which contributes to superficial gender-related activities that fail to produce meaningful change.[13] Similar challenges exist within multilateral organizations. For instance, UNDP often leads the implementation of multi-million-dollar electoral assistance programs, yet a 2015 evaluation of the organization's work found significant gaps in internal gender expertise, particularly with respect to integrating comprehensive gender analysis into program design.[14] At the same time, UN Women sometimes remains sidelined from electoral assistance or only receives limited funding for short-term gender and election initiatives.[15]

Enduring silos

Adding to donors' overreliance on short-term interventions is the siloed nature of gender equality funding. As we examined in the previous two chapters, advancing women's political power almost always requires fundamental changes beyond the political sphere. Sociocultural norms about women and girls' domestic responsibilities, their experiences of insecurity and violence, and entrenched socioeconomic inequities all shape women's ability and desire to engage in political life. Particularly for women from marginalized communities, gender inequalities are one of several axes of marginalization that diminish their political voice (see Chapter 10). A growing body of practice-oriented research therefore emphasizes that women's political empowerment initiatives are most effective when they target the interrelated economic, sociocultural, and political drivers of exclusion, with various interventions and reform initiatives at local, national, and regional levels reinforcing one another.[16] At the moment, however, bureaucratic and thematic silos often prevent such linkages and perpetuate arbitrary divisions between funding streams and programmatic initiatives.

Even international actors supporting women's political empowerment in the same country struggle to ensure that their activities add up to a coherent whole. In the worst cases, the result is duplication: different donors fund similar training programs targeting the same cohort of women while other priorities remain underfunded. Weak coordination also increases the logistical burden on local partners, who have to juggle multiple donors with varying priorities and administrative requirements. For example, the Association Démocratique des Femmes du Maroc (ADFM), a prominent advocacy group focused on women's political participation in Morocco, has previously received funding from eighteen different funders at once.[17]

To address these problems, bilateral and multilateral donors have sometimes relied on country-level coordination groups focused on gender equality, governance, or elections to share information about their activities. In other instances, they contribute to pooled electoral assistance funds or multidonor initiatives with objectives related to gender and democracy. Yet both coordination groups and pooled funds often struggle to reconcile competing priorities. As a policy issue that straddles gender equality and democratic governance, women's political empowerment occasionally falls through the cracks.[18] In Myanmar, for instance, a gender equality group cochaired by UN Women failed to include several democracy assistance organizations, which did not consider themselves to be part of the wider gender equality community.[19]

Since coordination among democracy aid actors can be challenging, it is not surprising that partnerships *across* aid sectors present even greater hurdles. Despite some efforts to move away from technical approaches to socioeconomic change, most donors still view their developmental and humanitarian goals as distinct from their more limited investments in political, prodemocratic change (Sweden, with its rights-based approach to development, represents somewhat of an exception in this regard). In many donor agencies, funding for socioeconomic development therefore flows through different bureaucratic units and channels than funding for democracy, rights, and governance.[20] Programs focus *either* on women's socioeconomic rights and empowerment or on women's political participation and leadership, rather than treating these domains as inherently linked. Although aid providers may hope that initiatives supporting women's access to land or reproductive health services in a postconflict society contribute to women's political voice and civic engagement, such interventions rarely link to democracy aid programs. Those working on democracy and rights issues note that these silos are not just the product of bureaucratic divisions. They also speak to persistent concerns among some development practitioners that engaging with questions of rights and democracy risks "politicizing" their work. Yet this segmented approach is out of sync with the reality that women's socioeconomic marginalization is often tied to their lack of political voice and vice-versa.

Similar divisions afflict donor funding for conflict prevention, stabilization, and postconflict recovery. Over the past decade, the WPS agenda, which seeks to bolster women's meaningful participation in conflict prevention and resolution, has gained traction within the foreign policy apparatuses of major donor governments, prompting the widespread adoption of WPS National Action Plans and related initiatives. However, these efforts remain marginalized from "mainstream" peace and stabilization initiatives. Donors rarely use gender analysis to strengthen their policy responses to conflict and fragility, for instance by asking how gender norms shape conflict and violence or how women's peacebuilding roles could contribute to political change.[21] Instead, gender-related issues are treated as a secondary concern, and gender-focused actors struggle to access peace and security funding that is not specifically earmarked for women's rights.[22]

Moreover, WPS programs and funds are often bifurcated from democracy and governance programs implemented in conflict-affected contexts, even though women's political participation is a core pillar of the WPS agenda. In Myanmar, for instance, many donor governments supported women's participation in the peace process through large multidonor funds such as the Joint Peace Fund and the Paung Sie Facility, which in turn issued grants to women's organizations advocating for inclusion in peace negotiations.[23] Yet these efforts unfolded separately from international support for democratic governance. "In a context like Myanmar, it doesn't make much sense to have those silos," one aid official working in Myanmar told us. "Cross-learning between [women's participation in peacebuilding and women's political empowerment] seems to have a lot of value, but there is less work on this. In that respect, there has been a challenge."[24]

Recently, several donors have taken steps to overcome coordination gaps. The European Commission's Gender Equality Action Plan III, for instance, requires EU delegations and EU member state embassies to develop joint country-level implementation plans that lay out gender equality policies and assistance objectives over multiple years, including their priorities related to women's political participation and leadership.[25] USAID has also launched a Network for Gender Inclusive Democracy intended to mobilize international resources for women's political empowerment and foster dialogue and knowledge-sharing among donors, intergovernmental organizations, and civil society partners. While it is too early to assess the impact of these mechanisms, they provide platforms for building greater coherence, especially if they facilitate coalition-building among local reform actors as well as international actors.

An externally driven agenda?

Short-term funding cycles and enduring thematic silos are symptomatic of a more fundamental challenge: current funding modalities are rarely designed to enable women leaders and organizations to set their own priorities, respond to changing political constraints and opportunities, and pursue long-term strategies. Instead, most assistance is structured around technical projects that tie local organizations to fixed activities and outputs and treat them as implementers rather than autonomous drivers of change. Faced with global democratic backsliding and growing government hostility toward transnational political aid, parts of the democracy assistance community have started to rethink this model. One overarching theme has been the need for "politically smarter" approaches: programs that are based on contextual power analyses rather than standard templates, that are more flexible and adaptive in their design, and that empower local reform actors rather than imposing external objectives and theories of change.[26]

It would be overly simplistic to characterize the goals of women's rights activists and movements in aid-recipient countries as determined by external funders. Existing research identifies multidirectional relationships linking domestic and international actors. For example, Restrepo Sanín (2022) describes how violence against women in politics emerged as an international policy priority in response to women councilors' activism in Bolivia, who lobbied legislators and feminist bureaucrats to advance legislative reforms. Various democracy aid organizations supported their activism by creating spaces for networking and by raising awareness in international fora; they have since developed research, advocacy tools, and policy recommendations that can be used by activists in other contexts (see Chapter 9).[27] The transnational diffusion of gender quotas followed a similar pattern. Quota reforms were pushed by women politicians and gender equality advocates in Europe and Latin America and then embraced and promoted by international organizations. Local political mobilization remains critical to their success. Kang and Tripp (2018), for instance, find that domestic advocacy coalitions have been the central drivers of electoral quota reforms across Africa, "above and beyond the efforts of international actors and pressures on governments."[28]

Yet, despite these pathways of bottom-up influence and mutual learning, our conversations with women's rights organizations and advocates across our four cases underscored recurring tensions and power imbalances between international donors and local actors. First, even though donors rhetorically recognize the role of local women's rights movements in driving gender equality change, many still channel a large share of their gender equality aid to INGOs based in the Global North, in addition to multilateral institutions and governmental partners.[29] In fact, the OECD reports that two-thirds of global gender equality aid flows through civil society organizations that are based in OECD member states.[30] Exemplifying this pattern, a 2018 evaluation of USAID funding for women's leadership found that twenty-five of forty-five analyzed programs were implemented by US organizations or for-profit contractors, whereas only five programs involved direct partnerships with civil society organizations in the aid-recipient country (and only one partnership was with a local women's rights organization).[31]

Not surprisingly, women's organizations based in the Global South often struggle to compete with INGOs for funding, with the latter benefiting from greater administrative capacity, human resources, and English-language skills as well as insider knowledge. Some funders also perceive international organizations as having greater technical expertise than local actors, even if their expertise comes at the expense of contextual knowledge. Although INGOs and multilateral organizations typically partner with civil society groups to carry out their programs, such partnerships can push local actors into implementation roles, while reducing their influence in the needs assessment and program design phase. These trends produce a striking gap in the international funding landscape. In 2018 only 1 percent of gender-focused international aid was allocated directly to women's rights organizations. Similarly, at the Generation Equality Forum held in 2021, only 7.5 percent of the $40 billion in financial commitments for gender equality even mentioned support to feminist movements and women leaders.[32]

Second, when aid providers do partner with local civil society groups, they still gravitate toward a small circle of professionalized, policy-oriented, and urban organizations with the administrative structures and skills needed to handle international grants. Most donor funding requires legal registration, proof of financial audits, and other administrative standards, which shuts out smaller, informal groups and those that have never accessed international resources before.[33] Even prior to the coup in Myanmar, for example, many women activists operating in the country's conflict-affected regions chose not to register their organizations with the central government. This informal status made it difficult for them to access international funds.[34] A similar imbalance exists in Nepal, where international grants are often awarded to larger organizations that are deemed less "risky" investments, especially those with preexisting ties to international donors.[35] This pattern produces a donor bias toward the narratives, priorities, and objectives of relatively privileged or professionalized women's groups, while sidelining those that are more radical, more explicitly political, or led by marginalized women (see Chapter 10).

Over time, an international focus on professionalized, policy-oriented NGOs can also weaken women's broad-based mobilization and movement-building, as these organizations are not always well connected to the majority of women voters and citizens. In Kenya, for instance, the country's most prominent women's organizations have spent the last decade advancing women's political representation by pushing for the implementation of the constitutionally mandated gender quota via policy advocacy and litigation. Yet in the face of continued resistance by the legislature and the executive, activists have started to question this pursuit of high-level reform. Some now wonder whether they should have invested more energy and resources into awareness-raising, social norm change, and grassroots political mobilization.[36]

Third, alongside these inequities in funding access, women's rights organizations lament that most international aid still takes the form of project grants rather than flexible, longer-term support.[37] In practice, this means that organizations receive funding based on specific proposals that lay out their goals, theories of change, and planned activities. The success of their projects is measured through indicators laid out in the initial proposal, or a refined version established during a midproject evaluation. Even when women's groups are fully involved in the project design phase, this approach has significant drawbacks. Not only is project funding likely to be short-term, it also impedes organizations' ability to invest in their own organizational growth and capacity, as grant funding typically cannot be used for their internal development and day-to-day operations. Moreover, following a set of predetermined activities makes it harder for organizations to adapt their priorities, goals, and tactics to evolving political conditions, unexpected hurdles and backlash, and sudden opportunities.[38]

Many of these challenges have long plagued international civil society assistance, which has been extensively criticized for its technical and depoliticizing bent. The constraints of results-oriented, projectized funding also weaken innovative work by international democracy organizations, including those working on sensitive issues such as political party dialogue and reform.[39] But the lack of accessible, long-term, and flexible support for frontline women's organizations is particularly striking given the overall increase in gender-related aid in recent years, most of which continues to circulate among governments, development agencies, and large INGOs. It is also at odds with donors' rhetorical commitments to "gender-transformative change," usually defined as change that tackles the systemic causes of gender inequality. Technical projects implemented through professional organizations can be well suited to influencing policy and legal change, but they are not necessarily set up to transform norms, attitudes, and informal practices or to foster women's grassroots agency and mobilization in the face of backsliding and resistance. Meanwhile, feminist and women's funds that support grassroots actors are simply too small to fill existing resource gaps. Between 2016 and 2018, Mama Cash—one of the biggest feminist funds—was only able to fund 3 percent of the eligible applications it received.[40] The problem, activists note, is not a lack of donor resources. It is that most aid is not designed to reach women's movements and does not allow women to challenge patriarchal structures on their own terms.[41]

Shifting resources and power

Confronted with these global inequities, feminist funds and other like-minded organizations have lobbied major donor governments for a more equitable global funding system. Drawing on scholarship documenting the critical role of feminist and women's rights movements in fighting misogyny, authoritarianism, militarism, and environmental destruction, they underscore that lasting gender equality change depends on the strength of these actors. Their calls for action revolve around three key demands: first, increased investments in local women-led groups, including in small and informal organizations led by marginalized women and groups focused on intersecting injustices; second, *better* funding for those actors, meaning funding that is multiyear and flexible and allows them to set their own priorities; and third, a stronger culture of partnership between donors, INGOs, and local women's rights activists.[42]

These advocacy efforts have triggered some positive responses by donors. Perhaps most notably, several aid agencies have created new funding mechanisms that move resources directly into the hands of local women's organizations. One of the forerunners in this area was the UN Fund for Gender Equality, which, following an initial endowment from Spain, provided $64 million in direct grants to women's organizations in 80 countries between 2009 and 2017, especially to groups led by and serving marginalized women.[43] More recently, a few bilateral donor governments, particularly Canada and the Netherlands, have also stepped up their financial support to women-led groups as part of their broader policy commitments to gender equality.

Their initial efforts relied on partnerships with INGOs and Western organizations to distribute smaller grants and other forms of support to local women's groups. For instance, in 2016, the Dutch government launched "Funding

Leadership Opportunities for Women II" (FLOW II), partnering with a small group of organizations and consortia (mostly based in the Global North) to invest 93 million euros in civil society groups working on violence against women, women's participation, and women's economic empowerment.[44] The Canadian government's global Women's Voice and Leadership Program (WVLP), a 182 million CAD fund launched in 2017 as part of Canada's Feminist International Assistance Policy, adopted a similar model. Using a range of Canadian, international, and local organizations as intermediaries, WVLP has provided multiyear core funding, rapid response grants, organizational capacity-strengthening, and support for alliance-building to local women-led groups across thirty countries.[45]

At the time of our data collection in 2020 and 2021, both programs served as important funding sources for grassroots women's groups in Myanmar. FLOW II funded IWDA's WAVE program, which we introduced in previous chapters. The program's innovative funding structure allowed IWDA to provide unusually flexible and sustained support to local women's groups, which proved particularly critical for supporting their advocacy activities. "You cannot really fund advocacy with a budget line: a lot of this work depends on informal relationship building," one of IWDA's program managers told us.[46] Canada's WVLP, on the other hand, partnered with the Nordic International Support Foundation to provide grants and capacity building to grassroots women's organizations working in remote parts of Myanmar.[47] WVLP has also supported dozens of women's rights groups in Kenya and Morocco. In contrast to most other forms of donor support, these resources have no predefined focus areas, allowing groups to choose their own priorities for action.

Despite these innovative features, both programs also replicated some shortcomings of traditional assistance models. For example, when WVLP was first established, aid officials received little guidance on applying the program's ambitious principles and goals to existing bureaucratic processes, especially since the overarching approach to risk management within Global Affairs Canada remained unchanged. Aid officials faced pressure to get the program off the ground quickly and, lacking time for systematic planning, ultimately selected partner organizations that were mostly Canadian or based in the Global North—despite the program's stated commitment to shifting more power to aid recipients.[48] The same problem arose with FLOW II. Most of the lead organizations selected by the Dutch Ministry of Foreign Affairs were from the Global North; meanwhile, the two partner organizations from the Global South received the smallest amounts of funding. This pattern triggered pushback from women's rights organizations, which argued that the process had excluded actors with fewer resources. They noted that feminist funding not only entailed making more money available to local actors but also shifting *control* over these resources into the hands of non-Western organizations and other nontraditional partners.[49]

Two recent initiatives highlight what this can look like in practice. In 2021, the Dutch government launched a new program called "Leading from the South" that is managed entirely by a consortium of feminist funds based in the Global South—an unprecedented recognition of these organizations' expertise and capacity to manage large amounts of bilateral funding (see Table 11.1). Another innovative feature is the program's emphasis on partnership. The consortium not only provides flexible grants and core funding support to feminist groups but also participates in strategic dialogues and joint monitoring and learning workshops with the Dutch Ministry of Foreign Affairs.[50] The program is running alongside a new "Power of Women" fund that is managed directly by the ministry and supports a smaller cohort of women's organizations with more sizable grants.

In Canada, advocates inside and outside of government have also advocated for shifting more power and resources directly to feminist movements. Their efforts have helped establish the Equality Fund, which builds on the lessons learned from WVLP. For one, the Fund was set up after extensive dialogues with women's rights activists and organizations around the world to ensure that its structure and operations matched their needs. It also combines an initial investment of 300 million CAD from the Canadian government with "gender lens investing" and philanthropy to generate new resources over time, with the ultimate goal of making the fund a self-sustaining and large-scale funding source for feminist movements rather than a one-off initiative.[51] Other innovations include a global panel of advisors from different backgrounds and regions that shortlists funding applications and a grantmaking portfolio that encompasses multiyear core funding for local groups alongside grants to women's funds, funding for coalition-building and networks, and dedicated support for feminist groups in conflict and disaster zones. Although these initiatives are still new, they represent innovative ways of working that could serve as models for other donors.

Reforming aid bureaucracies

At the same time, donor agencies face internal stumbling blocks to reform. This is not surprising. Shifting current assistance approaches toward more equitable partnerships with women's rights organizations and other local partners requires far-reaching changes in aid providers' ways of thinking and working.

First, reaching a diverse set of actors is labor- and time-intensive. Offering grants to large numbers of small and mid-sized women's rights organizations requires more administrative work than funding a few larger INGOs, and this

Table 11.1 **New Feminist Funding Models**

Name	Funding Modalities	Managed by	Funder	Budget
Leading from the South (2017–2025)	Flexible grants to women's organizations from the Global South	African Women's Development Fund; Fondo de Mujeres del Sur; International Indigenous Women's Forum; AYNI Fund Women's Fund Asia	Dutch Ministry of Foreign Affairs	40 million € (Phase 1) 80 million € (Phase 2)
Power of Women (2021–2025)	Grants to women-led organizations	Directly managed by the Dutch Ministry of Foreign Affairs	Dutch Ministry of Foreign Affairs	75 million €
Equality Fund (2018–ongoing)	Multiyear, core and flexible funding to women-led organizations Grants to women's funds and feminist funds Multiyear funding to coalitions and networks Grants for feminist groups working in conflict and disaster areas	African Women's Development Fund, Oxfam Canada, Community Foundations of Canada, MATCH International Women's Fund, Royal Bank of Canada, Toronto Foundation, and World University Service of Canada, Yaletown, Gender Funders CoLab	Global Affairs Canada and others	$300 million CAD (aims to be sustainable due to impact investing and philanthropic endowments)
Women's Voice and Leadership Program (2017–2022)	Core and flexible multiyear funding Smaller, short-term funding for piloting new approaches and emergency responses	In-country implementing partners	Global Affairs Canada	$182 million CAD

can be at odds with donors' desire to move funding quickly. In Myanmar, for example, Nordic International (the Canadian government's implementing partner for WVLP) held workshops in rural areas to help local organizations develop their ideas and guide them through the grant application process. This strategy sought to make WVLP funding accessible to actors that had never received international aid before. However, it also took significantly more time than standard calls for proposals.[52] Other participatory and adaptive programming approaches—such as codesigning programs with local partners, building feedback loops into program implementation processes, and involving grantees in monitoring and learning—similarly demand more staff time, capacity, and expertise than are typically made available by funders.

Second, working with nontraditional partners and providing flexible and longer-term support requires aid providers to change their approach to risk mitigation and results management. Greater space for experimentation has been a long-standing demand of democracy assistance practitioners, who note that rigid logframes may improve accountability but also stifle aid recipients' ability to work in politically responsive ways. Over the last decade, some aid actors have developed more creative ways to capture impact. Organizations such as the National Endowment for Democracy do not require logframes and instead ask grantees to develop their own evaluation plans. Others, including NDI and NIMD, have started using participatory evaluation tools, such as outcome harvesting.[53] Despite these advances, many aid officials still view flexible or unrestricted funding to civil society organizations as politically and financially risky.[54]

Risk aversion particularly stifles international support for feminist and women's rights *movements*. These movements are inherently political, focused on challenging systemic injustices and existing power structures. They often involve informal and unregistered collectives and organizations and, in some instances, engage in contentious action. They also tend to have long time horizons, as they usually encounter political resistance. These realities clash with many donors' preference for short-term policy wins and their reluctance to be seen as overtly political.

Finally, building a more feminist funding ecosystem also requires the aid community to re-think the role of INGOs, including those in the democracy assistance field. Most democracy aid initiatives rely heavily on partnerships with North American and European organizations, multiparty institutes, and political party foundations specialized in working with political parties, parliaments, and electoral bodies. Calls for more direct funding for women's groups do not imply that these actors have no role to play in advancing women's political empowerment globally. Yet to date, there has been little discussion of how these organizations could integrate feminist principles into their work.

As a starting point, democracy aid organizations could rethink their partnerships with women's rights organizations, to ensure that the latter are meaningfully involved in strategic planning and program design and benefit from the unique platform that international organizations provide. Internally, democracy assistance organizations could invest in the gender expertise of their staff, to ensure that even nonexperts understand the core tenets of gender-transformative program design. In our interviews, several staff members working in these organizations expressed frustration with inconsistent leadership commitments to this type of integration. Some had encountered colleagues who refused to work on gender issues because it was not part of their official job description or because they perceived gender equality to "no longer be an issue."[55]

Finally, recognizing that many hurdles to democratic inclusion are shared across borders, aid actors could explore new ways to extend their work on women's political empowerment into established democracies, thereby challenging existing divides between aid providers and recipients. Groups such as NDI are already engaged in cutting-edge global advocacy work in this vein, for instance on online violence against women in politics. These activities model new cross-national partnerships that could produce action-oriented research, advocacy campaigns, and knowledge exchanges spanning established and newer democracies.

A growing feminist tide

Crucially, many gender equality advocates note that reforming the international aid system alone is not enough. They would also like to see donors exert greater *diplomatic* pressure for women's political leadership and inclusion, leveraging their direct access to government counterparts. In Kenya, for example, women's rights organizations and feminist politicians found themselves frustrated with Western donors' reluctance to challenge political leaders on their failure to implement the two-thirds gender principle, despite several court rulings ordering the Kenyan parliament to do so. Although UN Women and other development actors pressured the parliament to pass a quota law, they refrained from publicly admonishing the parliament's unconstitutional composition in the aftermath of the 2017 and 2022 elections.

"Donors are sometimes scared to make difficult calls," argued one of the Kenyan activists who had taken the government to court for its failure to implement the quota. "Many of them didn't want to support adversarial action against the government. They don't want to be seen doing that, because the government considers it interference by international bodies."[56] A gender expert who had worked in Kenya echoed this concern, noting that international action had been too timid because aid actors were afraid of jeopardizing their relationships with government counterparts. "Maintaining access is everything. If you are pushing the envelope or threatening the power of the men who hold office at the moment, you are going to lose that. If you are really challenging campaign finance structures, questioning how security is organized, accusing folks of violating their own constitutions, and really holding them to account to those things— that's really disruptive, and you could lose your access and your funding."[57]

These critiques reflect what political scientist Sarah Bush has called the "taming of democracy assistance": the tendency of professionalized international aid actors to promote democracy in technical, nonpolitical ways, prioritizing their own organizational access and survival over political confrontation.[58] Yet whereas Bush categorizes initiatives related to women's rights as "non-confrontational" aid, our interviews with women's rights advocates underscore that challenging patriarchal institutions can be highly politically sensitive, particularly if doing so threatens the authority and power base of sitting male powerholders.

The disconnect between aid commitments and diplomatic action becomes more pronounced when we look beyond democracy assistance to the wider foreign policy field, including donor governments' defense, security, and trade policies. For instance, despite the proliferation of WPS action plans that emphasize the importance of women's participation in peace and security efforts, short-term security imperatives and elite deal-making continue to sideline women from peace negotiations as mediators and negotiators, most recently in Afghanistan. Between 1992 and 2019, women made up only 13 percent of negotiators, 6 percent of mediators, and 6 percent of signatories in major peace processes signed around the world.[59]

Many governments have also inconsistently integrated gender equality into their trade policy instruments or pushed for gender equality protections in multilateral forums.[60] A 2022 analysis by the Government Accountability Office found that only six of fourteen US free trade agreements and seven out of sixty-two Trade Investment Framework Agreements included provisions to promote women's rights and economic interests.[61] These omissions might seem disconnected from progress on women's political empowerment in any given country. However, they underscore that donor governments are not using the full spectrum of policy levers available to advance gender equality globally, thereby hindering the structural changes needed to ensure women's full political inclusion.

In light of these challenges, it has been encouraging to see a growing number of countries adopt feminist foreign policies (FFPs) in recent years. Sweden was the first to announce an FFP in 2014; as of 2022, several other countries— including Canada, Chile, Colombia, France, Germany, Liberia, Luxembourg,

Mexico, the Netherlands, and Spain—have followed suit. These policies reflect a growing political ambition to center gender equality in countries' external relations and to mitigate policy incoherence across development cooperation, diplomacy, trade, and security policy. The use of the word "feminist," pushed for by activists, is intentional: it aims to signal a more radical commitment to systemic transformation than traditional "gender mainstreaming" approaches.

What these policies entail in practice is more difficult to determine. To date, governments' FFP frameworks vary considerably in their level of detail and scope. Sweden's initial policy focused narrowly on women's rights and empowerment; more recently, some governments have broadened their approaches to encompass other dimensions of political and social inclusion.[62] Countries also vary in how far they extend their commitments across different policy areas, with some (like Canada) focusing on international assistance and others (like France and Mexico) putting the spotlight on diplomacy or emphasizing a holistic framework that spans development, diplomacy, and defense (Luxembourg). Not surprisingly, there have also been tensions between the radical ambitions of feminist activists that helped push for these frameworks and the reality of governments' partial or superficial implementation.[63]

While many FFP frameworks are still new, it is possible to discern some of their positive effects. In several countries, they have coincided with substantial funding increases for gender equality promotion.[64] Canada's Feminist International Assistance Policy, for example, includes a commitment to allocate 95 percent of Canadian foreign aid to programs with gender equality as a principal or significant goal, which has incentivized aid officials to make gender a more prominent part of every project they propose.[65] In France, gender-focused aid commitments have increased by 22 percentage points since the government adopted an FFP in 2019.[66] It is also no coincidence that the innovative funding models described earlier in this chapter were developed by governments committed to advancing feminist foreign policies.

It is more difficult to assess whether these policies have changed countries' diplomatic engagement or other aspects of their external relations. Some progress is visible at the multilateral level. Until it abandoned its FFP in 2022, Sweden played a prominent role in keeping gender equality on the agenda of the UN Security Council and of the Council of Europe, whereas both Canada and France made gender equality a political priority during their respective G7 presidencies.[67] Yet many governments have not systematically reported on and evaluated their implementation processes thus far. In some countries, FFP is also too new to draw firm conclusions about impact.

Generally, however, current debates about FFP among government officials and advocates have been strikingly silent on the topic of gender-inclusive democracy. For example, discussion papers compiled by civil society advocates to inform Canada's future FFP framework addressed peace and security, climate justice, globalization, and the care economy, yet paid negligible attention to democracy promotion.[68] In the United States, the policy priorities articulated by FFP advocates have focused on development aid, humanitarian assistance, trade policy, defense, and immigration, but they make almost no reference to US action to strengthen democracy domestically or abroad.[69]

Although both FFP frameworks and international democracy support are concerned with ensuring a more gender-equitable distribution of power, the connections between these two agendas remain underdeveloped. Women's rights advocates pushing for feminist foreign policies tend to focus on the structural drivers of women's exclusion, which they view as fostering women's political marginalization. They also, in some cases, lack strong organizational ties to the democracy aid community. Yet at a time when democratic backsliding threatens global gender equality progress, both communities of actors could benefit from and reinforce one another's work. On the one hand, a democracy lens invites women's rights advocates to focus on the political coalitions needed to advance and protect feminist policy change. On the other hand, a feminist lens could help strengthen the democracy aid community's attention to *substantive* democracy: democratic institutions and processes that reflect and respond to the interests of all citizens.

Conclusion

Democracy aid actors have become more attuned to the complexities of gender equality change in politics. Yet recurring weaknesses in current assistance models hinder their attempts to innovate. Aid programs continue to be characterized by short funding timelines and programmatic silos. Project-based aid often sidelines local women's rights organizations or pushes them into implementing roles, rather than empowering them to develop longer-term strategies and stronger constituencies. Recognizing these weaknesses, several donor governments in recent years have developed new funding models that move more money directly into the hands of grassroots women's organizations. Some have also adopted FFPs that aim to make gender equality a more central priority of their external engagement and align their diplomatic, policy, and assistance efforts on women's rights and inclusion.

These reforms, while encouraging, remain nascent and fragile. Many donor agencies are still hesitant to take on the risks involved in shifting more power and resources to local organizations. Bureaucracies can be difficult and slow to transform, and even reform-oriented actors face pressure to demonstrate short-term results or move funding quickly. Within the broader circle of international democracy aid organizations, the commitment to invest more staff, resources, and expertise into gender equality issues remains inconsistent.

Finally, international support for both democracy and gender equality faces strong political headwinds. Some donor governments, including the United Kingdom, have drastically cut their aid budgets in recent years and reoriented their foreign policies toward narrowly defined economic and security interests.[70] Others have decreased their engagement on gender equality issues after right-wing populist parties and leaders have come to power, as we witnessed in the United States under President Trump and more recently in Sweden. For Western donor governments, new geopolitical crises and heightened competition with Russia and China have made threats to democracy more politically salient, but rising security concerns also risk diluting their human rights commitments. In sum, advocates seeking to improve international support for women's political empowerment and gender equality still have a long road ahead of them, and face new hurdles and pushback.

12

Building Gender-Inclusive Democracies

Today, it is difficult to imagine democracies that disenfranchise and politically exclude half of their citizens. The idea that women's political empowerment is critical to both democracy and gender equality is now enshrined in multiple international and regional conventions and treaties, following years of local and transnational feminist mobilization and norm-building. Globally, the face of political leadership continues to change, gradually becoming more reflective of the diversity in our societies. At the same time, progress toward building truly gender-inclusive political systems has been slower than expected. As political change swept various regions of the world in the 1980s and 1990s, gradual and often partial democratic transitions enabled women to demand a stronger voice in decision-making. Yet after a period of rapid gains, this political momentum appears to have slowed in some countries and stalled altogether in others. In many parts of the world, women's political gains have been significant, but advocates and reformers still struggle to dislodge discriminatory norms, practices, and institutions.

International assistance has been an underexplored dimension of these processes of change. Over the past three decades, bilateral donors, multilateral organizations, and a wide range of international nongovernmental organizations have invested increasing resources into programs and initiatives that promote gender equality in politics, often as part of their broader support for democratic change and consolidation. In response to women's ongoing political mobilization, shifting international norms, and advocacy by gender experts within aid agencies and organizations, they have developed a wide-ranging programmatic toolkit to promote women's participation and influence as voters, activists, and elected representatives. As this area of international assistance has expanded, so too has academic research analyzing the difficulties of transforming patriarchal

Aiding Empowerment. Saskia Brechenmacher and Katherine Mann, Oxford University Press.
© Oxford University Press 2024. DOI: 10.1093/oso/9780197694275.003.0012

political systems and institutions. However, to date, most scholars have narrowly focused on specific components of international aid for women's political empowerment, particularly international actors' role in promoting gender quotas. Meanwhile, scholarship on democracy promotion has explored gender-related issues only in passing.

This book has therefore taken as its point of departure the need for more systematic research on this burgeoning field of democracy assistance. Studies of politically oriented aid tend to either dismiss it as insignificant or overstate its transformative impact. We have argued that a more nuanced and disaggregated assessment is needed. Recognizing the complexity that now characterizes the field, we set out to answer several questions. First, how has international support for women's political empowerment evolved over time and why? Second, what have practitioners learned about the strengths and weaknesses of the most common programming models and their underlying theories of change? And third, what are the new challenges facing this area of international support, and how do they unsettle existing assistance approaches? The book presents a number of significant findings about the current state of international support for women's political empowerment and offers pointers for further research and recommendations for reform.

Recapping our arguments

With respect to the field's evolution, our book traces a journey from early goals of "adding women and stirring" to more reflective and sophisticated efforts to transform exclusionary political institutions. Responding to a global wave of democratization in the early 1990s, the first generation of programs geared toward promoting women's empowerment was concerned with increasing women's participation as elected officials, voters, and civil society activists. Many early programs focused on bolstering the demand for and supply of women in politics, which, in practical terms, often translated into support for gender quota reforms, training programs targeting women candidates and politicians, and funding for politically oriented women's groups. These approaches prioritized women's descriptive representation and centered on formal political processes and institutions, such as elections and parliaments. They achieved some important successes: most notably, international actors helped advance the global proliferation and subsequent strengthening of gender quotas throughout the 1990s and 2000s. But these efforts were also limited in important ways. Women's rights advocates and their international backers quickly recognized that progress in women's political representation alone would be insufficient to overcome exclusionary political structures, weaken the power of male gatekeepers, and dismantle discriminatory norms. Moreover, first-generation programs often took the form of small-scale, stand-alone interventions that were divorced from broader democracy promotion initiatives, which limited their effectiveness and reach.

In response to these limitations, democracy support actors have spent the last decade developing a second generation of approaches to women's political empowerment. Their unifying feature is a focus on making the wider political ecosystem more gender-inclusive, rather than simply integrating women into exclusionary structures. Newer programming models not only provide capacity-building but also promote institutional reforms that make electoral processes, political parties, and parliaments more gender-sensitive. They also place greater emphasis on strengthening women's political influence. Some aid actors have turned their attention to harmful social norms and violence against women in politics. In parallel, advocates within aid organizations have pushed to mainstream gender across all areas of democracy assistance, in the hopes of overcoming siloed women-focused projects.

Practitioners today rely on a more sophisticated programmatic toolbox, which encompasses strategies that target formal legal frameworks and women's capacity alongside initiatives to reform political institutions and challenge patriarchal norms and resistance in the political sphere. However, our analysis also highlights several areas where changes in aid practice lag behind changes in thinking. For one, efforts to transform discriminatory gender norms and informal political practices, including by engaging men as allies, remain much more incipient and less common than interventions focused on technical legal reform and training for women. Second, practitioners have made less progress adapting standard assistance approaches to varying political settings, particularly contexts with entrenched inequities *between* women and countries experiencing democratic backsliding. Third, current assistance models are often at odds with an ecosystem approach, as most international funding is too fragmented, short-term, and inflexible to enable movement-building and experimentation.

In Chapters 6, 7, and 8, we took a closer look at the most common programming models implemented across Kenya, Morocco, Myanmar, and Nepal, their underlying theories of change, and their strengths and weaknesses in practice. Our research underscores that training for women candidates can provide important spaces for women to share their experiences and gain practical knowledge, particularly if they are political newcomers. However, programs too often rely on one-off, superficial training activities that arrive too close to elections, in part because aid providers seek to train as many women as possible within a short timeframe. More innovative models, in contrast, provide sustained mentorship and tailored accompaniment to smaller groups of women as they navigate their campaigns. Yet even well-designed training initiatives cannot overcome structural and institutional hurdles to women's political inclusion, such as undemocratic party nominations and women's financial constraints.

In the domain of political party aid, assistance organizations increasingly combine training for women party members and support for women's sections with advocacy for gender-sensitive party reforms and external party regulations. In some countries, they have successfully facilitated cross-party women's alliances as spaces for women to build solidarity and pursue joint legislative priorities. Some party aid initiatives have also spurred gender-related reforms in national party laws and party-internal gender assessments and action plans. However, this area of assistance suffers from recurring challenges, including insufficient reform incentives on the side of party officials and weaknesses in party institutionalization in new democracies. Aid organizations often treat parties' adoption of gender policies and action plans as successful program outcomes, without necessarily monitoring and assessing their subsequent implementation. Our case studies also highlight campaign finance as an area of limited progress. Although assistance providers have documented gendered financial hurdles to women's political engagement and identified various reform options, programs targeting this politically sensitive area remain rare.

Finally, within parliaments, we have described how training initiatives and support for women's caucuses have helped newly elected women learn about and assert their rights and, in some cases, advance joint legislative priorities. Like cross-party women's alliances, formal and informal women's networks within parliaments have served as fruitful platforms for training and coordination, though their effectiveness and sustainability depend on women's ability and willingness to work across party lines and other social cleavages. At the same time, our research underscores the importance of complementary entry points to strengthen women's substantive political representation that have received less donor attention and funding: nurturing feminist critical actors, supporting coalition-building between reform-oriented politicians, bureaucrats, and advocates, and promoting gender-sensitive parliamentary reforms.

In all three domains, we documented programming models that go beyond short-term capacity-building and injections of external knowledge and instead draw on more holistic theories of change, mirroring the field's overall evolution. However, across our cases, innovative programs focused on providing long-term mentorship and supporting gender-sensitive reforms within parties and parliaments were less common. Many aid providers still fall back on standard technical assistance and training initiatives.

Moreover, we observed a recurring disconnect between sophisticated programming tools focused on assessing and strengthening gender equality within parties, campaign finance frameworks, and parliaments, and a lack of program evaluations detailing whether and how these tools have been put into practice and what factors influence the success of different reforms. Our case studies draw attention to several system-level and institutional variables that are likey to mitigate the effectiveness of different reform approaches, including the role that money and clientelist politics play in elections, the degree of party institutionalization, party leaders' reform commitment, political constraints on women's collective mobilization, and the wider democratic context in which parties and parliaments operate. These findings underscore the importance of grounding interventions in gendered political economy analysis rather than relying on standard programmatic templates.

In the third and final part of the book, we turned our attention to three critical challenges facing the field: the persistence of patriarchal gender norms and informal practices, the relationship between women's political exclusion and intersecting forms of injustice and oppression, and weaknesses and inequities in current assistance modalities. In each domain, we identified budding areas of action that represent a natural deepening of second-generation approaches. These include emerging efforts to engage men as allies, prevent violence against women in politics, empower the most socially and economically marginalized women, and shift more resources and power into the hands of feminist and women's rights organizations. Some governments have also adopted feminist foreign policies that make gender equality a more central policy and assistance priority. Many of these initiatives are still new, and continued experimentation and learning are essential to strengthen them over time. They push aid providers and implementers into unfamiliar and challenging territory, asking them to look beyond formal reforms and institutions, beyond urban centers, and beyond thematic and funding silos. They also require donors to take on more political risk, whether to support feminist resistance in contexts of backsliding or to grant local movements and organizations the flexibility and resources needed to drive gender norm change. Across the board, these efforts face strong political and bureaucratic headwinds, including competing donor priorities, organizational roadblocks, and pushback by antidemocratic and antifeminist actors.

Some may wonder whether these challenges mean that international assistance no longer has a role to play in advancing women's political empowerment globally, just as some have wondered about the future of international democracy promotion more broadly. We argue that it does. Around the world, women and their allies are still pushing for change and mobilizing for greater political inclusion. This alone is a compelling reason for continuing to offer such support. At the same time, our analysis suggests that international assistance should adapt in important ways.

Strengthening the aid ecosystem

Bilateral and multilateral donor agencies play critical roles in shaping international support for women's political empowerment. Even though they are rarely the ones designing and implementing specific interventions, they wield tremendous power through their policies, political engagement, and funding practices. Our analysis suggests several high-level changes that bilateral and multilateral donors interested in advancing women's political rights and empowerment can take to strengthen their support moving forward (see Table 12.1).

Table 12.1 **Recommendations for Change**

Strengthening the Aid Ecosystem	Deepening Second-Generation Approaches	Tackling New Frontiers
Recognize the centrality of gender norms to global struggles for democracy	Support the implementation and enforcement of legislative reforms	Adapt assistance to varying political settings and intersecting vectors of exclusion
Increase funding to gender-focused democracy programs	Provide long-term, adaptive, and problem-oriented capacity-building for women leaders	Develop programs that extend beyond formal political processes and institutions
		Bridge entrenched silos between political and socioeconomic aid
Offer core and flexible support to local women's organizations	Tackle the financial barriers to women's political leadership	Confront resistance and backlash through targeted initiatives *and* long-term investments in structural and policy reform
Deepen gender integration by building in-house gender expertise	Support gender-sensitive reforms in parties and parliaments and investigate their practical outcomes	Treat movement-building as a goal
	Explore new channels to strengthen women's substantive political representation	Invest in learning and research partnerships
	Engage men and boys as allies and stakeholders	

Recognize the centrality of gender norms to democracy

In recent decades, the notion that gender equality is an important dimension of democratic health has gained ground in international policy circles. Most policymakers also recognize that women's equal political representation is not a natural byproduct of democratic institutions and processes: instead, it requires concerted advocacy and far-reaching reform. At the same time, however, advocates and gender experts note that some donor governments and multilateral organizations still treat gender equality as less important than other areas of democratic governance, such as free and fair elections, independent media, and effective oversight institutions. As new and pressing issues have risen on the global democracy agenda, from disinformation to digital authoritarianism and illicit finance, they fear that persistent problems of gender exclusion risk getting sidelined.

Critically absent from current policy debates is a more explicit recognition that gender hierarchies and norms are often leveraged as tools to erect and strengthen authoritarian power structures. In some countries, progress on women's rights has served as an authoritarian legitimation strategy, with governments adopting top-down gender equality reforms to build domestic and international support. Other leaders are cracking down on progressive gender norms to signal their rejection of the liberal international order and Western geopolitical influence. Authoritarian regimes in Russia and China are also manipulating "traditional values" to justify their hold on power, at a time when many Western democracies are negotiating new understandings of gender identity.[1] Meanwhile, women themselves play critical roles in mobilizing against patriarchal authoritarianism, both as participants of broad-based popular coalitions and in autonomous women's rights movements.

A clearer understanding of these linkages will strengthen international policy responses to democratic backsliding. Responses that ignore the voices of gender experts and women's rights activists, on the other hand, risk replicating existing inequities. This problem is evident in current global struggles over the information environment. Various authoritarian regimes use gendered disinformation to attack their critics and fuel hostility against progressive gender norms in Western democracies.[2] Any strategy designed to challenge disinformation that ignores these dynamics misses important opportunities for prodemocratic coalition-building.

Back rhetoric with investments

A second priority is to ensure that rhetorical and policy commitments to women's political empowerment are backed by adequate financial investments.

Nearly every major development aid donor has highlighted women's political participation as a core element of their gender equality strategies and democracy support portfolios. Yet even as high-level policy frameworks tout commitments to gender-transformative change, donor resources in this area remain limited in important ways. OECD data suggest that most of the recent increase in funding for women's political empowerment has been driven by programs with gender equality as a secondary objective. In contrast, there has not been a proportionate uptick in funding for democracy programs with gender equality as their *primary* goal.

While investments in gender mainstreaming are important, they rarely enable advocates to pursue multidimensional strategies for change, for instance by combining advocacy with political mobilization, training, and awareness-raising. To make progress on their commitments, donor governments should combine gender mainstreaming with increased investments in targeted, multiyear programs focused on women's political empowerment. They should also improve their internal tracking of money spent on democracy aid programs with gender-related objectives and ensure that all aid is screened using the OECD's gender equality marker (and that the marker is correctly applied). Collecting better data will enable aid officials and researchers to assess spending trends across donors and aid recipients and over time more easily.

From more to better funding

Yet as many women's rights activists emphasize, it is not enough for donor governments to make more money available. Instead, the *recipients* and *quality* of these resources matter. Building a holistic funding ecosystem for gender equality change requires aid providers to address the persistent funding gaps experienced by feminist and women's rights organizations, which currently receive only a small share of global gender equality resources. These organizations and movements play critical roles in pushing for the implementation of progressive laws, supporting women politicians and candidates, and challenging stereotypes about women leaders. They are also tackling the structural hurdles that hold back women's equal political engagement, from inadequate sexual and reproductive care and rights to insufficient investments in childcare and girls' education. However, current aid models, including in the democracy assistance sector, often push these organizations into implementing short-term projects, rather than empowering them to set their own priorities, invest in their organizational growth, and pursue multiyear strategies. Grassroots associations and informal groups struggle to access any form of international support at all.

Correcting these imbalances is no easy task. As we laid out in Chapter 11, adopting a more feminist approach to funding that centers the priorities of local reform actors and builds their long-term organizational capacity requires fundamental changes to donor governments' risk tolerance, time horizons, and evaluation approaches. But there are many short- and medium-term steps that aid providers can take to begin moving the needle. They can partner with feminist funds in the Global South to direct more flexible and multiyear support to women's rights organizations, using the model pioneered by (or partnering with) the Dutch government's Leading From the South program. They can also contribute to existing multidonor initiatives, such as the Canadian government's Equality Fund. Furthermore, they can revise their own grant-making mechanisms to ensure that they are more accessible to local women's organizations and enhance these actors' organizational strength. USAID's renewed focus on localization represents a welcome move in this direction, though the exact contours of the initiative are yet to be defined.

Beyond directing more unrestricted resources to local women's rights actors, donors should also prioritize flexible and longer-term funding in the democracy sector more broadly. This is not a new demand. Critics have repeatedly noted that rigid approaches to program implementation and results management are ill-suited to unpredictable political reform processes. The same basic insight applies to women's political empowerment. The terrain of gender equality change is complex: an intervention that is effective in one context may not work in another, and successful reforms often encounter new forms of resistance. It is therefore crucial that implementing organizations have the resources needed to carry out in-depth needs assessments, collect continuous feedback throughout the program implementation cycle, and adapt to emerging issues as they arise.

Advance gender integration

Advancing gender-transformative change abroad also requires donor governments and multilateral institutions to implement internal changes. Most UN organizations as well as foreign ministries and development agencies have not achieved gender equity in senior leadership roles, including in appointed ambassadorial positions. Prioritizing diversity across their own leadership and implementing gender-sensitive internal reforms—including with respect to childcare, parental leave policies, and sexual harassment protections—signals that these institutions are willing to walk the talk and examine their own practices with a critical lens.

For donor governments, a strong political commitment to domestic gender equality reform is equally important. The US government's first National Strategy on Gender Equity and Equality, which integrates domestic and international policy objectives, represents an important step in this regard. High-level integration of domestic and international priorities, which is also reflected in the UN's Sustainable Development Goals and in some countries' WPS National Action Plans, underscores that persistent gender inequities are shared across borders. By acknowledging domestic shortcomings and tracking the implementation of national reform commitments, aid-providing governments can support gender equality globally from a position of humility, solidarity, and shared interests, rather than one of political or cultural superiority.

Finally, bilateral and multilateral donors—as well as international democracy aid organizations—should expand their in-house gender expertise. Women's political empowerment sits at the intersection of two areas of international engagement: support for gender equality and women's rights on the one hand, and democracy assistance on the other. To strengthen their work in this area, aid agencies and organizations need to hire and support dedicated staff with knowledge of both gender and democracy issues. They must also empower these experts to work closely with colleagues across the democracy, rights, and governance sector (and beyond) to identify opportunities for advancing both women's political empowerment and wider democracy objectives, whether through diplomatic engagement and political pressure or through financial support.

Deepening second-generation approaches

Beyond these high-level policy, funding, and organizational changes, there are several practical steps that democracy support organizations and their local partners can take to deepen and expand second-generation programs focused on women's political empowerment.

Build on past legal gains

An initial priority is to reinforce and build on past legal reforms to ensure their full implementation and close persisting gaps in legal frameworks. Over the past two decades, dozens of countries have adopted gender quotas, primarily in response to the mobilization of women's rights activists. A growing number of countries, particularly in Latin America, have also criminalized violence against women in politics and integrated gender equality provisions into their electoral codes and political party laws.

Yet the implementation and enforcement of these legal measures often remain partial, and flawed quota designs at times actively undermine women's political influence. In Kenya, for instance, activists are still fighting for the implementation of the constitutional two-thirds gender principle, and some are pushing to reform a subnational gender quota that has been used by senior political leaders to reward their supporters and disincentivize women from entering competitive district races. In Morocco, advocates are asking for regulatory measures that would ensure full gender parity across all branches of government, and for a "zebra system" that would mandate the alternation of women and men on parties' candidate lists. A recurring theme across our interviews in Kenya, Morocco, and Nepal was the need to monitor how laws are transforming political practices and outcomes on the ground in order to identify and address blockages and covert resistance.

To this end, international actors can support women's rights organizations monitoring the implementation of gender equality reforms, including quota measures and laws criminalizing gendered political violence. They can leverage their comparative knowledge to identify obstacles to implementation and formulate enforcement mechanisms. They can also fund grassroots legal and political education campaigns and support local actors' advocacy for further regulatory or legal action. In places where quota measures are difficult to implement, they can research and support alternative reform avenues, such as changes to parties' candidate selection processes or to campaign financing rules, and facilitate knowledge exchanges with reformers in other countries. Rather than treating the adoption of new laws as the end goal, however, both international actors and local reformers should view legal or policy reform as the *beginning* of a protracted political struggle over implementation.

Revamp capacity-building

Aid providers and implementers must also rethink their continued reliance on capacity-building for women candidates and elected officials. Our research underscores that training can indeed be useful: women politicians often credit such activities with building their confidence and helping them develop new technical and political skills, particularly if they are first-time aspirants or newly elected officials. At the same time, current training models suffer from recurring pathologies. They take place too close to elections and are often divorced from real-life political processes. In some cases, they are not anchored in thorough assessments of women's needs and fail to confront the critical role of male gatekeepers. In fact, instead of challenging the exclusionary nature of political institutions, they can reinforce the assumption that women are somehow less qualified to lead than men.

Rather than abandoning training interventions entirely, aid providers and their local partners can take various steps to improve them. For one, these programs should become more problem- and action-oriented. Rather than teaching general background knowledge or abstract technical skills, they should help women navigate concrete challenges they face on their political journeys, from navigating party-internal candidate-selection processes to advancing specific bills. Such an approach requires carefully assessing women's individual and collective needs in partnership with local organizations and gender experts, and designing adaptive programs that can be adjusted as implementing organizations learn more about the hurdles facing women participants. This model also requires moving outside of hotel conference rooms. Women candidates, for instance, may benefit from initiatives that bring them into dialogue with community leaders, party officials, and potential voters. Elected women officials, on the other hand, may need support for constituency outreach. In Morocco, Nepal, and Kenya, women legislators have also asked for support in navigating the transition from quota seats or proportional representation lists to single member constituency seats.

Action-oriented capacity-building also calls for more sustained accompaniment and mentorship. Innovative programs have replaced one-off training sessions held a few months before an election with long-term coaching to help women build their political profiles. These constituency-building activities do not have to be tied to electoral assistance. Instead, they can also be integrated into programs focused on access to justice, economic empowerment, climate change, or democratic governance. Given the resources required for such in-depth support, assistance organizations should consider tiered participation models that recruit and mentor a smaller cohort of women from a larger initial participant pool. Whether they are working with women candidates or elected officials, however, aid providers should embed capacity-building into holistic interventions that also include training and dialogue with male gatekeepers within families, communities, and political parties, as well as political education targeting women and men voters alike.

Address financing gaps

In addition to updating capacity-building models, aid providers should pay greater attention to the financial barriers keeping women out of politics. Money is intertwined with political power: politicians need resources in order to run for office, gain party endorsements, and influence informal political negotiations. In clientelistic political contexts such as Kenya, candidates are also expected to spend their own money to win the support of voters and constituents. These patterns have gendered *and* economic implications. Political positions end up being dominated by wealthy individuals—who are more likely to be men. Current aid interventions largely sidestep these financial stumbling blocks, because international actors are reluctant to directly fund women candidates and thereby wade into debates about political interference. In some cases, they are also hesitant to raise politically sensitive campaign finance issues with government counterparts. The result is a disconnect between aid providers' emphasis on capacity-building and the resource barriers experienced by many women candidates and politicians.

To address this gap, aid organizations should learn from and build on innovative assistance models pioneered over the past several years. For instance, women politicians often appreciate in-kind support, whether in the form of media coverage, campaign materials, research interns, or town hall meetings that allow them to interact with their constituents. Some democracy support organizations have also worked with parties to reduce their nomination fees for marginalized groups. Although such measures are not transformative in and of themselves, they can be useful starting points.

In countries where resources constitute a systemic barrier to women's political participation, international actors can try to nurture wider-reaching reforms. They can support local reporting on political finance practices to uncover weaknesses in existing legal frameworks. They can also help convene reform-oriented legislators, party officials, and civil society actors to share information about the growing range of gendered electoral financing schemes that have been implemented across different contexts, and fund further research into their effectiveness. Where elections are mostly privately funded, aid providers can advocate for gender-sensitive campaign finance regulations and electoral system reforms, support efforts to reduce clientelist campaigning, and systematically link their interventions targeting women's economic and political empowerment (more on this below). No single project or reform can fix the distortions caused by money's outsized role in politics, and international actors' influence over certain financing and spending practices is inevitably limited. Nevertheless, international efforts should continue to document and support incremental policy and regulatory changes that contribute to making political systems more equitable and inclusive.

Advance gender-sensitive institutional reforms

Many practitioners and advocates now recognize that building gender-sensitive institutions involves more than changing formal rules or promoting more women into positions of leadership. It also requires shifting informal discriminatory practices and exclusionary organizational cultures that cater to the needs and interests of elite men. Efforts to address these internal practices are most advanced with respect to parliaments. Organizations such as the IPU, the OSCE, and the Commonwealth Parliamentary Association have developed valuable research and best practice guides to help parliaments around the world become more gender-inclusive and representative institutions. Some programs have also successfully worked with parties to develop gender equality action plans or implement new internal quota measures—although aid organizations to date have collected limited information about the longer-term impact of these initiatives.

More programming, experimentation, and learning are needed in this area. Whereas parliaments today have access to a wide range of diagnostic tools and reform recommendations, we still lack research investigating the effects of different gender-sensitive reforms on parliamentary practices and women's political influence, particularly in new democracies or hybrid regimes. Similarly, there is only limited evidence that political party support has brought about significant changes in women's status or power within parties, beyond bolstering the individual capacity of women party members. Future programs should continue collaborating with interested parliaments and parties on internal gender assessments and reform, but focus more explicitly on accompanying and supporting the *implementation* of gender equality actions plans and helping reform-minded politicians and civil society actors monitor their practical outcomes. It is also critical that aid providers engage male parliamentarians and party members in these change processes, to build their buy-in and understanding of gender-sensitive reforms and help mitigate patriarchal resistance. In the absence of political will or strong feminist critical actors within parliaments and parties, the most effective entry points may lie outside of the targeted institutions themselves, and instead involve regulatory agencies, civil society groups, or other actors. Effective programs therefore depend on a clear assessment of parliaments' and parties' actual functioning, structures, and incentives, and should avoid assuming that infusions of training and technical knowledge alone are sufficient to enact change.

Rethink women's substantive representation

Our analysis further underscores the need to explore new avenues to support women's substantive representation in political processes as a separate goal from advancing women legislators' presence, capacity, and power. Many aid interventions still implicitly assume a direct link between the influence and efficacy of women legislators and the representation of women's diverse political interests. To this end, they tend to support training and mentorship for women legislators as well as women's caucuses and networks. Our case studies suggest that the latter can provide important spaces for women politicians to share their experiences, develop their substantive knowledge, and forge common agendas—particularly during political transitions or other critical junctures. Even so, legislative collaboration among women is not guaranteed, as it is shaped by the degree of party discipline and cross-cutting cleavages among women representatives. Moreover, women legislators are not always capable or willing to advocate for gender equality reforms, nor are they necessarily representative of women's diverse perspectives and experiences in society.

While strengthening women legislators' individual and collective influence remain important goals, aid organizations and advocates should also orient their efforts toward other sites, actors, and channels involved in advancing gender-transformative policy change. As noted above, one important entry point are institutional reforms that integrate gender perspectives into legislative processes. Another promising avenue for change are "cooperative constellations" that bring reform-minded parliamentarians and change agents within state bureaucracies into dialogue with women's rights activists and movements and women constituents, including those from marginalized groups.[3] Finally, practitioners can also nurture and support critical actors: reform champions—men and women—who initiate feminist policy proposals and embolden others to act.

Engage men as stakeholders and allies

Across these various areas of action, aid providers and advocates can do more to engage men as stakeholders in building inclusive political systems. Although policymakers and practitioners frequently underscore the importance of working with men, our analysis uncovered few democracy aid programs that focus on transforming patriarchal attitudes and behaviors as core pillars of their theories of change. In recent years, several organizations (including NDI and IFES) have started closing this gap by piloting new programs that target male family members of women politicians and engage male party officials and civil society activists, often in parallel with workshops targeting women political leaders. Other groups, such as GROOTS Kenya, have recruited male champions that advocate for women's political engagement at the grassroots, accompany women's campaigns, and challenge harmful gender norms in their communities.

The wider democracy assistance community should replicate and expand these initiatives. The struggle for a more gender equitable world cannot be women's struggle alone—nor are women the only ones who stand to gain. Particularly young men, men from politically marginalized communities, and men who defy heteronormative notions of masculinity can benefit from transforming existing gender hierarchies. Any program that seeks to advance women's political empowerment should consider what changes are needed on the side of male gatekeepers, and how men and boys can contribute to reform. However, efforts to engage men must be designed with great care and with continuous feedback loops. Accountability to feminist actors and goals is imperative. The aim is to shift men's behaviors and practices in ways that advance gender equality, rather

Building Gender-Inclusive Democracies

than bolstering the authority and prestige of existing powerholders. Funding should not be diverted away from already underresourced women's rights organizations or platforms to support activities that center men and boys.

Tackling new frontiers

In this section, we turn to the new and daunting frontiers facing aid providers and practitioners who promote women's political empowerment. In light of the "stickiness" of traditional gender norms and hierarchies, the interconnectedness of gender inequality and entrenched socioeconomic and political injustices, and a global pattern of democratic erosion, we argue that international support for women's political empowerment must change in several ways. The priorities we outline here go beyond adjusting or improving specific program strategies. Instead, they require a fundamental rethinking of what it means to build more inclusive and gender-equitable political systems.

Pursue more differentiated approaches

The complexities of the current global political landscape demand greater strategic differentiation by democracy support actors.[4] First, democracy aid organizations should develop more nuanced strategies adapting their assistance approaches to varying political settings, including contexts experiencing political polarization and antifeminist backlash, dominant party authoritarianism, or clientelistic and violent electoral competition. Over the past decade, international organizations have produced a wide range of programming tools to assess the effectiveness of various quota designs across different electoral systems. They have also compiled and shared positive steps that political parties, parliaments, and electoral management bodies can take to become more gender inclusive. However, these documents rarely examine the contextual factors that shape the success or failure of these reforms, nor do they identify which entry points are most appropriate under different political conditions. To mitigate this problem, gender analyses, country assessments, and programming tools should not only examine a country's formal political characteristics, such as the electoral system or the presence of gender quotas, but also investigate how women's political inclusion interacts with informal institutions and practices, alongside potential openings or roadblocks to reform. Deeper political analysis is also needed to adapt assistance to contexts of democratic erosion or authoritarian co-optation, where women's formal political inclusion may not go hand in hand with meaningful decision-making power.

Second, aid providers' tools, analyses, and theories of change should account for the interaction between gender inequities and other vectors of exclusion. Women's political marginalization is rarely driven by gender discrimination alone. Rather, various sociocultural and political hierarchies interact to shape their access to power. Supporting the political rights and leadership of Amazigh women in Morocco, for instance, requires understanding how gender discrimination relates to the marginalization of rural and indigenous people in the country. Yet even though high-level gender strategies frequently reference intersectionality, there is little practical guidance for applying an intersectional lens to democracy support. As a first step, aid organizations and their local partners could collect and share their experiences tackling gender injustices in conjunction with other forms of exclusion, in addition to seeking out experts, organizations, and movements who can impart advice tailored to specific regions, countries, and communities. The goal is not to merge gender programs into broader inclusion initiatives (and thereby potentially dilute their impact), but rather to foster more holistic coalitions for gender justice that recognize the complexity of women's lives.

Move beyond formal politics

Our analysis suggests that one important entry point for responding to both democratic erosion and sociopolitical inequities *between* women is to embrace a broader understanding of women's political empowerment. To date, assistance carried out under this rubric has primarily targeted institutions and processes directly related to political representation, especially elections, political parties, and legislative bodies. Yet a narrow focus on women's formal political leadership may not be fruitful in all contexts. Promoting women's representation in dysfunctional and illiberal political institutions, for instance, is unlikely to yield transformative changes in gender equality or democratic governance. It can also reinforce and legitimize authoritarian governments' "gender-washing" practices. Highly unequal societies present a similar challenge: if elite women's political gains have not reinforced marginalized women's basic political agency, then a narrow focus on improving high-level representation risks widening existing social cleavages.

In these contexts, a greater emphasis on bottom-up participation and mobilization may be more effective. A useful first step would be to ask women from marginalized communities what political empowerment looks like in their local communities. In some places, women might emphasize their lack of financial autonomy and voice in community-level decision-making, or state authorities' unresponsiveness to their service needs. Responding to these and other concerns might involve seeking out nontraditional partners and supporting alternative spaces for building women's and girls' leadership and collective power, such as labor unions and professional associations, student groups, faith-based associations, and women's cooperatives. It may also entail shifting from a focus on formal political representation toward a stronger emphasis on women's political activism in civil society (more on this below). Importantly, such efforts should not be viewed as stepping away from politics, nor do they have to replace continued engagement on electoral participation and legislative reform. Instead, they should be treated as deeply political efforts to make democratic norms and principles meaningful in women's everyday lives.

Bridge political and socioeconomic aid

Advancing marginalized women's political engagement more effectively will also require aid providers to bridge the persistent divisions between democracy assistance and socioeconomic aid. Women's disproportionate care responsibilities and exclusion from critical financial assets often hinder their ability to engage in politics or take up leadership positions—a problem that is particularly acute for women from economically disadvantaged backgrounds and in political systems marked by expensive, candidate-driven elections. At the same time, a growing body of evidence suggests that women's improved access to leadership and their mobilization in feminist movements can advance women's economic rights and increase government investments in services that benefit women.[5] Tackling women's political and economic exclusion in isolation therefore makes little sense.

To overcome these enduring silos, aid providers should foster stronger linkages between their socioeconomic and politically oriented gender equality interventions. Civil society grants can directly support coalition-building between women's organizations addressing these interlinked issues. Aid programs can also empower individual partner organizations to work across both domains. Initiatives aimed at improving women's livelihoods and control over assets (and broader economic development efforts) should intentionally integrate a focus on women's political leadership and decision-making, whether at the local level or in national planning and implementation processes. Some development organizations, such as Oxfam, have developed expertise working at these intersections. Building on their work will require aid agencies to incentivize collaboration between experts in economic development, education, and health and those working on democracy, rights, and governance.

Confront resistance and backlash

The persistence of patriarchal gender norms presents another formidable challenge to women's equal political engagement, even in contexts of formal political and legal equality. Around the world, women in politics are routinely undermined by entrenched gender roles, including those that dictate family and care responsibilities or influence who is considered a strong and charismatic leader. In recent years, activists across different regions are also confronting renewed and more organized countermovements defending traditional gender hierarchies in the name of religion, nationalism, and "family values." Given these concerning trends, it is welcome to see donors, international aid organizations, and local civic groups take a greater interest in transforming harmful gender norms and addressing misogynistic violence and abuse targeting women in politics online and offline.

Yet when it comes to advancing gender norm change in the political sphere, democracy supporters currently have more questions than answers. Social norms change slowly, and not always in a progressive direction. Women's greater visibility in political leadership can serve an important symbolic function, but it does not guarantee shifts in deeply rooted norms and cultural practices. Moreover, narratives and stereotypes about women's political roles are often interwoven with wider social structures, including policies, norms, practices related to education, violence, and childcare. Interventions targeting the political domain alone are unlikely to uproot these barriers. Change is needed across multiple fronts, and reform actors must be patient and humble about what they can achieve in the short and medium term. Adopting a dual approach that simultaneously tackles pressing threats and promotes longer-term transformation is therefore vital.

In contexts where state and nonstate actors are actively mobilizing against progressive gender norm change, international actors should prioritize resourcing feminist resistance. This support should be anchored in ongoing consultations with local activists and organizations to ensure that international assistance does not play into political narratives that paint gender equality reform as a foreign imposition. At the international and regional levels, governments committed to gender equality can also invest more political capital into defending and strengthening existing multilateral commitments, rather than responding to reactionary attacks in an ad hoc manner. Donors and aid organizations should also build on burgeoning efforts to combat violence targeting politically active women both offline and online, including by facilitating dialogues between policymakers, civil society, law enforcement agencies, and tech platforms and by supporting awareness-raising, advocacy, and legal reform. However, transformative gender norm change will also require sustained investments in the structural enablers of women's political empowerment, including childcare, access to land and well-paying jobs, and education, alongside targeted interventions that challenge gender stereotypes about women politicians in the media, engage male allies, and support activists who are campaigning against harmful attitudes and practices.

Treat movement-building as a goal

Another avenue for moving the field forward is strengthening women's *collective* political mobilization and leadership. Although existing aid approaches often bolster women's political networks, including women's caucuses and women's wings, they rarely seek to strengthen women's movements as a goal in and of itself. Yet, as we have discussed throughout this book, feminist and women's rights movements serve as critical channels for women to negotiate and advance their diverse political interests, and to push for changes in gender norms and social structures that are critical for their equal access to political power. These spaces are particularly important for women who do not belong to elite social groups and are therefore more likely to be excluded from mainstream political organizations and institutions. Furthermore, as we have witnessed in Myanmar, women's rights activists are also at the forefront of mobilizing against authoritarian and illiberal regimes.

Support for movements and movement-building can take different forms. Channeling more flexible funding to women's organizations is one important step, including funding that reaches grassroots groups. Aid providers can also facilitate local and regional networking spaces for women's rights activists, support grassroots political education, and encourage coalition-building between their various partners. And they can integrate a strong feminist lens into their support for nonviolent collective action, such as USAID's new Powered by the People initiative.[6] Adopting and nurturing a "movement mindset" is a new terrain for many democracy aid providers, though there are initiatives—such as the WAVE program implemented by IWDA in Asia and the Pacific region—that offer helpful models.[7] Care should be taken to allow activists to define and drive their own causes, rather than undercutting their autonomy and flexibility. In some cases, the most useful forms of international support may not be financial, but instead offer access to high-level platforms, policy consultations, and diplomatic support.

Invest in learning

We conclude our recommendations by calling on the democracy aid community to invest in further learning. Throughout our research, we have found that the evidence base undergirding different intervention models remains thin or incomplete. This problem is particularly pronounced for newer areas of action, such as initiatives challenging gender norms about women's leadership by engaging male leaders. Evaluations are not always published, and when they are, they often describe activities and participant feedback rather than attempting to trace changes in women's agency and political influence.

One avenue for mitigating this problem is for aid providers and democracy support organizations to invest more resources in high-quality evaluations and to make their findings more accessible to researchers (when politically feasible). Some democracy aid officials have rightly been skeptical of the push for quantitative measurement in development aid, noting that it can become a straitjacket that inhibits flexibility and innovation. Activists also caution that in politically difficult contexts, donor pressure to demonstrate tangible outcomes is counterproductive: sometimes, holding the line in the face of resistance is a success. What types of learning models and outcome measurements are appropriate therefore depends on the goals of the program and the context. Yet organizations today have access to a wide range of possible evaluation methods, including participatory tools such as outcome harvesting that allow for political complexity and nonlinear change processes. These tools should be refined to better capture changes in behavior and practices over time, in addition to capturing "hard" outcomes such as the number of policies passed and women promoted into positions of leadership. When collaborating with women's organizations, one evaluation objective should also be to produce learning that is useful for local reform actors, rather than merely a check-the-box exercise for the donor.

However, even high-quality program evaluations remain limited tools, particularly as they rarely look at programs comparatively. Donors should therefore consider supporting new partnerships between democracy organizations and researchers. One promising line of inquiry might focus on behavioral and attitudinal changes among male politicians and gatekeepers who participate in awareness-raising and norm-change programs. Assistance programs would also benefit from more data elucidating whether civic education campaigns that promote women's political leadership influence public perceptions of women in office and citizen's voting practices. Additionally, future partnerships could examine the drivers and impacts of internal political party reforms, which remain poorly understood.

Taking a step back, the linkages between women's political and economic empowerment warrant further research, to help aid officials and advocates understand how gains in income, assets, and wealth influence women's individual and collective political participation and how these relationships vary across contexts. There is also much to learn about the relationship between women's formal political leadership and women's everyday political, social, and economic empowerment, particularly in developing democracies. In sum, we hope that this book will motivate other researchers to direct their attention to the assistance world and stimulate new initiatives to strengthen the evidence base informing women's political empowerment efforts.

Concluding reflections

As we finish writing this book, Jacinda Ardern, the prime minister of New Zealand and one of the few women heads of state around the world, announced that she would not seek re-election after two terms in office. In her resignation speech, she explained that she was burned out after five years in the job and felt that she would no longer be able to give her best. Throughout her time in office, Ardern gained praise for her empathetic leadership style, and many commentators celebrated her decision to voluntarily step back from a senior political role. Yet during her tenure, she also experienced exceptionally high levels of misogynistic online vitriol and real-life threats. One study found that between 2019 and 2022, she faced online abuse at a rate 50 to 90 percent higher than other high-profile figures in New Zealand; police data indicated that threats against her had tripled during that same period.[8] Although Ardern has stated that this online and offline harassment did not precipitate her departure, it is emblematic of the experience of many high-profile women leaders.

Meanwhile, thousands of miles away in Iran, women continue to protest. Since 22-year-old Mahsa Amini died in the custody of Iran's "morality police" in September 2022, thousands of women—and many men—have come out onto the streets to protest the country's strict religious rules that limit what women can do and wear in public. Yet many of the protesters' demands have gone even further. They are rejecting religious autocracy and police brutality and asking for full political citizenship, human rights, and dignity. Although antiregime protests have flared up in Iran in the past, this latest mobilization marks the first time in the country's history that an uprising has been spearheaded by women. The regime has cracked down on the protesters with full force, beating, jailing, and even executing its opponents. Yet resistance persists in more covert ways. Writing in *Foreign Affairs*, Iran analyst Ali Vaez observes that "what was once an anguished whim or a distant wish, which had turned into ravaging despair, has now turned into an irrevocable demand for fundamental political change and freedom."[9]

These two brief vignettes speak to the diversity and complexity of women's political struggles around the world today. Together, they reflect a picture of both disappointment and hope. Globally, more women hold positions of power and authority now than ever before. They are challenging long-standing ideas about what leadership looks like and transforming systems and institutions built on their exclusion, mobilizing and persevering under the most difficult of circumstances. But the hurdles they face are significant. In many countries, patriarchal authoritarianism continues to rear its ugly head. Even in the world's most gender-equal societies, sexist norms and attitudes persist and are sometimes fueled by political actors.

In light of these complex and varied challenges, how can international actors and institutions best support reformers and advocates fighting for women's political empowerment globally? Our book advances a pragmatic and incremental approach. Gender equality change is a long and arduous process, driven by structural, economic, political, and cultural forces far beyond the scope of a single project or program. It involves changes at the individual, household, community, and societal levels. Time and time again, we see that gender hierarchies survive even major societal and political upheavals, alongside other systems of domination and exclusion. Bringing about change in the political sphere can be particularly difficult. Those who benefit from an exclusionary status quo usually have access to powerful tools that can block or undermine meaningful reform.

But we also see that progressive changes do occur, sometimes quickly, and sometimes gradually. International assistance will never be the primary driver of transformation, but it can provide critical support to domestic reformers. Aid organizations can share information and research from various contexts and engage policymakers on reform possibilities. They can provide resources to local activists and organizations and facilitate platforms for coalition-building and learning. Our analysis helps illuminate the strengths and weaknesses of different support strategies, while emphasizing the need for persistence, humility, and long time horizons. Our hope is that it will give advocates and practitioners valuable tools and ideas to strengthen their work and illuminate productive new avenues for scholarly inquiry.

Although this book is concerned with international assistance, it is critical to remember that building gender-inclusive democracies remains a global challenge. Some countries have fared better along certain dimensions of women's political empowerment than others. Some have experimented with useful reforms from which advocates in other places can learn. But societies all around the world continue to wrestle with what it means to democratize the pathways to and exercise of political power. Getting more women into positions of leadership is an important, but ultimately limited part of the sweeping change that is necessary. Achieving gender equality in politics requires not only changing political institutions but also rethinking how we organize and divide caregiving, how we equalize economic power, and what forms of competence and experience we nurture and reward in political leaders. In other words, the fight for women's political empowerment has many fronts, and it is a shared struggle. This is a humbling realization, but also one that should inspire solidarity and hope.

NOTES

Chapter 1

1. Republica, "44,000 plus Vying for 13,556 Posts in First Phase Local Poll," *My Republica*, May 4, 2017, myrepublica.nagariknetwork.com/news/44-000-plus-vying-for-13-556-posts-in-first-phase-local-poll/.
2. Sarah Hewitt, "Money, Power and Muscles: Women in Nepalese Politics," Australian Institute for International Affairs, May 8, 2017, https://www.internationalaffairs.org.au/australianoutl ook/local-elections-womens-participation-nepal/.
3. Interview with a National Democratic Institute (NDI) official in Nepal, April 5, 2020.
4. We arrive at this measure using data collected by the Organisation for Economic Co-Operation and Development (OECD). To calculate what we term "democracy assistance," we add OECD sector codes 15150, 15151, 15152, 15153, and 15170 ("democratic participation and civil society," "elections," "legislatures and political parties," "media and free flow of information," "women's rights organizations and movements, and government institutions"), and use the OECD's gender equality marker to examine the total funding across these sectors that has gender equality and women's empowerment as a primary objective. Calculations are based on gross disbursements by DAC members; the unit is "US Dollar, Millions, 2020." OECD.Stat, "Aid Activities Targeting Gender Equality and Women's Empowerment (CRS)," https://stats.oecd.org/Index.aspx?DataSetCode=DV_DCD_GENDER.
5. Sarah Sunn Bush, *The Taming of Democracy Assistance: Why Democracy Promotion Does Not Confront Dictators* (Cambridge: Cambridge University Press, 2015), 4.
6. Thomas Carothers, *Aiding Democracy Abroad: The Learning Curve* (Washington, DC: Carnegie Endowment for International Peace, 1999).
7. The United Nations Fourth World Conference on Women, "Platform for Action," Beijing, September 1995, https://www.un.org/womenwatch/daw/beijing/platform/decision.htm.
8. United Nations General Assembly, "Transforming Our World: The 2030 Agenda for Sustainable Development," 2015, https://sustainabledevelopment.un.org/content/docume nts/21252030%20Agenda%20for%20Sustainable%20Development%20web.pdf.
9. Sweden announced in October 2022 that it would discontinue its feminist foreign policy.
10. Inter-Parliamentary Union (IPU) Parline, "Global and Regional Averages of Women in National Parliaments," accessed July 29, 2023, https://data.ipu.org/women-averages.
11. UN Women, "Facts and Figures: Women's Leadership and Political Participation," accessed July 29, 2023, https://www.unwomen.org/en/what-we-do/leadership-and-political-partic ipation/facts-and-figures.
12. Ibid.
13. IPU, "Women in Parliament in 2022," 2023, https://www.ipu.org/resources/publications/ reports/2023-03/women-in-parliament-2022.

14. IPU Parline, "Monthly Ranking of Women in National Parliaments," accessed July 29, 2023, https://data.ipu.org/women-ranking?month=7&year=2023.
15. Ana Laura Ferrari, "Women's Civil Liberties Worldwide: Much Achieved, More to Do," Varieties of Democracy, October 6, 2020, https://v-dem.net/weekly_graph/women-s-civil-liberties-worldwide-much-achiev.
16. Abdurashid Solijonov, "Voter Turnout Trends around the World" (Stockholm: International IDEA, 2016), https://www.idea.int/sites/default/files/publications/voter-turnout-trends-around-the-world.pdf.
17. Milan Vaishnav, "Indian Women Are Voting More Than Ever: Will They Change Indian Society?," Carnegie Endowment for International Peace, November 8, 2018, https://carneg ieendowment.org/2018/11/08/indian-women-are-voting-more-than-ever.-will-they-cha nge-indian-society-pub-77677.
18. Masum Momaya et al., "Feminist Activism Works! A Review of Select Literature on the Impact of Feminist Activism in Achieving Women's Rights" (Mama Cash, July 2020), https://www.mamacash.org/media/publications/feminist__activism_works_mama_cash.pdf.
19. UN Women, "Facts and Figures: Women's Leadership and Political Participation."
20. Mona Lena Krook, *Violence against Women in Politics* (New York: Oxford University Press, 2020).
21. Thomas Carothers and Saskia Brechenmacher, "Closing Space: Democracy and Human Rights Support under Fire" (Washington, DC: Carnegie Endowment for International Peace, 2014), https://carnegieendowment.org/files/closing_space.pdf.
22. World Economic Forum, "Global Gender Gap Report 2022," July 2022, https://www3.wefo rum.org/docs/WEF_GGGR_2022.pdf; and World Economic Forum, "Global Gender Gap Report 2023," June 2023, https://www3.weforum.org/docs/WEF_GGGR_2023.pdf.
23. World Bank, "Proportion of Seats Held by Women in National Parliaments (%)," accessed February 11, 2023, https://data.worldbank.org/indicator/SG.GEN.PARL.ZS.
24. Elin Bjarnegård and Pär Zetterberg, "How Autocrats Weaponize Women's Rights," *Journal of Democracy* 33, no. 2 (2022): 60–75.
25. See, for example, Emilie Combaz, "Donor Interventions on Women's Political Empowerment: Rapid Literature Review" (Birmingham, UK: GSDRC, August 2016), https://assets.publishing.service.gov.uk/media/585813dde5274a13070000e4/Donor-interventions-on-womens-political-empowerment.pdf; and UN Women, "Corporate Evaluation of UN Women's Contribution to Women's Political Participation and Leadership: Synthesis Report," April 2018, https://www.unwomen.org/sites/default/files/Headquarters/Attachments/Sections/Library/Publications/2018/Corporate-evaluation-Womens-political-participation-en.pdf.
26. For an overview, see Pamela Marie Paxton, Melanie M. Hughes, and Tiffany Barnes, *Women, Politics, and Power: A Global Perspective* (Lanham, MD: Rowman & Littlefield, 2020).
27. Sarah Sunn Bush, "International Politics and the Spread of Quotas for Women in Legislatures," *International Organization* 65, no. 1 (2011): 103–137; Amanda B. Edgell, "Foreign Aid, Democracy, and Gender Quota Laws," *Democratization* 24, no. 6 (2017): 1103–1141; and Mona Lena Krook, *Quotas for Women in Politics: Gender and Candidate Selection Reform Worldwide* (New York: Oxford University Press, 2010).
28. Daniela Donno, Sara Fox, and Joshua Kaasik, "International Incentives for Women's Rights in Dictatorships," *Comparative Political Studies* 55, no. 3 (2021): 451–492; and Alex Kroeger and Alice J. Kang, "The Appointment of Women to Authoritarian Cabinets in Africa," *Government and Opposition* (2022): 1–24.
29. Jennifer Piscopo, "The Limits of Leaning In: Ambition, Recruitment, and Candidate Training in Comparative Perspective," *Politics, Groups, and Identities* 7, no. 4 (2019): 817–828.
30. Carmen Geha, "The Myth of Women's Political Empowerment within Lebanon's Sectarian Power-Sharing System," *Journal of Women, Politics and Policy* 40, no. 4 (2019): 498–521; and Terence Wood, "Aiding Women Candidates in Solomon Islands: Suggestions for Development Policy," *Asia and the Pacific Policy Studies* 2, no. 3 (2015): 531–543.
31. Sheila Carapico, *Political Aid and Arab Activism* (Cambridge: Cambridge University Press, 2014).

NOTES

32. Bush, *The Taming of Democracy Assistance*; Catherine Herrold, *Delta Democracy: Pathways to Incremental Civic Revolution in Egypt and Beyond* (New York: Oxford University Press, 2020); and Carothers, *Aiding Democracy Abroad*.
33. Amy C. Alexander, Catherine Bolzendahl, and Farida Jalalzai, eds., *Measuring Women's Political Empowerment across the Globe* (London: Palgrave Macmillan, 2018), 4.
34. Louise Chappell and Fiona Mackay, "Feminist Critical Friends: Dilemmas of Feminist Engagement with Governance and Gender Reform Agendas," *European Journal of Politics and Gender* 4, no. 3 (2021): 321–340.
35. For a discussion of this dynamic, see Sarah E. Parkinson, "(Dis)courtesy Bias: 'Methodological Cognates,' Data Validity, and Ethics in Violence-Adjacent Research," *Comparative Political Studies* 55, no. 3 (2022): 420–450.
36. Peter Krause et al., "COVID-19 and Fieldwork: Challenge and Solutions," *Political Science and Politics* 54, no. 2 (2021): 264–269.
37. Jane Richardson, Barry Godfrey, and Sandra Walklate, "Rapid, Remote and Responsive Research during COVID-19," *Methodological Innovations* 14, no. 1 (2021):.
38. Marnie Howlett, "Looking at the 'Field' through a Zoom Lens: Methodological Reflections on Conducting Online Research during a Global Pandemic," *Qualitative Research* 22, no. 3 (2022): 387–402.
39. Andrew Gregory, "Covid Has Intensified Gender Inequalities, Global Study Finds," *Guardian*, March 2, 2022, https://www.theguardian.com/world/2022/mar/02/covid-intensified-exist ing-gender-inequalities-global-study-finds.

Chapter 2

1. Laura Clancy and Sarah Austin, "Fewer Than a Third of UN Member States Have Ever Had a Woman Leader," Pew Research Center, March 28, 2023, https://www.pewresearch.org/ short-reads/2023/03/28/women-leaders-around-the-world/; and World Bank, "Proportion of Seats Held by Women in National Parliaments (%)," accessed February 13, 2023, https:// data.worldbank.org/indicator/SG.GEN.PARL.ZS?most_recent_value_desc=true.
2. Pamela Paxton, "Women's Suffrage in the Measurement of Democracy: Problems of Operationalization," *Studies in Comparative International Development* 35, no. 3 (2000): 92–111.
3. Nitza Berkovitch, "The Emergence and Transformation of the International Women's Movement," in *Constructing World Culture: International Nongovernmental Organizations Since 1875*, eds. John Boli and George M. Thomas (Palo Alto, CA: Stanford University Press, 1999); and Pamela Paxton, Melanie M. Hughes, and Jennifer L. Green, "The International Women's Movement and Women's Political Representation, 1893–2003," *American Sociological Review* 71, no. 6 (2006): 898–920.
4. Berkovitch, "The Emergence and Transformation of the International Women's Movement."
5. Leila J. Rupp and Verta Taylor, "Forging Feminist Identity in an International Movement: A Collective Identity Approach to Twentieth Century Feminism," *Signs: Journal of Women in Culture and Society* 24, no. 2 (1999): 366.
6. Berkovitch, "The Emergence and Transformation of the International Women's Movement."
7. Pamela Paxton, Melanie M. Hughes, and Tiffany D. Barnes, *Women, Politics, and Power: A Global Perspective, Fourth Edition* (London: Rowman & Littlefield, 2021), 52; and Rupp and Taylor, "Forging Feminist Identity in an International Movement," 380.
8. Paxton, Hughes, and Green, "The International Women's Movement," 900, and Francisca de Haan, "A Brief Survey of Women's Rights," *UN Chronicle*, accessed November 8, 2023, https://www.un.org/en/chronicle/article/brief-survey-womens-rights.
9. Mona Lena Krook and Jacqui True, "Rethinking the Life Cycles of International Norms: The United Nations and the Global Promotion of Gender Equality," *European Journal of International Relations* 18, no. 1 (2010), 113–114; and Paxton, Hughes, and Green, "The International Women's Movement," 899.
10. Melanie Hughes, Mona Lena Krook, and Pamela Paxton, "Transnational Women's Activism and the Global Diffusion of Gender Quotas," *International Studies Quarterly* 59, no. 2 (2015), 359.

242   NOTES

11. "Convention on the Elimination of All Forms of Discrimination against Women," UN Women, accessed March 11, 2021, https://www.un.org/womenwatch/daw/cedaw/text/econvention.htm.

12. Paxton, Hughes, and Green, "The International Women's Movement," 898–920.

13. Hughes, Krook, and Paxton, "Transnational Women's Activism," 359.

14. "Beijing Declaration and Platform for Action" (United Nations, September 1995), https://www.unwomen.org/sites/default/files/Headquarters/Attachments/Sections/CSW/PFA_E_Final_WEB.pdf.

15. Liam Swiss and Kathleen M. Fallon, "Women's Transnational Activism, Norm Cascades, and Quota Adoption in the Developing World," *Politics and Gender* 13, no. 3 (2017): 458–487.

16. Judy El-Bushra, "Feminism, Gender, and Women's Peace Activism," *Development and Change* 38, no. 1 (2007): 131–147; and J. Ann Tickner and Jacqui True, "A Century of International Relations Feminism: From World War I Women's Peace Pragmatism to the Women, Peace and Security Agenda," *International Studies Quarterly* 62, no. 2 (2018), 7.

17. Women's International League for Peace and Freedom, "National Action Plans at a Glance," Women Peace and Security Programme of the Women's International League of Peace and Freedom, accessed November 7, 2023, http://1325naps.peacewomen.org/.

18. Sustainable Development Goals, "Decisions by Topic: Gender Equality and Women's Empowerment," https://sustainabledevelopment.un.org/topics/women/decisions.

19. Thomas Carothers and Diane de Gramont, *Development Aid Confronts Politics: The Almost Revolution* (Washington DC: Carnegie Endowment for International Peace, 2013), 3.

20. Shahrashoub Razavi and Carol Miller, "From WID to GAD: Conceptual Shifts in the Women and Development Discourse," UN Fourth World Conference on Women, Occasional Paper No. 1, United Nations Research Institute for Social Development (1995).

21. Carol Miller and Shahra Razavi, "Gender Mainstreaming: A Study of Efforts by the UNDP, the World Bank and the ILO to Institutionalize Gender Issues" (Geneva: United Nations Research Institute for Social Development, 1995), http://213.219.61.110/UNRISD/website/document.nsf/(httpPublications)/FC107B64C7577F9280256B67005B6B16?OpenDocument.

22. US Congress, *Foreign Assistance Act of 1973*, Pub. L. No. 93–189, S.1443 (1973), https://www.congress.gov/bill/93rd-congress/senate-bill/1443/text.

23. Eva M. Rathgeber, "WID, WAD, GAD: Trends in Research and Practice," *Journal of Developing Areas* 24, no. 4 (1990): 489–502.

24. This critical approach was sometimes termed "Women and Development" (WAD).

25. Thomas Carothers, *Aiding Democracy Abroad: The Learning Curve* (Washington DC: Carnegie Endowment for International Peace, 1999).

26. Ibid.

27. Patricia Ahern, Paul Nuti, and Julia M. Masterson, "Promoting Gender Equity in the Democratic Process: Women's Paths to Political Participation and Decisionmaking" (International Center for Research on Women and the Centre for Development and Population Activities, 2000), https://www.icrw.org/wp-content/uploads/2016/10/Promoting-Gender-Equity-in-the-Democratic-Process-Womens-Paths-to-Political-Participation-and-Decisionmaking.pdf; and Larry Diamond, "Promoting Democracy in the 1990s: Actors and Instruments, Issues and Imperatives" (Carnegie Corporation of New York, December 1995), https://www.carnegie.org/publications/promoting-democracy-in-the-1990s-actors-and-instruments-issues-and-imperatives/.

28. Peter Uvin, "From the Right to Development to the Rights-Based Approach: How 'Human Rights' Entered Development," *Development in Practice* 17, no. 4–5 (August 2007): 597–606.

29. Asian Development Bank, "Gender and Development," June 2003, https://www.adb.org/sites/default/files/institutional-document/32035/gender-policy.pdf, 27–28.

30. Miller and Razavi, "Gender Mainstreaming."

31. Jane S. Jaquette and Kathleen Staudt, "Women/Gender and Development," in *Women and Gender Equity in Development Theory and Practice*, eds. Jane S. Jaquette and Gale Summerfield (Durham, NC: Duke University Press, 2006): 17–52.

32. Caroline Moser and Annalise Moser, "Gender Mainstreaming since Beijing: A Review of Success and Limitations in International Institutions," *Gender and Development* 13, no.

NOTES 243

2 (2005), 18–19; and Jane Parpart, "Exploring the Transformative Potential of Gender Mainstreaming in International Development Institutions," *Journal of International Development* 26, no. 3 (2014): 382–395.

33. OECD, "Development Finance for Gender Equality and Women's Empowerment," accessed July 29, 2023, https://www.oecd.org/dac/financing-sustainable-development/developm ent-finance-topics/development-finance-for-gender-equality-and-women-s-empowerm ent.htm.

34. Margaret Besheer, "VP Harris: 'The Status of Women Is the Status of Democracy,'" *VOA News*, March 16, 2021, https://www.voanews.com/a/usa_vp-harris-status-women-status-democracy/6203379.html.

35. The OECD's Development Assistance Committee (DAC) includes twenty-nine member governments plus the European Union. For projects rated as "significant," gender equality should be "an important and deliberate objective but not the principal reason for undertaking the project or program." For projects rated as "principal," gender equality is "the main objective of the project or program and is fundamental to its design and objectives."

36. Parker Essick and Aria Grabowski, "Are They Really Gender Equality Projects? An Examination of Donors' Gender-Mainstreamed and Gender-Equality Focused Projects to Assess the Quality of Gender-Marked Projects" (Oxfam, February 5, 2020), https://policy-practice.oxfam.org/resources/are-they-really-gender-equality-projects-an-examination-of-donors-gender-mainst-620945/.

37. Ebba Henningsson, "The Devil Is in the Details: Challenges in Tracking ODA for Gender Equality," Donor Tracker, July 6, 2020, https://donortracker.org/insights/devil-details-cha llenges-tracking-oda-gender-equality.

38. Calculated by comparing the gross disbursements by DAC members to the government and civil society sector-general (Sector 151) to allocations in the same sector labeled as targeting gender equality and women's empowerment. Calculations are based on US Dollars 2020. Note: this excludes disbursements to conflict, peace, and security.

39. As noted in Chapter 1, our definition of "democracy assistance" encompasses OECD sector codes 15150, 15151, 15152, 15153, and 15170. Calculations were made based on gross disbursements (US Dollars 2020).

40. OECD, "Aid in Support of Gender Equality and Women's Empowerment: Donor Charts," (Paris: OECD, March 2023), https://www.oecd.org/dac/financing-sustainable-developm ent/Aid-to-gender-equality-donor-charts.pdf.

41. OECD netFWD, "Insights on Philanthropy for Gender Equality," (Paris: OECD Development Centre, 2019), https://www.oecd.org/development/networks/Final_Gender_WG_Polic y_Note_7319.pdf.

42. Ford Foundation, "Ford Foundation Commits $420 Million to Tackle Gender Inequality around the Globe Post COVID-19," June 30, 2021, https://www.fordfoundation.org/news-and-stories/news-and-press/news/ford-foundation-commits-420-million-to-tackle-gender-inequality-around-the-globe-post-covid-19/; and Open Society Foundations, "Open Society Commits $100 Million to Feminist Movements and Leaders," June 30, 2021, https://www.opensocietyfoundations.org/newsroom/open-society-foundations-commit-100-million-to-support-feminist-political-mobilization-and-leadership.

43. Kellea Miller and Rochelle Jones, "Toward a Feminist Funding Ecosystem: A Framework and Practical Guide" (Association for Women's Rights in Development, October 2019), https://awid.org/sites/default/files/2022-02/AWID_Funding_Ecosystem_2019_FI NAL_Eng.pdf.

44. UN Women, "Funding Partner Contributions," accessed November 7, 2023, https://open. unwomen.org/partners.

45. UN Women, "Corporate Evaluation of UN Women's Contribution to Women's Political Participation and Leadership," April 2018, https://www.unwomen.org/sites/default/files/ Headquarters/Attachments/Sections/Library/Publications/2018/Corporate-evaluation-Womens-political-participation-Brief-en.pdf.

46. United Nations Development Programme (UNDP) Evaluation Office, "Evaluation of UNDP Contribution to Strengthening Electoral Systems and Processes," United Nations Development Programme, August 2012.

244 NOTES

47. Interview with a staff member at NDI, January 15, 2020.
48. See, for example, Lisa Markowitz and Karen W. Tice, "Paradoxes of Professionalization: Parallel Dilemmas in Women's Organizations in the Americas," *Gender and Society* 16, no. 6 (2002): 941–958; Manal A. Jamal, "Western Donor Assistance and Gender Empowerment in the Palestinian Territories and Beyond," *International Feminist Journal of Politics* 17, no. 2 (2015): 232–252; and Sonia E. Alvarez, "Advocating Feminism: The Latin American Feminist NGO 'Boom,'" *International Feminist Journal of Politics* 1, no. 2 (1999): 181–209.
49. Tenzin Dolker, "Where is the Money for Feminist Organizing? Data Snapshots and a Call to Action," (Toronto: Association for Women's Rights in Development, 2021), 17.
50. Jamille Bigio et al., "Women's Participation in Peace Processes," Council on Foreign Relations, accessed June 20, 2022, https://www.cfr.org/womens-participation-in-peace-processes/.
51. Lejla Gačanica, Raba Gjoshi, and Sofija Vrbaški, "Women's Rights in Western Balkans" (Kvinna till Kvinna, November 2020), https://kvinnatillkvinna.org/wp-content/uploads/2020/11/The-KvinnatillKvinna-Foundation-report-WRWB_2020.pdf.
52. Brigitte Grésy et al., "Feminist Diplomacy: Moving from a Slogan to Rally Support to True Momentum for Change," (Haut Conseil à l'Égalité entre les Femmes et les Hommes, November 4, 2020), https://www.diplomatie.gouv.fr/IMG/pdf/20-3315-diplomatie_feministe_synthese_du_rapport_du_hce_en_v2_cle422caf.pdf; and Louise Rozès Moscovenko, "France's 'Feminist Diplomacy': Lots of Talk, Little Action," *EURACTIV*, November 23, 2020, https://www.euractiv.com/section/non-discrimination/news/frances-feminist-diplomacy-lots-of-talk-little-action/.
53. Essick and Grabowski, "Are They Really Gender Equality Projects?"
54. OECD.Stat, "Aid Activities Targeting Gender Equality and Women's Empowerment (CRS)."
55. Rosalind Eyben and Rebecca Napier-Moore, "Choosing Words with Care? Shifting Meanings of Women's Empowerment in International Development," *Third World Quarterly* 30, no. 2 (2009): 285–300; and Srilatha Batliwala, "Taking Power Out of Empowerment—An Experiential Account," *Development in Practice* 17, no. 4–5 (August 2007): 557–565.
56. Gabrielle Bardall, "A Feminist Approach to Supporting International Democracy: Canada's Contribution" (International Foundation for Electoral Systems and the Centre for International Policy Studies, February 22, 2019), https://www.ourcommons.ca/Content/Committee/421/FAAE/Brief/BR10364070/br-external/InternationalFoundationForElectoralSystems-e.pdf.
57. Interview with a staff member at NDI, January 15, 2020.
58. Amrita Basu, ed., *The Challenge of Local Feminisms: Women's Movements in Global Perspective*, 1st ed. (Boulder: Westview Press, 1995); and Aili Mari Tripp, "How African Feminism Changed the World," *African Arguments*, March 8, 2017, https://africanarguments.org/2017/03/how-african-feminism-changed-the-world/.
59. Thomas Carothers, "Look Homeward, Democracy Promoter," *Foreign Policy*, January 27, 2016, https://foreignpolicy.com/2016/01/27/look-homeward-democracy-promoter/.
60. Alvarez, "Advocating Feminism."
61. Zehra F. Kabasakal Arat, "Feminisms, Women's Rights, and the UN: Would Achieving Gender Equality Empower Women?," *American Political Science Review* 109 no. 4 (2015): 674–689.
62. Peace A. Medie and Alice J. Kang, "Power, Knowledge and the Politics of Gender in the Global South," *European Journal of Politics and Gender* 1, no. 1–2 (2018): 37–54.

Chapter 3

1. World Bank, "Proportion of Seats Held by Women in National Parliaments (%)," accessed July 29, 2023, https://data.worldbank.org/indicator/SG.GEN.PARL.ZS.
2. World Economic Forum, "Global Gender Gap Report 2022" (Geneva, July 2022), https://www3.weforum.org/docs/WEF_GGGR_2022.pdf.
3. World Bank, "Proportion of Seats Held by Women in National Parliaments (%) – Nepal," accessed November 9, 2023, https://data.worldbank.org/indicator/SG.GEN.PARL.ZS?locations=NP.
4. UN Women, "Nepal," Women Count Data Hub, February 14, 2023, https://data.unwomen.org/country/nepal.

NOTES

5. V-Dem in 2022 classifies Nepal as an electoral democracy, Kenya as an electoral autocracy, and Morocco and Myanmar as closed autocracies. Prior to the 2021 coup, Myanmar was classified as an electoral autocracy; the other countries' ratings were the same. See Varieties of Democracy (V-Dem), https://www.v-dem.net/publications/democracy-reports/.

6. Calculated by comparing allocations of gross disbursements by DAC members to "democracy assistance" (as defined in Chapter 1, endnote 4) that are labeled as targeting gender equality and women's empowerment as a "principal" or "significant" objective. All data is drawn from OECD.Stat (in 2020 US dollars). Figures are rounded to the nearest million.

7. K.C. Luna and Gemma Van Der Haar, "Living Maoist Gender Ideology: Experiences of Women Ex-Combatants in Nepal," *International Feminist Journal of Politics* 21, no. 3 (2019): 434–453; and Judith Pettigrew and Sara Shneiderman, "Women and the Maobadi: Ideology and Agency in Nepal's Maoist Movement," *Himāl Southasian*, January 1, 2004, https://www.himalmag.com/ideology-and-agency-in-nepals-maoist-movement/.

8. Punam Yadav, "Women in the Parliament: Changing Gender Dynamics in the Political Sphere in Nepal," in *Women in Governing Institutions in South Asia*, ed. Nizam Ahmed (Cham, Switzerland: Palgrave Macmillan, 2018)

9. Åshild Falch, "Women's Political Participation and Influence in Post-Conflict Burundi and Nepal," PRIO Paper (Oslo: Peace Research Institute Oslo, May 2010).

10. Bishnu Raj Upreti, Sharmila Shivakoti, and Kohinoor Bharati, "Frustrated and Confused: Mapping the Socio-Political Struggles of Female Ex-Combatants in Nepal," *Journal of International Women's Studies* 19, no. 4 (2018): 32–52.

11. Tara Kanel, "Women's Political Representation in Nepal: An Experience from the 2008 Constituent Assembly," *Asian Journal of Women's Studies* 20, no. 4 (2014): 39–62; and Women's Caucus et al., "Women Members of the Constituent Assembly: A Study on Contribution of Women in Constitution Making in Nepal" (International IDEA, 2011), https://www.idea.int/sites/default/files/publications/women-members-of-the-constituent-assembly.pdf.

12. Kanel, "Women's Political Representation in Nepal"; and Yadav, "Women in the Parliament."

13. Interview with a Nepali women's rights activist, June 15, 2020; and Interview with a representative from the Norwegian Embassy in Nepal, July 9, 2020.

14. Jill Cottrell, "The Constituent Assembly of Nepal: An Agenda for Women," International IDEA, June 2, 2008.

15. UN Women, "Final Evaluation of Project on Making Politics Work with Women (MP3W) in Nepal," July 2013, https://gate.unwomen.org/EvaluationDocument/Download?evaluatio nDocumentID=3645.

16. Interview with Nepali rights activists, November 2, 2020.

17. Nanako Tamaru and Marie O'Reilly, "How Women Influence Constitution Making after Conflict and Unrest" (Inclusive Security, January 2018).

18. Sangita Thebe Limbu, "Nepal's House of Cards: Are Women Included or Co-Opted in Politics?" London School of Economics, February 2, 2018, https://blogs.lse.ac.uk/southa sia/2018/02/02/nepals-house-of-cards-are-women-included-or-co-opted-in-politics-gen der-female-representation-caste/; and World Bank, "Proportion of Seats Held by Women in National Parliaments (%) – Nepal."

19. Swiss Confederation, "Provincial and Local Governance Support Program (PLGSP)," November 27, 2017, https://www.eda.admin.ch/countries/nepal/en/home/international-cooperation/projects.html/content/dezaprojects/SDC/en/2018/7F09921/phase1.

20. One exception is USAID's Niti Sambad program (2017–2022), which included a focus on party reform.

21. Kamal Dev Bhattarai, "Patriarchal Political Parties," *The Annapurna Express*, January 18, 2019, https://theannapurnaexpress.com/news/patriarchal-political-parties-1120.

22. YUWA, "Women and Gender Norms in Nepal's Parliament" (Advancing Learning and Innovation on Gender Norms (ALIGN), June 2021), https://www.alignplatform.org/sites/default/files/2021-07/yuwa_-_nepal-politics.pdf.

23. Asian Development Bank, "Gender Equality and Social Inclusion Diagnostic of Selected Sectors in Nepal," October 2020, https://www.adb.org/publications/nepal-gender-equality-social-inclusion-diagnostic.

NOTES

24. Nanjala Nyabola and Marie-Emmanuelle Pommerolle, eds., *Where Women Are: Gender and the 2017 Kenyan Elections* (Nairobi: Heinrich-Böll-Stiftung and Twaweza Communications, 2018).
25. Wanjiku Mukabi Kabira and Elishiba Njambi Kimani, "The Historical Journey of Women's Leadership in Kenya," *Journal of Emerging Trends in Educational Research and Policy Studies* 3, no. 6 (2012): 842–849.
26. Aili Mari Tripp, "Women's Movements and Constitution Making after Civil Unrest in Africa: The Cases of Kenya and Somalia," *Politics and Gender* 12, no. 1 (2016): 78–106; and Grace Maingi, "The Kenyan Constitutional Reform Process: A Case Study on the Work of FIDA Kenya in Securing Women's Rights," *Feminist Africa* 15 (2011): 63–81.
27. John W. Harbeson, "Putting the Third Wave into Practice: Democracy Promotion in Kenya," *African Studies Review* 59, no. 3 (2016): 129–137.
28. Interview with a staff member at NDI Kenya, April 10, 2020.
29. Pilar Domingo et al., "Women and Power: Shaping the Development of Kenya's 2010 Constitution" (Overseas Development Institute, March 2016), https://cdn.odi.org/media/documents/10338.pdf.
30. Marilyn Muthoni Kamuru, "The Missing Piece: The Legislature, Gender Parity and Constitutional Legitimacy in Kenya," in Nyabola and Pommerolle, *Where Women Are*, 193.
31. Ibid.
32. IPU Parline, "Monthly Ranking of Women in National Parliaments," accessed November 9, 2023, https://data.ipu.org/women-ranking?month=10&year=2023.
33. Echo Network Africa, "A Gender Audit & Analysis of Kenya's 2022 General Elections," February 6, 2023, https://democracytrustfund.org/download/gender-audit-analysis-kenyas-2022-general-elections/.
34. Afrobarometer, "Kenyans See Gains in Gender Equality, but Support for Women's Empowerment Is Still Uneven," March 8, 2017, https://afrobarometer.org/sites/default/files/ken_r7_presentation1_gender_equality.pdf.
35. Marilyn Muthoni Kamuru, "Kenya's Gender Bill: Battling Inequality, Saving the Constitution," *Al Jazeera*, March 17, 2019, https://www.aljazeera.com/indepth/opinion/kenya-gender-bill-battling-inequality-saving-constitution-190317093452466.html.
36. Yolande Bouka, Marie Berry, and Marilyn Muthoni Kamuru, "Women's Political Inclusion in Kenya's Devolved Political System," *Journal of Eastern African Studies* 13, no. 2 (2019): 313–333.
37. Matthew Gichohi, "With Hands Tied: A Woman's Presidential Bid," in *Women and Power in Africa: Aspiring, Campaigning, and Governing*, eds. Leonardo R. Arriola, Martha C. Johnson, and Melanie L. Phillips (Oxford: Oxford University Press, 2021): 117–140.
38. Marie Berry, Yolande Bouka, and Marilyn Muthoni Kamuru, "Implementing Inclusion: Gender Quotas, Inequality, and Backlash in Kenya," *Gender and Politics* 17, no. 4 (2020): 640–644.
39. NORC, "Assessment of USAID Support for Kenya's 2017 Elections: Final Report" (United States Agency for International Development, July 2018), https://pdf.usaid.gov/pdf_docs/PA00TCXK.pdf.
40. See, for example, International Foundation for Electoral Systems (IFES), "Kenyans Say 'We Are #BetterThanThis,' Aiming to Support Women's Participation in Elections," July 19, 2017, https://www.ifes.org/news/kenyans-say-we-are-betterthanthis-aiming-support-womens-participation-elections; and UNDP, "Strengthening Electoral Processes in Kenya: 2018 Annual Progress Report," 2018, https://info.undp.org/docs/pdc/Documents/KEN/2018%20Annual%20Report.Final.23Apr19.pdf.
41. Interview with a Kenyan women's rights advocate, May 6, 2020; and Interview with a US donor official in Kenya, June 26, 2020.
42. Interview with Kenyan women's rights advocates, June 3, 2020, and August 21, 2021.
43. Aili Mari Tripp, *Seeking Legitimacy: Why Arab Autocracies Adopt Women's Rights* (Cambridge: Cambridge University Press, 2019).
44. Moha Ennaji, "Women, Gender, and Politics in Morocco," *Social Sciences* 5, no. 4 (November 2016), 75.

NOTES 247

45. Clare Castillejo and Helen Tilley, "The Road to Reform: Women's Political Voice in Morocco" (Overseas Development Institute, April 2015), https://cdn.odi.org/media/documents/9606.pdf.
46. The voluntary reservation adopted by parties in 2002 reserved thirty out of the 325 seats in the lower house of the parliament for women. The seats were filled by women elected from a nationwide list. Hanane Darhour and Drude Dahlerup, "Sustainable Representation of Women through Gender Quotas: A Decade's Experience in Morocco," *Women's Studies International Forum* 41, no. 2 (2013): 132–142.
47. Carolyn Barnett and Marwa Shalaby, "Success Beyond Gender Quotas: Gender, Local Politics, and Clientelism in Morocco," The Program on Governance and Local Development Working Paper No. 48 (2021), https://gld.gu.se/media/2303/gld-working-paper48.pdf.
48. Thomas Carothers, "Struggling with Semi-Authoritarians," in *Democracy Assistance: International Co-Operation for Democratization*, ed. Peter J. Burnell (London: Routledge, 2000), 210–225.
49. Driss Maghraoui, "Constitutional Reforms in Morocco: Between Consensus and Subaltern Politics," *Journal of North African Studies* 16, no. 4 (December 2011): 679–699; and Anna Khakee, "Democracy Aid or Autocracy Aid? Unintended Effects of Democracy Assistance in Morocco," *Journal of North African Studies* 22, no. 2 (2017): 238–258.
50. Susanna McCollum, Kristin Haffert, and Alyson Kozma, "Assessing Women's Political Party Programs: Best Practices and Recommendations," (Washington, DC: National Democratic Institute, 2008), https://www.ndi.org/sites/default/files/Assessing-Womens-Political-Party-Programs-ENG.pdf.
51. International Republican Institute (IRI), "Morocco Overview" (Washington, DC: International Republican Institute, January 22, 2010), https://www.iri.org/sites/default/files/Morocco%202010-01-22.pdf.
52. Zakia Salime, "A New Feminism? Gender Dynamics in Morocco's February 20th Movement," *Journal of International Women's Studies* 13 no. 5 (2012): 101–114; and Karla Mari McKanders, "Anatomy of an Uprising: Women, Democracy, and the Moroccan Feminist Spring," *Boston University International Law Journal* 32, no. 1 (2014): 147–184.
53. Delana Sobhani, "Gender Quotas and Women's Political Representation: Lessons from Morocco," Georgetown Institute for Women, Peace and Security, July 21, 2021, https://giwps.georgetown.edu/gender-quotas-and-womens-political-representation-lessons-from-morocco/.
54. Interview with NDI representatives in Morocco, June 8, 2020.
55. European Parliament and UN Women, "Spring Forward for Women Conference" (Brussels, November 2014), https://arabstates.unwomen.org/sites/default/files/Field%20Office%20Arab%20States/Attachments/Publications/2015/English%20Spring%20Forward%20for%20Women%20Conference%20Report.pdf.
56. Reeda Kheder and Keri Zolman, "We Are ALL Heard: The Women's Support Network in Morocco," International Republican Institute, March 8, 2017, https://www.iri.org/news/we-are-all-heard-the-womens-support-network-in-morocco/.
57. IPU Parline, "Monthly Ranking of Women in National Parliaments," and Yana Gorokhovskaia, Adrian Shahbaz, and Amy Slipowitz, "Morocco," in *Freedom in the World 2023* (Washington, DC: Freedom House, 2023), https://freedomhouse.org/country/morocco/freedom-world/2023/.
58. Yamina El Kirat El Allame, "Gender Matters: Women as Actors of Change and Sustainable Development in Morocco," in *Women's Grassroots Mobilization in the MENA Region Post-2011*, ed. Kelsey P. Norman (Baker Institute for Public Policy, 2020), https://www.bakerinstitute.org/research/womens-grassroots-mobilization-mena-region-post-2011.
59. Darhour and Dahlerup, "Sustainable Representation of Women through Gender Quotas.".
60. Abderrafie Zaanoun, "The Impact of the Quota System on Women Parliamentary Representation in Morocco: A Series of Reforms or a Regressive Path?," Arab Reform Initiative, April 14, 2022, https://www.arab-reform.net/publication/the-impact-of-the-quota-system-on-women-parliamentary-representation-in-morocco-a-series-of-reforms-or-a-regressive-path/; and James Liddell, "Gender Quotas in Clientelist Systems: The Case of Morocco's National List," *Al-Raida Journal* Summer/Fall 2009, no. 126-127 (2009): 79–86.
61. Castillejo and Tilley, "The Road to Reform."

62. Silvia Colombo and Benedetta Voltolini, "'Business as Usual' in EU Democracy Promotion towards Morocco? Assessing the Limits of the EU's Approach towards the Mediterranean after the Arab Uprisings," *L'Europe en Formation* 371, no. 1 (2014): 41–57.

63. Interview with staff members at a US democracy organization in Morocco, June 8, 2020, and June 16, 2020; and Interview with a Moroccan gender equality advocate, August 24, 2020.

64. Aye Lei Tun, La Ring, and Su Su Hlaing, "Feminism in Myanmar" (Friedrich Ebert Stiftung, August 2019), https://asia.fes.de/news/feminism-in-myanmar.

65. Ibid.

66. Burma Lawyers' Council, "A Grim Perspective for Burmese Women," Social Watch, 2010, https://www.socialwatch.org/sites/default/files/B15Burma2010_eng.pdf; and Gabrielle Bardall and Elin Bjarnegård, "The Exclusion of Women in Myanmar Politics Helped Fuel the Military Coup," *The Conversation*, February 21, 2021, https://theconversation.com/the-exclusion-of-women-in-myanmar-politics-helped-fuel-the-military-coup-154701.

67. Thomas Carr, "Supporting the Transition: Understanding Aid to Myanmar since 2011" (The Asia Foundation, February 2018), https://asiafoundation.org/wp-content/uploads/2018/03/Supporting-the-Transition-Understanding-Aid-to-Myanmar-since-2011_ENG.pdf, 7.

68. Interview with staff members at international democracy assistance organizations in Myanmar, January 13, 14, and 19, 2021.

69. Shwe Shwe Sein Latt et al., "Women's Political Participation in Myanmar: Experiences of Women Parliamentarians 2011–2016" (The Asia Foundation and Phan Tee Eain, April 2017), https://asiafoundation.org/wp-content/uploads/2017/05/Womens-Political-Partic ipation-in-Myanmar-MP-Experiences_report-1.pdf. Note: These numbers reflect the proportion of *elected* representatives but does not include military appointees. The Tatmadaw retained the right to appoint 25 percent of legislative seats. If military appointees are included, then women only comprised 4.8 percent of all national MPs from 2011–2016 and 10.5 percent of all national MPs from 2016–2020.

70. Global Justice Center, "Myanmar's Proposed Prevention of Violence Against Women Law: A Failure to Meet International Human Rights Standards," *Global Justice Center Blog*, July 13, 2020, https://www.globaljusticecenter.net/blog/19-publications/1319-myanmar-s-propo sed-prevention-of-violence-against-women-law-a-failure-to-meet-international-human-rights-standards; and Hilary Faxon, Roisin Furlong, and May Sabe Phyu, "Reinvigorating Resilience: Violence against Women, Land Rights, and the Women's Peace Movement in Myanmar," *Gender and Development* 23, no. 3 (2015): 466.

71. Mollie Pepper, "Ethnic Minority Women, Diversity, and Informal Participation in Peacebuilding in Myanmar," *Journal of Peacebuilding and Development* 13 no. 2 (2018): 61–75.

72. Akanksha Khullar, "Dashed Hoped for Myanmar's Women," *The Diplomat*, August 9, 2019, https://thediplomat.com/2019/08/dashed-hopes-for-myanmars-women/.

73. Joint Peace Fund, "The JPF Backstory," accessed March 25, 2021, https://www.jointpeacef und.org/en/jpf-backstory.

74. Roslyn Warren et al., "Women's Peacebuilding Strategies amidst Conflict: Lessons from Myanmar and Ukraine" (Georgetown Institute for Women, Peace and Security, 2018), https://giwps.georgetown.edu/wp-content/uploads/2017/01/Womens-Peacebuilding-Str ategies-Amidst-Conflict-1.pdf, 27.

75. Netina Tan et al., "Party Building and Candidate Selection: Intraparty Politics and Promoting Gender Equality in Myanmar" (International Development Research Council of Canada, April 18, 2020), https://idl-bnc-idrc.dspacedirect.org/bitstream/handle/10625/58862/IDL-58862.pdf?sequence=2&isAllowed=y.

76. Zue Zue, "Proportion of Women in Myanmar's Legislatures Rises following Nov. 8 Election," *The Irrawaddy*, November 19, 2020, https://www.irrawaddy.com/elections/proportion-women-myanmars-legislatures-rises-following-nov-8-election.html.

77. Zarchi Oo, Billy Ford, and Jonathan Pinckney, "Myanmar in the Streets: A Nonviolent Movement Shows Staying Power," United States Institute of Peace, March 31, 2021, https://www.usip.org/publications/2021/03/myanmar-streets-nonviolent-movement-shows-stay ing-power.

78. Michelle Onello and Akila Radhakrishnan, "Myanmar's Coup Is Devastating for Women," *Foreign Policy*, March 23, 2021, https://foreignpolicy.com/2021/03/23/myan

NOTES 249

mar-coup-women-human-rights-violence-military/; and Nu Nu Lusan and Emily Fishbein, "'We Are Warriors': Women Join Fight against Military in Myanmar," *Al Jazeera*, November 16, 2021, https://www.aljazeera.com/news/2021/11/16/we-are-warriors-women-join-fight-against-military-in-myanmar.

79. Phyo Thet Tin, "Before We Go Dark: A Letter to the International Community," *Frontier Myanmar*, February 10, 2021, https://www.frontiermyanmar.net/en/before-we-go-dark-a-letter-to-the-international-community/; and May Sabe Phyu and Nang Moet Moet, "The Situation for Women in Myanmar: Statement at an Expert-Level Meeting for UN Security Council Members," Norway in the UN, May 12, 2021, https://www.norway.no/en/missions/un/news/123/the-situation-for-women-in-myanmar/.

Chapter 4

1. Maria Nzomo, "The Gender Dimension of Democratization in Kenya: Some International Linkages," *Alternatives: Global, Local, Political* 18, no. 1 (1993): 61–74.
2. Maria Nzomo, "Kenyan Women in Politics and Decision-Making," in *African Feminism: The Politics of Survival in Sub-Saharan Africa*, ed. Gwendolyn Mikell (Philadelphia: University of Pennsylvania Press, 1997): 232–254.
3. Ibid., 246.
4. Julie Ballington and Azza M. Karam, eds., *Women in Parliament: Beyond Numbers* (Stockholm: International IDEA, 2005), 216.
5. Drude Dahlerup, "The Story of the Theory of Critical Mass," *Politics and Gender* 2, no. 4 (2006): 511–522. See also Sarah Childs and Mona Lena Krook, "Critical Mass Theory and Women's Political Representation," *Political Studies* 56, no. 3 (2008): 725–736; and Sue Thomas, *How Women Legislate* (Oxford: Oxford University Press, 1994).
6. See, for example: Pippa Norris and Joni Lovenduski, *Political Recruitment: Gender, Race, and Class in the British Parliament* (Cambridge: Cambridge University Press, 1995); Rieko Kage, Frances M. Rosenbluth, and Seiki Tanaka, "What Explains Low Female Representation? Evidence from Survey Experiments in Japan," *Politics and Gender* 15, no. 2 (June 2019): 285–309; Kristin Wylie, "Taking Bread Off the Table: Race, Gender, Resources and Political Ambition in Brazil," *European Journal of Politics and Gender* 3, no. 1 (2020): 121–142; and Rachel Bernhard, Shauna Shames, and Dawn Langan Teele, "To Emerge? Breadwinning, Motherhood, and Women's Decisions to Run for Office," *American Political Science Review* 115, no. 2 (2021): 379–394.
7. Richard L. Fox and Jennifer L. Lawless, "Uncovering the Origins of the Gender Gap in Political Ambition," *American Political Science Review* 108, no. 3 (August 2014): 449–519; and Jessice Robinson Preece, "Mind the Gender Gap: An Experiment on the Influence of Self-Efficacy on Political Interest," *Politics and Gender* 12, no. 1 (2016): 198–217.
8. Susan Franceschet and Jennifer M. Piscopo, "Sustaining Gendered Practices? Power, Parties, and Elite Political Networks in Argentina," *Comparative Political Studies* 47, no. 1 (2014): 85–110; Elin Bjarnegård, *Gender, Informal Institutions, and Political Recruitment* (New York: Palgrave, 2013); Meryl Kenny, *Gender and Political Recruitment: Theorizing Institutional Change* (New York: Palgrave, 2013); Sylvia Tamale, *When Hens Begin to Crow: Gender and Parliamentary Politics in Uganda* (Boulder, CO: Westview Press, 1999); and Kristin Wylie, *Party Institutionalization and Women's Representation in Democratic Brazil* (New York: Cambridge University Press, 2018).
9. Pamela Paxton, Sheri Kunovich, and Melanie M. Hughes, "Gender in Politics," *Annual Review of Sociology* 33, no. 1 (2007): 263–284; and Cecilia Josefsson, "How Candidate Selection Structures and Genders Political Ambition: Illustrations from Uruguay," *European Journal of Politics and Gender* 3, no. 1 (2020): 61–78.
10. Interviews with former USAID officials, January 21, 2020 and January 23, 2020.
11. Interview with a gender advisor at a US democracy assistance organization, January 16, 2020.
12. Drude Dahlerup, "Comparative Studies of Gender Quotas" (International IDEA, 2003), https://citeseerx.ist.psu.edu/viewdoc/download?doi=10.1.1.493.6778&rep=rep1&type=pdf.

13. Mona Lena Krook, "Reforming Representation: The Diffusion of Candidate Gender Quotas Worldwide," *Politics and Gender* 2, no. 3 (2006): 303–327; Amanda B. Edgell, "Foreign Aid, Democracy, and Gender Quota Laws," *Democratization* 24, no. 6 (2017): 1103–1141; and Drude Dahlerup and Lena Freidenvall, "Quotas as the 'Fast Track' to Equal Political Representation for Women," *International Feminist Journal of Politics* 7, no. 1 (2005): 26–48.

14. Dahlerup and Freidenvall, "Quotas as a 'Fast Track' to Equal Representation for Women"; and International IDEA, "Ten Years of Supporting Democracy Worldwide," 2005, https://www.idea.int/sites/default/files/about_us/10-years-of-supporting-democracy-worldwide.pdf.

15. Sarah Bush, "International Politics and the Spread of Quotas for Women in Legislatures," *International Organization* 65, no. 1 (2011): 103–137.

16. Susan Franceschet and Jennifer M. Piscopo, "Gender and Political Backgrounds in Argentina," in *The Impact of Gender Quotas*, eds. Susan Franceschet, Mona Lena Krook, and Jennifer M. Piscopo (Oxford: Oxford University Press, 2012): 43-56.

17. Lena Wängnerud, "Women in Parliaments: Descriptive and Substantive Representation," *Annual Review of Political Science* 12, no. 1 (2009): 51–69.

18. Krook, "Reforming Representation," 317.

19. Ibid.

20. Salma Hasan Ali, "International IDEA: Democracy in the Making," International IDEA, 2001, https://www.idea.int/sites/default/files/reference_docs/annual_report_2000-1_scr een.pdf.

21. International IDEA, "Gender Quotas Database," accessed November 9, 2023, https://www.idea.int/data-tools/data/gender-quotas-database/about.

22. Tanya L. Domi, "Advancing Women's Political Rights in Bosnia-Herzegovina: Making a Difference Early in the Peace Process (A Case Study)," *Harriman Review* 14, no. 1–2 (November 2002): 36–46.

23. UN Women, "Corporate Evaluation of UN Women's Contribution to Women's Political Participation and Leadership: Synthesis Report," April 2018, https://www.unwomen.org/sites/default/files/Headquarters/Attachments/Sections/Library/Publications/2018/Corporate-evaluation-Womens-political-participation-en.pdf.

24. UNIFEM, "Building Women's Leadership in Governance, Peace, and Security," 2001, http://www.peacewomen.org/assets/file/Resources/UNReports/unifem_annualreportpart2_2001.pdf.

25. Management Innovation, Training and Research Academy (MITRA) Pvt. Ltd, "Final Evaluation of Project on Making Politics Work with Women (MP3W) in Nepal" (UN Women: 2013), https://gate.unwomen.org/EvaluationDocument/ReportDocIndex?evalu ationDocumentID=3645.

26. Dana Peebles, Awuor Ponge, and Jacinta K. Ndambuki, "Final Evaluation: Kenya Gender and Governance Programme (GGP III) 2009–2013" (UN Women, 2013); and Atsango Chesoni, Salome Muigai, and Karuti Kanyinga, "Promoting Women's Human Rights and Enhancing Gender Equality in Kenya," Sida, 2006, https://cdn.sida.se/publications/files/sida31176en-promoting-womens-human-rights-and-enhancing-gender-equality-in-kenya.pdf.

27. Bush, "International Politics and the Spread of Quotas for Women in Legislatures."

28. Rebecca J. Kreitzer and Tracy L. Osborn, "The Emergence and Activities of Women's Recruiting Groups in the US," *Politics, Groups and Identities* 7, no. 4 (2018): 842–852.

29. Susan J. Caroll and Kira Sanbonmatsu, *More Women Can Run: Gender and Pathways to the State Legislatures* (New York: Oxford University Press, 2013); and Jennifer M. Piscopo, "The Limits of Leaning In: Ambition, Recruitment, and Candidate Training in Comparative Perspective," *Politics, Groups and Identities* 7, no. 4 (2018): 817–828.

30. Interview with a staff member at UN Women, February 4, 2020; Interview with a gender advisor at a US democracy assistance organization, January 15, 2020. See also NDI, "Nominating for Change: Strengthening Women's Position within Political Parties," May 2003, https://www.pacwip.org/wp-content/uploads/2018/02/NDI-2003-Nominating-for-Change-Strengthening-Women%E2%80%99s-Position-in-Political-Parties-Training-for-Trainers-Manua.pdf; UN Women, "Corporate Evaluation of UN Women's Contribution to Women's Political Participation and Leadership"; Michelle Lokot, Jessica Kenway, and Chris Bradley, "Women's Leadership: Evidence Review" (Canberra: Department of Foreign

NOTES

Affairs and Trade, 2014), https://www.dfat.gov.au/sites/default/files/evidence-review-wom ens-leadership.pdf; and Mariz Tadros, *Women in Politics: Gender, Power, and Development* (London: Zed Books, 2014).

31. UNIFEM, "Building Women's Leadership in Governance, Peace, and Security," 2001, http:// www.peacewomen.org/assets/file/Resources/UNReports/unifem_annualreportpart2_ 2001.pdf; and Inclusive Peace & Transition Initiative, "Women in Peace and Transition Processes: Burundi (1996–2014)," December 2018, https://www.inclusivepeace.org/wp-content/uploads/2021/05/case-study-women-burundi-1996-2014-en.pdf.

32. Rohini Pande, Michael Callen, Binod Kumar Paudel, and Satish Wasti, "Strengthening Female Representation in Nepal's Local Governments," Yale Economic Growth Center, accessed November 12, 2023, https://egc.yale.edu/strengthening-female-representation-nepals-local-governments.

33. Susanna McCollom, Kristin Haffert, and Alyson Kozma, "Assessing Women's Political Party Programs: Best Practices and Recommendations" (Washington, DC: National Democratic Institute, 2008), https://www.ndi.org/sites/default/files/Assessing-Womens-Political-Party-Programs-ENG.pdf.

34. NDI, "Nepal: Training Women to Engage in the Constitution-Drafting Process through the Nepali Women's Leadership Academy," March 16, 2009, https://www.ndi.org/ our-stories/nepal-training-women-engage-constitution-drafting-process-through-nep ali-women%E2%80%99s.

35. Interview with a female Kenyan parliamentarian, July 22, 2020; and Interview with a staff member at the Society of Clerks at the Table (SOCATT), May 5, 2020.

36. Interview with a female Kenyan parliamentarian, July 22, 2020; and Jacinta Muteshi, "Mapping Best Practices: Promoting Gender Equality and the Advancement of Kenyan Women," Heinrich-Böll-Stiftung, 2006, https://ke.boell.org/en/2006/09/05/mapping-best-practices-promoting-gender-equality-and-advancement-kenyan-women.

37. IRI, "IRI and NDI Launch Women's Campaign Training in Morocco," March 21, 2009, https://www.iri.org/resource/iri-and-ndi-launch-women%E2%80%99s-campaign-training-morocco.

38. Sada Aksartova, "Why NGOs? How American Donors Embraced Civil Society after the Cold War," *International Journal of Not-for-Profit Law* 8, no. 3 (May 2006); and Christopher A. Sabatini, "Whom Do International Donors Support in the Name of Civil Society?," *Development in Practice* 12, no. 1 (February 2002): 7–19.

39. Aili Mari Tripp, "The New Political Activism in Africa," *Journal of Democracy* 12, no. 3 (July 2001): 141–155.

40. Maxine Molyneux, "Mobilization without Emancipation? Women's Interests, the State, and Revolution in Nicaragua," *Feminist Studies* 11, no. 2 (Summer 1985): 227–254.

41. Sonia E. Alvarez, "Advocating Feminism: The Latin American Feminist NGO 'Boom,'" *International Feminist Journal of Politics* 1, no. 2 (September 1999): 181–209; and James Richter, "Promoting Civil Society? Democracy Assistance and Russian Women's Organizations," *Problems of Post-Communism* 49, no. 1 (January 2002): 30–41.

42. David Everatt et al., "Evaluating the Gender & Governance Programme: Kenya 2008," South: Solutions from the Developing World, 2008, https://gate.unwomen.org/Evaluation/ Details?EvaluationId=4956; and Peebles, Ponge, and Ndambuki, "Final Evaluation: Kenya Gender and Governance Programme (GGP III) 2009–2013."

43. Data drawn from Melanie M. Hughes, Pamela Paxton, Amanda Clayton, and Pär Zetterberg, "Quota Adoption and Reform over Time (QAROT), 1947–2015," (Ann Arbor, MI: Inter-university Consortium for Political and Social Research, 2017); and International IDEA's "Gender Quotas Database," accessed November 10, 2023, https://www.idea.int/data-tools/ data/gender-quotas-database .

44. UN Women, "Why and How Constitutions Matter for Advancing Gender Equality," Policy Brief Nr. 8, 2017, https://www.unwomen.org/sites/default/files/Headquarters/Attachme nts/Sections/Library/Publications/2017/Why-and-How-Constitutions-Matter-en.pdf.

45. Aili Mari Tripp, *Women and Power in Postconflict Africa* (New York: Cambridge University Press, 2015), 175.

46. Alice J. Kang and Aili Mari Tripp, "Coalitions Matter: Citizenship, Women, and Quota Adoption in Africa," *Perspectives in Politics* 16, no. 1 (2018): 73–91.
47. On the interplay of international and domestic drivers, see Gretchen Bauer, "'A Lot of Head Wraps': African Contributions to the Third Wave of Electoral Gender Quotas," *Politics, Groups, and Identities* 4, no. 2 (2016): 196–213; Kang and Tripp, "Coalitions Matter"; Aili Mari Tripp, "Women's Mobilisation for Legislative Political Representation in Africa," *Review of African Political Economy* 43, no. 149 (2016): 382–399; and Krook, "Reforming Representation."
48. Aili Mari Tripp, Isabel Casimiro, Joy Kwesiga, and Alice Mungwa, *African Women's Movements: Changing Political Landscapes* (New York: Cambridge University Press, 2009).
49. Bush, "International Politics and the Spread of Quotas for Women in Legislatures."
50. Edgell, "Foreign Aid, Democracy, and Gender Quota Laws."
51. See Aili Mari Tripp and Alice Kang, "The Global Impact of Quotas: On the Fast Track to Increased Female Legislative Representation," *Comparative Political Studies* 41, no. 3 (2008): 338–361; and Leslie A. Schwindt-Bayer, "Making Quotas Work: The Effect of Gender Quota Laws on the Election of Women," *Legislative Studies Quarterly* 34, no. 1 (February 2009): 5–28.
52. International IDEA, *Women in Parliament: Beyond Numbers;* and IPU, "Women in Parliament in 2010: The Year in Perspective," accessed November 12, 2023, http://archive.ipu.org/pdf/publications/wmnpersp10-e.pdf.
53. International IDEA, "Gender Quota Database: Morocco," https://www.idea.int/data-tools/data/gender-quotas-database/country?country=151; and World Bank, "Proportion of Seats Held by Women in National Parliaments (%)—Morocco," accessed July 29, 2023, https://data.worldbank.org/indicator/SG.GEN.PARL.ZS?locations=MA.
54. Interview with an international aid official in Morocco, August 24, 2020.
55. Stina Larserud and Rita Taphorn, "Designing for Equality: Best-Fit, Medium-Fit, and Non-Favourable Combinations of Electoral Systems and Gender Quotas" (Stockholm: International IDEA, 2007), https://www.idea.int/sites/default/files/publications/designing-for-equality.pdf.
56. Pamela Paxton and Melanie M. Hughes, "The Increasing Effectiveness of National Gender Quotas, 1990–2010," *Legislative Studies Quarterly* 40, no. 3 (2015): 331–362.
57. Carmen Geha, "The Myth of Women's Political Empowerment within Lebanon's Sectarian Power-Sharing System," *Journal of Women, Politics and Policy* 40, no. 4 (2019): 498–521; and Jo-Anne Bishop, Sara Vaca, and Joseph Barnes, "Fund for Gender Equality: Meta Analysis 2011–2015" (UN Women, 2016), https://www.unwomen.org/sites/default/files/Headquarters/Attachments/Sections/Library/Publications/2016/FGE-Evaluation-Meta-Analysis-Report-2015-en.pdf.
58. Tripp et. al, *African Women's Movements.*
59. Association for Women's Rights in Development (AWID), "The State of Women's Organizations," FundHer Factsheet No. 1, March 2008, https://www.awid.org/sites/default/files/atoms/files/witm_-_factsheet_1.pdf.
60. Mona Lena Krook, "Contesting Gender Quotas: Dynamics of Resistance," *Politics, Groups, and Identities* 4, no. 2 (2016): 268–283.
61. Hanna Darhour and Drude Dahlerup, "Sustainable Representation of Women through Gender Quotas: A Decade's Experience in Morocco," *Women's Studies International Forum* 41, no. 2 (2013): 132–142.
62. James Sater, "Reserved Seats, Patriarchy, and Patronage in Morocco," in *The Impact of Gender Quotas*, 72–86.
63. Abderrafie Zaanoun, "The Impact of the Quota System on Women Parliamentary Representation in Morocco: A Series of Reforms or a Regressive Path?," Arab Reform Initiative, April 14, 2022, https://www.arab-reform.net/publication/the-impact-of-the-quota-system-on-women-parliamentary-representation-in-morocco-a-series-of-reforms-or-a-regressive-path/.
64. Tania Verge and Maria de la Fuente, "Playing with Different Cards: Party Politics, Gender Quotas and Women's Empowerment," *International Political Science Review* 35, no. 1 (2014): 67–79.

NOTES

253

65. Marie E. Berry, Yolande Bouka, and Marilyn Muthoni Kamuru, "Implementing Inclusion: Gender Quotas, Inequality, and Backlash in Kenya," *Politics and Gender* 17, no. 4 (2021): 640–664.

66. Gretchen Bauer, "Reserved Seats for Women MPs: Affirmative Action for the National Women's Movement or the National Resistance Movement," in *Women and Legislative Representation: Electoral Systems, Political Parties, and Sex Quotas*, ed. Manon Tremblay (New York: Palgrave Macmillan, 2012), 27–39; Timothy Longman, "Rwanda: Achieving Equality or Serving an Authoritarian State?" in *Women in African Parliaments*, eds. Gretchen Bauer and Hannah E. Britton (Boulder, CO: Lynne Rienner, 2006): 133–150; Vanessa Pupavac, "Empowering Women? An Assessment of International Gender Policies in Bosnia," *International Peacekeeping* 12, no. 3 (2005): 391–405; and Shirin Rai, Farzana Bari, Nazmunnessa Mahtab, and Bidyut Mohanty, "South Asia: Gender Quotas and the Politics of Empowerment," in *Women, Quotas, and Politics*, ed. Drude Dahlerup, Routledge Research in Comparative Politics 10 (New York: Routledge, 2006).

67. Krishna Kumar, "Aftermath: Women and Women's Organizations in Postconflict Societies— The Role of International Assistance," US Agency for International Development, July 2001, https://reliefweb.int/sites/reliefweb.int/files/resources/7B6A988FE30E9BE0C1256CC50 032A021-usaid-aftermath-jul01.pdf; and Lisa Markowitz and Karen W. Tice, "Paradoxes of Professionalization: Parallel Dilemmas in Women's Organizations in the Americas," *Gender and Society* 16, no. 6 (2002): 941–958.

68. Interview with a gender adviser at an international democracy aid organization, March 3, 2020; and Interviews with former USAID officials, December 16, 2019, and January 14, 2020.

69. Kumar, "Aftermath: Women and Women's Organizations in Postconflict Societies."

70. Everatt et al., "Evaluating the Gender & Governance Programme: Kenya 2008."

71. Interview with a former USAID official, January 14, 2020.

72. Ibid.

73. Interview with a staff member at the Netherlands Institute for Multiparty Democracy (NIMD), March 26, 2020.

74. Laure-Hélène Piron, "NIMD Country Programme Evaluation," September 20, 2015, https:// nimd.org/wp-content/uploads/2015/11/NIMD-country-programme-synthesis-final-rep ort.pdf.

Chapter 5

1. Thomas Carothers, "Democracy Assistance: Political vs. Developmental?," *Journal of Democracy* 20, no. 1 (2009): 5.

2. Andrea Cornwall and Anne Marie Goetz, "Democratizing Democracy: Feminist Perspectives," *Democratization* 12, no. 5 (2005): 783–800.

3. Audre Lorde, *Sister Outsider: Essays and Speeches* (New York: Crossing Press, 1984).

4. Mona Lena Krook, "Beyond Supply and Demand: A Feminist-Institutionalist Theory of Candidate Selection," *Political Research Quarterly* 63, no. 4 (2010): 707–720.

5. Ibid.

6. Interview with a USAID official, January 23, 2020.

7. Interview with a former USAID official, January 14, 2020.

8. Interview with a staff member at UNDP, February 13, 2020; Interview with a staff member at UN Women, February 3, 2020; Interview with a staff member at an international democracy assistance organization, March 3, 2020; and Interview with a gender advisor at a US democracy assistance organization, January 15, 2020.

9. USAID, "Gender Equality and Female Empowerment Policy," USAID Policy, 2012, https:// www.usaid.gov/sites/default/files/2022-05/GenderEqualityPolicy_2.pdf .

10. Interviews with current and former USAID officials, December 19, 2019; January 14, 2020; and January 21, 2020.

11. Interview with a former USAID official, January 21, 2020; Interview with USAID officials, December 19, 2019; Interview with a USAID official, January 14, 2020; and Interview with a USAID official, January, 23, 2020.

12. USAID, "Performance Evaluation of the Women's Leadership Portfolio," November 30, 2018, https://pdf.usaid.gov/pdf_docs/PA00TNBB.pdf.

13. United Nations Focal Point for Electoral Assistance, "Promoting Women's Electoral and Political Participation through UN Electoral Assistance," Policy Directive, December 24, 2013, https://dppa.un.org/sites/default/files/ead_pd_promoting_womens_electoral_political_participation_through_un_ea_20131224_e.pdf; and United Nations Focal Point for Electoral Assistance, "Guideline: United Nations Electoral Needs Assessments," May 11, 2012, https://dppa.un.org/sites/default/files/ead_guideline_un_electoral_needs_assessments_20120511_e.pdf.

14. Interview with UN Electoral Assistance Division (UNEAD) officials, February 21, 2020.

15. Interview with an NDI official, January 15, 2020.

16. See, for example, USAID, "Gender Integration in Democracy, Human Rights, and Governance (DRG)," Programming Toolkit, 2016, https://2017-2020.usaid.gov/sites/default/files/documents/2496/Gender%20Toolkit.pdf; UNDP, "Gender Equality and Justice Programming: Equitable Access to Justice for Women," December 17, 2015, https://www.undp.org/publications/gender-equality-and-justice-programming-equitable-access-justice-women; IPU, "Gender-Sensitive Parliaments: A Global Review of Good Practices," 2011, https://www.ipu.org/resources/publications/reports/2016-07/gender-sensitive-parliaments; NDI, "2019 Win with Women Assessment Toolkit," November 28, 2018, https://www.ndi.org/publications/2019-win-women-assessment-toolkit; and UNDP, "Promoting Gender Equality in Electoral Assistance: Lessons Learned in a Comparative Perspective 2011–2013," 2014, https://www.undp.org/sites/g/files/zskgke326/files/publications/2122-UNDP-GE-MAIN-English.pdf.

17. UNDP, "Promoting Gender Equality in Electoral Assistance," 4.

18. The ACE Electoral Knowledge Network, "Women and Voter Registration," November 7, 2013, https://aceproject.org/ace-en/focus/women-and-voter-registration/onePage.

19. Africanews, "Kenya: Right Groups Warn of Violence against Women during Elections," August 8, 2022, https://www.africanews.com/2022/08/08/kenya-right-groups-warn-of-violence-against-women-during-elections/.

20. Bimita GC, "Women Voters in Nepal: What Do We Need to Know about Women Voters?" Women for Politics, October 23, 2020, https://www.womenforpolitics.com/post/women-voters-in-nepal-what-do-we-need-to-know-about-women-voters.

21. Interview with a UN Women official, February 4, 2020; Interview with a UNDP official, February 14, 2020; and Interview with UNEAD officials, February 21, 2020.

22. Sophia Gomez Charlemagne, Malla Narayan Uttam, and Alexis Finley, "Mid-Term Review of the Electoral Support Project (ESP) to Nepal" (United Nations Development Programme, 2018), https://info.undp.org/docs/pdc/Documents/NPL/Mid%20Term%20Evaluation%20Report%20(MTER)ESPII.pdf.

23. Sue Nelson and Prakash Bhattati, "Electoral Support Project Phase II: Final Evaluation Support, UNDP Nepal," June 19, 2018, https://erc.undp.org/evaluation/documents/download/13734; and Interview with a UNDP official, February 20, 2020.

24. UNDP, "Electoral Support Project Phase II (ESP-II)," accessed November 12, 2023, https://www.undp.org/nepal/projects/electoral-support-project-ii.

25. Organization of American States (OAS), "Manual for Incorporating a Gender Perspective into OAS Electoral Observation Missions," 2013, https://www.oas.org/es/sap/deco/pubs/manuales/Manual_gender_e.pdf; and The Organization for Security and Co-Operation in Europe (OSCE), "Handbook for Monitoring Women's Participation in Elections" (Warsaw: OSCE Office for Democratic Institutions and Human Rights, 2004).

26. NDI, "Women in Elections," accessed July 13, 2021, https://www.ndi.org/dcc-elections; and Sarah Cooper, "Put Us in Your Place: Integrating Women into Election Observation," Democracy Works, August 3, 2016, https://demworks.org/poeci-gender-balance-election-observation.html.

27. Votes Without Violence, "Burma," June 21, 2022, https://www.voteswithoutviolence.org/burma.

28. Interview with an NDI official, January 15, 2020.

NOTES

29. Interview with a staff member at International IDEA, March 3, 2020; International IDEA, "A Record of Actions 2010," 2011, https://www.idea.int/sites/default/files/reference_docs/Annual-Report-2010-A-record-of-actions-PDF.pdf; and Rumbidzai Kandawasvika-Nhundu, "Political Parties in Africa through a Gender Lens" (International IDEA, 2013), https://www.idea.int/sites/default/files/publications/political-parties-in-africa-through-a-gender-lens.pdf.

30. International IDEA, "A Framework for Developing Gender Policies for Political Parties," 2016, https://iknowpolitics.org/sites/default/files/a-framework-for-developing-gender-policies-for-political-parties.pdf.

31. Julie Ballington et al., "Empowering Women for Stronger Political Parties" (United Nations Development Programme and National Democratic Institute, February 2012), https://www.ndi.org/sites/default/files/Empowering-Women-Full-Case-Study-ENG.pdf.

32. See, for example, International IDEA, "How Political Finance Is Hindering Women's Access to Politics in Colombia," December 21, 2017, https://www.idea.int/news-media/news/how-political-finance-hindering-women%E2%80%99s-access-politics-colombia/.

33. Julie Ballington and Azza Karam, eds., *Women in Parliament: Beyond the Numbers* (Stockholm: International IDEA, 2005).

34. Sonia Palmieri, "Gender-Sensitive Parliaments: A Global Review of Good Practice," Inter-Parliamentary Union, 2011, https://www.ipu.org/resources/publications/reports/2016-07/gender-sensitive-parliaments, 6.

35. See, for example, IPU, "Annual Report on the Activities of the Inter-Parliamentary Union in 2012," 2012, https://www.ipu.org/resources/publications/about-ipu/2016-07/annual-report-activities-inter-parliamentary-union-in-2012; and IPU, "Annual Report on the Activities of the Inter-Parliamentary Union in 2017," 2018, https://www.ipu.org/resources/publications/about-ipu/2018-03/annual-report-activities-inter-parliamentary-union-2017. The IPU self-assessment toolkit has also been used in Tanzania, Quebec, Sweden, Moldova, Georgia, Namibia, Colombia, Serbia, and the United Kingdom.

36. OSCE, "Realizing Gender Equality in Parliament: A Guide for Parliaments in the OSCE Region," (Warsaw: OSCE Office for Democratic Institutions and Human Rights, 2021), https://www.osce.org/odihr/506885; and UNDP, "Strategies and Good Practices in Promoting Gender Equality Outcomes in Parliaments," Guidance Note, May 2016, https://www.ohchr.org/Documents/Issues/Democracy/Forum2018/UNDP_3.pdf.

37. IPU, "Database on Women's Caucuses," accessed June 29, 2021, http://w3.ipu.org/.

38. UN Women, "Projet Maroc: Harmonisation de l'Arsenal Juridique Par Rapport aux Dispositions Constitutionnelles qui Consacrent la Suprématie des Normes Internationales sur le Droit National," 2017, https://morocco.unwomen.org/sites/default/files/Field%20Office%20Morocco/Documents/others/Fiches%20projets%202017/Fiche%20projet_Parlementaire_09062017.pdf.

39. Interviews with NDI officials in Nepal, October 22, 2019, February 7, 2020, and March 24, 2020; and Interviews with UN Women officials in Nepal, June 8, 2020, and July 14, 2020. See also: Bahar Kumar, "Transforming Nepal's Female Deputy Mayors: New Partnership with Women LEAD and the Asia Foundation," September 30, 2020, https://nepal.communitere.org/transforming-nepals-female-deputy-mayors-new-partnership-with-women-lead-and-the-asia-foundation/.

40. David Cownie, Mouna Hasehm, Rima Habasch, and Marta Balestrini, "United Nations Entity for Gender Equality and the Empowerment of Women (UN Women): Thematic Evaluation on Women's Political Participation," Lattanzio Advisory SpA, September 15, 2016.

41. Interviews with women candidates and politicians in Nyeri and Bungoma counties, Kenya, on September 2, 6, 7 and 13, 2021 and November 9 and 18, 2021.

42. UNDP, "Bridging the Gender Gap in Electoral Journalism," November 6, 2019, https://www.np.undp.org/content/nepal/en/home/presscenter/articles/2019/bridging-the-gender-gap-in-electoral-journalism.html; and Interview with staff at a Nepali women's civil society organization, November 25, 2020.

43. Interview with staff at a Nepali women's civil society organization, November 25, 2020.

44. Interview with staff members at UN Women, February 3, 2020, and February 4, 2020; Interview with a staff member at an international democracy aid organization, February 12,

2020; Interview with a representative from a US democracy assistance organization, February 20, 2020; and Interview with a Swedish aid official, January 1, 2020.

45. Interview with a gender advisor at a US democracy assistance organization, January 15, 2020.

46. Interview with a staff member at a European democracy assistance organization, March 22, 2020; Interview with a UNDP official, February 13, 2020; Interview with a Swedish aid official, January 1, 2020; and Interview with a staff member at UN Women, February 3, 2020.

47. Milli Lake and Marie E. Berry, "When Quotas Come Up Short," *Boston Review*, September 14, 2020, https://bostonreview.net/articles/marie-e-berry-milli-lake-when-quotas-come-short/.

48. Erica Chenoweth and Zoe Marks, "The Revenge of the Patriarchs: Why Autocrats Fear Women," *Foreign Affairs*, March/April 2022, https://www.foreignaffairs.com/articles/china/2022-02-08/women-rights-revenge-patriarchs.

49. Interview with a Swedish aid official, January 24, 2020; Interview with a gender advisor at a US democracy assistance organization, January 15, 2020; and Interview with a UN women official, February 4, 2020.

50. Interview with a former program officer at a US democracy assistance organization, January 16, 2020.

51. See, for example, Caroline Moser and Annalise Moser, "Gender Mainstreaming since Beijing: A Review of Success and Limitations in International Institutions," *Gender and Development* 13, no. 2 (2005): 11–22; and Jane L. Parpart, "Exploring the Transformative Potential of Gender Mainstreaming in International Development Institutions," *Journal of International Development* 26, no. 3 (2014): 382–395.

52. Email correspondence with a US aid official, October 28, 2022.

53. Peter Burnell (editor), *Evaluating Democracy Support Methods and Experiences* (Stockholm: International IDEA, 2007); and Thomas Carothers, *Aiding Democracy Abroad: The Learning Curve* (Washington DC: Carnegie Endowment for International Peace, 1999).

54. Outcome-harvesting consists of asking program participants to reflect on the most significant changes they have observed as a result of the program. The aim is to move toward more open-ended questioning and reflection in order to capture what meaning the project had and what changes it spurred, rather than simply asking whether it was useful or whether the participants learned something.

55. UNDP, "Promoting Gender Equality in Electoral Assistance"; Interview with a European Commission official, November 8, 2019; Interview with a Swedish aid official, January 24, 2020; and Interview with a staff member at IPU, February 12, 2020.

56. Interview with international aid officials in Nepal, July 1, 2020.

Chapter 6

1. Konrad-Adenauer-Stiftung, "A Training Manual for Women in Political Leadership," 2021, https://www.kas.de/documents/286528/0/Women+in+Leadership+Training+Manual.pdf/16b76ece-5c6b-ac7a-7a55-5daf90703e67?t=1627476447397.

2. Jennifer Piscopo, "The Limits of Leaning In: Ambition, Recruitment, and Candidate Training in Comparative Perspective," *Politics, Groups, and Identities* 7, no. 4 (2019): 817–828.

3. NDI, "In Nepal, Women Fight to Maintain Seats in the Constituent Assembly," January 24, 2014, https://www.ndi.org/nepal-women-fight-to-maintain-seats-in-parliament; and Interview with a staff member at NDI Nepal, February 7, 2020.

4. Interview with USAID officials, January 29, 2020; and Interview with a Kenyan civil society activist, May 5, 2020.

5. Mariz Tadros, ed., *Women in Politics: Gender, Power, and Development* (London: Zed Books, 2014); Susanna McCollom, Kristin Haffert, and Alyson Kozma, "Assessing Women's Political Party Programs: Best Practices and Recommendations" (Washington, DC: National Democratic Institute, 2008); and Rebecca Gordon et al., "Women's Political Careers: Leadership in Practice" (London: Westminster Foundation for Democracy, 2021).

6. Interview with a female candidate for the County Assembly in Nyeri County, Kenya, August 20, 2021.

7. Andrea Cornwall and Anne Marie Goetz, "Democratizing Democracy: Feminist Perspectives," *Democratization* 12, no. 5 (2005): 783–800.

8. See also Islah Jad, "Local Power and Women's Empowerment in a Conflict Context: Palestinian Women Contesting Power in Chaos," in *Women in Politics: Gender, Power, and Development*, ed. Mariz Tadros (London: Zed Books, 2014): 135–166; Darlene E. Clover, Catherine Mcgregor, Martha Farrell, and Mandakini Pant, "Women Learning Politics and the Politics of Learning: A Feminist Study of Canada and India," *Studies in the Education of Adults* 43, no. 1 (2011): 18–33; and NORC at the University of Chicago, "USAID/Liberia Elections and Political Transitions (LEPT), Getting Ready to Lead Activity Assessment," 2019, https://pdf.usaid.gov/pdf_docs/PA00TTX8.pdf.

9. Interview with a staff member of a multilateral organization in Kenya, May 4, 2020; Interview with Kenyan woman politician, July 17, 2020; Interview with aid official in Myanmar, April 14, 2021; and Interview women's rights activists in Kenya, June 3, 2020 and May 29, 2020.

10. Nic Cheeseman, Gabrielle Lynch, and Justin Willis, *The Moral Economy of Elections in Kenya: Democracy, Voting and Virtue* (Cambridge: Cambridge University Press, 2021).

11. Beatriz Tomé-Alonso, "Party of Justice and Development: A Strategy of Differentiation," Issue Brief (Baker Institute for Public Policy at Rice University, May 30, 2018), https://www.bakerinstitute.org/research/how-pjd-sets-itself-apart; and Saad Gulzar, Zuhad Hai, and Binod Kumar Paudel, "Information, Candidate Selection, and the Quality of Representation: Evidence from Nepal," *Journal of Politics* 83, no. 4 (October 1, 2021): 1511–1528.

12. Interview with Jennifer Riria of the Echo Network Africa, May 29, 2020.

13. Interview with an aid official in Kenya, June 20, 2020; Interview with a women's rights advocate in Nepal, October 15, 2020; Interview with a former staff member at an international democracy aid organization in Nepal, March 24, 2020.

14. Interview with a Kenyan women's rights advocate, June 3, 2020.

15. Interview with a Nepali women's rights activist, October 15, 2020.

16. Interview with a Kenyan women's rights advocate, June 3, 2020; Interview with a staff member at a multilateral organization in Kenya, June 8, 2020; Interview with an INGO staff member in Nepal, April 29, 2020; and Interview with staff at UN Women in Nepal, June 8, 2020.

17. Interview with Jen Clark, Program Manager at the International Women's Development Agency (IWDA), April 14, 2021.

18. Ibid.

19. Interview with an INGO official in Nepal, April 29, 2020; Interview with staff members at a multilateral organization in Nepal, June 8, 2020; Interview with a Kenyan women's rights advocate, June 3, 2020; Interview with Kenyan women candidates in Bungoma, November 11, 2021, and in Nyeri, August 30, 2021; and Interview with a Nepali women's rights advocate, August 18, 2020. See also: USAID, "Performance Evaluation of the Women's Leadership Portfolio," November 30, 2018, https://pdf.usaid.gov/pdf_docs/PA00TNBB.pdf.

20. Interview with IFES representatives, January 13, 2021.

21. Interview with the staff members of an international democracy assistance organization, August 28, 2020; and Interview with staff members at NDI Kenya, April 10, 2020.

22. Interview with staff members at NDI Kenya, April 10, 2020; and NORC at the University of Chicago, "Assessment of USAID Support for Kenya's 2017 Elections," July 2018, https://pdf.usaid.gov/pdf_docs/PA00TCXK.pdf.

23. Interview with a Nepali women's rights advocate, August 18, 2020.

24. Interview with a UN Women representative in Kenya, May 4, 2020; Interview with women candidates running for county assembly in Western Kenya, August 20, 2021; and Interview with a Kenyan women's rights advocate, June 3, 2020.

25. Interview with staff members of a US democracy aid organization in Morocco, June 17, 2020; and Interview with a Moroccan women's rights advocate, August 24, 2020.

26. Interview with a staff member of a multilateral organization in Nepal, June 8, 2020; Interview with a Western donor official in Nepal, July 1, 2020; Interview with a Nepali woman politician, October 26, 2020; Interview with a former woman Member of Parliament in Kenya, July 22, 2020; Interview with a female deputy mayor in Nepal, December 3, 2020; and Interview with a female mayor in Nepal, December 4, 2020.

27. Interview with a woman candidate in Western Kenya, May 6, 2022.

28. Devin Joshi and Ryan Goehrung, "Mothers and Fathers in Parliament: MP Parental Status and Family Gaps from a Global Perspective," *Parliamentary Affairs* 74, no. 2 (2021): 296–313.
29. Interview with a staff member at an INGO in Myanmar, March 31, 2021.
30. Interview with staff members at UN Women Nepal, June 8, 2020.
31. Interview with staff at the Heinrich-Böll-Stiftung in Kenya, June 4, 2020.
32. Interview with IFES representatives, January 13, 2021.
33. Ibid.
34. Piscopo, "The Limits of Leaning In." See also Shaun Hext and Kevin Deveaux, "Evaluation of the Westminster Foundation for Democracy (2012-2015)," https://www.oecd.org/derec/unitedkingdom/Westminster-Foundation-Democracy.pdf.
35. Interview with a Moroccan civil society activist, July 16, 2020.
36. Gulzar, Hai, and Paudel, "Information, Candidate Selection, and the Quality of Representation: Evidence from Nepal."
37. Tomé-Alonso, "Party of Justice and Development: A Strategy of Differentiation"; and Nyan Hlaing Lin, "NLD Candidate Selection Begins for 2020 Elections," *Myanmar Now*, June 2, 2020, https://myanmar-now.org/en/news/nld-candidate-selection-begins-for-2020-elections.
38. Richard Moego Bosire, "Political Parties' Strategy on Gender Equality in Candidates' Nomination in Kenya" (Nairobi: Center for Multiparty Democracy-Kenya, International IDEA, and NIMD, February 18, 2017), https://nimd.org/wp-content/uploads/2017/10/Political-parties-strategy-for-gender-equality-in-candidate-nominations-in-Kenya-CMD-Kenya-IDEA-NIMD.pdf.
39. Elin Bjarnegård and Meryl Kenny, "Comparing Candidate Selection: A Feminist Institutionalist Approach," *Government and Opposition* 51, no. 3 (2016): 370–392; and Niki Johnson, "Keeping Men In, Shutting Women Out: Gender Biases in Candidate Selection Processes in Uruguay," *Government and Opposition* 51, no. 3 (2016): 393–415.
40. Yale Economic Growth Center, "Evaluating the Effect of Increased Female Political Representation in Nepal," accessed June 18, 2022, https://egc.yale.edu/evaluating-effect-increased-female-political-representation-nepal.
41. See Elin Bjarnegård, *Gender, Informal Institutions and Political Recruitment: Explaining Male Dominance in Parliamentary Representation* (Basingstoke: Palgrave Macmillan, 2013); Christine Cheng and Margit Tavits, "Informal Influences in Selecting Female Political Candidates," *Political Research Quarterly* 64, no. 2 (2011): 460–471; Susan Franceschet and Jennifer Piscopo, "Sustaining Gendered Practices? Power, Parties, and Elite Political Networks in Argentina," *Comparative Political Studies* 47, no. 1 (2014): 85–110; and Meryl Kenny and Tania Verge, "Opening Up the Black Box: Gender and Candidate Selection in a New Era," *Government and Opposition* 51, no. 3 (2016): 359.
42. Interview with staff at an international democracy aid organization in Morocco, June 17, 2020; and Interview with a Moroccan women's rights advocate, August 24, 2020.
43. Binod Ghimire, "Alliance Politics May Trim Women's Representation in Local Government," *Kathmandu Post*, April 21, 2022, https://kathmandupost.com/politics/2022/04/04/alliance-politics-may-trim-women-s-representation-in-local-governments; and Sangita Thebe Limbu, "Nepal's House of Cards: Are Women Included or Co-Opted in Politics?" *South Asia @ LSE*, February 2, 2018, https://blogs.lse.ac.uk/southasia/2018/02/02/nepals-house-of-cards-are-women-included-or-co-opted-in-politics-gender-female-representation-caste/.
44. Nahomi Ichino and Noah L. Nathan, "Democratizing the Party: The Effects of Primary Election Reforms in Ghana," *British Journal of Political Science* 52, no. 3 (2022): 1168–1185.
45. Kenya National Commission on Human Rights, "The Fallacious Vote," 2018, https://www.knchr.org/Portals/0/CivilAndPoliticalReports/The%20Fallacious_B5_210518_2215.pdf?ver=2018-05-23-092645-480; and Fredrick O. Wanyama and Jorgen Elklit, "Electoral Violence during Party Primaries in Kenya," *Democratization* 25, no. 6 (2018): 1016–1032.
46. Interviews with former women candidates in Nyeri county, Kenya, August 20, 2021, August 24, 2021, and August 26, 2021; and Interviews with former women candidates in Kwale county, Kenya, February 8 and 9, 2022.
47. Interview with a Kenyan women's rights advocate, May 6, 2020. See also: Johnson, "Keeping Men In, Shutting Women Out."

NOTES 259

48. SAHAVAGI, DidiBahini, and Feminist Dalit Organization, *Progress of Women in Nepal (1995–2015), Substantive Equality: Non-Negotiable* (Chitwan, Nepal: UN Women Nepal, 2015), https://asiapacific.unwomen.org/en/digital-library/publications/2015/12/subs tantive-equality-non-negotiable, 167; and Sarah Hewitt, "A Situational Analysis of Women's Participation in Peace Processes," Monash University, July 2018, http://mappingpeace. monashgps.org/wp-content/uploads/2018/10/Nepal-Situational-Analysis_ART.pdf.

49. Ashok Dahal, "Rs 100 Billion: The Cost of Nepal's Next Parliamentary Election," *Annapurna Express*, January 21, 2021, https://theannapurnaexpress.com/news/rs-100-billion-the-cost-of-nepals-next-parliamentary-election-2984.

50. Election Observation Committee Nepal, "Study on the Election Campaign Finance: Local, Provincial and Federal Elections in Nepal, 2017" (The Asia Foundation, 2018), https://asi afoundation.org/wp-content/uploads/2018/10/Study-on-Election-Campaign-Finance-Election-Observation-Committee-Nepal.pdf.

51. Interview with a Nepali women's rights advocate, November 25, 2020.

52. Neelam Dhanuse, "FPTP Election: A Road Less Traveled by Women," *My Republica*, December 15, 2022, https://myrepublica.nagariknetwork.com/news/fptp-election-a-road-less-traveled-by-women/.

53. Karuti Kanyinga and Tom Mboya, "The Cost of Politics in Kenya: Implications for Political Participation and Development" (Westminster Foundation for Democracy and Netherlands Institute for Multiparty Democracy, July 2021); and Interviews with Kenyan women's rights activists on April 13, 2020; May 6, 2020; and July 1, 2020.

54. Kanyinga and Mboya, *The Cost of Politics in Kenya*, 16–17.

55. Interview with Dr. Regina Mwatha, Kenyan women's rights advocate, April 13, 2020.

56. Interview with a staff member of an international democracy aid organization in Kenya, April 13, 2020.

Chapter 7

1. Interview with a staff member at a Kenyan women's organization, April 29, 2020.

2. Interview with a Nepali women's rights advocate, June 16, 2020.

3. Diana Z. O'Brien, "Rising to the Top: Gender, Political Performance, and Party Leadership in Parliamentary Democracies," *American Journal of Political Science* 59, no. 4 (2015): 1022–1039.

4. Enlightened Myanmar Research Foundation, "Gender and Political Participation in Myanmar," October 2020, https://www.emref.org/sites/emref.org/files/publication-docs/ gender_and_political_in_myanmarenglish_online.pdf; and Interview with a civil society representative in Myanmar, January 17, 2021.

5. International IDEA, "National Dialogue on Political Parties' Internal Democracy in Kenya," October 18–19, 2016, https://www.idea.int/sites/default/files/publications/national-dialo gue-on-political-parties-internal-democracy-in-kenya.pdf.

6. Sana Benbelli, "Women's Experiences of Representation and Marginalization in Morocco: Taking Stock and Outlining Future Trajectories" (Arab Reform Initiative, April 6, 2023), https://www.arab-reform.net/publication/womens-experiences-of-represe ntation-and-marginalization-in-morocco-taking-stock-and-outlining-future-trajectories/; and Yale Economic Growth Center, "Evaluating the Effect of Increased Female Political Representation in Nepal," accessed June 18, 2022, https://egc.yale.edu/evaluating-effect-increased-female-political-representation-nepal.

7. Diana Z. O'Brien et al., "Letting Down the Ladder or Shutting the Door: Female Prime Ministers, Party Leaders, and Cabinet Ministers," *Politics and Gender* 11, no. 4 (December 2015): 689–717; Miki Caul Kittilson, *Challenging Parties, Changing Parliaments: Women and Elected Office in Contemporary Western Europe* (Columbus: Ohio State University Press, 2006); and Christine Cheng and Margit Tavits, "Informal Influences in Selecting Female Political Candidates," *Political Research Quarterly* 64, no. 2 (2011): 460–471.

8. Cecilia Josefsson, "How Candidate Selection Structures and Genders Political Ambition: Illustrations from Uruguay," *European Journal of Politics and Gender* 3, no. 1 (2020): 61–78; Tània Verge, "Political Party Gender Action Plans: Pushing Gender Change Forward beyond Quotas," *Party Politics* 26, no. 2 (2020): 238–248; and Elin Bjarnegård,

260 NOTES

Gender, Informal Institutions and Political Recruitment: Explaining Male Dominance in Parliamentary Representation (Basingstoke: Palgrave Macmillan, 2013).

9. Women's League of Burma, "Voices of the Female Candidates of the 2020 General Elections," January 2022, https://www.womenofburma.org/sites/default/files/2022-01/Voices-of-Female-Candidates-of-the-2020-Elections-Eng.pdf.

10. Nisha Onta and Pukar Malla, "Placing Nepali Women First Part the Post," *Nepali Times,* May 8, 2023, https://nepalitimes.com/opinion/placing-nepali-women-first-past-the-post; and Aakriti Ghimire, "Voters Favour Women, Party Leaders Don't," *Kathmandu Post,* September 29, 2022, https://kathmandupost.com/national/2022/09/29/voters-favour-women-party-leaders-don-t.

11. Mona Lena Krook, "Electoral Systems and Women's Representation," in *The Oxford Handbook of Electoral Systems*, eds. Erik S. Herron, Robert J. Pekkanen, and Matthew S. Shugart (Oxford: Oxford University Press, 2017), 175–192.

12. Interview with a former Kenyan parliamentarian, July 22, 2020; Interviews with female candidates in Kwale county, February 8, 2022 and May 31, 2022; and Interview with a Kenyan women's rights advocate, April 22, 2021.

13. Interview with a female County Assembly member in Bungoma county, May 4, 2022; Interview with a former woman MCA in Nyeri County, January 26, 2021; and Interview with a United Democratic Alliance party official, May 11, 2022.

14. Interview with Moroccan women's right advocates, August 24, 2020; and Interview with a representative at NDI Nepal, June 17, 2020. See also: Carolyn Barnett and Marwa Shalaby, "Success Beyond Gender Quotas: Gender, Local Politics, and Clientelism in Morocco," Program on Governance and Local Development in Morocco Working paper No. 48, October 2021.

15. Interview with a Moroccan women's rights advocate, August 20, 2020.

16. Interview with a former woman politician in Morocco, August 24, 2020.

17. Elisha Shrestha, "There Are More Women in Politics, but Few and Far Between at Decision-Making Level," *Kathmandu Post*, March 8, 2020, https://kathmandupost.com/politics/2020/03/08/there-are-more-women-in-politics-but-few-and-far-between-at-decision-making-level.

18. Interview with a staff member at NDI Morocco, July 1, 2020; Interview with a staff member at the Konrad-Adenauer-Stiftung in Morocco, June 10, 2020; Interview with a women's rights advocate in Kenya, September 14, 2021; and Interview with Nepali gender equality advocate, October 21, 2020.

19. Lars Svåsand, "International Party Assistance—What Do We Know about the Effects?" (Expertgruppen för Biståndsanalys, March 2014), https://www.oecd.org/derec/sweden/International-party-assistance.pdf.

20. The program was called "Get Involved! Women's Empowerment in Morocco and Benin" and was funded through the European Instrument for Democracy and Human Rights. Gonzalo Jorro Martinez, "How to Empower Female Politicians: The Case of Morocco," European Union, October 28, 2020, https://europa.eu/capacity4dev/articles/how-empower-female-politicians-case-morocco.

21. Interview with a USAID official in Nepal, July 7, 2020.

22. Interview with a gender consultant in Myanmar, May 11, 2021; Julie Ballington, "Empowering Women for Stronger Political Parties: A Guidebook to Promote Women's Participation" (New York: UNDP and National Democratic Institute, February 2012); iKnow Politics, "Consolidated Response on Establishing Women's Party Sections," accessed February 6, 2023, https://www.ndi.org/sites/default/files/iKNOW%20Politics%20Establishing%20Women%27s%20Party%20Sections.pdf; and Susanna McCollom, Kristin Haffert, and Alyson Kozma, "Assessing Women's Political Party Programs: Best Practices and Recommendations" (Washington, DC: National Democratic Institute, 2008).

23. Interview with staff at NDI Kenya, April 10, 2020.

24. Interview with a staff member at the Oslo Center in Kenya, May 5, 2020.

25. Interview with staff members at NDI Nepal on March 24, 2020, and April 5, 2020; McCollom, Haffert, and Kozma, "Assessing Women's Political Party Programs;" Leni Wild and Jiwan Subedi, "Review of International Assistance to Political Party and Party System

NOTES 261

Development: Case Study Report—Nepal" (Overseas Development Institute, August 2010), https://cdn.odi.org/media/documents/6873.pdf; and Interview with a European embassy official in Nepal, July 9, 2020.

26. Elina Hatakka and Anita Kelles-Viitanen, "Gender Equality within Political Parties and Women's Cross-Party Cooperation" (Helsinki: Demo Finland, 2015), https://nimd.org/wp-content/uploads/2016/02/Gender_equality_within_political_parties_and_womens_crossparty_cooperation_English.pdf; and Sergio Rodríguez Prieto and Sebastian Bloching, "Mind the Gap: NIMD's Work on Gender and Access to Power," Netherlands Institute for Multiparty Democracy, 2018.

27. Prieto and Bloching, "Mind the Gap."

28. Netherlands Institute for Multiparty Democracy (NIMD), "Annual Progress Report 2014," May 2015, https://nimd.org/wp-content/uploads/2017/10/NIMD-Annual-Progress-Report-2014.pdf; and Sergio Rodríguez Prieto, Sebastian Bloching, and Anna Zangrossi, "Respect for Women's Political Rights: Fostering Political Environments for Equal Participation and Leadership of Women in Political Parties (WPR)," Evaluation Report, Human Rights Fund of the Dutch Ministry of Foreign Affairs, March 2018.

29. Khin Thazin Myint and Hanne Lund Madsen, "Myanmar Multiparty Democracy Programme: Annual Report 2012–2013" (Danish Institute for Parties and Democracy, 2014), https://www.ft.dk/samling/20131/almdel/uru/bilag/152/1355046.pdf; and Interview with a staff member at the Danish Institute for Parties and Democracy (DIPD) in Myanmar, January 27, 2021.

30. Demo Finland, "Myanmar," accessed February 6, 2022, https://demofinland.org/en/our-work/myanmar/; and Doris Bartel et al., "Women's Action for Voice and Empowerment: Endline Evaluation" (International Women's Development Agency, December 2020), https://iwda.org.au/resource/womens-action-for-voice-and-empowerment-endline-evaluation-final-report/,

31. Interview with a USAID official in Nepal, July 7, 2020; McCollom, Haffert, and Kozma, "Assessing Women's Political Party Programs"; and CAMRIS International, "Final Evaluation of USAID/Nepal Strengthening Political Parties, Electoral and Legislative Processes Project" (United States Agency for International Development, January 26, 2017), https://cpb-us-w2.wpmucdn.com/campuspress.yale.edu/dist/b/405/files/2017/08/Consult09-HBlairEtAl-NepalSPPELP-FinalReport-Feb17-1r15t5a.pdf.

32. Interview with a female Constituent Assembly member in Nepal, November 19, 2020; CAMRIS International, "Final Evaluation of USAID/Nepal Strengthening Political Parties, Electoral and Legislative Processes Project"; Nicola Jones et al., "Evaluation of Norway's Support to Women's Rights and Gender Equality in Development Cooperation" (Swedish Institute for Public Administration, Overseas Development Institute, and the Chr. Michelsen Institute, 2015), https://www.oecd.org/derec/norway/Evaluation-of-norways-support-to-womens-rights-and-gender-equality-in-development-cooperation.pdf; Interview with a female Nepali parliamentarian, August 24, 2020; and Interview with staff at the Norwegian Embassy in Nepal, July 9, 2020.

33. See, for example, Georgina Waylen, *Engendering Transitions: Women's Mobilization, Institutions and Gender Outcomes* (Oxford: Oxford University Press, 2007).

34. Pirkko Poutiainen and Maaria Seppänen, "Evaluation 3 on the Programme-Based Support through Finnish Civil Society Organizations, Foundations and Umbrella Organizations" (Helsinki: Ministry for Foreign Affairs of Finland, 2017), https://um.fi/documents/384998/385866/demo_finland; Interview with a staff member at Demo Finland, March 22, 2020; and Demo Finland, "Dialogue Platforms—Supporting Women's Political Participation in Zambia," accessed February 10, 2023, https://demofinland.org/en/our-work/zambia/.

35. Interview with a staff member at Demo Finland, March 22, 2020; and Demo Finland, "Dialogue Platforms—Supporting Women's Political Participation in Zambia," November 2, 2021, https://demofinland.org/en/dialogue-platforms-supporting-womens-political-participation-in-zambia/.

36. CAMRIS International, "Final Evaluation of USAID/Nepal Strengthening Political Parties, Electoral and Legislative Processes Project."

37. Interview with a Nepali women's rights activist and gender expert, March 12, 2020.

38. Interview with staff at an INGO in Nepal, April 20, 2020.
39. Interview with a Kenyan women's rights advocate, May 28, 2020; and Interview with a staff member at UN Women in Kenya, May 4, 2020. See also: UN Women, "Annual Report 2011-2012," https://www.unwomen.org/sites/default/files/Headquarters/Attachments/Sections/Library/Publications/2012/UN-Women-AR-2012%20pdf.pdf.
40. UN Women Africa, "Kenya Elections: Ann Nderitu on Good Governance and Regulating the Country's Political Parties," May 25, 2022, https://africa.unwomen.org/en/stories/news/2022/05/kenya-elections-ann-nderitu-on-good-governance-and-regulating-the-countrys-political-parties.
41. Irene Mwangi, "Kenya: Lawyer Sues IEBC Over Two-Third Gender Rule for Lack of Public Views," *AllAfrica*, May 11, 2022, https://allafrica.com/stories/202205120122.html.
42. Interview with a representative at UN Women in Kenya, April 4, 2020; Interview with a UK aid official, June 29, 2020; and Interviews Kenyan women's rights advocates, June 3, 2020, and May 6, 2020.
43. "Elevating Women Leaders in Myanmar," International Development Research Centre, accessed February 5, 2023, https://k4dm.ca/2021/05/27/elevating-women-leaders-in-myanmar-2/; and Doris Bartel et al., "Women's Action for Voice and Empowerment: Endline Evaluation".
44. IWDA, "Annual Narrative Report 2020: Women's Action for Voice and Empowerment (WAVE) Program," accessed November 16, 2023, https://iwda.org.au/assets/files/WAVE-2020-Annual-report_IWDA.pdf.
45. Interview with a staff member at IWDA, April 14, 2021.
46. Internal report produced by Demo Finland/NIMD, accessed March 30, 2021.
47. Interview with a staff member at DIPD in Myanmar, February 2, 2021; and Interview with a Burmese civil society advocate, January 27, 2021.
48. Prieto and Bloching, "Mind the Gap."
49. Interview with an IRI official in Myanmar, January 14, 2021; and Interview with a Burmese civil society advocate, January 27, 2021.
50. Interview with a representative from Demo Finland, March 22, 2020.
51. Interview with a staff member at an international democracy aid organization in Myanmar, February 2, 2021.
52. Interview with staff at NDI Kenya, April 10, 2020.
53. Dzuya Walter, "Court Suspends IEBC Directive on Political Party Compliance to Two-Thirds Gender Rule," *Citizen Digital*, May 11, 2022, https://www.citizen.digital/news/city-lawyer-sues-iebc-over-the-implementation-of-two-third-gender-rule-n298052.
54. Management Innovation, Training and Research Academy (MITRA), "Final Evaluation of Project on Making Politics Work with Women (MP3W) in Nepal" (UN Women, July 2013), https://gate.unwomen.org/Evaluation/Details?evaluationId=4747.
55. Interview with a local staff member of a Western embassy in Kenya, August 10, 2021; and Interview with a Kenyan civil society advocate, August 11, 2021.
56. Verge, "Political Party Gender Action Plans."
57. NIMD, "Annual Progress Report 2016: Respect for Women's Political Rights: Fostering Political Environments for Equal Participation and Leadership of Women in Political Parties," May 2017, https://nimd.org/wp-content/uploads/2017/10/NIMD-Annual-Progress-Report-2016.pdf.
58. Interview with a staff member at an internatonal democracy assistance organization in Morocco, August 12, 2020.
59. See "Cost of Politics Reports," accessed February 9, 2023, https://www.costofpolitics.net/.
60. The WPR program run by NIMD and International IDEA in Kenya, Colombia, and Tunisia represents an exception in this regard. Interview with a representative from UNDP, February 14, 2020; Interview with a former staff member at an international democracy assistance organization, January 16, 2020; and Interview with a staff member at UN Women, February 3, 2020.
61. Interviews with women and men candidates in Nyeri, Kenya, February 2, 2022, in Kwale, Kenya, March 4, 2022, and in Bungoma, Kenya, February 26, 2022, and May 11, 2022.

62. Matthew K. Gichohi, "With Hands Tied: A Kenyan Woman's Presidential Bid," in *Women and Power in Africa*, ed. Leonardo Arriola, Martha Johnson, and Melanie Phillips (Oxford: Oxford University Press, 2021), 117–140.
63. Interview with European embassy officials in Nairobi, June 14, 2020, and June 19, 2020.
64. Melanie M. Hughes, Darcy Ashman, and Milad Pournik, "Women in Power Project: Summary Report" (United States Agency for International Development, April 2016), https://www.usaid.gov/sites/default/files/USAID-WiP-summary-report_FINAL.pdf.
65. Happy M. Kayuni and Ragnhild L. Muriaas, "Alternative to Gender Quotas: Electoral Financing of Women Candidates in Malawi," *Representation* 50, no. 3 (July 3, 2014): 393–404. See also Tam O'Neil et al., "Women and Power: Representation and Influence in Malawi's Parliament" (Overseas Development Institute, February 2016), https://cdn.odi.org/media/documents/10289.pdf.
66. Interview with a representative at the Center for Multiparty Democracy in Kenya (CMD-Kenya), April 13, 2020; and Mike Zuijderduijn, Irma Alpenidze, and Raphaël Pouyé, "Final Evaluation of the NIMD Strategic Partnership Dialogue and Dissent Programme" (MDF Training & Consultancy, November 2020), https://nimd.org/wp-content/uploads/2021/01/Final-Evaluation-NIMD-Strategic-Partnership.pdf.
67. Interview with a Kenyan women's rights advocate, August 18, 2021; and Rainbow Murray, Ragnhild Muriaas, and Vibeke Wang, "Editorial Introduction: Gender and Political Financing," *International Political Science Review* (September 2021), 6.
68. See, for example, Magnus Ohman, "Gender-Targeted Public Funding for Political Parties: A Comparative Analysis" (Stockholm: International IDEA, 2018), https://www.idea.int/sites/default/files/publications/gender-targeted-public-funding-for-political-parties.pdf, 21–22; and Lolita Cigane and Magnus Ohman, "Political Finance and Gender Equality," IFES White Paper (Washington, DC: IFES, August 2014), https://www.ifes.org/sites/default/files/migrate/political_finance_and_gender_equality.pdf.
69. Ragnhild Muriaas, Amy G. Mazur, and Season Hoard, "Payments and Penalties for Democracy: Gendered Electoral Financing in Action Worldwide," *American Political Science Review* 116, no. 2 (May 2022): 502–515; Francesca Feo and Daniela R. Piccio, "Doomed to Fail: The Adoption of Gendered Party Finance in Italy at an Inhospitable Time," *Contemporary Italian Politics* 12, no. 3 (2020): 287–299; and Murray, Muriaas, and Wang, "Editorial Introduction: Gender and Political Financing."
70. Interview with a Kenyan women's rights advocate, August 19, 2021.
71. Faith Kiboro, "Kenya's Election Jitters Have Roots in Campaign Financing. It's Time to Act," *The Conversation*, August 6, 2017, https://theconversation.com/kenyas-election-jitters-have-roots-in-campaign-financing-its-time-to-act-81693.
72. Interview with a European embassy official in Kenya, June 24, 2020; and Interview with a US aid official in Morocco, June 19, 2020.
73. Interview with a staff member at the Oslo Center in Kenya, May 5, 2020; Interview with a staff member at International IDEA Nepal, September 29, 2020; Interview with a former IRI staff member in Kenya, April 24, 2020; and Interview with a Moroccan women's rights advocate, August 20, 2020.
74. Internal report produced by Demo Finland/NIMD, accessed March 30, 2021; Prieto and Bloching, "Mind the Gap"; and Interview with a women's rights advocate in Kenya, June 3, 2020.
75. Verge, "Political Party Gender Action Plans."
76. Georgina Waylen, ed., *Gender and Informal Institutions* (Lanham, MD: Rowman & Littlefield, 2017).
77. Karen Celis and Joni Lovenduski, "Power Struggles: Gender Equality in Political Representation," *European Journal of Politics and Gender* 1, no. 1–2 (July 2018): 149–166.

Chapter 8

1. Name changed by the authors.
2. Interview with a vice chairperson in Nepal, November 18, 2020.

3. The Asia Foundation Partnership, "Nepal's Locally Elected Women Representatives: Exploratory Study of Needs and Capacity," July 19, 2018, https://asiafoundation.org/publication/nepals-locally-elected-representatives-exploratory-study-of-needs-and-capacity-assessment/.
4. Ibid.
5. Interview with a women's rights activist in Nepal, May 16, 2020.
6. Karen Celis and Sarah Childs, *Feminist Democratic Representation* (Oxford: Oxford University Press, 2020).
7. See Hanna F. Pitkin, *The Concept of Representation* (Berkeley: University of California Press, 1972).
8. UNDP, "Strategies and Good Practices in Promoting Gender Equality Outcomes in Parliaments," 2016, https://www.undp.org/sites/g/files/zskgke326/files/publications/GUIDANCE%20NOTE%20Strategies%20and%20good%20practices%20in%20promoting%20gender%20equality%20outcomes%20in%20parliaments_web.pdf.
9. Fiona Mackay, "'Thick' Conceptions of Substantive Representation: Women, Gender and Political Institutions," *Representation* 44, no. 2 (2008): 125–139.
10. Amanda Clayton, Diana Z. O'Brien, and Jennifer M. Piscopo, "All Male Panels? Representation and Democratic Legitimacy," *American Journal of Political Science* 63, no. 1 (2019): 113–129.
11. Celis and Childs, *Feminist Democratic Representation*.
12. Susan Franceschet and Jennifer M. Piscopo, "Gender Quotas and Women's Substantive Representation: Lessons from Argentina," *Politics and Gender* 4, no. 3 (2008): 393–425; Lisa A. Bryant and Julia Marin Hellwege, "Working Mothers Represent: How Children Affect the Legislative Agenda of Women in Congress," *American Politics Research* 47, no. 3 (2019): 447–470; and Amanda Clayton, Cecilia Josefsson, and Vibeke Wang, "Quotas and Women's Substantive Representation: Evidence from a Content Analysis of Ugandan Plenary Debates," *Politics and Gender* 13, no. 2 (June 2017): 276–304.
13. Kathleen A. Bratton and Leonard P. Ray, "Descriptive Representation, Policy Outcomes, and Municipal Day-Care Coverage in Norway," *American Journal of Political Science* 46, no. 2 (2002): 428–437; Amanda Clayton and Pär Zetterberg, "Quota Shocks: Electoral Gender Quotas and Government Spending Priorities Worldwide," *Journal of Politics* 80, no. 3 (2018): 916–932; Catherine Bolzendahl, "Making the Implicit Explicit: Gender Influences on Social Spending in Twelve Industrialized Democracies, 1980–99," *Social Politics: International Studies in Gender, State and Society* 16, no. 1 (2009): 40–81; Michael T. Koch and Sarah A. Fulton, "In the Defense of Women: Gender, Office Holding, and National Security Policy in Established Democracies," *Journal of Politics* 73, no. 1 (2011): 1–16; Sarah Shair-Rosenfield and Reed M. Wood, "Governing Well after War: How Improving Female Representation Prolongs Post-Conflict Peace," *Journal of Politics* 79, no. 3 (2017): 995–1009; and Valeriya Mechkova and Ruth Carliz, "Gendered Accountability: When and Why Do Women's Policy Priorities Get Implemented?" *European Political Science Review* 13, no. 1 (2020): 3–21.
14. Jane Mansbridge, "Should Blacks Represent Blacks and Women Represent Women? A Contingent Yes," *Journal of Politics* 61, no. 3 (1999): 628–657; Iris Marion Young, "Gender as Seriality: Thinking about Women as a Social Collective," *Signs* 19, no. 3 (1994): 713–738; and Mackay, "'Thick' Conceptions of Substantive Representation."
15. Karen Celis and Sarah Childs, "The Substantive Representation of Women: What to Do with Conservative Claims?" *Political Studies* 60, no. 1 (March 2012): 213–225.
16. Laurel S. Weldon, "Beyond Bodies: Institutional Sources of Representation for Women in Democratic Policymaking," *Journal of Politics* 64, no. 4 (2002): 1153–1174; and Celis and Childs, *Feminist Democratic Representation*.
17. Diana Z. O'Brien and Jennifer Piscopo, "The Impact of Women in Parliament," in *The Palgrave Handbook of Women's Political Rights*, eds. Susan Franceschet, Mona Lena Krook, and Netina Tan (New York: Palgrave Macmillan, 2018), 53–72; Roseanna Michelle Heath, Leslie A. Schwindt-Bayer, and Michelle M. Taylor-Robinson, "Women on the Sidelines: Women's Representation on Committees in Latin American Legislatures," *American Journal of Political Science* 49, no. 2 (2005): 420–436; and Josefina Erikson and Cecilia Josefsson, "The Parliament as a Gendered Workplace: How to Research Legislators' (UN)Equal Opportunities to Represent," *Parliamentary Affairs* 75, no. 1 (January 2022): 20–38.
18. Debra Dodson, *The Impact of Women in Congress* (New York: Oxford University Press, 2001).

NOTES 265

19. Shwe Shwe Sein Latt et al., "Women's Political Participation in Myanmar: Experiences of Women Parliamentarians 2011–2016" (The Asia Foundation and Phan Tee Eain, April 2017), https://asiafoundation.org/wp-content/uploads/2017/05/Womens-Political-Partic ipation-in-Myanmar-MP-Experiences_report-1.pdf. There was a similar pattern in Nepal's first CA: of the 197 women who were elected, only 26 had prior experience in legislative positions. Punam Yadav, "Women in the Parliament: Changing Gender Dynamics in the Political Sphere in Nepal," in *Women in Governing Institutions in South Asia*, ed. Nizam Ahmed (Cham: Palgrave Macmillan, 2017), 85.

20. Interview with a staff member at the Kenyan Women Parliamentary Association (KEWOPA), May 17, 2020; Interview with an international aid official in Kenya, May 4, 2020; Interview with a gender equality advocate in Kenya, July 1, 2020; and Interviews with staff members of international democracy assistance organizations in Myanmar, January 19, 2021, and April 14, 2021.

21. Interview with INGO officials in Nepal, April 29, 2020; Interview with staff at UN Women in Nepal, June 8, 2020; Interview with a journalist and women's rights activist at the Media Advocacy Group in Nepal, July 15, 2020; and Interview with a woman Member of Parliament in Nepal, August 17, 2020.

22. NDI, "Nepal: Training Women to Engage in the Constitution-Drafting Process through the Nepali Women's Leadership Academy," March 16, 2009, https://www.ndi.org/ our-stories/nepal-training-women-engage-constitution-drafting-process-through-nep ali-women%E2%80%99s; and NDI–Nepal, "Supporting Women's Participation in the Constituent Assembly Process," https://pdf.usaid.gov/pdf_docs/pnady396.pdf.

23. Interview with INGO officials in Nepal, April 29, 2020; and Interview with UN Women in Nepal, June 8, 2020; and Interview with European embassy officials, July 1, 2020.

24. Katie Ryan, "'She Leads' Women's Leadership Program Piloted in Nepal," International Foundation for Electoral Systems, July 18, 2019, https://www.ifes.org/news/she-leads-wom ens-leadership-program-piloted-nepal; and "She Leads – Women Leadership Programme," Schweizerische Eidgenossenschaft, accessed November 17, 2023, https://www.eda.admin. ch/countries/nepal/en/home/international-cooperation/projects.html/content/dezaproje cts/SDC/en/2019/7F10196/phase1?oldPagePath=/content/countries/nepal/en/home/ internationale-zusammenarbeit/projekte.html.

25. Frank Feulner, Pratap Chhatkuli, and Sarmila Shrestha, "Final Evaluation of the Parliament Support Project (PSP)—Phase 2, UNDP Nepal," June 2022, https://erc.undp.org/evaluat ion/documents/download/2141.

26. Newstone Global Consulting, "Learning Review: Myanmar Women Parliamentarians Mentoring Pilot Program" (International Women's Development Agency and Akhaya Women, August 2018), https://iwda.org.au/assets/files/IWDA-Myanmar-Women-Parli amentarians-Mentoring-Pilot_Learning-Brief.pdf.

27. Interview with a staff member at IWDA, April 14, 2021.

28. Ben Hillman, Prakash Bhattarai, and Kopila Rijal, "Mid-Term Review of Parliament Support Project (PSP) Phase-2" (United Nations Development Programme, 2020), https://erc. undp.org/evaluation/evaluations/detail/12423; and Feulner et al., "Final Evaluation of the Parliament Support Project (PSP)."

29. USAID, "Mid Term Evaluation of 'Nepal's Strengthening Political Parties, Electoral and Legislative Processes' Project," July 2014, https://pdf.usaid.gov/pdf_docs/PA00JZ7J.pdf; International IDEA, "Nepal's Constitution Building Process: 2006–2015," 2015, https:// www.idea.int/sites/default/files/publications/nepals-constitution-building-process-2006-2015.pdf; Women's Caucus et al., "Women Members of the Constituent Assembly: A Study on Contribution of Women in Constitution Making in Nepal," 2011, https://www.idea. int/sites/default/files/publications/women-members-of-the-constituent-assembly.pdf; Interview with a Nepali women's rights activist, June 16, 2020; and Interviews with female CA members, August 17, 2020, and October 26, 2020.

30. Interview with a Nepali deputy mayor, December 4, 2020; Interview with a women's rights advocate at the Media Advocacy Group in Nepal, July 15, 2020; Group interview with women CA members in Nyeri, September 7, 2022; Interview with a staff member at KEWOPA, May

17, 2020; and Interview with Pallavi Payal, a women's rights researcher in Nepal, October 21, 2020.

31. Newstone Global Consulting, "Learning Review: Myanmar Women Parliamentarians Mentoring Pilot Program."

32. UNDP, "Strategies and Good Practices," 23; and Interview with a representative of a multilateral organization in Myanmar, January 22, 2021.

33. Interview with a European embassy official in Kenya, April 30, 2020; and Interview with a staff member at KEWOPA, May 17, 2020.

34. Interview with a former staff member at a US democracy assistance organization in Kenya, April 24, 2020.

35. Newstone Global Consulting, "Learning Review: Myanmar Women Parliamentarians Mentoring Pilot Program."

36. Tara Kanel, "Women's Political Representation in Nepal: An Experience from the 2008 Constituent Assembly," *Asian Journal of Women's Studies* 20, no. 4 (2014): 39–62; and Yadav, "Women in the Parliament."

37. Neeti Aryal Khanal, "'I Can Speak': Navigating Masculine Spaces in Federal Nepal" (International Alert and Saferworld, December 2019), 12.

38. Seira Tamang et al., "Beyond 'Capacity': Gendered Election Processes, Networks, and Informality in Local Governments in Nepal" (The Asia Foundation, March 2022).

39. Group interview with women MCAs in Bungoma county, May 4, 2022; and Interview with a woman MCA in Kwale county, March 5, 2022.

40. Aili Mari Tripp, Catie Lott, and Louise Khabure, "Women's Leadership as a Route to Greater Empowerment: Kenya Case Study" (United States Agency for International Development, September 29, 2014), https://www.usaid.gov/sites/default/files/2022-05/WiP%20-%20Ke nya%20Case%20Study%20Report.pdf.

41. Management Innovation, Training and Research Academy (MITRA), "Final Evaluation of Project on Making Politics Work with Women (MP3W) in Nepal" (UN Women, July 2013), https://gate.unwomen.org/Evaluation/Details?evaluationId=4747.

42. Interviews with aid officials at democracy assistance organizations in Myanmar, January 19, 2021, and February 9, 2021.

43. "Arab Women Parliamentarians Network for Equality (Ra'edat)," accessed November 23, 2022, https://iknowpolitics.org/sites/default/files/raedat.

44. Interview with a staff member at KEWOPA, May 17, 2020; and Getrude Nthiiri, "The Contribution of the Kenya Women Parliamentary Association in Strengthening Democracy in Kenya" (University of Nairobi, 2014), http://erepository.uonbi.ac.ke/bitstream/handle/ 11295/100759/Nthiiri_The%20contribution%20of%20the%20Kenya%20women%20pa rliamentary%20association%20in%20strengthening%20democracy%20in%20Kenya. pdf?sequence=1.

45. KEWOPA has also advocated for a national-level gender quota, yet with no success to date. See Katherina Vittum et al., "Parliamentary Strengthening Program: Final Performance Evaluation" (USAID/Kenya Office of Democracy, Governance and Conflict, December 2015), https:// pdf.usaid.gov/pdf_docs/PA00KZ23.pdf; Tripp, Lott, and Khabure; "Women's Leadership as a Route to Greater Empowerment"; and Pamela Mburia, Jane Thuo, and Marceline Nyambala, "Journey to Leadership: Women Legislators in Kenya's Tenth Parliament" (Association of Media Women in Kenya, 2011), https://www.kewopa.org/wp-content/uploads/2015/04/ 10th-Parliament-Book.pdf.

46. Washington Onyango-Ouma et al., "The Making of the Kenya Sexual Offenses Act, 2006: Behind the Scenes" (Kwani Trust, 2009), https://knowledgecommons.popcouncil. org/cgi/viewcontent.cgi?article=2165&context=departments_sbsr-rh; and Interview with a staff member at SOCATT, May 5, 2020.

47. Niki Johnson and Cecilia Josefsson, "A New Way of Doing Politics? Cross-Party Women's Caucuses as Critical Actors in Uganda and Uruguay," *Parliamentary Affairs* 69, no. 4 (2016): 845–859; Monica Costa, Marian Sawer, and Rhonda Sharp, "Women Acting For Women: Gender-Responsive Budgeting in Timor Leste," *International Feminist Journal of Politics* 15, no. 3 (2013): 333–352; Vibeke Wang, "Women Changing Policy Outcomes: Learning from Pro-Women Legislation in the Ugandan Parliament," in

Women's Studies International Forum 41 (2013): 113–121; Gisela G. Geisler, "Women and the Remaking of Politics in Southern Africa: Negotiating Autonomy, Incorporation, and Representation" (Nordiska Afrikainstitutet, 2004); Elizabeth Pearson, "Demonstrating Legislative Leadership: The Introduction of Rwanda's Gender-Based Violence Bill" (The Initiative for Inclusive Security, April 2008), https://inclsvescurity.wpenginepowered.com/wp-content/uploads/2012/08/1078_rwanda_demonstrating_legislative_leadership_updated_6_20_08.pdf; and Jennie E. Burnet, "Gender Balance and the Meanings of Women in Governance in Post-Genocide Rwanda," *African Affairs* 107, no. 428 (2008): 361–386.

48. Women's Caucus et al., "Women Members of the Constituent Assembly," 74–75; and Interview with an aid official at a democracy assistance organization in Myanmar, January 19, 2021.

49. Interviews with women MCAs in Bungoma county, Kenya, November 5, 2021, and November 18, 2021; and Interview with women MCAs in Kwale county, Kenya, February 7, 2022, and March 5, 2022.

50. Interview with a women's rights advocate in Morocco, June 18, 2020; and Interview with staff at a US democracy assistance organization in Morocco, July 1, 2020.

51. Amanda Clayton, "Electoral Systems and the Process of Substantive Representation: Lessons from Namibia and Uganda," in *Women and Power in Africa*, eds. Leonardo Arriola, Martha Johnson, and Melanie Phillips (New York: Oxford University Press, 2021), 163–186.

52. Rita Manchanda, "Nepali Women Seize the New Political Dawn: Resisting Marginalisation after Ten Years of War" (Centre for Humanitarian Dialogue, December 2010), https://www.files.ethz.ch/isn/125619/2010_12_Nepali%20women%20seize%20the%20new%20political%20dawn.pdf; and Women's Caucus et al., "Women Members of the Constituent Assembly," 86, 91.

53. Kanel, "Women's Political Representation in Nepal."

54. Interviews with a Kenyan women's rights advocate, April 22, 2021; Interview with a woman candidate in Nyeri county, Kenya, September 8, 2021; and Interview with a woman MCA in Nyeri county, Kenya, August 27, 2021.

55. Interview with an international aid official in Myanmar, February 9, 2021; Mi Ki Kyaw Myint, "What Advice Do Myanmar's Female MPs Have for Women Candidates in 2020?" (Asia Foundation, October 23, 2019), https://asiafoundation.org/2019/10/23/what-advice-do-myanmars-female-mps-have-for-women-candidates-in-2020/; and Interview with a civil society advocate in Myanmar, January 28, 2021.

56. Latt et al., "Women's Political Participation in Myanmar."

57. Agora Parliament and International Knowledge Network of Women in Politics, "Women's Caucuses," 2011, http://old.agora-parl.org/sites/default/files/e-discussion_summary_-_womens_caucuses.pdf, 3.

58. Women's Caucus et al., "Women Members of the Constituent Assembly."

59. Jaemin Shim, "Substantive Representation of Women and Policy-Vote Trade-Offs: Does Supporting Women's Issue Bills Decrease a Legislator's Chance of Reelection?," *Journal of Legislative Studies* 28, no. 4 (April 5, 2021): 1–21.

60. Interview with an aid official at The Asia Foundation, February 9, 2021.

61. Mackay, "'Thick' Conceptions of Substantive Representation," 128.

62. Karen Celis, Sarah Childs, Johanna Kantola, and Mona Lena Krook, "Rethinking Women's Substantive Representation," *Representation* 44, no. 2 (2008): 99–110.

63. Karen Celis, Sarah Childs, and Jennifer Crutin, "Specialised Parliamentary Bodies and the Quality of Women's Substantive Representation: A Comparative Analysis of Belgium, United Kingdom, and New Zealand," *Parliamentary Affairs* 69, no. 4 (2016): 812–829.

64. Johnson and Josefsson, "A New Way of Doing Politics?"

65. Sarah Childs and Mona Lena Krook, "Analysing Women's Substantive Representation: From Critical Mass to Critical Actors," *Government and Opposition* 44, no. 2 (2009): 125–145; and Karen Celis and Silvia Erzeel, "Beyond the Usual Suspects: Non-Left, Male and Non-Feminist MPs and the Substantive Representation of Women," *Government and Opposition* 50, no. 1 (January 2015): 45–64.

66. Interview with an aid official at an international organization in Myanmar, January 27, 2021; and Interview with a civil society advocate in Myanmar, January 28, 2021.

67. Interview with a civil society advocate in Myanmar, January 28, 2021.
68. Women's Caucus et al., "Women Members of the Constituent Assembly," 91.
69. Interview with a staff member at SOCATT, May 5, 2020; and Interview with a staff member at KEWOPA, May 17, 2020.
70. Interview with a Kenyan women's rights advocate, September 14, 2021.
71. Interview with an international aid official in Morocco, August 24, 2020; Sana Benbelli, "Women's Experiences of Representation and Marginalization in Morocco: Taking Stock and Outlining Future Trajectories," Arab Reform Initiative, April 6, 2023, https://www.arab-ref orm.net/publication/womens-experiences-of-representation-and-marginalization-in-moro cco-taking-stock-and-outlining-future-trajectories/.
72. Interview with a European embassy official in Morocco, June 12, 2020; Interview with an official at a US democracy organization in Morocco, July 1, 2020; Interviews with Moroccan women's rights activists, July 16, 2020; July 14, 2020; and August 20, 2020; and Interview with a German political foundation official in Morocco, June 10, 2020.
73. Interview women candidates in Nyeri, August 20, 2021, September 2, 2021, and September 6, 2021.
74. Interview with a staff member at SOCATT, May 5, 2020; Interview with a Kenyan women's rights advocate, April 20, 2021; and Interview with a staff member at democracy assistance organization in Morocco, July 1, 2020; Interview with Moroccan women's rights advocates, July 14, 2020.
75. Anne Maria Holli uses the term "women's co-operative constellations" to describe the multiple actors involved in processes of substantive representation. Anne Maria Holli, "Feminist Triangles: A Conceptual Analysis," *Representation* 44, no. 2 (2008): 169–185.
76. See, for example, Anne Marie Goetz and Shireen Hassim, eds., *No Shortcuts to Power: African Women in Politics and Policy Making* (London: Zed Books, 2003); Mala Htun and S. Laurel Weldon, *The Logics of Gender Justice: State Action on Women's Rights around the World* (New York: Cambridge University Press, 2018); and Sohela Nazneen, Samuel Hickey, and Eleni Sifaki, eds., *Negotiating Gender Equity in the Global South: The Politics of Domestic Violence Policy* (London: Routledge, 2019).
77. Alice J. Kang and Aili Mari Tripp, "Coalitions Matter: Citizenship, Women, and Quota Adoption in Africa," *Perspectives on Politics* 16, no. 1 (March 2018): 73–91; Juliana Restrepo Sanín, "Criminalizing Violence Against Women in Politics: Innovation, Diffusion, and Transformation," *Politics & Gender* 18, no. 1 (2022): 1–32; and Kaden Paulson-Smith and Aili Mari Tripp, "Women's Rights and Critical Junctures in Constitutional Reform in Africa (1951-2019)," *African Affairs* 120, no. 480 (2021): 365–389.
78. Weldon, "Beyond Bodies."
79. See also Wang, "Women Changing Policy Outcomes;" and Holli, "Feminist Triangles: A Conceptual Analysis."
80. Interview with a Department of Foreign Affairs and Trade (DFAT) representative and adviser in Myanmar, March 30, 2021.
81. Interview with a staff member at IWDA, April 14, 2021; and Interview with DFAT representative and adviser in Myanmar, March 30, 2021.
82. Newstone Global Consulting, "Learning Review: Myanmar Women Parliamentarians Mentoring Pilot Program."
83. Doris Bartel et al., "Women's Action for Voice and Empowerment: Endline Evaluation" (International Women's Development Agency, December 2020), https://iwda.org.au/resou rce/womens-action-for-voice-and-empowerment-endline-evaluation-final-report/.
84. Colleen Lowe Morna, Susan Tolmay, and Mukayi Makaya, "Women's Political Participation: Africa Barometer 2021," (Stockholm: International IDEA, 2021), https://www.idea.int/sites/default/files/publications/womens-political-participation-africa-barometer-2021.pdf, 138.
85. Interview with a women's rights advocate at Mobilizing for Rights Associates in Morocco, July 16, 2020; and Interview with an official at a European embassy in Morocco, July 12, 2020.
86. Andrea Krizsán and Conny Roggeband, "Reconfiguring State–Movement Relations in the Context of De-Democratization," *Social Politics: International Studies in Gender, State and Society* 28, no. 3 (2021): 604–628.

NOTES   269

87. IWDA, "WAVE Movement Series: How Do You Build Movements?," October 9, 2019, https://iwda.org.au/wave-movement-series-how-do-you-build-movements/; and IWDA, "Women's Action for Voice and Empowerment (WAVE): Research, Evidence and Learning Framework," 2017, https://aidstream.org/files/documents/WAVE-RELF-V3-2017050 1020510.0-2017.pdf.

88. Joni Lovenduski, *Feminizing Politics* (Cambridge: Polity, 2005); Josefina Erikson and Tània Verge, "Gender, Power and Privilege in the Parliamentary Workplace," *Parliamentary Affairs* 75, no. 1 (January 1, 2022): 1–19; and Sonia Palmieri, "Feminist Institutionalism and Gender-Sensitive Parliaments: Relating Theory and Practice," in *Gender Innovation in Political Science: New Norms, New Knowledge*, eds. Marian Sawer and Kerryn Baker (Cham: Palgrave Macmillan, 2019), 173–194.

89. Lena Wängnerud, *The Principles of Gender-Sensitive Parliaments* (New York: Routledge, 2015); and Palmieri, "Feminist Institutionalism and Gender-Sensitive Parliaments: Relating Theory and Practice."

90. Sonia Palmieri, "Gender-Sensitive Parliaments: A Global Review of Good Practice," Inter-Parliamentary Union, 2011, http://archive.ipu.org/pdf/publications/gsp11-e.pdf; OSCE, "Realizing Gender Equality in Parliament: A Guide for Parliaments in the OSCE Region" (OSCE Office for Democratic Institutions and Human Rights, 2011), https://www.osce.org/files/f/documents/3/b/506885_2.pdf; and UN Women and IPU, "Gender-Responsive Law-Making," 2021, https://www.unwomen.org/sites/default/files/2021-11/Handbook-on-gender-responsive-law-making-en.pdf.

91. IPU, "How Do Parliaments Follow Up on IPU Resolutions and Initiatives?," October 14, 2022, https://www.ipu.org/news/case-studies/2022-10/how-do-parliaments-follow-up-ipu-resolutions-and-initiatives; and OSCE, "Realizing Gender Equality in Parliament."

92. OSCE, "Realizing Gender Equality in Parliament."

93. Parliament of Kenya, "Commonwealth Parliamentary Association (CPA) Benchmarks for Democratic Legislatures—Report of Self-Assessment of the Parliament of Kenya" (Commonwealth Partnership for Democracy and the Westminster Foundation for Democracy, May 2022), http://www.parliament.go.ke/sites/default/files/2022-05/Ass essment%20of%20Parliaments%20against%20the%20CPA%20recommeded%20Ben chmarks%20for%20Democratic%20Legislature.pdf; and IPU, "Kenyan Parliament Hosts Gender Mainstreaming Workshop," June 30, 2017, https://www.ipu.org/ar/node/8648.

94. Interview with a staff member of a regional international organization, November 21, 2022.

95. UN Women, "Corporate Evaluation of UN Women's Contribution to Women's Political Participation and Leadership: Synthesis Report," April 2018, https://www.unwomen.org/sites/default/files/Headquarters/Attachments/Sections/Library/Publications/2018/Corporate-evaluation-Womens-political-participation-en.pdf, 46; and UNDP, "Strategies and Good Practices in Promoting Gender Equality Outcomes in Parliaments," 11.

96. European Institute for Gender Equality, "Gender-Sensitive Parliaments," accessed November 23, 2022, https://eige.europa.eu/gender-mainstreaming/toolkits/gender-sensit ive-parliaments.

97. Interview with a staff member of a regional international organization, November 21, 2022.

98. Interviews with staff members at SOCATT, May 5, 2020 and June 17, 2022; and Annette Ittig and Caspar Merkle, "Kenya 2014–2018 Country Portfolio Evaluation: Final Report" (UN Women, September 21, 2018), https://gate.unwomen.org/Evaluation/Details?Evalu ationId=4916.

99. UN Women, "Harmonisation de L'Arsenal Juridique Par Rapport Aux Dispositions Constitutionelles Qui Consacrent La Suprematie Des Normes Internationales Sur Le Droit National," 2017, https://morocco.unwomen.org/sites/default/files/Field%20Office%20 Morocco/Documents/others/Fiches%20projets%202017/Fiche%20projet_Parlementai re_09062017.pdf.

100. Interview with an international aid official in Morocco, August 24, 2020.

101. Feulner et al., "Final Evaluation of the Parliament Support Project (PSP)."

102. YUWA, "Women and Gender Norms in Nepal's Parliament" (Advancing Learning and Innovation on Gender Norms (ALIGN), June 2021), https://www.alignplatform.org/sites/default/files/2021-07/yuwa_-_nepal-politics.pdf.

103. OSCE, "Realizing Gender Equality in Parliament;" and UNDP, "Strategies and Good Practices in Promoting Gender Equality Outcomes in Parliaments."

104. Interview with a staff member of a regional international organization, November 21, 2022.

105. Sarah Childs and Jessica C. Smith, "Written Evidence Submitted by Professor Sarah Childs and Dr Jessica C. Smith [GSP0012]" (The Parliament of the United Kingdom, 2021), https://committees.parliament.uk/writtenevidence/25329/pdf/.

106. OSCE, "Realizing Gender Equality in Parliament"; Commonwealth Parliamentary Association UK, "Westminster Workshop on Gender Sensitive Scrutiny: Official Report" (The Parliament of the United Kingdom, June 2019), https://www.uk-cpa.org/media/3364/westminster-workshop-on-gender-sensitive-scrutiny-report.pdf; and Palmieri, "Gender-Sensitive Parliaments."

107. UNIFEM, "UNIFEM's Work on Gender-Responsive Budgeting: Morocco," Evaluation Report, 2009, https://www.unwomen.org/sites/default/files/Headquarters/Media/Publications/UNIFEM/Evaluation_GRB_Programme_Morocco_en.pdf; and Interview with a representative of an international organization in Myanmar, January 27, 2021.

108. Interview with a representative of an international organization in Myanmar, January 27, 2021.

Chapter 9

1. Independent Electoral and Boundaries Commission, "Electoral Code of Conduct," 2020, https://gck.or.ke/wp-content/uploads/2020/08/ELECTORAL-CODE-OF-CONDUCT.pdf.

2. Name changed by the authors. Interview with a female MCA in Kenya, September 1, 2021.

3. Mona Lena Krook, *Violence against Women in Politics* (Oxford: Oxford University Press, 2020).

4. Mona Lena Krook, "Contesting Gender Quotas: Dynamics of Resistance," *Politics, Groups, and Identities* 4, no. 2 (2016): 268–283.

5. Cynthia H. Enloe, *The Big Push: Exposing and Challenging the Persistence of Patriarchy* (Oakland: University of California Press, 2017).

6. Caroline Harper et al., "Gender, Power and Progress: How Norms Change" (Advancing Learning and Innovation on Gender Norms and Overseas Development Institute, December 2020).

7. "World Values Survey Data Analysis Tool," accessed January 28, 2023, https://www.worldvaluessurvey.org/WVSOnline.jsp.

8. UNDP, "Uncertain Times, Unsettled Lives: Shaping Our Future in a Transforming World," Human Development Report 2021–2022 (New York, 2022), https://hdr.undp.org/content/human-development-report-2021-22.

9. Afrobarometer, "Kenyans Want Women to Have Equal Chance of Being Elected, Approve of Government Efforts to Close Gender Gaps," September 23, 2022, https://www.afrobarometer.org/wp-content/uploads/2022/09/R9-News-release-Kenyans-endorse-gender-equality-in-politics-Afrobarometer-22sept22.pdf.

10. Tyler G. Okimoto and Victoria L. Brescoll, "The Price of Power: Power Seeking and Backlash against Female Politicians," *Personality and Social Psychology Bulletin* 36, no. 7 (July 2010): 923–936; and Alice H. Eagly and Steven J. Karau, "Role Congruity Theory of Prejudice toward Female Leaders," *Psychological Review* 109, no. 3 (2002): 573–598.

11. Tània Verge and Maria de la Fuente, "Playing with Different Cards: Party Politics, Gender Quotas, and Women's Empowerment," *International Political Science Review* 35, no. 1 (2014): 67–79.

12. Cecilia L. Ridgeway, *Framed by Gender: How Gender Inequality Persists in the Modern World* (New York: Oxford University Press, 2011).

13. Pippa Norris, "The State of Women's Participation and Empowerment: New Challenges to Gender Equality" (New York: UN Women, 2020), https://www.unwomen.org/sites/default/files/Headquarters/Attachments/Sections/CSW/65/EGM/Norris_State%20of%20Womens%20Participation%20and%20Empowerment_BP1_CSW65EGM.pdf.

NOTES 271

14. Stephanie Seguino, "Plus Ça Change? Evidence on Global Trends in Gender Norms and Stereotypes," *Feminist Economics* 13, no. 2 (April 2007): 1–28; Marie E. Berry, *War, Women, and Power: From Violence to Mobilization in Rwanda and Bosnia-Herzegovina*, 1st ed. (Cambridge: Cambridge University Press, 2018); and Alice Evans, "Cities as Catalysts of Gendered Social Change? Reflections from Zambia," *Annals of the American Association of Geographers* 108, no. 4 (July 4, 2018): 1096–1114.
15. Juan J. Fernández and Celia Valiente, "Gender Quotas and Public Demand for Increasing Women's Representation in Politics: An Analysis of 28 European Countries," *European Political Science Review* 13, no. 3 (August 2021): 351–370; Peter Allen and David Cutts, "How Do Gender Quotas Affect Public Support for Women as Political Leaders?," *West European Politics* 41, no. 1 (January 2, 2018): 147–168; and Lori Beaman, Raghabendra Chattopadhyay, Esther Duflo, Rohini Pande, and Petia Topalova, "Powerful Women: Does Exposure Reduce Bias?," *Quarterly Journal of Economics* 124, no. 4 (November 2009): 1497–1540.
16. Jeong Hyun Kim and Yesola Kweon, "Why Do Young Men Oppose Gender Quotas? Group Threat and Backlash to Legislative Gender Quotas," *Legislative Studies Quarterly* 47, no. 4 (November 2022): 991–1021; and Krook, "Contesting Gender Quotas."
17. Interview with a staff member at the IPU, February 12, 2020.
18. Search for Common Ground, "Madam President: Screenings and Dialogues," April 29, 2016, https://www.sfcg.org/madam-president-screenings-jordan/; and Interview with a staff member at NDI, February 7, 2020.
19. European Union External Action, "Ms President: Reality TV Show Winner Announced," July 30, 2019, https://www.eeas.europa.eu/node/66017_en.
20. Darcy Ashman et al., "Performance Evaluation of the Women's Leadership Portfolio" (United States Agency for International Development, November 30, 2018), https://pdf.usaid.gov/pdf_docs/PA00TNBB.pdf.
21. Ali Cheema et al., "Canvassing the Gatekeepers: A Field Experiment to Increase Women Voters' Turnout in Pakistan," *American Political Science Review* 117, no. 1 (February 2023): 1–21.
22. Carla Beth Abdo, "The Future of Female Mobilization in Lebanon, Morocco, and Yemen after the Arab Spring," Elliott School of International Affairs: The Project on Middle East Political Science, March 11, 2016, https://pomeps.org/the-future-of-female-mobilization-in-leba non-morocco-and-yemen-after-the-arab-spring.
23. A. Glinski, C. Schwenke, L. O'Brien-Milne, and K. Farley, *Gender Equity and Male Engagement: It Only Works If Everyone Plays* (Washington, DC: International Center for Research on Women and Cartier Philanthropy, 2018), https://www.icrw.org/wp-content/uploads/2018/04/ICRW_Gender-Equity-and-Male-Engagement_Full-report.pdf.
24. Interview with a USAID official, January 22, 2020.
25. Interview with USAID officials, January 19, 2019; and Interview with a SIDA official, January 24, 2020.
26. Cheema et al., "Canvassing the Gatekeepers."
27. Interview with a Kenyan women's rights activist, May 2, 2020; and iKnow Politics, "Engaging Male Champions to Support Women's Political Participation," December 2017, https://www.iknowpolitics.org/sites/default/files/consolidated_reply_male_champions_e-discuss ion_december_2017_1.pdf.
28. UN Women, "Corporate Evaluation of UN Women's Contribution to Women's Political Participation and Leadership," 2018, https://www.unwomen.org/en/digital-library/publi cations/2018/4/corporate-evaluation-womens-political-participation-and-leadership.
29. Ibid.; and GROOTS Kenya, "Champions for Transformative Leadership," April 20, 2017, https://grootskenya.org/project/champions-for-transformative-leadership.
30. Interview with a Kenyan women's rights activist, May 2, 2020; and Jo-Anne Bishop, Sara Vaca, and Joseph Barnes, "Fund for Gender Equality Evaluations 2011–2015: Meta Analysis," 2016, https://www.unwomen.org/en/digital-library/publications/2016/8/fund-for-gen der-equality-evaluations-2011-2015-meta-analysis.
31. Rachel Jewkes et al., "Hegemonic Masculinity: Combining Theory and Practice in Gender Interventions," *Culture, Health and Sexuality* 17, no. sup2 (October 16, 2015): 112–127; and Christine Ricardo, "Men, Masculinities, and Changing Power: A Discussion Paper on

Engaging Men in Gender Equality from Beijing 1995 to 2015" (MenEngage Alliance, UN Women, and UNFPA, 2019).

32. Interview with an aid official at IFES, November 6, 2020.

33. Glinski et al., *Gender Equity and Male Engagement*, 39.

34. Tazreen Hussain, "Male Allies for Leadership Equality: Learning from Nigeria's Experience" (IFES, March 15, 2016), https://www.ifes.org/news/male-allies-leadership-equality-learning-nigerias-experience.

35. IFES, "Engaging Male Allies to Advance Women's Voter Registration in Khyber," March 8, 2021, https://www.ifes.org/news/engaging-male-allies-advance-womens-voter-registration-khyber.

36. Interview with an aid official at IFES, November 6, 2020.

37. Caroline Hubbard and Alan Greig, "Men, Power and Politics: Program Guidance" (Washington, DC: NDI, 2020), https://www.ndi.org/sites/default/files/Men%2C%20Power%20and%20Politics%20Program%20Guidance%2011_20_2020%206.pdf.

38. Remarks by Alan Greig, speaking at an event hosted by NDI and MenEngage Alliance on NDI's Men, Power, and Politics manual, March 22, 2021.

39. Caroline Hubbard and Alan Greig, "Men, Power and Politics." NDI has since also piloted the same program with youth activists in Lebanon, as part of its Youth Activism for Lebanese Accountability program.

40. Interview with a staff member at US democracy assistance organization, January 15, 2020.

41. Interview with Kenyan civil society activist, May 6, 2020; and Interview with staff member at Kenyan women's rights organization, May 12, 2020. See also: Bishop, Vaca, and Barnes, "Fund for Gender Equality Evaluations 2011–2015."

42. Interview with a staff member at a Kenyan NGO, May 5, 2020.

43. Interview with a Kenyan aid official, May 20, 2020.

44. David Duriesmith, "Engaging Men and Boys in the Women, Peace and Security Agenda: Beyond the 'Good Men' Industry," *LSE Centre for Women, Peace and Security*, November 2017, https://blogs.lse.ac.uk/wps/2017/12/15/engaging-men-and-boys-in-the-women-peace-and-security-agenda-beyond-the-good-men-industry-david-duriesmith-112017/.

45. Glinski et al., *Gender Equity and Male Engagement*.

46. Ibid., and Stephen R. Burrell and Michael Flood, "Which Feminism? Dilemmas in Profeminist Men's Praxis to End Violence Against Women," *Global Social Welfare* 6 (2019): 231–244.

47. Interview with an aid official at IFES, November 6, 2020.

48. Glinski et al., *Gender Equity and Male Engagement*.

49. Rachael S. Pierotti, Milli Lake, and Chloé Lewis, "Equality on His Terms: Doing and Undoing Gender through Men's Discussion Groups," *Gender and Society* 32, no. 4 (August 2018): 540–562.

50. Hubbard and Greig, "Men, Power and Politics."

51. Krook and Restrepo Sanín distinguish between physical violence, psychological violence, sexual violence, economic violence, and semiotic violence. Mona Lena Krook and Juliana Restrepo Sanín, "The Cost of Doing Politics? Analyzing Violence and Harassment against Female Politicians," *Perspectives on Politics* 18, no. 3 (September 2020): 740–755.

52. Kirsten Zeiter, Sandra Pepera, and Molly Middlehurst, "Tweets That Chill: Analyzing Online Violence against Women in Politics" (NDI, June 14, 2019), https://www.ndi.org/tweets-that-chill.

53. Interview with staff members at a US democracy organization in Myanmar, January 14, 2021.

54. Elin Bjarnegård, "The Continuum of Election Violence: Gendered Candidate Experiences in the Maldives," *International Political Science Review* 44, no. 1 (2021): 107–121; and Elin Bjarnegård, Sandra Håkansson, and Pär Zetterberg, "Gender and Violence against Political Candidates: Lessons from Sri Lanka," *Politics and Gender* 18, no. 1 (March 2022): 33–61.

55. Bjarnegård, "The Continuum of Election Violence"; Bjarnegård, Håkansson, and Zetterberg, "Gender and Violence against Political Candidates"; Sandra Håkansson, "Do Women Pay a Higher Price for Power? Gender Bias in Political Violence in Sweden," *Journal of Politics* 83, no. 2 (April 1, 2021): 515–531; Rebekah Herrick and Sue Thomas, "Not Just Sticks and Stones: Psychological Abuse and Physical Violence among U.S. State Senators," *Politics*

and Gender 18, no. 2 (June 2022): 422–447; and Sofia Collignon and Wolfgang Rüdig, "Harassment and Intimidation of Parliamentary Candidates in the United Kingdom," *Political Quarterly* 91, no. 2 (April 2020): 422–429.

56. Amnesty International UK, "Black and Asian Women MPs Abused More Online," accessed February 10, 2023, https://www.amnesty.org.uk/online-violence-women-mps; Amnesty International India, "Troll Patrol India: Exposing Online Abuse Faced by Women Politicians in India," 2020, https://decoders.blob.core.windows.net/troll-patrol-india-findings/Amnesty_International_India_Troll_Patrol_India_Findings_2020.pdf; and Ludovic Rheault, Erica Rayment, and Andreea Musulan, "Politicians in the Line of Fire: Incivility and the Treatment of Women on Social Media," *Research and Politics* 6, no. 1 (2019).

57. Krook, *Violence against Women in Politics.*

58. Ranjana Kumari et al., "Violence against Women in Politics: A Study Conducted in India, Nepal and Pakistan" (UN Women, 2014), https://www.unwomen.org/en/digital-library/publications/2014/6/violence-against-women-in-politics.

59. Interviews with women candidates in Nyeri county, Kenya, September 2, 2021, September 9, 2021, and February 1, 2022; and Interviews with a woman MCA in Kwale county, Kenya, June 7, 2022.

60. Krook, *Violence against Women in Politics*; and Kirsten Zeiter et al., "Tweets That Chill."

61. Juliana Restrepo Sanín, "Criminalizing Violence against Women in Politics: Innovation, Diffusion, and Transformation," *Politics and Gender* 18, no. 1 (March 2022): 1–32.

62. Krook, *Violence against Women in Politics.*

63. Gabrielle Bardall, "Breaking the Mold: Understanding Gender and Electoral Violence" (IFES, December 2011), https://ciaotest.cc.columbia.edu/wps/usak/0031612/f_003161 2_25631.pdf; Jessica Huber and Lisa Kammerud, "Violence against Women in Elections: A Framework for Assessment, Monitoring, and Response," (IFES, September 2016), https://www.ifes.org/publications/violence-against-women-elections-framework; and IFES, "Violence against Women in Elections Online: A Social Media Analysis Tool," September 30, 2019, https://www.ifes.org/publications/violence-against-women-elections-online-soc ial-media-analysis-tool.

64. NDI, "No Party to Violence: Analyzing Violence against Women in Political Parties," March 19, 2018; Kirsten Zeiter et al., "Tweets That Chill"; and NDI, "Votes without Violence: A Citizen Observer's Guide to Addressing Violence against Women in Elections," September 21, 2016.

65. IPU, "Sexism, Harassment and Violence against Women Parliamentarians," Issues Brief, October 2016; and UN Women, "Data and Violence against Women in Politics: Expert Group Meeting Report and Recommendations," 2019, https://www.unwomen.org/en/digital-library/publications/2020/08/egm-report-data-and-violence-against-women-in-politics.

66. See, for example, Political Party Peer Network, "Preventing Violence against Women in Politics: Benchmarks for Political Parties" (International IDEA, NDI, The Oslo Center, and Demo Finland, December 7, 2022), https://www.idea.int/publications/catalogue/pre venting-violence-against-women-politics; and UN Women, "Guidance Note: Preventing Violence against Women in Politics" (New York, July 2021), https://www.unwomen.org/en/digital-library/publications/2021/07/guidance-note-preventing-violence-against-women-in-politics.

67. Krook, *Violence against Women in Politics.*

68. NDI, "#NotTheCost: Stopping Violence against Women in Politics," 2018, https://www.ndi.org/sites/default/files/NDI%20Submission.pdf.

69. UN General Assembly, "Intensification of Efforts to Prevent and Eliminate All Forms of Violence against Women and Girls: Sexual Harassment" (New York, January 11, 2019), https://digitallibrary.un.org/record/1660337?ln=en.

70. Interview with a UN Women official, February 3, 2020.

71. They also followed up with a model protocol for political parties in the region. Inter-American Commission of Women: Follow-up Mechanism to the Belém do Pará Convention, "Inter-American Model Law on the Prevention, Punishment and Eradication of Violence against

Women in Political Life" (Organization of American States, 2017), http://www.oas.org/es/cim/docs/ViolenciaPolitica-LeyModelo-EN.pdf.

72. Restrepo Sanín, "Criminalizing Violence against Women in Politics."
73. Beyond Latin America, Tunisia became the first Arab country to incorporate into its laws a provision on gender-based political violence, following a long campaign by activists.
74. Interview with a UN Women official, February 3, 2020.
75. NIMD, "Colombia's Observatory on Violence against Women in Politics," November 21, 2022, https://nimd.org/colombias-observatory-on-violence-against-women-in-politics/.
76. Interview with a women's rights activist in Nepal, October 15, 2020.
77. A 2022 report supported by USAID and NDI found that politically active women in Nepal routinely face misogynistic attacks online: Panos South Asia, "Analysis of Gendered Violence in Social Media against Women in Politics in Nepal" (National Democratic Institute and U.S. Agency for International Development, July 2022), https://southasiacheck.org/wp-content/uploads/2022/07/Analysis-of-Gendered_web.pdf.
78. Interview with a UN Women representative, May 4, 2020; and Beverline Ongaro et al., "Breaking Cycles of Violence: Gaps in Prevention of and Response to Electoral Related Sexual Violence" (OHCHR, UN Women, and Physicians for Human Rights, December 2019), https://www.ohchr.org/sites/default/files/Documents/Countries/KE/OHCHRPHRUNWOMENKenya GapAnalysisDec20191.pdf.
79. UN Women Africa, "UN and Kenya Police Host Forum towards Peaceful 2022 Elections," January 26, 2022, https://africa.unwomen.org/en/stories/news/2022/01/un-and-kenya-police-host-forum-towards-peaceful-2022-elections.
80. UN Women Africa, "Police Training Rolled out across Kenya Ahead of Elections," July 26, 2022, https://africa.unwomen.org/en/stories/news/2022/07/police-training-rolled-out-across-kenya-ahead-of-elections.
81. UN Women Africa, "Kenya's Strides towards Eradicating Violence against Women and Girls in Elections," December 23, 2022, https://africa.unwomen.org/en/stories/feature-story/2022/12/kenyas-strides-towards-eradicating-violence-against-women-and-girls-in-elections.
82. Echo Network Africa, "A Gender Audit and Analysis of Kenya's 2022 General Elections," 2023, https://democracytrustfund.org/Gender-Audit-Analysis-Kenya-2022-GE.pdf, 39.
83. Ibid., and Interviews with women aspirants and candidates in Nyeri, Nairobi, and Bungoma counties between August and December 2021.
84. Kofi Annan Foundation, "Online Gender-Based Political Violence in Kenya: The Road towards a Code of Conduct for Digital Behaviour," December 19, 2021, https://www.kofiannanfoundation.org/supporting-democracy-and-elections-with-integrity/online-gender-based-political-violence-kenya/.
85. Interview with staff members at a US democracy organization in Myanmar, January 14, 2021; Interview with a Burmese civil society activist, January 28, 2021; and Interview with a staff member of an international organization in Myanmar, February 9, 2021.
86. Interview with staff members at a US democracy organization in Myanmar, January 14 and 19, 2021.
87. Interview with a staff member of an international democracy aid organization in Myanmar, January 13, 2021.
88. Interview with a staff member of an international democracy aid organization in Myanmar, February 9, 2021.
89. Interview with a staff member at UNDP, February 14, 2020; NDI and Meedan, "Interventions for Ending Online Violence against Women in Politics," October 2022, https://www.ndi.org/sites/default/files/NDI%20Interventions%20to%20End%20OVAW-P.pdf; and Lucina Di Meco, "Online Threats to Women's Political Participation and the Need for a Multi-Stakeholder, Cohesive Approach to Address Them" (Sixty-Fifth Session of the Commission on the Status of Women, New York: UN Women, 2020), https://www.unwomen.org/sites/default/files/Headquarters/Attachments/Sections/CSW/65/EGM/Di%20Meco_Online%20Threats_EP8_EGMCSW65.pdf.
90. Nina Jankowicz et al., "Malign Creativity: How Gender, Sex and Lies Are Weaponized against Women Online" (Washington, DC: The Wilson Center, January 2021), https://www.wilso

NOTES 275

ncenter.org/publication/malign-creativity-how-gender-sex-and-lies-are-weaponized-agai nst-women-online.

91. Ellen Judson et al., "Engendering Hate: The Contours of State-Aligned Disinformation Online" (London: Demos, October 2020), https://www.ndi.org/sites/default/files/Enge ndering-Hate.pdf.

92. Rachel Kleinfeld, "The Rise of Political Violence in the United States," *Journal of Democracy* 32, no. 4 (2021): 160–176; and Daniel L. Byman, "How Hateful Rhetoric Connects to Real-World Violence," The Brookings Institution, April 9, 2021, https://www.brookings. edu/blog/order-from-chaos/2021/04/09/how-hateful-rhetoric-connects-to-real-world-violence/.

93. Colleen Scribner, "Why Strongmen Attack Women's Rights," Freedom House, June 18, 2019, https://freedomhouse.org/article/why-strongmen-attack-womens-rights; and Peter Beinart, "The New Authoritarians Are Waging War on Women," *The Atlantic*, February 2019, https://www.theatlantic.com/magazine/archive/2019/01/authoritarian-sexism-trump-duterte/576382/.

94. Juliana Restrepo Sanín, "Violence against Women in Politics: Latin America in an Era of Backlash," *Signs: Journal of Women in Culture and Society* 45, no. 2 (January 2020): 302–310; and Flávia Biroli, "Violence against Women and Reactions to Gender Equality in Politics," *Politics & Gender* 14, no. 4 (2018): 681–685.

95. Nina Jankowicz, Sandra Pepera, and Molly Middlehurst, "Addressing Online Misogyny and Gendered Disinformation: A How-To Guide" (NDI, 2021), https://www.ndi.org/publicati ons/addressing-online-misogyny-and-gendered-disinformation-how-guide.

96. Interview with a staff member at UN Women, February 4, 2020; and Victoria Scott, "Understanding the Gender Dimensions of Disinformation: Current Approaches to Countering Gendered Disinformation and Addressing Gender Dimensions of Disinformation," Countering Disinformation, April 2, 2021, https://counteringdisinformat ion.org/topics/gender/3-current-approaches-countering-gendered-disinformation-and-add ressing-gender.

97. Mala Htun and S. Laurel Weldon, "Feminist Mobilization and Status Politics: Combatting Violence against Women," in *The Logics of Gender Justice: State Action on Women's Rights around the World* (Cambridge: Cambridge University Press, 2018), 28–83; Diana Jiménez, Caroline Harper, and Rachel George, "Mobilising for Change: How Women's Social Movements Are Transforming Gender Norms" (Advancing Learning and Innovation on Gender Norms and Overseas Development Institute, November 2021), https://odi.org/en/publications/mob ilising-for-change-how-womens-social-movements-are-transforming-gender-norms/; and UNDP, "Uncertain Times, Unsettled Lives."

Chapter 10

1. Name changed by the authors.

2. Interview with a Dalit women's rights activist, November 23, 2020.

3. Sinduja Raja, Marie E. Berry, and Milli Lake, "Women's Rights after War," FBA Research Brief (Folke Bernadotte Academy, December 2020), https://fba.se/contentassets/7a174aaa5 85e41038daee227e12d9907/womens-rights-after-war.pdf.

4. Farida Jalalzai, "Women Rule: Shattering the Executive Glass Ceiling," *Politics and Gender* 4, no. 2 (June 2008): 205–231; and Mark R. Thompson, "Dynasties' Daughters and Martyrs' Widows: Female Leaders and Gender Inequality in Asia," *Disruptive Asia* 5 (February 2022), https://disruptiveasia.asiasociety.org/dynasties-daughters-and-martyrs-widows-female-leaders-and-gender-inequality-in-asia.

5. Melanie M. Hughes and Joshua Kjerulf Dubrow, "Intersectionality and Women's Political Empowerment Worldwide," in *Measuring Women's Political Empowerment across the Globe: Strategies, Challenges and Future Research*, eds. Amy C. Alexander, Catherine Bolzendahl, and Farida Jalalzai, Gender and Politics (New York: Springer International Publishing, 2018), 77–96.

6. Kimberlé Crenshaw, "Demarginalizing the Intersection of Race and Sex: A Black Feminist Critique of Antidiscrimination Doctrine, Feminist Theory and Antiracist Politics," *University*

of Chicago Legal Forum 1989, no. 1(1989): 139–167; Nira Yuval-Davis, "Intersectionality and Feminist Politics," *European Journal of Women's Studies* 13, no. 3 (August 2006): 193–209; and Pamela Marie Paxton, Melanie M. Hughes, and Tiffany Barnes, "Intersectionality and Difference," in *Women, Politics, and Power: A Global Perspective*, 4th ed. (Lanham, MD: Rowman and Littlefield, 2020), 92–112.

7. Interview with a former UN official in Nepal, November 2, 2020.

8. Hughes and Dubrow, "Intersectionality and Women's Political Empowerment Worldwide."

9. Melanie M. Hughes, "Intersectionality, Quotas, and Minority Women's Political Representation Worldwide," *American Political Science Review* 105, no. 3 (August 2011): 604–620.

10. Francesca R. Jensenius, "Competing Inequalities? On the Intersection of Gender and Ethnicity in Candidate Nominations in Indian Elections," *Government and Opposition* 51, no. 3 (July 2016): 440–463; and Karen Celis et al., "Quotas and Intersectionality: Ethnicity and Gender in Candidate Selection," *International Political Science Review* 35, no. 1 (January 1, 2014): 41–54.

11. Bhola Paswan, "How Quotas Provided a Footing but Left Inequality Unresolved: Dalits in the Local Election," *The Record*, October 29, 2017, https://www.recordnepal.com/how-quo tas-provided-a-footing-but-left-inequality-unresolved-dalits-in-the-local-election.

12. Srijana Nepal, "Nepal Survey: Does a Seat at the Table Guarantee Gender Equality?" The Asia Foundation, May 8, 2019, https://asiafoundation.org/2019/05/08/nepal-survey-does-a-seat-at-the-table-guarantee-gender-equality/; and "Madhesi Dalits and Janajatis Want Quota within Quota," *The Himalayan*, June 24, 2019, https://thehimalayantimes.com/nepal/madh esi-dalits-and-janajatis-want-quota-within-quota.

13. Paswan, "How Quotas Provided a Footing but Left Inequality Unresolved."

14. Marie E. Berry and Milli Lake, "Women's Rights after War: On Gender Interventions and Enduring Hierarchies," *Annual Review of Law and Social Science* 17, no. 1 (October 13, 2021), 460.

15. European Commission, "Together towards a Gender Equal World: EU Gender Equality Action Plan III," November 25, 2020, https://international-partnerships.ec.europa.eu/sys tem/files/2021-01/join-2020-17-final_en.pdf.

16. USAID, "2023 Gender Equality and Women's Empowerment Policy" (Washington, DC: US Agency for International Development, 2023).

17. See, for example, Shreejana Pokhrel and Gopal Krishna Siwakoti, "Promoting Gender Equality and Social Inclusion: Nepal's Commitments and Obligations" (INHURED International, United States Agency for International Development, and The Asia Foundation, 2018).

18. Interview with civil society activists in Kenya, April 13, 2020, and May 17, 2020.

19. Interview with a Moroccan women's rights advocate, May 18, 2020.

20. Interview with a representative of IRI in Morocco, July 10, 2020.

21. The program was designed and implemented by the Feminist Dalit Organisation, Tewa, Women for Human Rights, and Womankind Worldwide. Feminist Dalit Organisation (FEDO) et al., "Participation and Voice for Excluded Women (PAVE): Learning Report," September 2022, https://www.womankind.org.uk/wp-content/uploads/2022/09/PAVE-Learning-report-September-2022-1.pdf.

22. Interview with staff at a multilateral organization in Morocco, August 24, 2020; and Interview with a UN Women, February 3, 2020.

23. Interview with an aid official at a US development contractor, February 21, 2020; and Interview with staff at a multilateral organization in Morocco, August 24, 2020.

24. Interview with a staff member at US democracy assistance organization in Nepal, April 5, 2020; and Interview with Saloni Singh, a Nepali women's rights activist, October 15, 2020.

25. Jenny Enarsson, "Repoliticising Intersectionality," Intersectionality Series (Oxfam, 2015), https://s3.amazonaws.com/oxfam-us/www/static/media/files/Repoliticising_Intersectio nality_-_Enarsson__fmkAQFP.pdf.

26. Interview with a gender studies professor at Tribhuvan University in Nepal, November 2, 2020; Interview with staff at the Alliance for Social Dialogue, July 26, 2020, and with Sancharika Samuha, November 25, 2020; and Interview with a Nepali female vice chair-person, November 18, 2020.

NOTES

27. Berry and Lake, "Women's Rights after War"; and Daniela Donno and Anne-Kathrin Kreft, "Authoritarian Institutions and Women's Rights," *Comparative Political Studies* 52, no. 5 (April 1, 2019): 720–753.

28. Gretchen Bauer and Jennie E. Burnet, "Gender Quotas, Democracy, and Women's Representation in Africa: Some Insights from Democratic Botswana and Autocratic Rwanda," *Women's Studies International Forum* 41, no. 2 (2013): 103–112; and Aili Mari Tripp, "The Instrumentalization of Women Opposition Leaders for Authoritarian Regime Entrenchment: The Case of Uganda," *Politics and Governance* 11, no. 1 (2023): 152–163.

29. Interview with a former gender consultant for the UN Mission in Nepal, November 2, 2020; and Interview with staff at an international democracy assistance organization in Nepal, November 29, 2020.

30. Shradha Ghale, "Backlash against Inclusion," in *Two Steps Forward, One Step Back: The Nepal Peace Process*, eds. Deepak Thapa and Alexander Ramsbotham, Accord 26 (London: Conciliation Resources, 2017), 123–124.

31. Lynn Bennett, "Gender First: Rebranding Inclusion in Nepal," in Thapa and Ramsbotham, *Two Steps Forward, One Step Back*, 114–117.

32. Anna Lührmann and Staffan I. Lindberg, "A Third Wave of Autocratization Is Here: What Is New about It?," *Democratization* 26, no. 7 (October 3, 2019): 1095–1113.

33. Thomas Carothers and Benjamin Press, "Understanding and Responding to Global Democratic Backsliding," Carnegie Endowment for International Peace, October 20, 2022, https://carnegieendowment.org/2022/10/20/understanding-and-responding-to-global-democratic-backsliding-pub-88173.

34. Nicolas Bouchet, Ken Godrey, and Richard Youngs, "Rising Hostility to Democracy Support: Can It Be Countered?," Carnegie Europe, September 1, 2022, https://carnegieeurope.eu/2022/09/01/rising-hostility-to-democracy-support-can-it-be-countered-pub-87745.

35. Suparna Chaudhry, "The Assault on Civil Society: Explaining State Crackdown on NGOs," *International Organization* 76, no. 3 (2022); and Marlies Glasius, Jelmer Schalk, and Meta De Lange, "'Illiberal Norm Diffusion: How Do Governments Learn to Restrict Nongovernmental Organizations?" *International Studies Quarterly* 64, no. 2 (June 2020): 453–468.

36. Conny Roggeband and Andrea Krizsán, "The Selective Closure of Civic Space," *Global Policy* 12, no. 5 (July 2021): 23–33; and Swiss Agency for Development and Cooperation (SDC), "Gender and Rising Authoritarianism," SDC Synthesis Note, March 2022, https://www.swisspeace.ch/assets/publications/downloads/Gender-and-Rising-Authoritarianism_SDC.pdf.

37. Conny Roggeband and Andrea Krizsán, "Democratic Backsliding and the Backlash against Women's Rights: Understanding the Current Challenges for Feminist Politics" (UN Women, June 2020), https://www.unwomen.org/sites/default/files/Headquarters/Attachments/Sections/Library/Publications/2020/Discussion-paper-Democratic-backsliding-and-the-backlash-against-womens-rights-en.pdf; Flávia Biroli and Mariana Caminotti, "The Conservative Backlash against Gender in Latin America," *Politics and Gender* 16, no. 1 (March 2020); and Sonia Corrêa, David Paternotte, and Roman Kuhar, "The Globalisation of Anti-Gender Campaigns," *International Politics and Society*, May 31, 2018, https://www.ips-journal.eu/topics/democracy-and-society/the-globalisation-of-anti-gender-campaigns-2761/.

38. Erica Chenoweth and Zoe Marks, "Revenge of the Patriarchs: Why Autocrats Fear Women," *Foreign Affairs* March/April 2022, https://www.foreignaffairs.com/articles/china/2022-02-08/women-rights-revenge-patriarchs.

39. Flávia Biroli, "Violence against Women in Politics and Public Life, Democratic Backsliding, and Far-Right Politics," Paper prepared for an Expert Group Meeting, Sixty-Fifth Session of the Commission on the Status of Women, October 5–8, 2020, September 2020, https://www.unwomen.org/sites/default/files/Headquarters/Attachments/Sections/CSW/65/EGM/Biroli_Violence_EP9_EGMCSW65.pdf; and Lucina Di Meco, "Monetizing Misogyny: Gendered Disinformation and the Undermining of Women's Rights and Democracy Globally," #ShePersisted, February 2023, https://she-persisted.org/wp-content/uploads/2023/02/ShePersisted_MonetizingMisogyny.pdf.

40. Emily Brown, "Women, Voice, and Power: How Transformative Feminist Leadership Is Challenging Inequalities and the Root Causes of Extreme Vulnerability" (Oxfam, 2021), https://oxfamilibrary.openrepository.com/bitstream/handle/10546/621202/dp-women-voice-power-061021-en.pdf; and Andrea Krizsán and Conny Roggeband, "Reconfiguring State–Movement Relations in the Context of De-Democratization," Social Politics: International Studies in Gender, State and Society 28, no. 3 (November 12, 2021): 604–628.

41. Lara Owen and Ko Ko Aung, "Myanmar Coup: The Women Abused and Tortured in Detention," BBC World Service, December 9, 2021, https://www.bbc.co.uk/news/world-asia-59462503; and Kathleen Kuehnast and Gabriela Sagun, "Myanmar's Ongoing War against Women," United States Institute of Peace, November 30, 2021, https://www.usip.org/publications/2021/11/myanmars-ongoing-war-against-women.

42. Nathalie Ebead and Atsuko Hirakawa, "Inclusion and Gender Equality in Post-Coup Myanmar," Constitution Assessment for Women's Equality Brief (International IDEA, May 2022), https://www.idea.int/sites/default/files/publications/inclusion-and-gender-equality-in-post-coup-myanmar-CAWE4_0.pdf.

43. Elisabeth Olivius, Jenny Hedström, and Zin Mar Phyo, "Women, Peace and Security in Myanmar after the 2021 Military Coup" (Umeå University, 2022), https://www.diva-portal.org/smash/get/diva2:1633147/FULLTEXT01.pdf.

44. International Crisis Group, "The Deadly Stalemate in Post-Coup Myanmar," October 20, 2021, https://www.crisisgroup.org/asia/south-east-asia/myanmar/b170-deadly-stalemate-post-coup-myanmar.

45. Ken Godfrey and Richard Youngs, "Strengthening Democracy Support in Regimes with Dominant Parties," Carnegie Europe, September 13, 2021, https://carnegieeurope.eu/2021/09/13/strengthening-democracy-support-in-regimes-with-dominant-parties-pub-85288.

46. Bouchet, Godfrey, and Youngs, "Rising Hostility to Democracy Support"; and Alina Rocha Menocal and Samuel Sharp, "Politically Smart Support to Democracy: Staying the Course in the Long Road" (Overseas Development Institute, May 10, 2022), https://odi.org/en/insights/politically-smart-support-to-democracy-staying-the-course-in-the-long-road/.

47. Interview with a UNDP official, February 19, 2020.

48. Interview with a civil society activist in Nepal, October 20, 2020; and Interview with an INGO official in Nepal, September 29, 2020.

49. See, for example, Oxfam Canada, "Oxfam Canada Launches New Program to Advance Women's Empowerment in Myanmar," June 20, 2022, https://www.oxfam.ca/news/oxfam-canada-launches-new-program-to-advance-womens-empowerment-in-myanmar/.

50. NIMD, "Myanmar: The Resilience of Democratic Values in a Conflict Setting," August 24, 2022, https://nimd.org/myanmar-the-resilience-of-democratic-values-in-a-conflict-setting.

51. Scot Marciel, "It's Time to Help Myanmar's Resistance Prevail," United States Institute of Peace, August 22, 2022, https://www.usip.org/publications/2022/08/its-time-help-myanmars-resistance-prevail; and David Hutt, "Myanmar Resistance Movement Calls for More EU Support," Deutsche Welle, May 10, 2022, https://www.dw.com/en/eu-support-for-myanmar-resistance/a-63341502.

52. Olivius, Hedström, and Phyo, "Women, Peace and Security in Myanmar after the 2021 Military Coup."

53. Donno and Kreft, "Authoritarian Institutions and Women's Rights."

54. Ibid., and Daniela Donno, Sara Fox, and Joshua Kaasik, "International Incentives for Women's Rights in Dictatorships," Comparative Political Studies 55, no. 3 (2021): 451–492.

55. Ibid.; and Sarah Sunn Bush and Pär Zetterberg, "Gender Quotas and International Reputation," American Journal of Political Science 65, no. 2 (April 2021): 326–341.

56. Donno and Kreft, "Authoritarian Institutions and Women's Rights"; and Elin Bjarnegård and Pär Zetterberg, "How Autocrats Weaponize Women's Rights," Journal of Democracy 33, no. 2 (2022): 60–75.

57. Aili Mari Tripp, Seeking Legitimacy: Why Arab Autocracies Adopt Women's Rights (Cambridge: Cambridge University Press, 2019).

58. Hanane Darhour, "Whose Empowerment? Gender Quota Reform Mechanisms and De-Democratization in Morocco," in Double-Edged Politics on Women's Rights in the MENA Region, eds. Hanane Darhour and Drude Dahlerup, Gender and Politics (Cham: Springer International Publishing, 2020), 279–302.

NOTES

279

59. Eric Goldstein, "Morocco's Hidden Repression: Shrinking Space for Dissent, Independent Journalism," July 29, 2022, https://www.hrw.org/news/2022/07/29/moroccos-hidden-repression.

60. Elin Bjarnegård and Pär Zetterberg, "How Autocrats Use Women's Rights to Boost Themselves," *Foreign Policy*, June 3, 2022, https://foreignpolicy.com/2022/06/03/autocrats-gender-equality-women-rights-rwanda.

61. "Repression against Women: The Regime's Anti-Feminist Efforts in Nicaragua," Expediente Público, January 8, 2021, https://www.expedientepublico.org/repression-against-women-the-regimes-anti-feminist-efforts-in-nicaragua/.

62. Niki Johnson and Cecilia Josefsson, "A New Way of Doing Politics? Cross-Party Women's Caucuses as Critical Actors in Uganda and Uruguay," *Parliamentary Affairs* 69, no. 4 (October 1, 2016): 845–859; and Lihi Ben Shitrit, "Authenticating Representation: Women's Quotas and Islamist Parties," *Politics and Gender* 12, no. 4 (December 2016): 781–806.

63. Lindsay J. Benstead, "Why Quotas Are Needed to Improve Women's Access to Services in Clientelistic Regimes," *Governance* 29, no. 2 (April 2016): 185–205.

64. Aili Mari Tripp, "Political Systems and Gender," in *The Oxford Handbook of Gender and Politics*, eds. Georgina Waylen et al. (Oxford: Oxford University Press, 2013), 514–535.

65. Charla Britt et al., "Gender Analysis and Assessment: USAID/Egypt Final Report" (United States Agency for International Development, November 2020), https://pdf.usaid.gov/pdf_docs/PA00X46M.pdf; and Nora Noralla, "Inside Egypt's Feminist Washing," The Tahrir Institute for Middle East Policy, September 26, 2022, https://timep.org/commentary/analysis/inside-egypts-feminist-washing/.

66. Carolyn Barnett and Marwa Shalaby, "Success beyond Gender Quotas: Gender, Local Politics, and Clientelism in Morocco," Working Paper No. 48 (Program on Governance and Local Development at the University of Gothenburg, 2021), https://gld.gu.se/media/2303/gld-working-paper48.pdf; and Abderrafie Zaanoun, "The Impact of the Quota System on Women Parliamentary Representation in Morocco: A Series of Reforms or a Regressive Path?" (Arab Reform Initiative, April 14, 2022), https://www.arab-reform.net/publication/the-impact-of-the-quota-system-on-women-parliamentary-representation-in-morocco-a-series-of-reforms-or-a-regressive-path/ .

67. Mohammed Drif, "Gender Policy and Authoritarian Flexibility: The Women's Quota in Morocco as an Instrument of Regime Support," *Rowaq Arabi* 27, no. 1 (February 9, 2022): 5–22.

68. European Court of Auditors, "EU Support to Morocco—Limited Results so Far," 2019, https://www.eca.europa.eu/Lists/ECADocuments/SR19_09/SR_Morocco_EN.pdf; and Ghita Tadlaoui, "EU Support for Women's Political Participation and Leadership under the EU's Gender Action Plan: A Case Study on Morocco" (The European Democracy Hub, 2021), https://epd.eu/content/uploads/2023/08/GAP-Morocco.pdf .

69. Delegation of the European Union to Egypt, "EU Gender Champions Working with Egypt to Support Women Empowerment," October 14, 2019, https://www.eeas.europa.eu/delegations/egypt/eu-gender-champions-working-egypt-support-women-empowerment_en; and Loes Debuysere, "What Egypt's El-Sisi and the EU Have in Common When It Comes to Women's Rights," Centre for European Policy Studies, October 30, 2018, https://www.ceps.eu/ceps-publications/what-egypts-el-sisi-and-eu-have-common-when-it-comes-womens-rights/.

70. Ken Godfrey, "How the EU Can Better Avoid Bankrolling Authoritarianism," Carnegie Europe, March 4, 2021, https://carnegieeurope.eu/2021/03/04/how-eu-can-better-avoid-bankrolling-authoritarianism-pub-83992.

71. Working Group on Elite Capture and Corruption of Security Sectors, "Elite Capture and Corruption of Security Sectors," United States Institute of Peace, 2023, https://www.usip.org/sites/default/files/2023-02/20230217-elite-capture-corruption-security-sectors.pdf.

72. Chenoweth and Marks, "Revenge of the Patriarchs."

73. Interview with a US democracy assistance official, October 31, 2022.

74. Pilar Domingo et al., "Assessment of the Evidence of Links between Gender Equality, Peacebuilding and Statebuilding" (Overseas Development Institute, December 17, 2013),

https://odi.org/en/publications/assessment-of-the-evidence-of-links-between-gender-equality-peacebuilding-and-statebuilding-literature-review/; and Émilie Combaz, "Effectiveness of Donor Support to Women in Formal Political Leadership—Annotated Bibliography," K4D Helpdesk Report, October 3, 2018, https://assets.publishing.service.gov.uk/media/5be95c15ed915d6a13d1de4f/Helpdesk_annot_biblio_Pol_leadership.pdf.

75. Chenoweth and Marks, "Revenge of the Patriarchs."
76. Lana Woolf and Emily Dwyer, "Managing Backlash against Women's and LGBT+ Rights Movements in the Commonwealth" (Edge Effect and Equality and Justice Alliance, January 2020), https://www.edgeeffect.org/wp-content/uploads/2020/04/EdgeEffect_Backlash_Full-Report.pdf; Natália Maria Félix de Souza and Lara Martim Rodrigues Selis, "Gender Violence and Feminist Resistance in Latin America," *International Feminist Journal of Politics* 24, no. 1 (January 1, 2022): 5–15; and Roggeband and Krizsán, "Democratic Backsliding and the Backlash against Women's Rights."
77. Sohela Nazneen and Awino Okech, "Introduction: Feminist Protests and Politics in a World in Crisis," *Gender and Development* 29, no. 2–3 (September 2, 2021): 231–252.
78. Sara E. Davies and Jacqui True, "Follow the Money: Assessing Women, Peace, and Security through Financing for Gender-Inclusive Peace," *Review of International Studies* 48, no. 4 (October 2022): 668–688; and Elisabeth Olivius, Jenny Hedström, and Zin Mar Phyo, "Feminist Peace or State Co-Optation? The Women, Peace and Security Agenda in Myanmar," *European Journal of Politics and Gender* 5, no. 1 (February 2022): 25–43.
79. Olivius, Hedström, and Phyo, "Women, Peace and Security in Myanmar after the 2021 Military Coup."

Chapter 11

1. Interview with a Moroccan women's rights advocate, June 18, 2020.
2. Catherine Herrold, *Delta Democracy: Pathways to Incremental Civic Revolution in Egypt and Beyond* (New York: Oxford University Press, 2020); Sarah Sunn Bush, *The Taming of Democracy Assistance: Why Democracy Promotion Does Not Confront Dictators* (Cambridge: Cambridge University Press, 2015); and Jeroen de Zeeuw, "Projects Do Not Create Institutions: The Record of Democracy Assistance in Post-Conflict Societies," *Democratization* 12, no. 4 (August 2005): 481–504.
3. Elisabeth Olivius, Jenny Hedström, and Zin Mar Phyo, "Feminist Peace or State Co-optation? The Women, Peace and Security Agenda in Myanmar," *European Journal of Politics and Gender* 5, no. 1 (2022): 25–43; and Alba Boer Cueva, Keshab Giri, Caitlin Hamilton, and Laura J. Shepherd, "Funding Precarity and Women's Peace Work in Colombia, Nepal, and Northern Ireland," *Global Studies Quarterly* 2, no. 3 (July 2022): 1–13.
4. Interview with an aid official at a multilateral organization in Myanmar, January 18, 2020.
5. Thomas Carothers, *Aiding Democracy Abroad: The Learning Curve* (Washington, DC: Carnegie Endowment for International Peace, 1999); Bush, *The Taming of Democracy Assistance*; and de Zeeuw, "Projects Do Not Create Institutions."
6. Interview with NDI officials in Washington, DC, June 8, 2020, and in Morocco, June 17, 2020; and Interview with an aid official at a multilateral institution in Myanmar, January 18, 2020.
7. Interview with a Kenyan women's rights advocate, June 3, 2020.
8. Interview with staff at UN Women in Kenya, May 4, 2020; and Interview with a staff member at Kvinna till Kvinna, June 12, 2020.
9. Interview with a gender equality advocate in Nepal, November 2, 2020.
10. Interview with a US government official, October 31, 2022.
11. Interview with a staff member Kvinna till Kvinna, June 12, 2020; and Interview with a Kenyan women's rights activist, June 3, 2020.
12. UNDP, "Evaluation of UNDP Contribution to Gender Equality and Women's Empowerment," Independent Evaluation Office, August 2015, https://erc.undp.org/evaluation/documents/download/8794; OECD, "Gender Equality and Women's Empowerment in Fragile and Conflict-Affected Situations: A Review of Donor Support," October 2017, https://read.oecd-ilibrary.org/development/gender-equality-and-women-s-empowerment-in-frag

NOTES

ile-and-conflict-affected-situations_b75a1229-en; and Interview with a US government official, October 29, 2022.

13. Interview with a US government official, October 29, 2022; and Interview with a former USAID official, December 17, 2019.

14. UNDP, "Evaluation of UNDP Contribution to Gender Equality and Women's Empowerment."

15. UN Women, "Corporate Evaluation of UN Women's Contribution to Women's Political Participation and Leadership: Synthesis Report," April 2018, https://www.unwomen.org/sites/default/files/Headquarters/Attachments/Sections/Library/Publications/2018/Corporate-evaluation-Womens-political-participation-en.pdf, 59.

16. Émilie Combaz, "Effectiveness of Aid Interventions to Strengthen Collective Action That Facilitate Women's Political Empowerment: Executive Summary" (K4D, October 2018), https://opendocs.ids.ac.uk/opendocs/bitstream/handle/20.500.12413/14106/K4D_Exec Summ_CollectiveAction_Final.pdf?sequence=1&isAllowed=y; Oussematou Dameni et al., "Journeys from Exclusion to Inclusion: Marginalized Women's Successes in Overcoming Political Exclusion" (International IDEA, October 1, 2013), https://www.idea.int/publicati ons/catalogue/journeys-exclusion-inclusion-marginalized-womens-successes-overcoming; and Pilar Domingo and Tam O'Neil, "Women and Power: Overcoming Barriers to Leadership and Influence" (Overseas Development Institute, February 2016), https://odi.org/en/publi cations/women-and-power-overcoming-barriers-to-leadership-and-influence/.

17. Clare Castillejo and Helen Tilley, "The Road to Reform: Women's Political Voice in Morocco" (Overseas Development Institute, April 2015).

18. Interview with a representative of a European embassy in Kenya, June 19, 2020.

19. Interview with an aid official at a multilateral organization in Myanmar, January 18, 2021.

20. Thomas Carothers and Diane de Gramont, *Development Aid Confronts Politics: The Almost Revolution* (Washington, DC: Carnegie Endowment for International Peace, 2013).

21. Clare Castillejo and Pilar Domingo, "Gender-Responsive Reforms in Transitions from Conflict" (London: Overseas Development Institute, June 2022), https://cdn.odi.org/media/docume nts/ODI-MR-WPS-Synthesis-Report-Jun22_v2.pdf; Alexis Henshaw, "Gendered Labor in the Making of United States Policy on Women, Peace and Security: An Interagency Perspective," *International Feminist Journal of Politics* 24, no. 5 (October 20, 2022): 767–789; and OECD, "Gender Equality and Women's Empowerment in Fragile and Conflict-Affected Situations."

22. Interview with a staff member at Kvinna till Kvinna, June 12, 2020.

23. Interview with a representative of a Western donor agency in Myanmar, January 20, 2021.

24. Interview with a staff member at an INGO in Myanmar, February 9, 2021.

25. European Commission, "Country Level Implementation Plans (CLIPs) and Gender Country Profiles (GCPs)," Capacity4dev, accessed January 6, 2023, https://capacity4dev.europa.eu/groups/country-level-implementation-plans-clips-gender_en.

26. Susan Dodsworth and Nic Cheeseman, "Ten Challenges in Democracy Support—and How to Overcome Them," *Global Policy* 9, no. 3 (April 30, 2018): 301–312.

27. Juliana Restrepo Sanín, "Criminalizing Violence against Women in Politics: Innovation, Diffusion, and Transformation," *Politics and Gender* 18, no. 1 (March 2022): 1–32.

28. Alice J. Kang and Aili Mari Tripp, "Coalitions Matter: Citizenship, Women, and Quota Adoption in Africa," *Perspectives on Politics* 16, no. 1 (March 2018): 73–91.

29. Emily Esplen, Olivier Bouret, and Janina Fischer, "Donor Support to Southern Women's Rights Organisations: OECD Findings" (OECD DAC Network on Gender Equality, November 2016), https://www.oecd.org/dac/gender-development/OECD-report-on-womens-rights-organisations.pdf.

30. OECD, "Gender Equality and the Empowerment of Women and Girls: Guidance for Development Partners," May 6, 2022, https://www.oecd.org/development/gender-equal ity-and-the-empowerment-of-women-and-girls-0bddfa8f-en.htm.

31. Darcy Ashman et al., "Performance Evaluation of the Women's Leadership Portfolio" (US Agency for International Development, November 30, 2018), https://pdf.usaid.gov/pdf_d ocs/PA00TNBB.pdf.

32. Pamela Shifman et al., "Lighting the Way: A Report for Philanthropy on the Power and Promise of Feminist Movements" (Shake the Table and The Bridgespan Group, May 5,

2022), https://www.bridgespan.org/bridgespan/Images/articles/philanthropy-and-femin ist-movements/full-report-philanthropy-and-feminist-movements.pdf.

33. Interview with a Nepali gender equality advocate, July 16, 2020.

34. Interview with a staff member of an INGO in Myanmar, March 31, 2021.

35. Interviews with Nepali gender equality advocates, October 20, 2020, and November 2, 2020; and Interview with a Western embassy official in Nepal, July 9, 2020.

36. Interviews with Kenyan women's rights advocates, April 20, 2021, and August 5, 2021.

37. Esplen, Bouret, and Fischer, "Donor Support to Southern Women's Rights Organisations: OECD Findings."

38. Interview with a Kenyan women's rights activist, May 6, 2020; Angelika Arutyunova and Cindy Clark, "Watering the Leaves, Starving the Roots: The Status of Financing for Women's Rights Organizing and Gender Equality" (Association for Women's Rights in Development, October 7, 2013), https://www.awid.org/publications/watering-leaves-starving-roots; Mary O'Neil, "Strengthening Women's Rights Organizations Through International Assistance" (Ottawa: Nobel Women's Initiative and The MATCH International Women's Fund, March 10, 2017), https://www.international.gc.ca/gac-amc/assets/pdfs/campaign-campagne/ Strengthening-Womens-Rights.pdf; and Gender Action for Peace and Security (GAPS) et al., "The Key to Change: Supporting Civil Society and Women's Rights Organisations in Fragile and Conflict Affected Contexts," December 2020, https://www.womankind.org.uk/wp-cont ent/uploads/2021/01/The-Key-to-Change-Supporting-Civil-Society-and-Womens-Rights-Organisations-in-Fragile-and-Conflict-Affected-Contexts-Overarching-Report-1.pdf.

39. See, for example, European Partnership for Democracy, NIMD, and Club de Madrid, "Inspiring Democracy: Operating Model for Inclusive and Participatory Policy Dialogue," November 2016, https://nimd.org/wp-content/uploads/2016/11/INSPIRED-Handboo k_final.pdf.

40. Kasia Staszewska, Kellea Miller, and Esther Lever, "Moving More Money to the Drivers of Change: How Bilateral and Multilateral Funders Can Resource Feminist Movements" (The Association for Women's Rights in Development and Mama Cash, November 2020), https:// www.mamacash.org/media/publications/movingmoremoney_mama_cash_awid_cmi. pdf, 9.

41. Mama Cash, "Feminist Foreign Policy: Stronger Action Needed to Resource Feminist Movements," November 2022, https://www.mamacash.org/media/221128_mc_policy_br ief-eng_artfinal.pdf.

42. Ibid.; and Staszewska, Miller, and Lever, "Moving More Money to the Drivers of Change."

43. Over time, the Fund struggled to attract new resources, particularly since its design placed it in fundraising competition with UN Women. It wrapped up its operations in 2021. Caroline Horekens et al., "Independent Global Programme Evaluation of the Fund for Gender Equality, 2009–2017: Final Evaluation Report" (UN Women, 2018), https://www.unwo men.org/sites/default/files/Headquarters/Attachments/Sections/Library/Publications/ 2018/FGE-evaluation-2009-2017-en.pdf.

44. The partners were ActionAid, Creating Resources of Empowerment in Action, Hivos, Impunity Watch and Oxfam IBS, IWDA, Panos Institute West Africa, Rutgers, SIMAVI, SNV, and Women for Women International. IOD Parc, "Final Evaluation of Funding Leadership Opportunities for Women (FLOW 2) 2016–2020" (The Netherlands Ministry of Foreign Affairs, February 3, 2022), https://www.government.nl/topics/gender-equal ity/documents/reports/2022/02/03/final-evaluation-of-funding-leadership-opportunit ies-for-women-flow-2-2016-2020.

45. Global Affairs Canada, "Canada's Feminist International Assistance Policy," 2017, https:// www.international.gc.ca/world-monde/assets/pdfs/iap2-eng.pdf, 19; Flavie Halais, "Canada's New Foreign Aid Policy Puts Focus on Women, Rights," *Devex*, June 12, 2017, https://www. devex.com/news/canada-s-new-foreign-aid-policy-puts-focus-on-women-rights-90458; and Government of Canada, "Women's Voice and Leadership Program," accessed November 17, 2023, https://www.international.gc.ca/world-monde/issues_development-enjeux_develo ppement/gender_equality-egalite_des_genres/wvl_projects-projets_vlf.aspx?lang=eng.

46. Interview with a staff member at IWDA, April 14, 2021.

NOTES

47. Global Affairs Canada, "Project Profile—Women's Voice and Leadership—Myanmar," June 2022, https://w05.international.gc.ca/projectbrowser-banqueprojets/project-projet/deta ils/D004987001.
48. Renée Gendron and Andréanne Martel, "An Analysis of Civil Society Organizations' Experiences with the Women's Voice and Leadership Program" (Ottawa: Canadian Council for International Co-operation and Women's Rights Policy Group, 2020), https://cooperat ion.ca/wp-content/uploads/2020/07/WVL-report.pdf.
49. Dutch Ministry of Foreign Affairs, "Good Practices and Lessons Learned from the Diverse Funding Modalities in the Field of Women's Rights and Gender Equality: The Dutch Example," April 2018, https://www.mamacash.org/media/conferences/dutch_mfa_ good_practices_funding_modalities_1_.pdf; and IOD Parc, "Final Evaluation of Funding Leadership Opportunities for Women (FLOW 2) 2016–2020."
50. Staszewska, Miller, and Lever, "Moving More Money to the Drivers of Change."
51. Equality Fund, "Shared Hopes: The Equality Fund's Response to the High Hopes, High Expectations Consultation Recommendations," April 2021, https://equalityfund.ca/wp-content/uploads/2021/07/SharedHopes-English_reduced.pdf.
52. Interview with a Canadian embassy official in Myanmar, March 17, 2021.
53. Richard Smith, "Use of Outcome Harvesting for Monitoring in Dialogue and Dissent Alliances: Findings from a Survey and Discussions" (Cordaid, Hivos, NIMD, Oxfam Novib, PAX, SNV, Wetlands International, World Wildlife Fund, 2020), https://www.outcome mapping.ca/download/en_Use%20of%20Outcome%20Harvesting%20for%20monitor ing%20REPORT%20rev1-with%20Logos.pdf.
54. Staszewska, Miller, and Lever, "Moving More Money to the Drivers of Change."
55. Interview with a former gender advisor in a US democracy aid organization, January 16, 2020; and Interview with a gender advisor at an international democracy aid organization, November 6, 2020.
56. Interview with a Kenyan women's rights activist, April 28, 2020.
57. Interview with a former gender advisor in a US-based democracy aid organization, January 16, 2020.
58. Bush, *The Taming of Democracy Assistance*.
59. The Council on Foreign Relations, "Women's Participation in Peace Processes," accessed January 18, 2023, https://www.cfr.org/womens-participation-in-peace-processes/.
60. Harald Aspelund and Javier A. Gutiérrez, "We Must All Work Together to Ensure Gender Equality in Trade," International Institute for Sustainable Development, March 2, 2022, https://www.iisd.org/articles/work-together-ensure-gender-equality-trade.
61. US Government Accountability Office, "Trade Agreements Increasingly Promote Women's Rights and Economic Interests, but Barriers Remain," May 2022, https://www.gao.gov/ass ets/gao-22-104711.pdf.
62. Saskia Brechenmacher, "Germany Has a New Feminist Foreign Policy. What Does it Mean in Practice?" Carnegie Endowment for International Peace, March 8, 2023, https://carnegieen dowment.org/2023/03/08/germany-has-new-feminist-foreign-policy.-what-does-it-mean-in-practice-pub-89224.
63. Ekatherina Zhukova, Malena Rosén Sundström, and Ole Elgström, "Feminist Foreign Policies (FFPs) as Strategic Narratives: Norm Translation in Sweden, Canada, France, and Mexico," *Review of International Studies* 48, no. 1 (January 2022): 213–214.
64. Foteini Papagioti, Lyric Thompson, and Spogmay Ahmed, "Feminist Foreign Policy and Development Finance for Gender Equality: An Assessment of Commitments" (Washington, DC: International Center for Research on Women, 2022), https://www.icrw.org/wp-cont ent/uploads/2022/09/Feminist-Foreign-Policy-and-Development-Finance-for-Gender-Equality_web-version_rev.pdf.
65. Interview with aid officials at Global Affairs Canada, January 21, 2021.
66. Papagioti, Thompson, and Ahmed, "Feminist Foreign Policy and Development Finance for Gender Equality: An Assessment of Commitments."
67. Swedish Presidency of the Council of the European Union, "Swedish EU Presidency Takes Part in UN Meeting on Gender Equality – CSW67," March 6, 2023, https://swedish-preside ncy.consilium.europa.eu/en/news/swedish-eu-presidency-takes-part-in-un-meeting-on-gen

der-equality-csw67/; Government of Canada, "Canada and the G7," accessed Novermber 17, 2023, https://www.international.gc.ca/world-monde/international_relations-relati ons_internationales/g7/index.aspx?lang=eng; John Ruthrauff, Lyric Thompson, and Mitchell Cahill, "France Called for a Feminist G7, but Did the G7 Deliver? A Report Card on the 2019 G7 Commitments to Gender Equality" (Washington, DC: International Center for Research on Women and Center for Democratic Education, 2019), http://www.g8.utoronto. ca/w7/2019-G7-2019-Report_FINAL.pdf.

68. Feminist Foreign Policy Working Group, "Conversations on Canada's Feminist Foreign Policy: Background Document" (Global Affairs Canada, 2020), https://live-amnesty.panth eonsite.io/sites/default/files/CSO%20Backgrounder%20Canada%20FFP.pdf.

69. Lyric Thompson et al., "Toward a Feminist Foreign Policy in the United States" (Washington, DC: International Center for Research on Women, 2020), https://www.icrw.org/wp-cont ent/uploads/2020/05/FFP-USA_v11-spreads.pdf.

70. William Worley and David Ainsworth, "UK Aid Faces Third Major Cut in 3 Years, with £1.7B to Be Cut," Devex, November 23, 2022, https://www.devex.com/news/uk-aid-faces-third-major-cut-in-3-years-with-1-7b-to-be-cut-104513.

Chapter 12

1. Colleen Scribner, "Why Strongmen Attack Women's Rights," Freedom House, June 18, 2019, https://freedomhouse.org/article/why-strongmen-attack-womens-rights; and Emil Edenborg, "Anti-Gender Politics as Discourse Coalitions: Russia's Domestic and International Promotion of 'Traditional Values,'" *Problems of Post-Communism* 70, no. 2 (2023): 175–184.

2. Nina Jankowicz, Jillian Hunchak, Alexandra Pavliuc, Celia Davies, Shannon Pierson, and Zoë Kaufmann, "Malign Creativity: How Gender, Sex and Lies are Weaponized against Women Online" (Washington, DC: Wilson Center, 2021).

3. Anne Maria Holli, "Feminist Triangles: A Conceptual Analysis," *Representation* 44, no. 2 (2008): 169–185.

4. For more thinking along these lines, see Thomas Carothers, "Democracy Support Strategies: Leading with Women's Political Empowerment" (Washington, DC: Carnegie Endowment for International Peace, 2016), https://carnegieendowment.org/2016/09/14/ democracy-support-strategies-leading-with-women-s-political-empowerment-pub-64534.

5. See, for example, Thushyanthan Baskaran, Sonia Bhalotra, Brian Min, and Yogesh Uppal, "Women Legislators and Economic Performance," *Journal of Economic Growth* (2023); Carmen Diana Deere, "Women's Land Rights, Rural Social Movements, and the State in 21st-century Latin American Agrarian Reforms," *Journal of Agrarian Change* 17, no. 2 (2017): 258–278; and Nam Nyu Kim, "When Does Women's Political Power Matter? Women's Representation and Legal Gender Equality of Economic Opportunity Across Contexts," *European Political Science Review* 14, no. 4 (2022): 583–599.

6. USAID, "USAID Announces Initiatives to Advance Democracy in Support of Presidential Initiative for Democratic Renewal," December 9, 2021, https://www.usaid.gov/news-info rmation/press-releases/dec-09-2021-usaid-announces-initiatives-advance-democracy-supp ort-presidential-initiative-democratic-renewal.

7. Maria J. Stephan, Sadaf Lakhami, and Nadia Naviwala, "Aid to Civil Society: A Movement Mindset," United States Institute of Peace, 2015, https://www.usip.org/sites/default/files/ SR361_Aid_to_Civil_Society_A_Movement_Mindset.pdf.

8. Tess McClure, "Abuse, Death Threats and Riots: New Zealand Reckons with a Toxic Political Discourse," *Guardian*, January 27, 2023, https://www.theguardian.com/world/2023/jan/ 28/abuse-death-threats-and-riots-new-zealand-reckons-with-a-toxic-political-discourse/; and Chris Wilson, "Data Reveals Level of Online Hatred for Jacinda Ardern," January 24, 2023, https://www.auckland.ac.nz/en/news/2023/01/24/data-shines-a-light-on-the-onl ine-hatred-for-jacinda-ardern.html.

9. Ali Vaez, "The Long Twilight of the Islamic Republic: Iran's Transformational Season of Protest," *Foreign Affairs*, February 2, 2023, https://www.foreignaffairs.com/iran/long-twili ght-islamic-republic?utm_medium=social.

INDEX

For the benefit of digital users, indexed terms that span two pages (e.g., 52–53) may, on occasion, appear on only one of those pages.

Tables and figures are indicated by *t* and *f* following the page number

"Advancing Women's & Girls' Civic and Political Leadership Initiative" (USAID), 200–1
aid ecosystem. *See* global aid ecosystem
Alexander, Amy, 13
Amini, Mahsa, 235
Ardern, Jacinda, 235
Argentina, gender quotas in, 65–66
Asia Foundation, 54, 134, 138, 140–41
assistance modalities. *See also* global aid ecosystem
  chronic short-termism and, 196–98
  feminist funding models and, 207*t*
  gender mainstreaming and, 198, 210–11
  international nongovernmental organizations and, 202, 203–5, 206–8
  issues with project-based grants and, 203
  overview of, 195–96, 212–13
  power imbalances between international donors and local actors and, 202
  privileging of professional civil society organizations and, 76, 203
  reforming aid bureaucracies and, 206–9
  siloed approaches and, 198–201
  under-funding of local women's rights organizations and, 32, 197–98, 202–6, 208
Association Démocratique des Femmes du Maroc (ADFM) (Morocco), 199
autocracy, 9, 11–13, 41, 43, 52–55, 68, 93–94, 150–51, 164–65, 175–76, 182–83, 187–92, 193, 229, 235
autocratic co-optation, 11–13, 164–65, 182–83, 187–90, 193, 229

backlash to empowerment. *See* patriarchal backlash; violence and harassment of women in politics
Beijing Platform for Action, 5, 23–24, 27, 82–83
Berry, Marie, 178

Bolivia, 91, 167, 169, 201–2
Bolzendahl, Catherine, 13
Bush, Sarah, 72–73, 210

candidate selection, 103, 105, 106, 110–12, 117–18, 123, 126, 224–25
candidate training programs *See also* capacity-building, first-generation approaches
  broadening the scope of, 106–9
  exclusionary candidate selection process and, 110–12
  innovative practices of, 102*t*
  investing in long-term accompaniment and, 104–6
  Kenya and, 100, 101–2, 103, 105–6, 107, 108, 110–13
  measuring the success of, 100–2
  Morocco and, 69–70, 106, 109, 110
  Myanmar and, 69–70, 104–5, 107–9, 110
  Nepal and, 69–70, 100, 103, 104, 107–8, 110–11, 112–13
  one-off initiatives and, 103–4
  overview of, 98–99, 113–14
  recurring pitfalls of, 102*t*
  resource constraints and, 112–13
  supply-side model and, 99–100, 106–7
  theories of change and, 68–69, 100
  training of trainers model and, 99–100
capacity-building. *See also* candidate training programs
  effectiveness of, 100–2, 139–41
  first-generation approaches and, 68–70
  goals of, 102, 119, 137–39
  narrow focus on women's capacity as limitation and, 109, 139–40
  overview of, 68–70
  revamping of, 224–25

285

286 INDEX

Carapico, Sheila, 9
Center for Dalit Women Nepal, 138
Centre for Rights Education and Awareness
(CREAW) (Kenya), 101–2
Chappell, Louise, 17
Cheema, Ali, 161
Chenoweth, Erica, 192
civil liberties, 7, 41, 187
Clinton, Hillary, 82–83
Consortium for Elections and Political Process
Strengthening (CEPPS), 54
Convention on the Elimination of All Forms of
Discrimination against Women (CEDAW),
23, 49–50
cooperative constellations for change, 146–48, 228
cost of politics. See political funding and cost of
politics
Covid-19 pandemic, 17–19, 49
Crenshaw, Kimberlé, 177
critical actors, 143–46, 217, 227–28
cross-party women's networks, 120–21

Danish Institute for Parties and Democracy
(DIPD), 31–32, 54, 118–19, 121, 124–25
Decade for Women (UN), 23
Demo Finland, 31–32, 118–19, 121, 123, 124–
25, 186–87
democracy assistance, 5, 7–9, 13–14, 178–79,
214–16, 221, 223, 228–29, 231
democratic backsliding, 7–8, 35–36, 93–94, 176,
183–87, 190–92, 195, 201, 212, 220
Department for International Development
(DFID) (United Kingdom), 86–87, 183
descriptive representation (of women), 61, 75–
76, 78, 88–89, 96–97, 187, 215–16
Development Assistance Committee (DAC), 29
Donno, Daniela, 187

ecosystem approach to women's political
empowerment, 11–12, 92, 94, 97, 216
Egypt, 189, 190
Electoral Commission of Nepal (ECN), 86
EMILY's List, 68–69
engaging men as stakeholders and allies. See also
patriarchal backlash; tackling patriarchal
gender norms
allyship model, 160–62, 160t
awareness-raising model, 160–61, 160t
capacity-building and, 106–8
family resistance and, 106–7
recommendations for, 228–29
norm transformation model, 160–61, 160t,
162, 218
overview of, 159–63, 160t
tackling patriarchal gender norms and, 90–
91, 159–62
Equality Fund (Canada), 206, 222

European Instrument for Democracy and Human
Rights, 32
expanded toolbox of aid for women's political
empowerment, 81–85, 84t

feminist and women's funds, 30–31, 74–75, 122,
203–4, 205–6, 207t, 208, 222
feminist foreign policy, 5–6, 27, 29–30, 210–12, 218
feminist funding models, 204–6, 207t, 208
Feminist International Assistance Policy
(Canada), 29–30, 204–5
feminist or women's movements
authoritarian co-optation of, 5, 188, 189–90
challenges of funding, 189–90, 202, 203–6,
207t, 208
first-generation approaches and, 60, 63–65,
72–75
international collaboration of, 21, 35
movement-building as a goal, 192–93, 206, 233
Morocco and, 145, 188
Myanmar and, 233
role in democratic resistance, 188, 189–90, 233
substantive representation and, 146–47
shifting resources and power to, 204–6, 212–13
fighting violence and backlash. See patriarchal
backlash; violence and harassment of women
in politics
first-generation approaches to women's political
empowerment
adding women and stirring and, 75–76
assistance to women's organizations and, 70–71
bolstering women's political participation
and, 61–65
capacity-building and, 68–70
descriptive and substantive representation and, 61
drivers of women's political exclusion and, 61–62
gender quotas and, 62–63, 65–68, 72f, 72–73
intersectionality and, 62–63
limitations of, 75–76
overview of, 59–60, 64t, 78
siloed approaches and, 76–78
formal legal gains and, 72–75
supply of and demand for women in politics
and, 61–63, 62f, 63f
UN Women and, 67–69
first-past-the-post electoral systems, 40–41, 54–
55, 72, 74, 112–13, 117, 125, 142. See also
majoritarian electoral systems
Ford Foundation, 30–31
Foreign, Commonwealth & Development Office
(FCDO) (United Kingdom), 86
Fourth World Conference on Women (1995), 5
"Funding Leadership Opportunities for Women II"
(FLOW II) (Netherlands), 204–6

Geha, Carmen, 9
Gender Equality Action Plan III (EU), 179, 200–1

INDEX

Gender Equality Network (Myanmar), 53–54
gender mainstreaming, 33, 82–83, 85–86, 95, 198, 210–11, 221
gender norms. *See* patriarchal backlash; tackling patriarchal gender norms
Gender Plan of Action (USAID) (1996), 82–83
gender quotas
  Beijing Conference and, 66
  development of, 65–66
  effectiveness of, 73
  first-generation approaches and, 62–63, 65–68, 72*f*, 72–73
  global aid ecosystem and, 23–24
  global push for, 65–68, 72*f*
  Kenya and, 67–68, 75–76, 121, 145–46, 223–24
  limitations of, 72–73, 144–45
  Morocco and, 49–52, 67–68, 70, 73, 75, 145, 188, 223–24
  Myanmar and, 124–25
  Nepal and, 3–4, 40–41, 67–68, 73, 111, 118, 134, 138
  overview of, 7, 11
  political parties and, 118, 121
  reasons for adoption of, 68
  second-generation approaches and, 80–81, 88–89, 137–38
  UN Women and, 67–68
gender-sensitive parliaments, 89, 148–51, 216, 217, 226–27
Generation Equality Forum (2021), 30–31, 202
Global Affairs Canada, 205–6
global aid ecosystem. *See also* assistance modalities
  critiques of, 35–36
  current assistance landscape and, 27–31, 28*t*, 30*f*
  democratic backsliding and, 35–36
  fragile consensus and, 32–35
  Gender and Development approach and, 26
  gender mainstreaming and, 33
  gender quotas and, 23–24
  evolution of, 25–27
  intrinsic vs. instrumental approaches and, 34–35
  key actors in, 31–32
  overview of, 21–22, 27–31, 28*t*, 30*f*, 37
  private philanthropic foundations and, 30–31
  rise of a new global norm and, 22–24
  top ten donors of gender-related democracy aid and, 29–30, 30*f*
  United Nations and, 23, 31
  UN Women and, 31
  Women in Development approach and, 25–26, 34
  Women, Peace and Security agenda and, 24, 33
GROOTS Kenya, 161–62, 228

harassment of women in politics. *See* violence and harassment of women in politics
Harris, Kamala, 27

#HeforShe Campaign (UN Women), 161–62
Howlett, Marnie, 18

International Foundation for Electoral Systems (IFES)
  development of, 26, 31–32
  engaging men and, 162–63
  Myanmar and, 53–54, 105, 108–9
  Nepal and, 86, 138
  online violence and harassment and, 171
  political funding and, 129
  "She Leads" program of, 54, 108–9, 138
  violence and threats against women in politics and, 167–68, 171
International Institute for Democracy and Electoral Assistance (International IDEA)
  development of, 26, 31
  gender quotas and, 66–67, 74
  Kenya and, 87–88
  need to go "beyond numbers" and, 88–89
  Nepal and, 44–45, 140–41
  political funding and, 129
  political parties and, 87
  second-generation approaches and, 87
International Labour Organization, 22–23
international nongovernmental organizations (INGOs), 31–32, 81–82, 103–4, 143, 202, 203–5, 206–8
International Republican Institute (IRI), 31–32, 50–51, 54, 70, 118–19, 180
International Woman Suffrage Alliance, 22
International Women's Development Agency (IWDA), 105, 121, 124–25, 138–39, 140–41, 147–48, 205
International Women's Year (UN), 23
Inter-Parliamentary Union (IPU), 226–27
  as a key actor, 31, 35–36
  gender-sensitive parliaments and, 89, 226–27
  gender quotas and, 66–67, 148–49
  violence against women in politics and, 158–59, 167–68
Inter-Party Women's Alliance (IPWA) (Nepal), 69–70, 120–21, 122, 123
intersectionality
  assistance modalities and,
  definition of, 177
  depoliticized approach to, 181–83
  first-generation approaches and, 62–63
  gender quotas and, 187
  hierarchies between women and, 176–78
  LGBTQ+ individuals and, 185
  logic of inclusion and, 182–83
  Kenya and, 179–80, 181–82
  Morocco and, 179–80, 230
  Myanmar and, 179–80
  Nepal and, 177, 179–80, 181–82, 183
  overview of, 175–83, 177*t*

intersectionality (*cont.*)
  aid actors' privileging of elite groups and, 178–79
  second-generation approaches and, 12–13, 93–94
  translating into practice, 177t, 178–81, 230

Jalalzai, Farida, 13
Jo Cox Foundation, 180
Johnson, Niki, 143–44
Josefsson, Cecilia, 143–44

Kang, Alice, 201–2
Karua, Martha, 128
Kayuni, Happy, 128–29
Kenya
  assistance to women's organizations in, 71
  barriers to political representation in, 59
  candidate training in, 100, 101–2, 103, 105–6, 107, 108, 110–13
  capacity-building approaches in, 69–70, 119–21, 126, 128–30, 139–42
  confronting "winner-takes-all" politics in, 46–49
  constitutional reform in, 47, 71, 124, 223–24
  critical actors in, 144–45
  engaging men in, 161–62, 164, 228
  gender quotas in, 67–68, 75–76, 121, 145–46, 223–24
  gender-sensitive media coverage in, 158–59
  gender-sensitive parliaments and, 148–49
  International IDEA and, 87–88
  intersectionality and, 179–80, 181–82
  local governance in, 89–90
  majoritarian electoral system in, 40–41, 117
  marital discord resulting from political ambitions in, 107
  National Democratic Institute and, 70, 105–6
  Netherlands Institute for Multiparty Democracy and, 87–88, 113, 121, 127–28
  overview of politics in, 41, 46–49
  patriarchal backlash in, 157, 166–67, 169–70
  political funding in, 113, 127–29, 197, 225–26
  political parties in, 87–88, 115–18, 119–20, 121, 124, 126
  proportion of women in parliament in, 39f, 40–41
  protracted fight for democratic inclusion in, 46–49
  reluctance of donors to challenge political leaders in, 209–10
  share of assistance that is gender-related in, 43f
  short-term aid programs in, 197
  total gender-related democracy aid to, 41–42, 42f
  United States Agency for International Development and, 47, 49
  UN Women and, 47, 49, 67–68, 71, 124, 209
  violence and harassment of women in politics in, 85, 155, 166–67, 169–70
  women's caucuses and, 140–42

Kenyan African National Union, 47
Kenya Women Parliamentary Association (KEWOPA), 140–42, 144
Konrad-Adenauer-Stiftung, 100, 119
Kreft, Anne-Kathrin, 187
Krook, Mona Lena, 81, 92

Lake, Milli, 178
"Leading from the South" (Netherlands), 206, 222
League of Kenyan Women Voters, 70
League of Nations, 22–23
LGBTQ+ individuals, 7–8, 14, 180, 185
limits of candidate training programs. *See* candidate training programs

Mackay, Fiona, 17
majoritarian electoral systems, 40–41, 54–55, 72, 74, 112–13, 117, 125, 142. *See also* first-past-the-post electoral systems
"Making Politics Work with Women" (UN Women), 125–26
Malawi, 128–29
"Male Allies for Leadership Equality" (IFES), 162
Mama Cash, 30–31, 203–4
Marks, Zoe, 192
masculinities, transforming, 162–63
"Men, Power and Politics" (NDI), 163
men as stakeholders and allies. *See* engaging men as stakeholders and allies
methods and sources 14–17
Mohammed VI, 41, 49–50, 68, 188
Moi, Daniel arap, 59
monitoring, evaluation, and learning, 8–10, 95–96, 206–8, 217–18, 224, 234–35
Montenegro, 148–49
Morocco
  aid actors' responses to democratic decline in, 50, 189–90
  aid funding in, 199
  Arab Spring in, 50–51
  autocratic co-optation in, 41, 188
  barriers to women's political empowerment in, 51–52
  candidate training in, 69–70, 106, 109, 110
  challenge of partial reform in, 49
  cooperative constellations for change in, 147
  democratic reform in, 49
  engaging men in, 156–59
  feminist movement in, 145, 188
  gender biases in political parties in, 115–16, 118, 119–20, 128
  gender quotas in, 49–52, 67–68, 70, 73, 75, 145, 188, 223–24
  gender-sensitive media coverage in, 158–59
  intersectionality and, 179–80, 230
  International Republican Institute and, 50, 70
  local governance in, 89–90

INDEX 289

National Democratic Institute and, 50, 70
overview of politics in, 49
patriarchal backlash in, 169–70
proportion of women in parliament in, 39f, 40–41
restrictions on women's mobility in, 159
share of assistance that is gender-related to, 43f
total gender-related democracy aid to, 41–42, 42f
United States Agency for International
 Development and, 51, 158–59
UN Women and, 51, 89–90, 140–41
violence and harassment of women in politics
 in, 169–70
women's caucuses in, 89, 140–41
Muriaas, Ragnhild, 128–29
Myanmar
 aid actors' response to democratic decline
  in, 186–87
 barriers to women's political empowerment
  in, 54–55
 candidate training in, 69–70, 104–5, 107–9, 110
 challenges for activists in accessing international
  aid in, 202–3
 cooperative constellations for change
  in, 146–47
 critical actors in, 144
 democratic backsliding in, 52–55, 185–86, 192
 democratic opening in, 52–53
 election monitoring in, 86–87
 engaging men in, 159
 feminist movement in, 233
 gender quotas in, 124–25
 internal armed conflict in, 41
 International Foundation for Electoral Systems
  and, 53–54, 105, 108–9
 intersectionality and, 179–80
 National Democratic Institute and, 54, 140–41
 National League for Democracy in, 53–
  55, 124–25
 online violence in, 171
 overview of politics in, 52–55
 patriarchal backlash in, 166, 169–70, 171
 patriarchal gender norms in, 156–57
 political parties in, 115–18, 121, 124–25
 popular democratic resistance in, 53–55
 proportion of women in parliament in,
  39f, 40–41
 reforming aid bureaucracies in, 206–8
 resurgence of autocracy in, 52–55
 Saffron Revolution in, 53
 share of assistance that is gender-related to, 43f
 shifting resources and power to local actors in, 205
 total gender-related democracy aid to, 41–
  42, 42f
 training and mentoring programs for women
  parliamentarians in, 137–40
 United States Agency for International
  Development and, 53–54

UN Women and, 199
 violence and harassment of women in politics
  in, 166, 169–70, 171
 women's caucuses in, 140–42

National Democratic Institute (NDI)
 data collection on gendered electoral violence
  by, 167–68
 evaluation tools of, 208
 engaging men and, 163, 165–66
 Kenya and, 70, 105–6
 as a key actor, 31–32
 Morocco and, 50, 70
 Myanmar and, 54
 Nepal and, 3, 69–70, 100, 119–20, 122, 138
 #NotTheCost Campaign by, 91, 168–69
 training programs of, 3–4, 100, 118–21,
  138, 140–41
 violence against women in politics and, 91
 "Win with Women" tool of, 121
National Endowment for Democracy, 208
National League for Democracy (NLD)
 (Myanmar), 53–55, 116, 124–25
National Strategy on Gender Equity and Equality
 (United States), 222–23
National Women in Politics Platform
 (Zambia), 123
Nepal
 aid actors' responses to democratic decline
  in, 186–87
 barriers to women's political
  empowerment in, 46
 candidate training in, 69–70, 100, 103, 104,
  107–8, 110–11, 112–13
 challenges facing women voters in, 85–86
 Constituent Assembly of, 44–45, 67–68, 73,
  100, 122, 138, 139–40, 142
 cross-party women's networks in, 120–
  21, 122–23
 Dalit community in, 3, 45, 138, 175, 177–78
 disarmament, demobilization, and reintegration
  process in, 44
 decentralization in, 3, 43–46, 89–90, 138, 183
 discrimination and exclusion of women
  parliamentarians in, 149–50
 engaging men in, 159
 ethnic differences in, 142
 gender mainstreaming in, 86
 gender quotas in, 3–4, 40–41, 67–68, 73, 111,
  118, 134, 138
 gender-sensitive media coverage in, 90–
  91, 158–59
 instrumentalization of women's rights reforms
  in, 183
 International Foundation for Electoral Systems
  and, 53–54, 86, 105, 108, 138
 International IDEA and, 44–45, 140–41

Nepal (*cont.*)
intersectionality and, 177, 179–80, 181–82, 183
minority quotas in, 3, 45, 177–78
National Democratic Institute and, 3, 69–70, 100, 119–20, 122, 138
overview of politics in, 43
patriarchal backlash in, 167, 169–70
political funding in, 112–13, 128
political parties in, 115–18, 119–21, 122–23, 125–26
proportional representation system in, 142
proportion of women in parliament in, 39*f*, 40–41
share of assistance that is gender-related to, 43*f*
struggle for postconflict inclusion in, 43
total gender-related democracy aid to, 41–42, 42*f*
training and mentoring programs for women parliamentarians in, 138–40
United States Agency for International Development and, 158–59
UN Peace Fund for, 44
UN Women and, 45, 67–68, 90–91, 107–8, 125–26, 138
violence and harassment of women in politics in, 167, 169–70
women's caucuses in, 140–42
Nepal Federation of Indigenous Nationalities (NEFIN), 183
Netherlands Institute for Multiparty Democracy (NIMD)
evaluation tools of, 208
gender mainstreaming and, 77–78
Kenya and, 87–88, 113, 121, 127–28
as a key actor, 31–32
political funding and, 127–28
violence against women in politics and, 169
Network for Gender Inclusive Democracy, 200–1
Nordic International, 205, 206–8
#NotTheCost campaign (NDI), 91, 168–69
Nzomo, Maria, 59

Open Society Foundations, 30–31
Organization for Security and Co-operation in Europe (OSCE), 67, 89, 148–49, 226–27
outline of book, 19–20

parliaments, 89, 148–51, 216, 217, 226–27
"Participation and Voice for Excluded Women" (PAVE), 180, 181–82
patriarchal backlash. *See also* engaging men as stakeholders and allies; tackling patriarchal norms
gender norms and, 166–68, 232–33
Kenya and, 166–67, 169–70
Morocco and, 169–70

Myanmar and, 166, 169–70, 171
Nepal and, 167, 169–70
overview of, 7–8
recommendations for counteracting, 232–33
second-generation approaches and, 91
substantive representation and, 140
Piscopo, Jennifer, 9
political funding and cost of politics
addressing financing gaps and, 225–26
challenges posed by, 107–8, 112, 127–29
financial support for women candidates and, 123–24, 127–30
gender-sensitive campaign finance reforms and, 121, 129–30, 217–18, 225–26
Kenya and, 113, 127–29, 197, 225–26
overview of, 127–30
political parties and, 127–30
Malawi and, 128–29
Nepal and, 128
Netherlands Institute for Multiparty Democracy and, 127–28
second-generation approaches and, 87–88
political parties. *See also* political party aid
engagement with, 87–88, 92–93
exclusionary nature of, 110–12
gender biases in, 116–18
Kenya and, 115–18, 119–20, 121, 124, 126
Morocco and, 115–16, 118, 119–20, 127
Myanmar and, 115–18, 121, 124–25
Nepal and, 115–18, 119–21, 122–26
political party aid. *See also* political parties
candidate selection processes and, 117–18, 123, 126
cross-party networks and, 120–21, 122–23
effectiveness of gender-related political party aid, 122–25, 129
electoral system design and, 117
organizational change and, 118–22
gender biases in political parties and, 116–18
gender quotas and, 118, 121
limitations of, 125, 127
measurement challenges of, 122
need for pragmatism and, 130–32
overview of, 115–16, 132–33
political funding and, 127–30
women's wings and, 120–21
"Power of Women" fund (Netherlands), 206
"Powered by the People" (USAID), 233
proportional representation, 45–46, 72, 112–13, 117, 142, 224–25

recognizing the centrality of gender norms to democracy, 220
reforming aid bureaucracies, 206–9
representation. *See* descriptive representation; substantive representation (of women)

INDEX 291

"Respect for Women's Political Rights"
Programme (International IDEA and
NIMD), 87–88, 121, 124–25, 127
Restrepo Sanín, Juliana, 201–2
Rwanda, instrumentalization of reforms in, 182–83, 188
women's political inclusion as a global
norm, 22–24

Samuha Sancharika, 45, 90–91
scholarship survey, 8–10
second-generation approaches. *See also* ecosystem
approach to women's political empowerment
shift toward, 81, 82*f*
continuity with first generation of, 84–85
countering resistance and violence and, 90–91
definition of, 79, 80–81, 92
democratic backsliding and, 93–94
elections and, 85–87
electoral management bodies and, 85–87
expanded toolbox and, 81–85, 84*t*
gender mainstreaming and, 82–83, 85–86, 95
gender quotas and, 80–81, 88–89, 137–38
gendered institutions as a focus of, 81, 89
insufficient strategic differentiation and, 93–94
intersectionality and, 12–13, 93–94
limitations of, 91–97
local governance and, 89–90
male allies and, 91
monitoring, evaluation, and learning
and, 95–96
nascent engagement with informal rules and
norms and, 92–93
overview of, 79–81, 96–97
patriarchal backlash and, 91
political funding and, 87–88
political parties and, 87–88
supply of and demand for women in politics
and, 80–81
United States Agency for International
Development and, 82–83
UN Women and, 90–91
weaknesses of, 94–95
women-in-politics programs and, 79, 81–82
women's caucuses and, 89
women's political influence as a focus of, 88–90
Shan Nationalities League for Democracy
(SNLD), 124–25
"She Leads" program (IFES)
Myanmar and, 54, 105, 108–9
Nepal and, 138
short-termism of aid programs, 11–12, 102–3,
161, 172–73, 216, 217, 224
siloed approaches in international aid, 198–201
substantive representation (of women)
challenges of defining women's political
interests and, 136–37

cooperative constellations and, 146–48
critical actors and, 143–46
feminist movements and, 146–47
gender quotas and, 137–38
gender-sensitive parliaments and, 148–51
indirect link between women legislators and
gender equality and, 135–37
institutional constraints and, 137
overview of, 134–35, 151
patriarchal backlash and, 140
training and mentoring programs and, 137–40
transforming parliamentary institutions
and, 148–51
women's caucuses and, 140–43
Summit for Democracy, 191
Sustainable Development Goals (SDGs) (UN),
5–6, 24, 222–23
Suu Kyi, Aung San, 53–54, 116
Sweden, 29–30, 211

tackling patriarchal gender norms. *See also*
engaging men as stakeholders and allies;
patriarchal backlash; violence against women
in politics
accountability in, 165
adapting to new threats and, 171–73
countering resistance and violence and, 90–91
data collection efforts and, 167–68
engaging men and, 90–91, 159–62
gender-sensitive media coverage and, 158–59
entrenchment of patriarchal norms and, 156–59
flexibility in assistance required for, 195, 203
models of male engagement and, 160–62, 160*t*
multidimensional problem and, 168–71
need for learning and, 164–66
norm transformation model and, 160–61, 160*t*,
162, 218
overview of, 155–56, 173–74
process of gender norm change and, 157–59
recommendations for, 228–29
risk of co-optation in, 164–65
transforming masculinities and, 162–63
UN Women and, 161–62
violence and harassment of women in politics
and, 90–91, 155, 166–68
threats against women. *See* violence and
harassment of women in politics
Tin Ei, Daw, 144
training and mentoring programs. *See* candidate
training programs, capacity-building
Tripp, Aili Mari, 72, 201–2

Uganda, instrumentalization of reforms
in, 182–83
UN Electoral Assistance Division (EAD), 83
UN Fund for Gender Equality, 204
UN Security Council Resolution 1325, 5–6, 24

292 INDEX

UN Women
  establishment of, 31
  focus of, 31
  funding of, 31
  gender quotas and, 67–68
  gender-sensitive parliaments and, 149
  global aid ecosystem and, 31
  #HeforShe Campaign, 161–62
  Kenya and, 47, 49, 67–68, 71, 124, 209
  Morocco and, 51, 89–90, 140–41
  Myanmar and, 199
  Nepal and, 45, 67–68, 90–91, 107–8, 125–26, 138
  patriarchal gender norms and, 161–62
  "Spring Forward for Women" and, 51
  violence and harassment of women in politics and, 167–68, 169–70
United Nations (UN)
  Decade for Women, 23
  establishment of, 23
  global aid ecosystem and, 23, 31
  International Women's Year, 23
  Sustainable Development Goals of, 5–6, 24, 222–23
United Nations Development Programme (UNDP), 31, 86, 198
United States Agency for International Development (USAID)
  gender mainstreaming and, 82–83
  gender strategy of, 83
  Kenya and, 47, 49
  Morocco and, 51, 158–59
  Myanmar and, 53–54
  Nepal and, 158–59

Varieties of Democracy, 7, 41
violence and harassment of women in politics
  data collection on, 91, 167–68
  fighting against, 90–91, 166–67, 169–70
  International Foundation for Electoral Systems and, 167–68, 171
  Kenya and, 166–67, 169–70
  Morocco and, 169–70
  Myanmar and, 166, 169–70, 171
  multidimensional nature of, 168–71
  National Democratic Institute and, 91, 167–68
  Nepal and, 167, 169–70

  online violence and disinformation and, 171
  tackling patriarchal gender norms and, 90–91, 166–68
  UN Women and, 167–68, 169–70

Women, Peace, and Security (WPS) agenda, 5–6, 13–14, 192–93, 195, 200, 210, 222–23
"Women and Constitution Building Initiative in Nepal" (International IDEA), 45
Women in Development approach (WID), 25–26, 34, 77 78
Women in Parliament (International IDEA), 88–89
women-in-politics programs, 60, 76–77, 79, 81–82
"Women's Action for Voice and Empowerment" (WAVE) (Myanmar), 138–40, 146–48, 205, 233
women's caucuses, 3–4, 9, 60, 69, 89, 126, 140–44, 151, 217, 227–28, 233
"Women's Initiative Platform" (Myanmar), 105
Women's International League for Peace and Freedom, 22
women's movements. *See* feminist or women's movements.
women's rights organizations
  autocratic crackdown on, 185, 188
  funding gaps of, 188, 192–93, 202–4, 221, 228–29
  increased spending on, 29–31, 70–71
  partnerships with international donors, 32, 70–71, 201–4
  project grants and, 192–93, 203, 212
  professionalization of, 76
  recommendations for supporting, 218, 221, 224
  reforming aid bureaucracies and, 206–8
  shifting power and sources to, 204–6, 212–13, 218
Women's Political Empowerment Index (WEF), 7–8
"Women's Political Rights" (WPR) (Kenya), 87–88, 121
Women's Voice and Leadership Program (WVLP) (Canada), 204–8
Women's wings, 87, 115–16, 119–21, 126–27, 233

Zambia, 123, 125
Zambian National Women's Lobby, 123

The manufacturer's authorised representative in the EU for product safety is Oxford University Press España S.A. of El Parque Empresarial San Fernando de Henares, Avenida de Castilla, 2 – 28830 Madrid (www.oup.es/en or product.safety@oup.com). OUP España S.A. also acts as importer into Spain of products made by the manufacturer.

Printed in the USA/Agawam, MA
March 28, 2025

885041.005